MW00462028

FINAL CONFESSIONS
of NFL ASSASSIN
Jack Tatum

by Jack Tatum with Bill Kushner

Quality Sports Publications

Cover and dustjacket design by
Mick McCay

All photographs compliments of
Jack Tatum

For information write:
Quality Sports Publications
24 Buysse Drive
Coal Valley, IL 61240
(309) 234-5016

Duane Brown, Project Director
Melinda Brown, Designer
Susan Smith, Editor

Printed in the U.S.A

ISBN 1-885758-07-3

Table of Contents

"I was paid to be a warhead – and anyone who came near me should get knocked into hell!"
– Jack Tatum

"If professional football is really about some of the things he says it is, then maybe those of us who really enjoy the game had better ask ourselves who we are and what we are about."
– Jerry Izenberg
New York Post

"It's frightening, it casts doubt on a whole way of life, and it indicts a national institution... a casebook study on the destruction of a young athlete by a cruel system."
– Jim Murray
Los Angeles Times

"It will make you wince... It may well be the most interesting sports book ever written."
– Bob Padecky
Sacramento Bee

"Courageously frank... uncommonly sharp... The shock and anger people feel over Tatum's book has been running wild... Everybody grab the sides of the chair and hold on."
– Mike Antonucci
San Jose Mercury

THEY CALL ME
ASSASSIN

by Jack Tatum with Bill Kushner
Original © 1979

*The original confessions
of the NFL's
most feared hit man!
Back by popular demand!
The book
they tried to ban!*

Contents

1

I Plead Guilty,
But Only to
Aggressive Play

When you're a two-time All-American from Ohio State, you expect to be drafted into professional football. I certainly felt that one of the NFL teams would draft me, and in the first round, too. In college, and even in high school, I had developed a reputation as a devastating hitter. Whenever I'd hit a running back or receiver with a good shot, the man usually didn't get up. I've always had an affinity for controlled violence and contact sports. Professional scouts look for athletes who have an appetite for contact, so they were looking at me.

Before the draft, the All-American team did a television show with Mr. Bob Hope. He introduced the team members and cracked jokes about each player. When my turn came, he said, "Jack Tatum ... what a hitter. Tatum can straighten your spine quicker than Ben Casey. Why, he's so tough that even his fingernails have muscles. I became a Jack Tatum fan when I saw him play in the Rose Bowl. Jack hit O. J. [Simpson] so hard that he knocked me out of my fifty yard line seat and into the parking lot. Imagine how the Juice felt ... squeezed. Jack's mother told me that he was just a normal kid ... except he liked to ram his head into fire hydrants. Normal kid, eh?"

Mr. Hope glanced at me and saw that I was laughing and enjoying his teasing. He paused for a second and then said, "Sorry we don't have any fire hydrants on stage, Jack. Oh, what the hell, if you want to have some of your kind of fun, then go ahead and ram your head into the walls."

Neither Mr. Hope nor anyone in the audience realized what was really making me laugh, but the conception most people have of aggressive football players seems so funny to me. They think a man has to be mentally unbalanced to play football violently. I know me better than anyone else knows me, and I'm no psychopath. But I and others like myself learned early in our careers that in football, the name of the game is hitting, and to play it well, you have to play it hard.

High school football was the beginning of my career. I quickly learned that it hurt more to get hit than it did to actually do the hitting. That might sound strange, but let me explain. Most high school defensive players are passive. They sit back and wait for the opposition to come to them. This is bad, because a young player can get seriously hurt. When you lay back, the offensive man builds up his momentum and is doing the hitting while the defensive man is getting hit.

Good defensive football amounts to mass times velocity. The faster I can move toward impact, and the more violently I can drive my body through a target, the more effective my hit will be. This way I'm doing the hitting and the offensive player is absorbing the punishment. Most running backs and receivers never run full speed. They're either cutting or dodging tacklers. So once I figure out where the man is trying to go, it just becomes a matter of building up a full head of speed and driving through him. My method is similar to a karate punch. I concentrate on a point one yard or so behind the man I'm going after, and on impact, I drive hard to that point.

I played my first game of football as a sophomore in high school, and even then I was effective. My coach, John Federici, said, "Jack, when you see the quarterback dropping back to pass, go after him."

I did something right because in the fourth quarter, the team we were playing ran out of quarterbacks. They had to finish the game with a tight end taking snaps from the center. After the game, I was a hero. The fans loved my style of play.

In college I developed quickly. I grew stronger and faster, and became a more aggressive and vicious tackler. Naturally, I still practiced the basics of sound football, but in addition, I also learned other important defensive fundamentals. Coach Woody Hayes was a teacher of body control. He believed that a great athlete could thoroughly control his body. Through Woody's drills I learned how to start and stop on a dime and generate maximum power in my tackles. An important part of body control was also, as Woody called it, mind control. This meant no late hits or cheap shots out of bounds. It was still rough and violent football, but my style of aggressive play was within the rules and regulations of the game.

In my first collegiate game I won no All-American honors, but I did make the other teams on our schedule wary of me. I was only a sophomore, but I had earned a starting assignment as a linebacker. We were playing Southern Methodist, a school known for putting the ball in the air. That meant people would be running pass patterns in my area looking for the ball instead of the linebackers. Believe me, when you catch someone with a good shot who isn't expecting it, you're going to hurt him.

Early in the fist quarter I spotted a wide receiver running a quick slant over the middle. The receiver was concentrating on making the catch and never saw me coming. He was my fist collegiate knockout victim.

Later in the same period, I saw a running back slip over the middle and look back for the pass. He became my second knockout. The 85,000 fans watching the game were delighted. The action was gruesome, but that's what the fans love, violent contact. The Ohio State fans loved the action I had provided and so did my coaches. Once again I was a hero.

By the time my college career ended, I had more knockouts than Joe Louis and Muhammad Ali combined. I won every defensive award the Big Ten had to offer and more. Three times I was among the top vote-getters for the Heisman Trophy, and twice I was voted the nation's best defensive player. I was certain that my next adventure would be professional football.

I have mentioned a word that is synonymous with boxing: Knockout. Actually, though, knockouts do occur in many of the nonpassive sports. It's just that the very purpose of a boxing match is built around one's ability to knock his opponent into a senseless mass of blood and flesh. Football and the other contact sports do have a different purpose. In football there are various degrees of violence and contact, but the two basic objectives of the game are to score points and prevent points from being scored, and not to knock people out cold. However, when you put an offensive team on the field for the purpose of advancing the ball forward, and the defensive team has quite the opposite purpose, it all becomes a war, and I am simply a warrior in a very physical way. As a warrior I must discourage running backs and receivers whenever they attempt to gain yardage against the defense. It is a physical and a violent job, and quite often the end results are knockouts or serious injuries to my opponent. But it is just part of a very risky business.

The first round of the college draft went as I expected, and I became the property of the Oakland Raiders. After eight years of hard work in high school and college, I was at last part of the NFL.

Several weeks after the draft, I flew out to Oakland for contract talks with Al Davis, a partner and general manager of the Raiders. Al Davis talked my language. I asked, "How much?" and he answered with a $50,000 bonus check and a three-year, no-cut contract worth six attractive figures. I signed the contract.

When the paperwork was finished, there was a statement in the press to the effect the Raiders had just hired the Assassin that no winning team could be without ... and his name was Jack Tatum.

"Assassin?" I thought. "That makes me sound like a gangster." But, actually, I was a "hit man." I didn't rush out and buy a dark suit or a fedora, but I did think about my career. The Raiders had invested in me and I had to produce. Professional football is vicious and brutal; there's not much time for sentiment. I was being paid well for a service, and if I didn't deliver, they'd go and find someone else who would.

I was committed to play my first professional game with the College All-Stars against the World Champion Baltimore Colts. The game was an annual charity affair held each year in Chicago, but it was also much more.

As All-Americans we wanted to prove to the Colts that we belonged in the NFL. We weren't concerned with showing off or pretending that we were already professional superstars. We just wanted to go out, play a good game, and earn the respect of the best team in professional football. But for some reason the old pros turned nasty and tried to beat our heads in. Every time they got off a good play, they would smart-mouth us or cuss. I thought it was very unfair of them to treat us as if we didn't belong in the same stadium. We had only played together for ten days, and the Colts had years behind them. I don't think that any of the All-Stars seriously believed that we could win the game, but still, we didn't expect to be disgraced.

Before very long, the Colts had a seven-point lead but were acting as though they had a seventy-point lead. On a third down and eight play, I started thinking that maybe Earl Morrall would look for his tight end, John Mackey. Earlier in the game Morrall tried a quick pass to the tight end, and it had worked for good yardage. That first time, as I went after Mackey, someone had partially blocked me and I hadn't made good contact. Mackey got up, shrugged his shoulders, and walked back to the huddle laughing and hollering in my direction, "Hard-hitting rookie ... what a joke."

Morrall took the snap and dropped straight back looking for the tight end. I carefully avoided the blind side blocks and drew a bead on Mackey's rib cage. Morrall hadn't thrown one of his better passes, and I could have easily intercepted, but I had other plans. I wondered if John Mackey would still think I was a joke after he was really hit. As Mackey reached back for the ball, I drove my helmet into his ribs and knocked him to the ground. It was a good hit. Mackey was on the ground flopping around like a wounded duck and gasping for air. Standing over him, I glared down and asked, "How funny was that joke?" Of course, I admit I cussed at him, too.

John Mackey wasn't the only Colt I ran into on that particular night. Later in the game I found another tight end, Tom Mitchell, roaming in my area trying to catch one of Morrall's terrible wobbly passes. I introduced myself to Tom, but I don't think he heard the name. Tom was my second professional knockout.

Immediately, sportswriters started comparing me with Dick Butkus, a linebacker for the Chicago Bears. Butkus was supposedly the meanest, dirtiest, hardest-hitting football player to ever put on a pair of cleats and walk out onto the field. I resented the comparison because I had seen Butkus play. I admit that Butkus was mean and there was strong evidence he played dirty (teeth marks on running backs' ankles), but for anyone to think he was a hitter was absurd. Butkus even admitted that he couldn't hit. When he traveled across the country doing TV shows, he said, "Whenever I get a clear shot at the ball carrier, I don't want him turning around to see who did the hitting. I want him to know without looking that it was Dick Butkus."

Any fool knows that when you hit someone with your best shot and he is still able to think, then you're not a hitter. My idea of a good hit is when the victim wakes up on the sidelines with train whistles blowing in his head and wondering who he is and what ran over him. I'm not saying that Butkus wasn't a fair linebacker, because, after all, he was an All-Pro. But in my estimation, Butkus was most definitely not a hitter.

As a defensive player I had resigned myself to the fact that I would never rush for 1,000 yards during a season and I would never score many touchdowns. But at the same time I vowed to earn my reputation in pro football with aggressive tackling. I knew that in professional football or even high school football, the team that can dominate physically will usually win. Punishment is demoralizing, and few teams can withstand a painful beating without it warping their will to win. I never make a tackle just to bring someone down. I want to punish the man I'm going after and I want him to know that it's going to hurt every time he comes my way.

Violent play can make a defensive team much sharper, but there is a limit. I believe that running backs and receivers are fair game once they step onto the field. If they want to run out of bounds to avoid the tackle, then fine, let them run away from the action. But anyone who comes near me is going to get hit. I like to believe that my best hits border on felonious assault, but at the same time everything I do is by the rule book. I don't want to be the heir to Butkus' title, because his career had shadows. Some people say that Butkus bit, while others say he didn't. My style of play is mean and nasty and

I am going to beat people physically and mentally, but in no way am I going down in the record book as a cheap-shot artist.

After the All-Star game I joined the Raider training camp at Santa Rosa, California. I guess it was surprising that my helmet still fit over my head. I was starting to believe everything the press wrote about me, and I'm afraid I became overconfident. After all, I was considered a superstar in high school and I was a collegiate All-American two times. Then came the All-Star game and my two professional knockouts. It was a lot for a twenty-one-year-old man to grasp and still keep both feet on the ground. The Oakland Raiders had a man named Fred Biletnikoff, now retired, who put things in proper perspective for me, however.

Fred Biletnikoff was a balding but hippy-looking wide receiver for the Oakland Raiders. When I was instructed by my coaches to cover Fred one-on-one during a pass defense drill, I laughed to myself. Fred Biletnikoff had a great pair of hands and could catch anything near him, but he was slow by NFL standards. I've played against big receivers, small receivers and fast receivers, and they couldn't burn me. Now, for my first test in an Oakland Raider camp, they put me against a slow receiver.

Fred ran his first pattern and I showed him why I was All-American. Covering him like a blanket, I nearly intercepted the ball, and after the play I told Fred, "You're lucky that we aren't hitting."

On the next play Fred drove off the line hard and made a good move to the outside. I was too quick for him though and reacted like an All-Pro. But then he broke back across the middle and left me tripping over my own feet. Needless to say, the quarterback laid a perfect pass into Fred's hands, and he scored. On the way back to the huddle, Fred showed me the football and asked, "Were you looking for this, Rookie?"

That got me upset and I started cussing. I told him, "Try me again and see what happens, Chump!"

Fred came at me again with about five different fakes and just as I went left, he went right and scored again. Fred Biletnikoff started running patterns that quickly deflated my ego and taught me humiliation. He burned me time and time again so bad that I went back to the locker room feeling very uncertain as to whether or not I had what it takes to make it in professional football. Deep down inside my pride was scorched.

Later that same evening I bumped into Fred and we started talking about practice. Fred turned out to be a pretty good guy. After a few minutes we were talking like old friends. Fred told me that he grew up in Erie, Pennsylvania, and it didn't sound like paradise.

While he was talking about the mills and factories of Erie, I was picturing the filth and dirt of my hometown, Passaic, New Jersey. After a great high school career in Erie, Fred accepted a scholarship to attend Florida State University, and there earned All-American honors. The more we talked, the better I liked the man.

"A man has to adjust," Fred was saying about the NFL, " and if he doesn't he's gone. The difference today was that I know you could knock me out if you hit me with a good shot, but you didn't know that I could burn you. Now it comes down to respecting each other and adjusting."

I listened to everything Fred told me, because he had the experience and wanted to help my career. He told me that receivers are the biggest bunch of cons going. Fred warned, "Some receivers will fake with their hips, feet, head, shoulders, eyes or anything to gain a liberated step. Don't be sucked in by a fake; go after what's real. Remember, Jack, all the quarterbacks in this league can hit the one-on-one pass. If some receiver gives you a fake and you trip over your own feet going after nothing, then it's just God and green grass between that man and six points."

Fred started working with me and taught me how to think like a receiver. By the time the exhibition season opened up, I didn't have all the answers, but I gave my best. Maybe if Fred hadn't given me some of his time, my stay in the NFL would have been a short one.

I got burned a few times, but luck was with me. It seemed that if a receiver caught a pass over me, I was able to stick the next attempt in his rib cage. Still, though, I was undisciplined enough to be hazardous. Aggressiveness is as common to football as helmets and shoulder pads, but I had yet to learn how to channel my aggressive style of play into aspects of the game where it would do the team the most good.

In one game we were holding a 21-14 lead over the New Orleans Saints. Late in the fourth period the Saints quarterback threw over the middle for his wide receiver, Danny Abramowicz, who was well-covered by our strong safety, George Atkinson. In my eagerness to assist, I blasted in from the weak side and creamed everyone. It was a double knockout. I got Abramowicz, but I got George, too.

After that my play became sloppy. I'd go after the ball and slam into anyone that got in the way. It was early in the season and I had already knocked out seven men. That would have been a good start, except that four of those knockouts were Oakland Raiders. I knocked out our Captain, Willie Brown, got Nemiah Wilson and cut his eye pretty bad, too, and then there was George Atkinson. I knocked out George twice. It got to the point where our defensive people were starting to worry more about me than the real enemy.

After George recovered from his second knockout, he took me aside and said, "Damn, Tate, are you color-blind or something? I wear the same color jersey as you do. I'm on your side and the deal is gettin' the other team."

After he felt that I was sure which team I played for, George started teaching me some of his techniques. I learned how to anticipate the offensive man. For example, if a running back went wide on a play and there was good outside pursuit, then I'd position myself inside and hope the back would cut against the flow. That way I'd be waiting, and from there it was a matter of building up my speed and hitting the enemy. On passing situations I talked with the other defensive backs and asked how they were going to play a particular receiver. That way I sort of knew where my people were going to be and how they were going to play the situation. For example, if Willie Brown said he was going to play his man loose and go for the ball, then I went for the receiver. It started working so well that most of the time I let the other backs go for the interception and I'd punish the receiver.

George Atkinson started teaching me a few more of his other tricks. George said, "I was going to teach you the 'Hook' when you first came into the league but you were having identification problems. Now that you seem to know who's who, let me show you the best intimidator in the business, the Hook." Of course, the rules governing the Hook have changed recently, but back then it wasn't just legal but an important weapon in a good hitter's arsenal.

The Hook is simply flexing your biceps and trying to catch the receiver's head in the joint between the forearm and upper arm. It's like hitting with the biceps by using a headlock type of action. The purpose of the Hook was to strip the receiver of the ball, his helmet, his head, and his courage. Of course, you only use the Hook in full-speed contact, and usually from the blind side. Using the Hook effectively was not as easy as it may sound. Very few defensive backs used the Hook because if you were a little high with your shot, the receiver would slip under and get away. Also, if you weren't careful and you hit with the forearm, it became an illegal tactic.

Another trick that George taught me was the "Groundhog." The Groundhog is a perfectly timed hit to the ankles just as the receiver is leaping high to catch a pass. The Groundhog isn't as devastating as it looks on TV but it does have a tendency to keep the receiver closer to the ground on high passes.

As the free safety for the Raiders, I never have a specific responsibility. I am given the freedom to help out wherever we feel the offense is going to concentrate its attack. If a team is running good against us, then I move closer to the line of scrimmage and try to get a good hit on a running back. Most of the time one good hit will slow down any running back and wake up the defense. That's what I mean about punishment demoralizing and warping a team's will to win.

I started feeling comfortable about halfway into the season. It seemed as though everything was falling into place rather nicely, and best of all, I hadn't knocked out any of my teammates for three games. I worked hard at practice, studied game films of coming opponents, and showed improvement weekly. My career was getting off to a solid start, and I felt good about the overall development I had shown. I was doing my job, getting well-paid, and no one had any complaints. At least, no one on the Oakland Raiders had any complaints.

If ever a man did have a reason to complain about my style of play, it had to be Riley Odoms, a tight end with the Denver Broncos. During a game at Denver's Mile High Stadium, I leveled the best shot of my career against Riley. It was a clean hit, not a cheap shot, but I was upset because I really thought I had killed the man.

Late in the game we had built a 27-16 lead, but Denver's offense was getting fancy. They singled out Nemiah Wilson, our left corner-back, as the man in the secondary to exploit. Nemo was small, only about 170 pounds, and he was playing with an injured leg. This seemed to be an invitation for Charley Johnson, Denver's quarter-back, to do his passing around Nemo. Denver positioned both of their wide receivers on opposite sides of the field, away from Nemo, and put him one-on-one with Riley Odoms. Riley is one of the best tight ends in professional football. He's big, standing 6 feet 4 inches and weighing 235 pounds; he would be a lot of man for Nemo on this particular Sunday, or any day of the week, for that matter.

Since I had the option of roaming around and policing the secondary, I decided to help Nemo. When the play started to develop, I dropped back a few steps to give Riley the impression I had deep coverage. Riley saw me dropping off and made a quick move over the middle. It was a great move because Riley had Nemo off balance and he broke open by five yards. Quarterbacks love to see that type of a situation, and Charley Johnson wasted little time releasing the ball toward Riley. I just timed my hit. When I felt I could zero in on Riley's head at the same time the ball arrived in his hands, I moved. It was a perfectly timed hit, and I used my Hook on his head. Because of the momentum built up by the angles and speed of both Riley and myself, it was the best hit of my career. I heard Riley scream on impact and felt his body go limp. He landed flat on his back, and the ball came to rest on his chest for a completion, but Riley's eyes rolled back in his head and he wasn't breathing. I had another knockout, and maybe this time, I had even killed a man.

God knew that I didn't want something like that to happen.

I've used the word "kill," and when I'm hitting someone I really am trying to kill, but not like forever. I mean I'm trying to kill the play or the pass, but not the man. Football is a violent game, and people are seriously injured; sometimes they are killed. But any man that puts on a uniform and doesn't play hard is cheating. The players of the NFL are paid good money and risk serious injuries because the structure of football is based on punishing your opponent. There is nothing humorous or even vaguely cheerful about playing in the NFL. It is a high-risk but high-salaried job.

Riley was scraped off the field and carried to the sidelines. He was shaken and hurt, but thank God he was still alive. After the game I went over to the Denver locker room and talked with Riley. He said, "Damn, Tate, don't ever hit me like that again. You nearly killed me." Then he laughed and I slapped him on the back and smiled with relief. Very few people understand the camaraderie and mutual respect professional athletes feel for each other. We admire each other's abilities and appreciate the man who has the guts to do his job well. My coaches, sportswriters, and even football fans talked about how hard I hit Riley. People called that hit everything from vicious to brutal but I never heard anyone say it was a cheap shot.

During the years that have followed I have continued my style of play and have registered many more knockouts. I remember one game, again it was against Denver, when the Broncos' best running back, Floyd Little, took a hand-off and swept around left end with a herd of blockers leading the way. As he turned the corner, the reds and blues of Denver had gone south and I was coming up fast. Floyd didn't see me coming and there was a collision at mid-field near the sidelines, right in front of the Denver bench. I whipped my Hook up under Floyd's face mask and landed a solid shot flush on his jaw. Floyd looked like a magician practicing levitation just before all the lights went out. His head snapped back, his feet straightened out, and the ball and one of his shoes shot into the stands. I was coming so hard that my momentum carried both of us into the Denver bench.

The play had started close to the sidelines and I could have pushed Floyd out of bounds, but instead, I hit him with everything I had to offer because if you just push a guy like Floyd Little out of bounds, then he'll start getting some bad ideas about you. Floyd would probably start thinking that I was soft, and that would lead to him wanting to take advantage of me. Before long every team in the NFL would be gunning their game plans at me, and when that happened the Raiders would get someone else, someone who would beat a running back out of bounds rather than give him a sissy push.

Some of the players moaned when I hit Floyd and a few of them even cussed at me, but once again no one even suggested that I hit Floyd with a cheap shot.

My ferocity seemed to influence the entire Raider defense. Everyone started talking about getting a "knockout." Guys who used to tackle just to bring someone down started to punish people, and that made the defense much sharper. If a running back got off a good play and picked up, say, fifteen yards but go his head rattled so badly that he had to leave the game, it was worth the fifteen yards. I started taking shots at everyone wearing a different colored uniform. I'd take shots at every receiver and running back. They didn't like it, and sometimes they'd send a lineman after me, but I didn't care; I'd take a shot at him, too. I would initiate a demoralizing kind of punishment on the opposing offense and it picked our defensive team up. The Raiders had become a nasty group of men. The Oakland Raiders have never tried to look lovable. As soon as they run on the field, they radiate villainy. The black-shirted Raiders, with their crossed swords and pirate decals, immediately bring to mind the bad guys in the old movies. Every team in professional football seems to consider the Raiders their arch-rival. They all treat the Raider malice with a special intensity, and football fans love it. I was enjoying my job with the Raiders and proud to be a part of the organization regardless of what the national image was. I knew in my heart that it was professional football and there wasn't any on-field charm connected with the game.

During my second year George Atkinson suggested that he and I start a contest for who would get the most knockouts over the course of the season. It sounded like a good idea, and we agreed on a set of rules. First of all, neither of us wanted to get penalties called against us so we agreed that our hits must be clean shots and legal. Next, the man you hit would have to be down for an official injury time-out and he had to be helped off the field. That would be considered a "knockout" and it was worth two points. Sometimes, one of us would hit a man and he'd take the injury time-out but would limp off the field under his own power. We called that a "limp-off" and it was worth one point. When the season started, so did we. Actually, it was all part of our job, but we made a game out of it. Guess who won?

The seasons had a way of piling up, and before I knew it, I was a veteran of seven years. When I stopped to look back and see what had happened over the course of my career, I was shocked. I came into the NFL wanting to be the most intimidating hitter in the history of the game. At this stage of my career, people were scared of me because they knew I was accomplishing my objective. But something else was also happening and I resented it. Some people considered me a dirty player and a cheap-shot artist. I can live with rumors, but when I see my name published in the *San Diego Union* along with football's top ten dirty players, I get upset. When my attorney calls me from Pittsburgh and tells me that Sam Nover of Channel 2 and Myron Cope of Channel 4 are doing specials on my dirty tactics, I become angry. After a few questionable incidents, everything has mushroomed into a problem serious enough for Howard Cosell to dedicate one of his half-time shows on *Monday Night Football* to George Atkinson and me and our "cheap shots." Even NBC Sports used prime time for a special, "Violence in Sports."

It started with a normal football game, a few good hits, a knock-out, and a certain coach's "criminal elements" speech. From there it was picked up by the press and traveled into the office of the Commissioner of the NFL. From there some fines were issued, which then I refused to pay, and now every official in the NFL is throwing quick flags in my general direction. However, I doubt that I'm going to change how I live my life or how I play the game because, as I told the commissioner, "I plead guilty, but only to aggressive play."

2

The Criminal Elements

In all sports there are bitterly contested rivalries. Ali and Frazier fought three time with a ferocious intensity that would have had lesser men crying for mercy. Connors and Borg swatted tennis balls as though they were beating each other's heads in with racquets. And each year, late in November, Ohio State and Michigan duel in a death struggle that usually determines the Big Ten Championship. But when the game is over, a great athlete realizes the battle is also over and walks away with a genuine feeling of respect for his opponent.

During my career, I have often risen to the heights of a tremendous effort when it came time to battle the rival gang, the rival high school football team, or whatever. As I grew in physical size and developed techniques and mental abilities, my competition also seemed to grow, and the rivalry became a much more serious situation. In college the rival was Michigan; I was a winner twice and a loser once. However, in college victory or defeat was only a matter of pride, whereas in professional football it is quite another story.

In professional football every team becomes another team's natural enemy whenever they play against each other. Still, there are special rivalries that seem to bring a higher level of intensity to the contest. Personally, I play every game hard and violently, but when I go against the Pittsburgh Steelers, a different style of aggression seems to come over me. In fact, an intensely aggressive mood sweeps through the entire Raider team. The same feeling overcomes the Pittsburgh players as they ready themselves to go against us. When this type of situation develops, you have a very special game. Both Pittsburgh and Oakland consider themselves the best in professional football, and when we meet we spend a violent Sunday afternoon trying to convince the other team of that point. Those are the games that become more than just a matter of pride or winning and losing.

The professional success, security, and esteem of every individual on both the Steelers and the Raiders depends on his performance in "the big one." Any player can be having the best season of his career, but if he muffs it in this game, everyone – the fans, his teammates and the owners – will quickly forget all his previous accomplishments and remember only that this was the season when he threw the interception, or fumbled, or missed a tackle in the Oakland –Pittsburgh game. Yes, we call it a game, but it just happens to be our livelihood and a segment of our future existence. With stakes so high, the game becomes a serious situation. I, for one, would rather get burned ten times against the New York Giants than once against the Steelers.

September 5, 1976, wasn't a typical Sunday in my life. I started the day off in a normal fashion with a shower and a light breakfast, but I was moody and much quieter than usual. I was still trying to shake some of the cobwebs from those conscious chambers of my mind and get serious. The previous night we had had a party with some of my teammates and a few of the Pittsburgh Steelers. It wasn't a wild drinking party, just sort of a get-together with a few ladies, a few laughs, and a glass or two of a mild wine. Even then I could feel the tension building, and that wasn't normal. Usually, whenever we get together with the Steelers for a game, Saturday night and Sunday afternoon become two separate segments of life. We share the mutual friendship and respect of athletes on Saturday night with the under-standing that we will be temporary enemies on Sunday. But some-how this particular Saturday night seemed to have a little Sunday flavor in it. It wasn't a good party, because everyone was tense. We joked and laughed a little, but most of it was phony. Everyone could sense it, and we all knew, right there, Sunday afternoon was going to be hell.

I want to be alone before the game. I don't want to talk with reporters or teammates, I just want to be alone. I spend that time in my own way mentally getting ready for the game. Sports fans can never realize the pressure on a professional athlete. I work and train a lifetime for two or three hours that put my talents against the best receivers and running backs in the world. I know they will try to burn me, and my job is to discourage them. It is a war in every sense of the word, and I am a warrior. Those hours before the game are lonely and tough. I think about, and even fear, what can happen. I know that in a split second of contact someone could get seriously injured or even killed, but at the same time I realize it is my job and the way of my life I have chosen. To back down or even think about backing down would be cheating. So when the ball is set for play, I am ready to use whatever means of my physical or mental ability it will take to protect myself and be effective in my job.

While driving to the stadium I started thinking about our game with the Steelers last season. Late in December we had played in Pittsburgh for the championship of the American Football Conference. Pittsburgh won the game and went on to win the Super Bowl. That really dug at me, even though I had played a great game. I wanted to win. I wanted the Super Bowl and the extra money, but Pittsburgh was there. I stayed home and sullenly watched the game on television.

Then I started thinking about Lynn Swann. Last year on the ice of Three Rivers Stadium, I caught Lynn Swann running a pattern across the middle. I hit him! I hit him hard and he went down. Then several plays later George hit him. In fact, Lynn spent a week in the hospital with a serious concussion, but still he recovered in time to win the MVP award at the Super Bowl..

My collision with Lynn Swann was, I admit, premeditated. I saw him coming across the middle for a pass, and even though Terry Bradshaw had thrown the ball in a different direction, Swann was still a fair and legal target. I don't want Lynn Swann or anyone in my area trying to catch passes. Most receivers know I earn my money and reputation with devastating hits. I don't care, but when the receiver operates as the primary target, I'm going to make him pay the price. A receiver needs concentration to succeed. If by using demoralizing hits I can get the receiver to start thinking about me instead of catching the ball, I will win the battle.

Against the Steelers last season I was only doing a job, but before the game was over I had been hit in the knees with a cheap shot because of the Swann action. Ray Mansfield, the Steelers' center, saw me cream Swann and, in what he thought to be an act of big-brother justice, hit me with a spearing cheap shot. Several plays after Swann had been carried off the field, George Atkinson and I smashed into Rocky Bleier and he fumbled. Bodies were all over the ground scrambling for the ball, but instead of Mansfield thinking about recovering the fumble, he speared me in the knee. Some of the teams in the NFL try to intimidate defensive backs by sending linemen at them, but I don't think it was a Steeler plan as much as a Mansfield idea. Still, the end result was an injury to my knee.

There is a difference between my hit on Swann and Mansfield's hit on me. Swann was a legal target, and so was I. What I mean is that on that particular play, Lynn Swann could have blocked me. On the other hand, I had the right to take him out of the play. I admit it was full speed, and I did hit him high with a Hook, but still, it was legal. There was an official on the play, no flag. Mansfield, on the other hand, admits he tried to "get me" because I got Swann. Ray Mansfield succeeded, but there was still today.

Often I think about getting even for myself or one of my teammates who was blasted insensible, but that's not the purpose of the game. Sure I think about Mansfield hitting me with a cheap shot, but I'm not going into the game looking to break his neck. It still comes back to the fact that if Lynn Swann runs across the middle, he's liable to get hit again. Only next time I'll be watching Big Brother a little more closely, too.

Dressing for a game, any game, is a ritual with me. I take great care with my shoes because they are important. I make sure my cleats are tight and new because I don't want to slip. Next, I put on two pairs of socks and jam my foot into the shoe. I want a tight fit. Then I tape my shoes on tight. This way there is no chance of my shoe giving way under the stress of stopping and starting. I believe that every ounce of running power can be generated into my body. It seems to make for an explosive start and maximum speed on contact.

Of course, I take care with my other articles of equipment, but I stress taping my wrists and forearms. I use rolls of tape on my wrists and forearms for protection, and the tape gives a more solid feel during contact.

After all the gear is on and I'm taped, I channel all my attention to the game and the people I'll be going up against. There are passive teams in the NFL that try to win with pure execution rather than aggressive and violent play. Execution has a place in the NFL, but unfortunately passive teams usually lose while physical teams usually win. That is simply the basic rule of football or any other contact sport. In any contact sport it behooves the athlete to be physical.

The Vikings, Browns, and Bengals are just a few of the passive teams that can hang in there for a quarter or two against the heavyweights, but in the end pain and punishment have a way of warping their will to win. I've played against the nonphysical teams, and for a few quarters it was a respectable game. But when the final gun went off, the Raiders usually won.

When playing against a passive team, one hit, a good hit, will usually discourage the entire offensive line from getting fancy. I mean that if the linemen open up a big hole and the running back picks up some good yardage but in the process gets severed from reality, it all has a way of demoralizing the entire offensive team and picking up the defense. It might be hard to accept, but even in professional football there are some individuals and even teams that back down from brutal contact. I don't like that type of game, because I have a tendency to let down a little myself. I realize that my paycheck is dependent on my ability to inflict a demoralizing punishment to the opponent, but still, in a passive semi-contact game, I get sloppy.

However, the Pittsburgh Steelers are far from passive and they are not easily intimidated. Then again the Raiders have a reputation for being a rather surly bunch that thrives on brutal contact themselves. When two football giants such as the Steelers and Raiders get together, there isn't any backing down on either side.

When playing in a big game against a physical team such as the Steelers, I look for individual keys in the personality of the athletes in the primary positions. I realize that the Steelers as a whole will not be intimidated any more than will the Raiders. I accept that fact and look to channel my aggression directly toward the weaker athletes on the team. Sometimes in an important physical game little things, such as a dropped pass or a running back slipping down short of the first down, will mean the difference between a win or a loss.

Several years ago we were playing Miami in a very important game. During the first half we were doubling Paul Warfield, the Dolphins' All-Pro wide receiver. Warfield is a great athlete and has a tendency to deliver the big play at the right time. My assignment in that particular game was to discourage him from attempting to make the big play against us. On a third-down play Warfield bolted off the line of scrimmage and made a good outside move. Just as Nemo Wilson moved to cover him outside, Warfield cut back over the middle and was open by five yards. Bob Greise threw a perfect pass, but Paul caught more than just the ball. From my deep position I had nearly seven yards to build up my momentum and I caught Paul with a devastating shot in the ribs and throat. Warfield was scraped off the field unconscious. Later in the game, to my surprise, Paul Warfield returned to the action. At the time we were hanging on by a one-point lead, but the Dolphins were driving. On a critical fourth-down play, Greise dropped back to pass and looked for Warfield, who by now had beaten Nemo again on a good out pattern. The ball was in flight, but just as it was about to drop into Paul's hands, he turned and looked for me. Well, I was there and I caught him in the back with a pretty good shot. Warfield dropped the ball, one that he usually would have caught easily, and the Dolphins lost the game.

Under normal conditions Warfield would have caught that pass one hundred times in a row. But playing against the Raiders, Paul found himself in a different situation. For a split second Paul Warfield lost his concentration. In that little period of mental lapse, my physical presence had paved the way for his mistake. Whenever I can get a receiver or running back worried about me, his concentration is finished and I will win.

With the Steelers, I look for these particular areas to channel my violence through. I must be brutal, but legal, because infractions of the rules and the resultant penalties only tend to hurt the defense rather than help it. My objective against the Steelers is to find their weak links and move from there but still respect the rules of the game.

The Pittsburgh Steelers have balance. The offensive team can move the ball while the defensive team is, at times, impossible to beat. However, I don't analyze the Steelers on paper and look for the weakness that way. I have analyzed the Steelers by playing against them, and the experience of battle has made me a wiser player. For example, on paper Franco Harris is big, fast and devastating as a running back. On paper his stats look good, but in reality Franco is a big man who will sometimes back down. If Franco had the aggressiveness of a Gayle Sayers, Jimmy Brown, Walter Payton, Earl Campbell, or a hundred more great running backs, his achievements would be unequaled. But Franco runs from sideline to sideline instead of aggressively straight ahead. Some coaches may argue that Franco is concerned with his personal safety and runs with his particular style for self-preservation. From my point of view a running back is paid to carry the ball forward, and if that means running through, over, or around the defense, he ought to make the effort. Franco either runs for the sidelines when it gets a bit sticky or he gives way to one of his patented slips.

Therefore, Franco becomes a target for me and the entire Raider defense. We know that by pounding him hard and often, Franco's will to win is going to be warped. It may not be important, but then again the ballgame could rest on Franco's courage. I've seen Franco against less physical teams just blast away for those third down and short yardage plays and I've seen him slip and fall down short of the first down on similar plays against the more physical teams. It pays to get physical with running backs and receivers.

Lynn Swann, although a great receiver, lacks consistency on patterns over the middle. Against some teams he runs a sharp quick pattern, but against the Raiders he rounds everything off and looks for openings in the zone rather than making those bold dashes across the middle.

I can't fault these people for playing their style of football, because in their own way they might be right. Franco has been around many years and has seemed to avoid serious injuries. Lynn Swann is still doing a great job, and also trying to keep himself out of the hospital. It's all a matter of style, but nonetheless, it remains an area for me to exploit once the whistle starts the game.

The game itself started the way I figured – violent and brutal. When playing against the Steelers or any of the physical teams, one comes to expect solid contact and flaring tempers, but somehow this game immediately started getting out of hand. Early in the game our wide receiver, Cliff Branch, caught a short turn-in pass and was quickly scooped up by a Steeler defensive back, Mel Blount. Cliff isn't a very physical receiver, and when Mel had him shackled, that should have been the end of the play. Unfortunately, it wasn't. Instead of just making the tackle, Mel grabbed Cliff, turned him upside down, and then tried to pile-drive his head into the ground. It was obviously a deliberate attempt to hurt the man and it got some of our defensive people talking about getting the Steelers' receivers. Personally, I don't believe in the big brother routine. I don't like to see a man like Blount, or anyone for that matter, try to maim a fellow player and friend, but it still does not warrant my going after one of the Steelers' receivers. However, an event such as Blount's hit does adversely affect the mood of the game because some individuals are going to get mad and start taking other cheap shots.

Before long it became more serious than Mel Blount putting a little extra in his shots. Both teams started. On a dive play, a Steeler tight end, Randy Grossman, hit me after the whistle. I defended myself by throwing Grossman to the ground and punching him. I was mad, and it was just a reaction and not a premeditated act, but I ended up on the short end of a penalty flag. Naturally, I protested the call, but the officials didn't listen. My point was that Grossman hit me late, and the films bear testimony to that fact. I don't believe that Randy's hit was a deliberate infraction of the rules, but I still resented the shot. When I fought back I became the villain. I realize two wrongs can never make a right, but in the heat of an important battle, tempers are going to fire up. It was wrong that I punched Grossman, but during the tension of an important game, an athlete reacts erratically. I just think the official should have used more judgment in the call. After all, under normal conditions I don't punch and kick my opponent. The official should have realized that something serious had caused the incident, but it just didn't work out that way.

I should have guessed that the officiating was only going to become more one-sided as the game continued. After all, Mel Blount had hit Cliff with a cheap shot and there wasn't a flag. Grossman had hit me late, and no flag. Then I fire back with a natural reaction and it's fifteen yards against the Raiders.

Later in the game the Steelers were driving for a touchdown. Franco took the ball and tried the middle. There wasn't a hole, so I knew he would either fall down or run for the sidelines. Since the last few attempts on Franco's part had been no-gain slips in the backfield, he moved outside and made a straight path for the sidelines. I had a good angle, and Franco was going to get busted before he reached safety. He realized that fact, too, and before I could get within five yards of him, Franco slipped and fell to the ground. Damn! If a man is going to put on a uniform and play football, he should at least play it like a man. Under the NFL rules a ball carrier isn't officially down until a defender either has made the tackle or has physically touched and downed a man. Franco still had the chance to get up and run because no defensive man had yet touched him. I realized that Franco wasn't going to attempt to get up and I really wanted to blast into him. I wanted to stick my helmet in his ribs or face or anything. I just wanted to hit him, but instead I lazily downed him with a light slap on his helmet. I didn't give the incident a second thought until I got up and saw the penalty flag. Once again I was a villain. The official felt that I had hit Franco too hard and he flagged me for unnecessary roughness. That was a ridiculous call! I wasn't even moving half-speed when I fell over Franco, and I had slapped at him open-handed with more of a disgusted effort than anything else, but still, I was hit with a fifteen-yard penalty. It happens that way, though. Sometimes you get on the wrong side of an official and he drops the flag every chance he gets. It's not fair, but it's still part of the game.

Shortly after that penalty the Steelers tried a sweep to my side. I had the outside responsibility and as I started to move into position I spotted Rocky Bleier coming at me from the blind side. He was coming low, going for my knee. Ever since last season and Ray Mansfield's cheap shot at my knee, I've been sensitive about those cheap shots. I reacted. I know that Bleier was surprised when I turned quickly and blasted him with a fist and forearms up under his face mask. Standing over Rocky I glared down and said, "I don't like people getting into my knees." Rocky is tough and man enough to know that if the situation had been reversed, he would have blasted me to protect his knees. He jumped up and said, "No problem," and ran back to the Steelers' huddle. I looked around to see whether another flag had been thrown, but the man in stripes had missed this one. I guess if the official is a poor enough one to make mistakes of the flags he throws, he can miss a legitimate call, too.

Later the Steelers tried to make the same play, but Rocky Bleier wasn't in my area. This time I spotted Lynn Swann nonchalantly roaming over the middle, and I drew a bead on his rib cage. But then

I saw George Atkinson homing in on Lynn, and with one quick swipe of a forearm, George sort of pulled Lynn down using a club-like action across the head and side of the neck. Lynn went down and George moved in toward the ball carrier. The shot to Swann was by no means an overpowering one. In fact, I thought that it had simply caught Lynn off guard and he had lost his balance. But Lynn needed some assistance getting off the field. The entire incident was, at the time, so insignificant that George wasn't even credited with a "knockout" or even a "limp-off." It was nothing, absolutely nothing. While the action was going on, I could see Lynn running back and forth behind the Steelers' bench.

Shortly thereafter the Steelers scored a go-ahead touchdown, making the score 21-14. It had been that kind of day. One team would score and then the other team would score.

On the next series the Steelers stopped us cold and had the ball again. When their offensive unit came out of the field, Swann stayed behind and ran lazy patterns behind the bench. He seemed perfectly healthy, and I wondered why he wasn't in the game. Then, on the first play, I got John Stallworth. Stallworth caught the ball over the middle and a split second later, I hit him hard. As a result of the contact, John twisted his knee and had to be helped off the field. George gave me credit for a "limp-off." Now, when Lynn Swann was called up and told to go back into the game, he collapsed on the side-lines. One second he was perfectly normal and the next second he was supposedly out cold. It could be that it took George's shot a long time to register, but then again, I really wonder.

Even without Swann and Stallworth, the Steelers went in for another score and built their lead to 28-14. Bradshaw had a great time running up and down the sidelines showing the ball to Raider fans. Evidently, Terry thought the game was over even though there were still over five minutes on the clock. Unfortunately for Bradshaw and the entire Steeler team, five minutes was more than enough for us to come back.

When Kenny Stabler got his hands on the football, he started performing feats of magic. Within a minute the scoreboard was lighting up and now read, Steelers 28, Raiders 21.

We stopped the Steelers on their next series and they kept us in our own territory when we got the ball back. With a little more than three minutes to play, Coach Madden decided to kick the ball deep and ask the defense to come up with the big play. After three running plays the Steelers were faced with a fourth down and ten. Bobby Walden, the Steelers' punter, was rushed into a bad kick and once again Stabler was operating from good field position.

In a matter of seconds the game was tied at 28, but the Steelers were going to have another chance. After kicking deep, the Steelers took over on their own twenty and from there Bradshaw decided to try some magic of his own. One play later Terry Bradshaw made the ball disappear from the Steelers' offense. Actually, Bradshaw was under fire; he threw a wild pass into the strength of our secondary, and linebacker Willie Hall made a great interception. From there we ran a few running plays to use up the time and then kicked a last-second field goal.

The game was over and the Raiders won 31-28. It's strange that professional football players can be brutal enemies during the contest but once the final gun sounds, the animosities are usually over. Everyone realized it had been a great game and even a greater come-from-behind win. In a semi-serious tone some of the Steelers warned us that they would return for the playoffs later in the year. Actually, there was a lot of truth in that statement because the Raiders and Steelers usually do meet in the playoff games. In all, I would say that most of the players left the field pretty good friends, in spite of every-thing that had happened. Naturally, I thought it was a good game, a great game, but there was always next week to start considering.

Early Monday morning I received a call from my attorney, Tony DeCello. Tony lives in Pittsburgh, a strange place for me to have an attorney, but that's the way it worked out. Anyway, Tony called and asked, "Tate, did you hear the news?"

"Damn, Tony, what time is it?" I asked. "It's still dark."

Tony told me it was eight o'clock in the morning ... Pittsburgh time. That meant it was five o'clock in Oakland.

For my attorney to call me at five in the morning means that something serious must have happened. As he was telling me the story, I started to wake up. I didn't understand everything the first time so I asked Tony to run it by me again. He said, "Tate, Lynn Swann is in the hospital with a serious concussion and Chuck Noll is blasting the hell out of you and George. Noll is claiming that there are 'criminal elements' in professional football. The commissioner has already called my office and they are going to take legal action – fines, I think."

Well, I still couldn't make heads or tails out of the situation. First of all, I hadn't touched Swann in the game. I was looking for him, but he never came anywhere near me. And the "criminal element" talk I simply couldn't understand.

"Tony," I said, "call me later. I'm going back to sleep."

That was how serious I thought the situation was. I didn't know what was going on, and quite frankly, I didn't care. Commissioner

Pete Rozelle has the right to sound off. After a tough game I need my sleep, and that was much more important to me than another publicity stunt.

Later in the morning George Atkinson called me and laughed about Chuck Noll's comments. George said, "Tate, the coach in Pittsburgh has referred to you and me as criminals and he wants us put in jail."

At the time I still had no idea of the impact the game and the accusations were having on the public. I thought that it wasn't serious because nothing had really happened. But as the day went on, I began to realize that a few isolated incidents were getting blown up by the press, Steeler coach Chuck Noll, and Commissioner Pete Rozelle.

Later that afternoon I found out that Lynn Swann really was in the hospital with a concussion. I had seen George hit Swann and at the time it didn't look that serious. After all, even after the hit, I had seen Lynn running up and down the sidelines apparently in fairly good health, but somewhere between Oakland and Pittsburgh he had evidently developed a serious concussion. Regardless of Swann's condition, I still couldn't figure out why my name was dragged into the mess. After all, I didn't hit Swann. I remembered that last year when I got Swann, Chuck Noll had made the statement that I should be barred from ever playing football in the NFL, but that was last year.

It took some time, but all parts of the puzzle started falling into place. I found out that Rocky Bleier – the same Rocky Bleier who had taken a shot at my knee during our miraculous win over the Steelers – had written a letter to Commissioner Rozelle regarding my tactics. In the letter, which I later read, I was accused of willfully trying to hurt receivers and running backs. I was accused of being a cheap-shot artist and of employing tactics designed to seriously injure my opponents. The letter also implied that many players feared for their lives when playing against me and that some type of disciplinary action should be taken immediately.

There were rumors that other Steelers had written the commissioner complaining about my style. My first reaction was, "Where's Franco's letter?" But I soon found out he never sent one in. To say the least, I was surprised. But a greater surprise was the shock I felt about Rocky Bleier being part of such trash. Rocky has a certain amount of courage and he knows about the game. More important than all that, he knows why I fought back against him. Sure, I go out and use the Hook and I hit hard, but it's all part of the game. Given the same opportunity, any player would try to blast me into the nickel stands, too. The point is that my job is based upon my ability to be intimidating and violent. Yet my every action is well within the structure of the NFL rules. If and when the rules change, I'll change my style. But for now, I prevent the opposition from scoring by destroying their confidence. A running back cannot run toward the goal line and away from me at the same time. Likewise, a receiver can't concentrate on catching a pass while listening for my footsteps.

I have never faulted Rocky for running too fast or blocking too hard, because I realize why he is paid. Randy Grossman is said to have a great pair of hands and can catch anything near him. Should I cry because Grossman can make great catches? Or maybe I should look into the physical aspects of playing tight end? Okay, Grossman is a down lineman. He can catch a pass or he can come down the field and block. There is no rule that tells Grossman how fast he can run or how hard he can block. If his job calls for coming at me full speed and knocking me over hard and violently, and he does it, then fine. I accept that as part of the game. Playing free safety is a job of hitting and getting hit. I've been hit by linemen who outweigh me by eighty or ninety pounds. When one of those beasts hits you straight on or from the blind side while moving full speed, it hurts! I literally bounce along the ground after getting smacked by an offensive guard or tackle but I still realize it's all part of the game. I have never cried about anyone hitting me too hard or getting blind-sided, because it's a chance I take every time I suit up to play football. Even when Mansfield speared me in the championship game of 1975 and my knee was injured, I didn't complain. Even when I was hit in Denver's Mile High Stadium after the play was over with a cheap shot that cost me knee surgery, I didn't complain.

I cannot stress enough the fact that football is a violent and brutal game. When people start pounding each other, they bleed. When running backs moving full speed slam into defensive people, bones often break and men find themselves severed from reality. Look into the basic objective of a football game and you'll see what I mean. An offensive team is put on the field and given the responsibility to move the ball forward and score points. But a defensive team is also out there trying to counteract every offensive move. The human body was not designed with a football game in mind, but nonetheless this type of violence seems to satisfy a psychological need of our society. The Romans had the gladiators, hungry lions and Christians; and we have boxing, hockey and football.

Whenever I step onto the field for a game, I expect to get knocked around, and I consider the possibility I will sustain a serious injury. If I get hit and injured, whether by a clean block or a cheap shot, I just consider it part of the game. I know that in the heat of battle there are going to be individuals who let their emotions get the best of them, and from time to time I'll get hit late or clipped. But it doesn't mean I have to cry to the press about criminals in football, and it certainly doesn't require a letter to the commissioner. I get hit and I hit because it's part of football. Sometimes the hits will be late or questionable, but it happens. I guess that's why we have rules and officials – just to make sure everyone gets busted up according to the book. Fast running, great catches, hard hits, late hits and cheap shots are all just part of the game, and I don't believe any rules of the commissioner can control these areas of football. Any time you put two or more athletes together and let them engage in a contact sport, tempers will flare and violence will prevail. When you consider that on a typical play during a football game twenty-two men, at the combined weight of better than two tons, engage in violent physical action against each other, it's really no wonder that the game is brutal. Any athlete in the NFL who expects something less than brutality is thinking like a fool or hiding from reality.

Lynn Swann has great natural athletic ability. Swann can leap high and make great catches, and he has the speed and quickness to beat you long or short. But when it comes to hitting or getting hit, Lynn has a tendency to shy away. I would expect him to write the commissioner a letter, but I never imagined that Grossman and Bleier would do such a thing. I was certain I had done nothing wrong, but because of letters to the commissioner and several questionable calls, I was faced with a problem. Public opinion was being manipulated against my style of play.

Even though Howard Cosell dedicated a half-time show on "Monday Night Football" to George and me, the commissioner's office would only state that action would be taken in the near future. According to Cosell, George and I were worse than the Prince of Darkness himself, but we both felt the validity of any statement Cosell made would be questionable at best. The show and the comments were simply a part of Cosell's plan to build sensationalism into a small part of a football game while portraying himself as the crusader against violence and brutality in football. Football is a violent and brutal game, but for the news media to devote any time to cheap shots and cheap-shot artists is absurd. Still, though, all the undesirable publicity did have a bad effect on George and me. Every time we came anywhere near contact, the officials started throwing penalty flags for unnecessary roughness. In a game against New England several weeks after the Swann incident, George and I attempted to bring down their running back, Jess Philips. Several years before, Jess had been a Raider, and we knew back then he was a very difficult man to tackle. Neither George nor I made a good hit, and Jess was bucking and dragging us along for extra yardage. Finally, I got in a position to flip him and slam him to the ground. The official immediately threw a flag. It was ridiculous, and everyone knew it. When George protested, the official threw another flag, and on a play that started out to be a six-yard gain, the officials helped to make it a quick thirty-six yards. Even Jess jumped up and asked the official, "Man, what the hell are you doing? There wasn't anything cheap about that shot. What gives, anyway?"

Even the man who was getting hit and knocked to the ground thought it was a quick and unjustifiable call, but the official said, "Tatum, I'm not going to let you get away with a damn thing. I'm watching you all the way!"

During another game I was clipped, and the official was standing right on the spot watching the play. Naturally, I asked the official about the clip, and he replied, "I'm not watching anyone except you."

Most of the players and coaches know and understand about the game, but once in a while someone will come along who cries and complains loud enough and long enough until the news media listens. When that happens, it becomes an uphill struggle to prove your point. I am not a cheap player. I hit hard, but I've never taken an illegal shot at anyone. Sure, I've caught receivers close to the sidelines, but never out of bounds. It's also true that I used the Hook, but the technique was legal then. It might sound strange, but there is a legal and an illegal way to use the Hook. Using a straight forearm and swinging it into a player is illegal, but I would keep my arm in tight against my body. I would attempt to strip the ball from the offensive man while at the same time trying to catch his head in between my biceps and forearms. Believe me, it was legal, and what's more, the Hook was always the best intimidator in the business. I've probably used the Hook at one time or another on every receiver and running back in the NFL. Every time I've been called on the carpet by the commissioner, the tactic was never questioned. So the Hook was legal, and until the rules were rewritten I stung people with that particular technique.

I guess it was several weeks later that I actually received a certified letter from Pete Rozelle stating that I was being fined $750. The letter explained that because I punched Grossman, slapped Franco and slugged Bleier, the commissioner deemed it necessary to fine me $250 for each incident. I wasn't about to pay the fines and demanded a hearing. By shelling out $750 to the NFL, I would have been giving in to the worst kind of autocracy. I have never believed that the commissioner has the right to set fines without hearings, and I filed a formal protest.

Even if I had been wrong about those three incidents, I still would have refused to pay the fines because of my right to have a hearing. The truth of the matter was that I did slug Grossman after being provoked, but the Franco Harris incident was absurd. If they wanted to penalize me for anything, then drop the flag because of the Bleier hit and step off fifteen yards. If the commissioner intended to start fining every player because of action during the game then we might just as well hang up the gear and start playing ping-pong.

If Rozelle felt the fines were justifiable, then let him prove it through his attorneys and make me pay the money.

Rozelle accepted the challenge and arranged a date that fit into our schedule. After a Sunday game in New England, which we lost 48-17, I flew into New York for a Monday morning hearing. Using game films, Pete tried to prove that I was guilty of infractions. When he started with the Grossman incident, the films proved that Randy hit me late. Still, the commissioner contended that I had punched and kicked a man. Next he tried to get me on the Franco Harris slap, but the films proved that I had the right to hit the man. More than just hit or slap at Franco, I could have blasted into him without mercy. At that point the score seemed to be even at 1-1, but the commissioner came up with the Bleier movies and I openly admitted my guilt during that particular play. I tried to bring up the previous season when Mansfield injured my legs and explain that I was sensitive about low crack back blocks, but the man just wasn't listening. I felt as though the walls were closing in on me. I was in a hostile environment, and regardless of the facts, I was to be guilty as charged.

Although the news media seemed to know and understand everything about the "criminal element" incident, quite frankly, I didn't. Even after my hearing with Pete Rozelle, I knew little or nothing about the deal. First of all, there were, as I explained, three separate charges against me: Franco, Grossman and Bleier. At the hearing Rozelle said that the charges were "unnecessary roughness," and then he said that I had acted "unprofessionally." Pete Rozelle and his lawyers were vague about everything.

Next, I was shown the famous letters, but wasn't permitted copies. I was just told to read the letters from the Steelers, and when my attorney asked for copies the answer was a polite, "No!" To me the hearing had shades of the Old West. The bad guy was in the courtroom at his hearing while the hangman was knotting the rope securing it over the nearest tree.

Of course, we looked at the game films, but they only proved my incident with Grossman was provoked by Grossman, that Franco actually hadn't been down, and the hit on Rocky could have been passed off as part of the game or maybe my bending the rules. But in all, the entire hearing was so damn vague that I was upset for several days. I believe that in view of the Atkinson-Swann action, the NFL felt that Jack Tatum's name should be mentioned, too. But that's the kind of ink in the paper I'm trying to get away from.

I'm getting a little ahead of myself, but much later Pete Rozelle sent down a $500 fine for my "unnecessary roughness" charges. Evidently, Pete felt a little compassion for me and reduced my sentence by $250. But that's not the issue or the point. I wasn't guilty of unnecessary roughness or unsportsmanlike conduct. I was a victim of the system and resented it. I resented even more the fact that Rozelle wasn't interested in my side of the story. The verdict was in and I was guilty regardless of favorable evidence or the NFL's lack of proof that a crime had been committed.

As I flew back to Oakland I started thinking about my life and how dramatically it had changed from farm boy in North Carolina to "paid assassin" for the Oakland Raiders. While deep in thought about those early years, I began to realize that someone was staring at me. As I looked across the aisle I saw a young boy looking back expressionlessly.

"What's happenin', Pal?" I asked.

He never answered the question. The kid just sat there looking at me. "Are you going for a vacation in California or do you live there?" I asked, trying to get the little dude going.

Then this little man's mother said, "Tell Mr. Tatum that you live in Oakland and you watch all his football games."

Well, this little fellow wouldn't say a word. He just sat there and stared, but his mother and I started talking. She said, "We've seen you play on television and at the stadium. You know, we are Oakland Raider fans."

It was small talk, but a nice conversation. Finally, the lady got around to saying, "You know, I've pictured you much differently. I guess when you put on your equipment and play in a game you have to be a different personality. I half expect all football players to be brutes in real life, but you're real people, too."

Just then the little dude said, "Jack, can I have your autograph? You're my favorite player. You wear number thirty-two in the games, but how's come on my bubble gum card you wear number thirty-one?"

I signed the little man an autograph first and then said, "Come over here and sit beside me. Now, let me tell you the story about my rookie year and why I was number thirty-one."

3

In the Ghetto

I would have been perfectly content to have spent my childhood listening to my grandfather, Wesley Starr, telling me stories of the great Civil War. With a particular fondness I remember Grandpa telling me how he and General Grant, riding white chargers, sent a hundred or more Johnny Rebs fleeing for their lives. I'd sit for hours on hours beneath the green tapestry of a willow tree as Grandpa rambled on about the Great War and many other actual events in history on which he had had a direct bearing. Why, Grandpa even told me that he had helped row General Washington across the Delaware on a winter's night in the first war he ever fought.

Grandpa Starr had a way of painting stories with simple words that could mesmerize a young boy, but as I grew older and much more knowledgeable, it began to seem that the old gentleman had a tendency to exaggerate a little. For if he and Grant actually did send those rebels fleeing, and if in fact he did row Washington across the Delaware, then my grandfather was remarkably well-preserved for a man closing in on two hundred years of life. I learned much later that Grandpa was a sharp-witted gentleman of some sixty odd years who had a fancy for history. However, it had still been a delightful experience for a young barefoot country boy to sit in the shade on those hot summer days and be whisked away by the magic of an old man's words to exciting eras of history.

I was born in Crouse, North Carolina, on November 18, 1948. My early childhood memories are filled with a special contentment because my early life encompassed the peaceful Carolina countryside and those fantastic journeys of the mind I made while listening to Grandpa. With all this, and good food, a roof overhead, and parents who loved me, what more could a little boy really expect?

In those early years I never actually sat down and thought about my future, but I'm sure if a decision were to have been made, I probably would have trotted off over the countryside with my Grandpa and gone into the next battle he and Grant, or Washington, or even Patton were planning. Then again, maybe I would have just sat in the shade and waited for Grandpa to return and let him tell me about the fighting. My experience in Crouse typified the lazy half-asleep movements of the humid and sticky South. Unlike most young boys, I had no ambition of growing up and becoming a cowboy or fireman. I guess I would have been perfectly content to just remain a happy child who vicariously rushed into adventure through a journey of the mind.

When I was nearing six years of age, my parents started talking about moving to New Jersey. Some of our relatives, my mother's brother Jim and his family, had left the South several years ago and found New Jersey to their liking. When they wrote about the higher-paying jobs and better school systems in the North, my parents grew more serious about moving.

North Carolina suited my style of life, and I just wasn't interested in moving anywhere. After all, my father had a good job as a welder, and our home was comfortable and always filled with the scent of good things cooking. But nonetheless the rumors of a move to New Jersey persisted. We were a family of seven, but democracy did not exist within the structure of the Tatum household. Although my parents, Lewis and Annie Mae, were quite set on moving up to New Jersey, my two brothers, Manuel and Samuel, along with my two sisters, Peggy and Mabel, protested against the idea. I was the youngest, and for the most part, not expected to understand the intricacies of moving to another state, but I still filed my protest along with my older sisters and brothers.

Instead of taking a vote about whether or not we were actually going to move, my father simply sat us down and explained his decision without even considering the unanimous disapproval of his five children. He informed us that we were making the move to New Jersey and anyone who didn't like the idea could stay behind with my mother's parents, Delzora and Wesley Starr. I remember thinking that was all quite fine with me and quickly decided to tell my parents, "Have a nice trip and come back and visit with me sometime."

But just as I began to wonder how much I would miss my parents, I heard my dad say, "That applies to everyone except John David and Mabel." I was John David and Mabel was the youngest of my sisters. "You two are just kids and can't take on the responsibility of caring for yourselves," my father went on to explain.

There were times when my father's voice had the ring of authority to it, and those were the times you never said, "But, Daddy..." You learned early in life when a subject wasn't open for discussion. Mabel and I realized that Samuel, Manuel and Peggy would be staying behind while the rest of us would be heading north into a new adventure.

The imagination of a six-year-old boy can be fantastic. It was always quite easy for me to picture in my mind the stories Grandpa had told, and now I was letting that same imagination run to New Jersey. I envisioned new friends, naturally, but I also anticipated as my new swimming hole a quiet lake shimmering in the sunshine. I further imagined a river lined with green and golden trees and a small, but rather nice-looking pier that jutted out over the exact spot where a school of catfish spent their time just waiting to be caught by a little boy like me. There were some bass and a few trout, too. "Yes," I thought, "New Jersey will be a nice place." I carried those thoughts and visions into my sleep as the night fell and my father drove northward.

As morning broke, the reality of Paterson, New Jersey, slapped me to consciousness. I peered out the window of our car at gaunt stacks belching the black smoke and soot that was falling over the crowded tenement dwellings. The cotton land of Carolina had been traded for a maze of chipped concrete, broken glass, and a serrated mass of towers and spires standing silently against a faded red sky. I was scared and already longing for my home.

We moved in with Uncle Jim and Aunt Billie Starr. My aunt and uncle had a small but quite nice home in Paterson. I must admit that with my two cousins, Leon (he was the oldest) and Rayvon (he was my age), and the five of us, plus Uncle Jim and Aunt Billie, it was very crowded. We all managed to live together and get along, but I do believe sanity prevailed only because everyone knew that as soon as my dad found work, we would move into our own place.

Rayvon was a blessing for me in my attempts at justifying the move from Crouse to Paterson. It was quite obvious that Paterson was different from Crouse and if not for Rayvon, I would have had great difficulty in adjusting to my new world. There were plenty of kid things to do around Paterson. We could go down to the railroad yard and throw rocks at passing commuter trains or play in the wreckage and ruins of old buildings. I wasn't opposed to throwing rocks, but aiming at trains bothered me. After taking me to the railroad yard, Rayvon said, "I like to throw rocks but it's not much fun hitting the train." We both agreed that someone could get hurt. More than the chance of one of the passengers on the train getting hurt, Rayvon and I considered the possibility of getting caught. Then, for sure, someone would get hurt, and in all probability, it would be two little dudes named John David and Rayvon. After a couple of days of throwing rocks at the trains I asked, "Rayvon, why do we have to do this?" He answered, "Because everyone does." Although we were young, the reason behind "everyone does" wasn't strong enough to keep us at the railroad yard. There were other things to do, and we went on to explore the rest of the city.

Playing in the wreckage and ruins of the old buildings wasn't bad except for the warning Uncle Jim had issued when we first arrived. Uncle Jim said, "Rayvon, if you take J.D. down by those old buildings and I catch ya, I'll beat the hell out of both of you."

The buildings were ideal for our war games, but Uncle Jim's warnings constantly rang somewhere in the deep chambers of my mind. With each passing day, the excitement of climbing around the piles of bricks, broken glass and rusted-out pipes caused us to forget Uncle Jim's threats, and the old buildings became our playground. I was particularly fond of exploring the condemned buildings with rotted-out flooring and weak and creaky staircases. When we would carry our war games into one of those old buildings, it would sometimes take hours to sight the enemy. But I learned to listen for the sound of a floorboard creaking under the weight of the enemy and then plan my attack.

After several weeks of playing and exploring the old buildings, Uncle Jim's warnings faded completely from my mind. In the evenings, when he would fix himself a drink from his bottle of I.W. Harper, Uncle Jim would usually ask, "What did you boys do today?" Rayvon or I would answer, "Nothin' special, just played outside." Every so often he would ask, "You guys don't play in the old buildings, do you?" Rayvon and I would both answer, "Oh no, a kid could get hurt down there."

Well, we were right about a kid getting hurt down there. Unfortunately, our fears about a kid getting hurt even more when he got home were also correct. One day Rayvon went through a rotted area of flooring. One second he was on the fourth floor moving in on me (I was hiding in a closet), and the next thing I knew, Rayvon screamed, fell through the flooring, and landed on the third floor. My first reaction was to run downstairs and shoot him with my gun made from a rusted pipe, but then I realized he could be hurt, seriously hurt. I yelled in terror and ran down the stairs to help him. When I reached Rayvon, he was lying face down over a pile of splintered boards and dusty plaster. I stood frozen with fear as terrible images flashed through my mind. He could have broken his neck, or leg, or even had a piece of sharp floor board sticking in his side. I felt weak with anxiety as I approached Rayvon's motionless body. Then Rayvon whirled over and said, "Bam, you're dead!" He got me, but that wasn't the end of the battle. Rayvon had actually hurt himself. He had cut and twisted his leg and had bruises all over his body, head and face. He got me, but when we got home, Uncle Jim got him.

That day ended our war games in the old buildings forever, but it was still a big city with other areas to explore.

We tried playing the games that other kids in our neighborhood played, but it wasn't much fun. Most of the other kids thought stealing things from the stores in the area was great fun and a true test of one's manhood. Sometimes they stole items they could use or eat, but usually it was a game of stealing for the sake of stealing, and I just couldn't understand it at all. Actually, I couldn't even understand stealing food and things you could use, because I realized that someone was going to have to pay for the merchandise in the long run. One time Rayvon and I went into a small grocery store. The plan was for Rayvon to keep the storekeeper busy while I sneaked around to a side aisle and stole something. I was trying to keep an eye on Rayvon and the storekeeper and at the same time grab something off the shelf. We were smooth and I slipped out the door with a big box tucked under my shirt. I ran around the corner and started to laugh with relief. Seconds later Rayvon ran out of the store and we beat it on down the road. After running several blocks, we were sure it was cool to check out the merchandise. Rayvon said, "Wow, J.D., that's a big box you got under your shirt, what didya get?"

"I don't know," was my reply. I tugged out the box and we both stood there and looked. "What is it, J.D.? What's it used for?" Rayvon asked me.

Hell, I didn't know, and since neither of us could read, we tried to figure it out. Rayvon felt that maybe these pads were used for cleaning cars or something like that but I figured they were for shining shoes. Except for the fact that they were white and thick, they did look very much like the cloths the shoeshine boys used. We both eventually agreed that they were for shining shoes and decided to do a good deed. The plan was to go home and shine everyone's shoes. At the time I couldn't figure it out, but when my aunt came home and saw us shining shoes with those pads, she became a little uptight. Rayvon and I figured that she had found out we stole the pads, and when she asked, "What are you guys doing?" Rayvon screamed out, "Don't hit me! J.D. stole 'em!"

Throwing rocks at trains wasn't my bag, and after the incident at the building, I realized there must be a safer way to spend the summer. Then, when my father explained why a person doesn't steal, I understood that the life of crime could be a painful experience. There just had to be something else for us to do. When we sat around the house complaining that there wasn't anything to do, Aunt Billie found a few things to keep us busy. Washing windows, dusting tables, cleaning the cellar, working in the yard ... after a day or so of her idea of fun and games, Rayvon and I moved out into the streets again in search of other adventures.

Before long, my father found work and we moved. Then we moved again and again. In the space of three months, we had moved four times and were planning yet another move. These moves were spurred by different reasons: one because of better housing in another section of town; another because of a different job my father found; but regardless, it was becoming a difficult life. I would get settled in school, make a few friends, and the next day we would move into another area of Paterson. Then the moves involved greater distances. Instead of moving around Paterson, my father found a job in Clifton, and we moved. After a few months in Clifton, my parents realized the rent was too high and we moved back into Paterson. I was about eight or nine years old and had moved more times than I could remember.

After a few years, my father's work became more secure and we sort of settled down in one area. It was a tough neighborhood, but I honestly tried to mind my own business and keep out of trouble. I wasn't happy with our situation and even though it had been years since I left Crouse, I still had a strong desire to return to my true home. Because of my loneliness and longing for the countryside, I became shy and reserved. It wasn't that my grades in school were bad or anything like that, I just never said much and became a loner for the most part.

One morning on my way to school, several young neighborhood hoodlums mistook my reserved ways for cowardice. I guess you could say that we lived on the other side of the tracks because every morning on my way to school, I had to walk through an underpass as trains would steam and whistle their way overhead. To cross over the tracks above the underpass would be dangerous, and only a fool would try such a thing. The trains would speed by at fifty and sixty miles an hour and several people had been killed shortcutting over the tracks. My father only had to tell me once about the importance of the underpass, and I knew that if anyone ever caught me up on the tracks, either the train or my father would kill me. So walking to and from school through the underpass was a daily ritual for me.

That particular morning I was jumped by these two young hoods just as I came out of the underpass. They roughed me up a little and then the biggest one said, "Hey man, we own the underpass and any dude that uses it got to pay toll. Out with your milk money or we'll beat you."

They were both a little older than me and a little bigger, but I really wasn't scared. And to this day I don't know why I gave in to their demands, but I reached in my pocket and took out a dime. That was the money my dad had given me for milk and cookies, and the biggest one grabbed the dime and pushed me to the ground. They ran off laughing while I picked myself up and went on to school.

When it was time for our class to have a milk and cookies break, I sat back and watched the others enjoying themselves while I started to burn deep down inside.

I didn't like the idea of someone stealing from me. It not only hurt my feelings, but the more I thought about the incident, the more angry I became. I realized how the merchants felt when we stole from them. Although I was never what you would call an active thief, I still occasionally took little items that were not mine. That day I made a vow to never again take anything that wasn't mine from anyone. And by the same vow I wasn't going to treat with favor anyone that stole from me. I hoped the little thugs would never try me again. It hadn't been very enjoyable watching other kids eat cookies and drink milk, and I felt certain I would never let it happen again.

On my way out of the underpass the very next morning I was accosted by the same two bullies, and once again I gave in to their demands. This time I felt more angry with myself than with the thugs because I had failed to live up to my vows. I needed a plan. My first alternative was to avoid any future confrontation. I started thinking about another route to school but I didn't want to get caught on the tracks by either a train or my father, so that was out of the question. I could have walked nine blocks or so in the other direction and crossed the tracks by using another underpass, but that would mean getting up at least forty-five minutes earlier in the morning. Being mugged two days in a row wasn't much fun, and there was always tomorrow morning, when I believed they would make it three. I had to do something. I knew I couldn't go to the police or anyone else for help, since squealing on anyone in my neighborhood was an unforgivable act of cowardice. My course of action was obviously to attack the attackers.

The next morning I found a piece of pipe about eighteen inches long. The pipe would more or less even up the odds. There were two of them, and now, two of me. As I walked through the underpass I hoped the thugs would not be there, because I really didn't want to hit anyone with that piece of pipe, but I certainly didn't relish the thought of being mugged every morning. "Maybe," I thought to myself, "just maybe they were satisfied and won't even be there today."

I also considered the possibility that I wouldn't be able to use the pipe and I pictured the two of them pounding little me into the ground and then stealing my dime. I even thought about turning around in the middle of the underpass and going over the tracks or even back home. But then I started thinking about my grandfather's stories and how he talked about bravery. "Sometimes," he would say, "sometimes a man has got to face danger. If he turns and runs, he isn't worth his weight in salt but if he fights for a cause, he's a man even if he loses the battle."

As I looked toward the far end of the underpass at the daylight I could see the silhouetted figures of the toll collectors. At that point, I made up my mind to face the danger and become a man.

When I reached the end of the tunnel, the biggest thug said, "Okay, fool, you know what to do next. Be out with the dime or I'll smack you in the mouth."

I reached inside my jacket for the security of the pipe tucked in my belt and said, "Kiss off, chump!"

There was wavering in both of the little thugs' confidence, and they paused for a second. Then the biggest one reached out for me and I blasted him with the pipe. I hit him on the hand first and then started swinging wildly. I caught him with a good shot on the head, a couple times on the shoulder, and they both took off running and crying. I chased after the other one, too, and beat him a couple of times on the back. As I chased them down the street, I could hear the small one screaming, "He's crazy! He's crazy!"

Well, crazy or not, I was never again asked to pay a toll at the end of the underpass, but there was another occasion when I had to prove my manhood. While I was growing up I had to prove myself only twice in fights. Actually, I consider piping the toll collectors only a matter of self-preservation, but there was one time in my early life that required a knockdown, drag-out fight. Of course, there were many fights in the ghetto, but for the most part, I was always able to bluff my way out. Most of the kids my age were scared to death of me for some reason, and I never had any problems with them. Once in a while some of the older guys would try to rough us up, but my confidence and assertiveness enabled me to bluff my way out of actually fighting. I wasn't afraid to fight, and it wasn't having to kick someone's teeth in or get mine kicked in that restrained me from being a street fighter. It was just that I always looked on fighting as a silly waste of energy. And besides, more times than not, two dudes would get into a fight and seconds later they were buddies. So within my street gang I never had any serious problems. But one time the Crackers from the other side of the tracks came into our neighborhood looking for trouble. We found the Crackers or they found us, but regardless, we met in an alley face to face, getting ready to go at it. One of the Crackers made the statement, "Stanley Petrokoski can kick the hell out of any nigger in Niggertown."

The word "nigger" didn't bother me, but I didn't like the tone of his statement. I moved to the front and said, "I'm no nigger, but will a black do?"

All my friends were shocked to hear me pipe off like that because I wasn't the biggest member of the gang and I never started fights. Stanley pushed his way out of the crowd of Crackers and said, "You look like a nigger to me."

Stanley was big and I sort of stepped back a bit expecting one of the older stronger guys in our gang to jump in and accept the challenge. But Rayvon said, "Tate, he's talking to you. He just called you a nigger."

I had to choose whether to back down and be a coward or fight and get the hell beat out of me. Once again the voice of Grandpa Starr rang in my mind, and it came back to the point of being a man. Winning or losing the fight wasn't important, but proving yourself a man was what life was all about.

I fought and to my surprise, Stanley was a pussy. He was big and maybe even strong, but I was so damn fast that I sucker-punched him before he had a chance to blink. In all probability the fight was over after my first punch. Blood was gushing from around Stanley's mouth where his two front teeth had previously been and the light of confidence in his eyes had dulled to a fixed and stupid gaze, but I was riled up and decided to give Stanley a serious whipping. All the Crackers kept screaming, "Hit him, Stash, kick 'em, Stash," but Stash was getting punched up the alley toward the street. I admit that I didn't have to beat him so badly, but it was going to be a lesson no one would ever forget. My father and even my Uncle Jim used to say, "Don't start a fight, but if you've got to fight, then fight to beat the hell out of him." By the time we reached the street, Stanley's face was a mass of unfamiliar bumps and bruises. Somehow I got him up on my shoulder and threw him in the street in my final fit of rage. That was the last time I ever fought or had to bluff my way out of a fight while living in the ghetto. By the time my friends and the Crackers had finished adding to the story and developing my reputation as a ferocious fighter, I would have backed down from myself.

Street fighting was a common practice in the ghetto, but as I grew older and much wiser, I could never justify fighting. There was no purpose behind any of the fights I watched, and it all seemed a waste of time. To fight with someone because he was white, or black, or because he lived on the opposite side of town was utterly ridiculous. Fighting for self-preservation, or because you were a professional boxer, or maybe for the love of a woman had some merit, but street fights in the ghetto were ludicrous.

During the last half of my eighth year in school, my parents moved again. My father hadn't received a raise for several years and the rent on our apartment had tripled. We simply couldn't afford to live in the "classy" area of Paterson's ghetto, so we moved into the bottom of Passaic's ghetto. This was a most difficult time for my family and myself but even under these extreme conditions, I tried to do the right things in life. I realized my parents had enough problems and I didn't want my actions to add to their growing list.

Passaic, New Jersey, or at least my part of Passaic, was a cluttered, noisy neighborhood. It was a belligerent environment that clamored with the noises of trains, factories, traffic, and kids playing in the street. When we had first moved to New Jersey everything at least looked respectable. Now that I was looking at my world through more mature eyes, I wanted out. Life to the residents of the Passaic ghetto was a deep, throbbing pain, and the escape routes from this world were marked with drugs and crime. Most of my friends became thieves, and worse, many others turned to hard drugs as their way out. I didn't want to live in a ghetto for the rest of my life, and I wanted something better for my parents, too. But there were times when I felt my world was a cell and we were all sentenced to life imprisonment.

I avoided trouble as though it were the plague and my grades in school were good. Some of the guys in the neighborhood considered me strange because I was quiet and reserved and hardly ever went along with the gang's idea of fun and excitement. Occasionally, I would take a drink of wine and I did start to smoke, but that was it. I had a burning desire to get out of the ghetto, and I realized that education, not crime, was my ticket.

By the time I became a sophomore in high school, my physical abilities and size were impressive. Weighing 185 pounds and standing nearly five feet ten inches, no one ever questioned me or my ideas about getting out of the ghetto. I knew that my strength was natural and there wasn't anyone in the neighborhood who was stronger or faster. My once-skinny arms had developed into solid ridges of muscle and my reflexes were unbelievably quick. Some people thought I would become a boxer, but I didn't have that type of desire. Then my Uncle Jim and my father started talking about football. I had always like football and knew my skills in that game were far above average. In fact, most of the kids in the neighborhood didn't like to play tackle football against me. I was the fastest and hardest runner, and when I tackled, everyone (even the older guys) complained that I hit too hard. Until football practice started in our sophomore year, I had always considered myself abnormal. Something had to be wrong with me. It just wasn't normal to be the fastest, hardest-running guy in town when most of the people I played against were much older and bigger. And when it came time to make the tackles, I wasn't afraid, but actually enjoyed bone-crunching contact. Hard tackling involved something I couldn't figure out. Usually, there are two bodies involved in a tackle. When those two bodies collide, it seemed natural to assume that both would feel the effects of the shock, but when I'd hit someone, they usually didn't get up right away, and I would hardly feel a thing. It got to a point where I was becoming afraid of football. The contact had no effect on me, but I worried about what I might do to others. I just never really wanted to hurt anyone.

When I put the pads on for the first time, my coach, John Federici, started off the practice with a tackling drill. I didn't know much about technique, but I liked his tackling philosophy. My coach said, "When you go after a ball carrier, hit him hard and with everything you have. Good tackling is projecting yourself through a target. This way, you are hitting and the offensive man is getting hit. Now a couple of you jump in here and try it."

Some of the guys were making pretty good tackles and some weren't. When my turn came to make a tackle, everyone quieted down. Coach Federici had never seen me tackle before and he sort of wondered what was about to happen. Then in a split second of clashing pads and painful screams, Coach Federici understood the silence before my first tackle. Actually, it was no big deal, even though I did knock the ball carrier out. Everyone who knew me expected a knockout because of the type of drill the coach had set up. One man ran the ball straight at another man, who would attempt to make the tackle. This drill was for me only because it was straight-ahead football. It simply amounted to building up your speed and smashing the ball carrier. For the most part, the running back is usually a little apprehensive about head-on tackles and he tends to back off. Any man who has the courage to really drive his body through the target while making the tackle is going to hurt the other person. Needless to say, Coach Federici never let me participate in that particular drill again. I think his decision made a lot of guys on our football team very happy.

My early practice sessions were unusual. Everyone else was permitted to go full speed while I was restrained from tackling. The coach said he didn't have enough bodies on the team to risk injuries to anyone (we only had twenty-four players). He said, "Jack, you take it easy. Just play touch football with the ball carrier because I don't want you hurting yourself."

"Coach," I said in reply, "I'm not scared of getting hurt. In fact, it doesn't hurt to tackle people and I really like to hit."

The coach sort of smiled in a peculiar way and said with a big grin, "I know, Jack, I know."

The business about not being allowed to make tackles started to bore me so I asked if I could try some offense. The coach consented, and once again, at least for a couple of plays, I was the terror of the gridiron. At first I was used as a running back. I figured if making tackles by driving through a target was effective, then running with the same driving force would work, too. I therefore went out of my way trying to run people over. My theory worked, and I became a one-man wrecking crew. At the time I never realized why I was so effective as both tackler and runner, but I later learned it was just a matter of the proper use of speed. Since I was the fastest man on the team, speed became my advantage. Tackling is mass times velocity. As I said before, the faster and more violently I can drive my body into a target, the more effective my hit will be. In high school I had the ability to start out with quick, strong bursts. I was able to achieve full speed in two steps, and regardless of whether I was running the ball or tackling the ball carrier, I always became the driving force. I was always able to do the hitting instead of getting hit. That was my idea of defensive football.

Still, there was a limit to my aggressiveness. I was aware that tackling and even running the ball required a full-speed style if the end results were to be effective, but I had mixed emotions about actually hurting people. I know it might sound strange, but after I would bust into someone and knock that man cold, it sort of hurt me emotionally. And yet when I seemed to slack off a little, someone would simply run me over, and that hurt even more. Unfortunately, there seemed to be no happy medium in my style of play. After making several flat-footed, half-hearted approaches at tackling and finding myself getting bulled over, I became Mr. Devastation. I was a brutal tackler, but the first lessons I learned were the structures of the rules.

Ghetto football is tougher than a high school football game. Playing around the various towns in New Jersey, you had to be tough or you could get killed. The guys, I guess, because of their backgrounds, seemed to be nastier and would take cheap shots. Sometimes one or two guys would try to hold you up while another would try to tear your head off with a high tackle. There was an old saying that you were supposed to step on legs that were sticking out of a different colored uniform. Also, if you didn't get blood on your jersey, someone else's blood, then you weren't doing your job. I wasn't scared to play the game hard, but in my estimation there was a difference between rough football and insanity.

I had a lot of respect for my high school coach. Our coach taught sportsmanship, and it made me proud to play for that type of person, when many other coaches actually encouraged cheap-shot animalism. As a sophomore and a junior, I received some minor bumps because of cheap shots. It wasn't uncommon for another team to pile on, or you could be tackled five yards out of bounds, or you could get hit ten seconds after the whistle. Dirty play was more dominant in the games against the wealthier schools or better areas we went into. For some reason, many of these schools seemed to resent a team made up of mostly blacks and boys who came from the ghetto, and the officiating also reflected the prejudiced attitude. One time we ran over one team and scored touchdown after touchdown. But every scoring play we had was called back for one infraction or another. We were called dirty names, and played the game without the aid of a fair judge. During this game I began to hate the other players, but it never entered my mind to play dirty against the other team. I played hard and made several violent tackles, but I just couldn't bring myself to hit a man who was out of bounds or to make a hit after the whistle. I guess my attitude was a reflection of the coaching I was receiving and the influence of my parents. I know it wasn't much fun getting hit late but I can honestly say that I never went out and tried to take a cheap shot. It hurt me to see one of our guys get injured because of a late hit, but even in high school I tried to keep my aggression channeled within the structure of the rules. Sometimes, I admit, I did things differently, but nonetheless I was always a fair player.

I remember playing a scrimmage with an all-white team. We were taking a terrible physical beating. It wasn't because the team was good or hard-hitting, it was because of their expertise in late hits, clipping, biting and kicking. Even though the other team was cheating and doing everything rotten, we were still running up the scores. All during the game one of their defensive backs was taking cheap shots and hitting late. He really got on my nerves. In all the football games I have ever played, this was one guy I wanted to really get, but as it was, he seemed to avoid the real action and was busy looking for other people when their backs were turned. Well, on one play, I broke out around the end with the ball and had about seventy yards of green grass between myself and the goal line. Just as I was ready to turn on the burners, I saw him coming after me. Actually, he had no chance of catching me and he knew it, but he was making it look good. He was pumping his arms and legs and running like some fool trying to cut me off. Somewhere between six points and the forty yard line, I got this inspiration to cut back and run the dirty player over. I slowed down a little and gave him the proper angle on me. When he was about five yards from me, I cut back against the grain, put my head down, and buried the man. That was the only time in my career that I can honestly remember trying to hurt a man. Other times, I tackled hard and violently, but it wasn't for the purpose of injuring my opponent.

During my junior year I started thinking that maybe I had a future in football. Already I was an All-State player and had even made the high school All-American team. But between the ghetto and professional football was college. It was easy to see that if I didn't work hard in school and pay the price with athletics, my future was going to be bleak. I've seen how the ghetto can reach up and grab you by the throat, but then again, all the losers I knew actually wanted to lose. Sure, it was a tough lifestyle and there isn't anything pretty about garbage rotting in the streets and ten people living together in a three-room apartment. But just about everyone in the ghetto stays there because they want to spend their days feeling sorry for themselves instead of working their way out. My parents were poor and we had it tough, but my father went to work every day and was trying to improve. I know there were times when he looked around at his world and how his children were living and it hurt, but he realized, too, that it was only going to be temporary. To me, my father was a king because he believed in better days to come and went out and worked toward this goal, and my mother was a queen because she kept our clothes clean, the house in good order, and taught us children about the Good Lord and the better things that life had to offer. I knew that in spite of my environment I could get out, but I would have to work and work. It probably would have been easier to give in to the screams of the ghetto, start running the streets with the gangs, and take trips on drugs, but my highs came from football and doing well in school. Even though I grew up in the ghetto, I always believed that I was the luckiest guy in the world. Someday I was going to work my way from the hell of this broken cluttered world out into that area where the sun would shine a little brighter. I wasn't going to let the ghetto own my soul.

When my senior year came along, I had developed into one of the top high school players in the country. I was 5 feet 11 and weighed 205 pounds. Physically, I had reached full maturity, in fact, I still carry the same weight. There were people who said I looked out into the world from narrowed slits in a hardened face. They said I was mean and nasty and had no regard for my personal safety or the safety of others around me. But they mistook grim determination for meanness; I was only a young man with a mission in life. I wanted out of the ghetto; and football and education were my road toward success. Because of my purpose, I dedicated myself to helping my parents, my brothers and sisters, and of course, me, from the dirt and filth of the ghetto. Every day was another day closer to the time when we could leave, and I never gave up. It was hard work in the classroom and on the practice field. But then, one day, my high school career had ended and college scouts and recruiters came from all over the country to talk with me about the future. Finally, after three years of hard work on the football field and solid grades in the classroom, I was taking my first step out of the ghetto and into a better world.

4

Recruiting Wars

I have often been asked which phase of football in my career has been the most demanding. Some people think it is trying to cover a quick receiver, while others might consider it trying to bring down a big running back. The truth of the matter is that the real strain of my career has never come from the physical or mental combat of battle. The most pressure I ever faced during my football career was trying to decide which college I wanted to attend. Part of the pressure came from the fact that I had enough intelligence to realize that college could be the chance to launch a career in the NFL, but more important, it was an opportunity for me to receive an education. Football is a fine and wonderful game, but between high school and professional football were many ifs. I wasn't about to put my future on thin ice. I wanted my future to be on solid ground, and education was my primary reason for college. Football was important, but not as important to me as preparing myself for a career in a good, paying profession.

I guess letters started piling up in my coach's office during my junior year in high school. Although it was flattering to think colleges were interested enough to start writing me when I was only a junior, Coach Federici felt it wasn't the time for me to even begin to consider which college I wanted to attend. My coach simply filed all the letters in a big box with the promise I could start reading them after my football career at Passaic High School was over.

Several times during my junior year a coach or scout from one of several universities broke through my coach's defense and actually approached me. But whenever Coach Federici got wind of what was going on, he quickly took a broom to anyone near me. In a way it was good because one year of maturing means a lot to a high school kid. I know that in one year many of my values changed, and by the time I was a senior, I had my priorities in proper order – education first, then football. As a junior I had been thinking about All-Pro status in the NFL without even considering four years of college football as the necessary stepping stone between high school and professional football.

When Coach Federici finally opened the door and let the recruiters in, my headaches only just began. At first I felt it was going to be quite simple. I wanted my parents to see my college games so I picked Syracuse. It was a major college, had a good academic program, and had produced some of the great running backs in the game. Jim Brown, Floyd Little, and the late Ernie Davis had all starred for the Orangemen and gone on to professional fame. I liked the idea of following in their footsteps.

When I started talking to coaches and recruiters from the different colleges around the country, it suddenly became quite frustrating and confusing. One school in the South, a white school, wanted a token black. That was during the height of the equality bunk that was spreading across the country and the recruiter from that school said, "If we have to start putting blacks into uniform, we may as well go after the best talent in the country." I didn't know whether to consider myself flattered or to smack the man in the mouth. I mentioned the incident to my coach, and he had that school barred from talking to any of the athletes on the Passaic team.

Then there was the all-black school and its recruiter, who felt black athletes were better than white athletes. He was in the process of building a National Championship team from colored stars across the country. His remark was something like, "We'll teach them hunky bastards about football!" That was another recruiter who eventually was barred from Passaic.

Still, I kept my head squarely on my shoulders and made my first visit to Syracuse. It was a delightful weekend. I received something like $300 in cash for expenses, a car to drive around and even a girl. And the girl was something else! She explained what Syracuse had to offer differently than the coaches did, and to be quite honest, I liked her reasoning. I had almost definitely decided that I would make Syracuse my university for the next four years and that young lady certainly figured into my plans. What made the Syracuse offer even more enticing was the fact that they were going to let me wear number 44. Anyone who knows anything about Syracuse and number 44 knows that all the great running backs in the history of the school wore that number. For many reasons at that time, number 44 meant something to me. It was like being able to follow in Jim Brown's footsteps or maybe even indicated confidence that I would eventually play in the NFL. Whatever, it was special to me, and the memory of my new lady friend and knowledge of that famous jersey number had me thinking Orange and Syracuse.

When I arrived back in Passaic, I told Coach Federici everything that had happened. He was a little disappointed when I told him how I was lured in by the young lady but I assured my coach that even without her, Syracuse was still a very attractive school. He suggested that I think about everything and in the meantime I should get out and see some of the other schools. He said, "After all, they pick up the expenses and I think it's good for you to see what some of the other universities have to offer. That way, you can compare the differences." It was good advice and I took it.

My next stop was Michigan State and a rather rude awakening. At Michigan State I met a young running back from Thomas Jefferson High School in Brooklyn, John Brockington. John and I had the same type of career, All-Everything in high school, and even had the same recruiters after us. We got to rapping about the differences between the various schools, and I started picking up some information. John had been out visiting quite a number of schools and, compared to me, seemed to be an expert. Then he started talking about his trip to Syracuse and a certain young lady. I listened and by the time he finished talking, I could have sworn that he was listening in on my date with my lady. She said the same things to him that she had said to me. They even did the same things that she and I did! What's more, John said, "They'll even give me number 44 if I go there."

Well, it hurt for a little while, but I really didn't have that much time for pain because Michigan State had provided me with another young lady who had a way of making me fall in love with the Spartans. But now I was starting to seriously consider what my coach had said about looking around before I decided at what university I planned to spend the next four years of my life.

I came away from my MSU trip believing that all schools would tell a young athlete anything to get him signed up. It seemed like bending the rules or outright lies and made me extremely cautious. If a school was willing to bend the rules to get me there on a four-year athletic scholarship, then maybe they would also break the rules to get rid of me should I fail to measure up to expectations. It became a serious concern of mine.

After several more trips I had something like $700 in cash left over, five new young ladies who were madly in love with me, the promise of high-paying off-season jobs and any type of car I wanted. I got to the point where I really enjoyed visiting a university and found little ways of getting more money from them. It all became a big game and the cash kept flowing in. One school gave me a job in Passaic working at a drug store – one of their alumni members owned the store and they really wanted me. Another school promised me $200 a week under the table, a better-paying job for my father and something special for my mother. I never found out what they meant by something special for my mother, but they hinted about new furniture. It was becoming unbelievable, and then came my trip to Notre Dame. I figured that if the other schools were making all these wild promises, then Notre Dame was really going to offer a fantastic deal.

I arrived in South Bend on a rather cold and snowy day. That sort of put a damper on everything, because I hate cold weather. They took me over to meet Coach Ara Parsegian. Thus far no one had made any special promises, so I naturally figured Ara would make the full presentation.

Sitting in his office, I noticed there were several other players waiting to go in to see him, and I really didn't like the idea of wasting time. I waited for a half hour and noticed that he was taking exactly fifteen minutes per player. That was strange. Then my turn came. To be honest, when I walked into his office, I didn't know if I should kiss his ring or shake his hand. Everything seemed so pious and upright, and then there were all these priests scattered here and there throughout the campus. Well, it made me feel like I was in a big church or even in the Vatican City and Ara was His Holiness.

Ara was calm and cool as he rattled off his Notre Dame pep talk. I could see that there was little or no sentiment attached to the deal and he offered nothing special. The meeting was quite matter-of-fact, and when my fifteen minutes had expired, so had the meeting.

The next stop was the gym. The assistant coach had me fitted with gym clothes and tennis shoes. For what, I didn't know, but then we went out on the main floor. The coach said, "Jump up and touch the rim."

"What?" I asked.

"Jump up and touch the rim. I want to see how high you can jump."

I wasn't interested in basketball and I wasn't interested in jumping in the air. When I stopped for a few seconds to think about the situation, I realized I wasn't interested in Notre Dame, either. I didn't jump up and attempt to touch the rim.

When I started out, selecting a college seemed a very easy decision, but now, after having made many trips to the different schools, it was becoming a mind-boggling experience. I didn't know what school I liked. The pressure was going to be overwhelming. I almost got to a point where I was ready to say the hell with it and go work on the garbage truck. Every time I turned around, there was a coach or scout knocking at the front door with a thousand reasons why I should attend his university. It all began to sound like a big recording: a different face, a different voice, but the same old story. I needed a change of pace. I needed something different that would help me decide, and I didn't know what the answer was going to be.

During the early spring, Joe Paterno from Penn State called me, and he was different. Joe explained that Penn State was a highly accredited learning institution with an excellent football program. Joe slanted his talk toward the emotional aspects of my career, with football as his number-two concern. He was a down-to-earth type of guy, and we talked about making plans for a trip to Penn State. Just talking with the man on the phone had me excited, and I started thinking that maybe Penn State was the answer to my situation. Joe never promised any girl or money under the table, and nothing was mentioned about wearing any special jersey. I liked the way Paterno presented himself and the university.

Then, about a week after the Paterno call, I was playing basketball with several of the guys when a young dude came up to me and said, "Hey, Tate, I think a sweeper salesman just went up to your house and your mother let him in."

There had been this slicker going around the neighborhood trying to get people signed up for sweepers. It was one of those $10 down and $5 a month for the next 50 years deals. It was also rumored that the sweeper salesman was a con artist who ripped people off for the $10 down and never delivered the sweeper. If it was that sweeper salesman talking to my mother, then I was going home and do some talking to him. My mother has one of those hearts that won't say no. I don't care what the deal is, she'll buy it, and I didn't like the idea of a slicker trying to con her.

I dropped the ball and took off over fences and through the alleys. Half the guys in the neighborhood took off after me. Everyone thought that if I caught up with the dude, there would be trouble, and they all wanted to watch the action. Actually, I really didn't have any plans to get physical with the dude unless he started giving me some lip, but still, I was going to let him know that the suckers don't live on this side of town.

I banged open the front door and heard my mother say, "There's John David now." I walked into the kitchen real cool, but I stopped in my tracks when I saw Woody Hayes. Hell, he wasn't a sweeper salesman.

My mother said, "J.D., this is the nicest man I have ever met.

He's Coach Woody Hayes. My, what a prince this man is!"

I leaned over the back of the chair where my mother was sitting and simply said, "Hi." After all, I had met nearly every coach in the country, so Woody Hayes wasn't anything special to me.

But then Woody quickly let me know I wasn't anything special either when he said, "Hi," and went back to talking with my mother. "Mrs. Tatum, that was the best piece of pie I have ever tasted. You'll just have to give the recipe to my wife."

"Why! Coach Hayes, you say the nicest things. That's our favorite pie. It's banana cream and I make this special crust..."

My mother went on to explain her secret recipe, and Woody stuffed his mouth with another piece of pie and listened. I got the feeling he had come in from Columbus to visit my mother, and the way she was talking to him made it seemed like they were lifelong friends. After five or ten minutes, I couldn't see any sense in my leaning on the back of my mother's chair and listening to their conversation. They didn't need me in the room, so I left. To my surprise, no one missed me.

After Woody and my mother talked for about an hour, I went back into the kitchen. The pie was completely gone and Woody was sitting there picking at the crumbs and telling my mother about General Patton and World War II. Then my mother started telling Woody about her father's claims of fighting in the Civil War. It was amazing. Once again, I felt very much out of place.

Several hours later, Woody left. He said good-bye and told me he would see me soon, but that was it. I was shocked. Woody Hayes couldn't have come all the way to Passaic to recruit my mother, and yet he never go around to talking to me. I just couldn't figure it out. I half expected him to lay some money on me or at least give me some pep talks about the Buckeyes and the Rose Bowl, but there was nothing.

After supper I began to realize what actually had happened. My mother said, "You know, John David, I think it would be nice if you went to Columbus and paid Coach Hayes a visit. I think it is a wonderful school and he's so kind."

It wasn't long afterward that I arrived in Columbus to see what Woody Hayes was all about. But I went there maintaining the attitude that Jack Tatum was something special. After all, almost every school in the country had put in a bid for my talents, and some of them were willing to pay a big dollar to get me. I couldn't help but think that Ohio State would make the best offer of all. When you think about hard-nosed football and a winning tradition, Ohio State ranks up at the top. They always seem to get their share of great athletes, so there had to be some payola involved. I wanted to see the color of Woody's money, even though I still entertained thoughts of visiting Penn State.

It was a surprise when Woody started out by saying, "I don't know what the hell the other schools promised you, but I'll make only two promises ... and I'll keep both of them. When you come here, expect to study. No one gets any grades handed out to them. That way, you'll leave a better man than when you came. That's my first promise – to make you a better man. And secondly, I'll make you a better football player. I'm not promising that you'll go off and play in the NFL; I'm only saying that you'll be a better football player. In fact there isn't a school in the country that will give you a better education in the classroom and better training on the football field. It's just that simple."

I was amazed at Woody's presentation. He was overpoweringly blunt and to the point. There was no mention of money under the table, no young lady to entertain me, no fancy car, no sugar daddy; just education and football. I started talking with some of the other players who had actually spent time under Woody. Everyone said the same thing: "He's a monster." I couldn't understand. If the man was such a monster, why did all these players stick it out?

So I asked the obvious question, "If that's so, then why stick?"

Everyone looked at me like I was some kind of a fool. Then one guy stood up and said, "We stick 'cause Coach Hayes is a great man. He doesn't lie, doesn't cheat, and he wants to win."

I couldn't figure out the difference between my conception of a "monster" and how the term was supposed to be applied to the character of Woody Hayes, but there was obviously some difference. Everyone said he was a bastard, but everyone said he was a great guy, too. It was strange but intriguing.

When I went back home, my mother was the first to ask what I thought about Woody, and all I could say was, "Different."

After a few phone calls and my parents' visit to the school, my mother made up her mind; I was most definitely going to OSU.

Recruiting to me was, and always has been, a war. I realize that the NCAA has changed many rules and has really tried to clamp down on any illegal activity, but still, all the high school stars getting ready to consider a college have my sympathy. Selecting a university to attend on a full athletic scholarship is an exhausting experience. I don't think any kid in the world is actually ready for that type of pressure, but it happens every year. After the high school football season, every university in the United States fires up their recruiting machine and begins digging up the talent.

I know that Ohio State considers their methods the best, and Alabama thinks their way is the best; along with Notre Dame, Purdue, Arizona, UCLA and even Slippery Rock. Every school has a technique for recruiting high school athletes, but it all comes down to basically the same idea: Get the athlete to sign a letter of intent.

In the state of Ohio there are more than 40,000 high school boys participating in football. When you consider that more than 750 high schools have a football program in the state and that only about 100 of the school boys are considered blue chippers, finding that talent can become a tremendous job. I have only mentioned the state of Ohio, and OSU football covers more than just the Buckeye State. Let's consider that in an average year, Ohio State's scouting system gets into several thousand schools across the country, and that is probably an underestimation. But using that figure, it means that Ohio State scouts actually look at over 100,000 kids across the country. And from that number it will come down to getting serious about only two or three hundred of the best athletes.

The recruiting process all starts with the committeemen. These are the people who have graduated from Ohio State and go into their particular walk of life without forgetting the scarlet and gray. They are always trying to make a contribution to their beloved university. A good example of what I'm talking about occurred in the sleepy little town of Brookfield in northeastern Ohio. Brookfield High School has a total enrollment of possibly five hundred students in the top three grades but they had something very special: a State Championship football team. Winning state championships usually means talent, and Brookfield is loaded. But long before Brookfield won statewide honors, college committeemen, coaches and scouts flocked to this small town and began verbally attacking the young players. I don't mean it in a bad way, but still, it becomes a verbal attack when every one of the scouts and coaches have their own special talk about the school they represent. After a while the kids start ducking every time someone mentions their name. Hell, when I was in school, I wanted to go out and play some basketball or run around with my lady friends. At first I really wasn't interested in some scout or coach taking up my time. Being a teenager can be a wonderful time of any man's life, and I believe the pressure these young kids receive from big-time colleges is a little ridiculous. At Brookfield they had three blue chippers, Marc Marek, Darwin Ulmer, and John Lott. An average day for these kids consisted of six hours of classroom studies and twelve hours of bullshit from college scouts and coaches. Committeemen called me from Ohio State and asked me to talk with these young fellows from Brookfield, but I didn't believe in that type of interference. I have met the coach at Brookfield, John Delserone, and his prize athletes, but I won't interfere in anyone's life. I told the coach and his boys, "Ohio State is a nice place. It suited me but you go and look for yourself. Make up your own mind and don't let anyone sway you into a bad decision." But it's tough for these young men to always make the right decision. I know that a lot of universities actually do care about the young people they approach, and I firmly believe Ohio State is one of these schools, but day after day, hour after hour, it becomes a real headache for any young man to try to make the right decision.

I had received over three hundred letters from different colleges and universities. I never realized that there were so many different universities in the country, but they all knew about me. When my coach opened the door and let the scouts in, it became a serious problem. I said before that I was so overwhelmed that I almost threw in the towel, and I wasn't kidding.

I honestly believe that a new system of recruiting should be developed. A high school coach should grade his talent and then, for the blue chippers, let them pick out six major schools and three Division II schools to visit. It should be the athlete's selection, and not some coach or scout who starts the meeting. This way, the coach writes to possibly Ohio State and five other schools and tells them about his number-one running back. If any of the schools are interested in the young man, then arrangements are made for a visit. The young athlete would be able to visit several schools, get a pretty good overall picture of the situation, and then start making up his mind. If he feels that he would like to look into another university, then his high school coach would make the contact. I believe these young athletes are still kids, even though some of their bodies would argue that point. Still, we should treat this matter with some intelligence, and, most important, give the kids a little consideration and some room to breathe. If someone doesn't begin to change the rules on recruiting in favor of the young athlete, then I can see people actually getting beaten up and shot at over the whole issue. The pressure to win at any level of college football is overcoming our ability to reason. With hundreds of schools participating in the annual chase for the high school talent, it's going to come down to a matter of broken bones for the recruiters and nervous breakdowns for the kids. Think about it: Every major school has its committeemen, and even Brookfield, Ohio, has its Penn State grads, Ohio State grads, Pitt grads, Maryland, Michigan, Bowling Green, etc., grads. Well, I think you see what I mean. All I can say is that I really thank God for guiding me in the right direction and into the correct decision.

If I were to give any young athlete advice on how to select a school, I think it would first start with honesty. How honest is the recruiter? If the recruiter is filling your head with wild promises, then be wary, because the more promises a person makes, the more difficult it becomes to keep those promises. The next thing to consider is your education. The likelihood of a professional football career is a distant and improbable dream for most athletes, but educating yourself for a workable career is a strong possibility for anyone who has the persistence to work at it. Therefore, education is more important than any football program. But still, there are many quality schools that offer excellent academic programs and still compete on a major level in collegiate football. Ohio State is just one of those schools, and I guess I was just one of those lucky guys who spent four years educating himself and developing into a football player. I knew that if something happened, an injury or whatever, and I wasn't able to participate in sports, I would still have the education to fall back on. Like I said, I was lucky.

Raider Warriors: George Atkinson (43) and Jack Tatum (32).

5

Different Strokes for Different Folks

Woody Hayes was the head football coach at Ohio State for twenty-eight years. But he's much more. Ask anyone. Just mention his name on the street and the reaction is everything from "prince" to "prick."

My father always calls Woody "Coach Hayes" and my mother referred to him as the "royal prince." She only made that statement once, but Woody is my parents' main man. They trust him and believe in him.

Other folks around the country have different opinions of Woody. Once I heard a little guy say to his friend, "I'm gonna get me the autograph of Mr. Nasty."

He went up to Woody and asked him to sign the program he was holding. Woody did. Then he looked Woody right in the eye and asked, "Are you really nasty all the time?"

Woody sort of smiled and said, "No, just most of the time."

Another time when I was out for dinner with a lady friend, we got on the subject of strange people we knew. Right away I blurted out, "Woody Hayes!"

The lady sat up and said, "Oh yes, Woody Hayes. He's the governor of Ohio."

Just about everyone from coast to coast knows the name Woody Hayes but most people have never met the man or taken the time to find out about him. The fact is, Woody Hayes is just about everything he has ever been called, but you have to know the man to understand his story. The whole story isn't something you see on TV or read about on the sports page.

Until now the only public statement I have ever made concerning Woody was: "Woody is different. You've got to know the man to understand the man."

Woody Hayes is a man of personality and character, and he can change quicker than the snap of a finger. I've seen Woody travel from his Sunday-morning, go-to-church best to the other side of normal in the time it took him to sucker-punch someone for not paying attention.

At half-time during one game against Northwestern, Woody was talking to the offensive unit about its poor showing. The score was only 21-0, and Woody felt we should have scored at least 40 points in that first half. He was upset but he was cool as the paced the locker room pointing out mistakes.

Then my roommate, Phil Strickland, stood up to fix his shoulder pad strap. Phil, an offensive guard, should have been paying attention, because he had made plenty of mistakes, often pulling the wrong way and running over our quarterback. But then, Phil also comes under the heading of strange people I know.

Phil was standing up playing around with his straps when Woody moseyed over toward him. The tone of Woody's voice never changed. When he stood about an arm's length from Strick, the old man lashed out with four or five quick jabs to Phil's head. Then Woody went on talking as if nothing had happened, but Phil had been knocked over backward from the punches to his head. The rest of us helped him get his seat, and to this day I believe Phil still wonders what happened. So do I.

That was just a common type of coaching sucker-punch. It wasn't serious. A lot of coaches use a sucker-punch, or even a solid kick in the can, as an attention-grabber. However, every once in a while Woody will stray from the ranks of normality, and you don't have to play football at Ohio State to see the old man throw a fit. Woody's all-time best performances may have come before live TV audiences during the heat of battle. There's just something about a TV game that brings out the worst in Woody. Most coaches dress up for the TV game and say cool things in front of the cameras. Not Woody. He always wears the same old black pants, wrinkled white shirt, 1939 Sears & Roebuck skinny necktie, and baseball cap. If Woody thinks the situation calls for a cuss word, he will cuss. Or if he thinks heavier action is needed, Woody will do everything from chase the officials to kick the fans or even beat up on a cameraman and his camera.

I'm an Ohio State fan and I watch OSU football on TV because I like the action. Don't get the idea that I'm praising the football action, because that's not the action I'm talking about. I watch Ohio State football because of Woody Hayes. The old man is unpredictable, and it's exciting trying to figure out what he's going to do next.

Several years ago the team went up north for a game with Michigan. It was tough going throughout the game, but Woody was keeping himself under control. He was doing normal things like cussing, stomping up and down on the sidelines, and throwing his clipboard. Then came a five-yard penalty, and Woody went off like a big cannon.

I could see Woody's old heart start pumping the blood and the heat coming off his back hit the cold air and turn to steam. The old man was boiling in a few seconds, and everyone around him knew it. When his face turned three shades of red, the other coaches jumped him. It was a funny scene, Woody dragging the coaches across the field swinging and cussing up a storm in the direction of the man who threw the flag.

I believe that if several players hadn't jumped in and helped out, Woody would have dragged the coaches back to Ohio chasing after the official. Finally, the coaches and players got the old man down and wrestled him back to the sidelines. Everything seemed under control, but Woody got to his feet just in time to see the official stepping off the last few yards of another penalty against Ohio State. Lip readers from coast to coast saw Woody ask, "What the hell was that all about?"

An unthinking young freshman player informed Woody, "Coach Hayes, the dude laid the flag on you for coming after him."

Woody let the statement register for a second and then he went berserk, screaming and cussing. He threw his baseball cap at the ground and ran along the sidelines shaking his fist at the official and cussing him out. The official wasn't listening and paid no attention to Woody's verbal assault. I felt Woody was going to sucker-punch the official or at least give him a kick in the tail, but he fooled me. This was a big TV game, and Woody had one better up his sleeve.

The old man ran over to the yardage markers, grabbed them up like a bundle of sticks, and threw them onto the playing field. That got everyone's attention, including the man with the yellow flag. It was fifteen more yards against Ohio State.

In a final fit of defiant rage, Woody stormed onto the field and started jumping up and down on the yardage markers. This time the other coaches and players let him alone. Everyone was so amazed or shocked at Woody's action that they decided it would be safer to stand back and let the old man burn himself out beating up on some metal poles.

That was a dark day in the career of Wayne Woodrow Hayes. Woody lost all the arguments with the officials; he lost the game;

and, most likely, he gave up any claim to the good fellowship award for the best-behaved college coach.

Most of Woody's career has been sunshine and roses, but there have been a few other dark spots worth mentioning. I'd say that November 19, 1977, might be one date in history that Woody scratched out with a black crayon. That was the day he took the team up to Ann Arbor for the big game with Michigan.

To appreciate exactly what did happen on that day, a person must understand the rivalry between Ohio State and Michigan. Part of the football season's bitterness between the two schools comes from the fact that for about the last ten years this game has decided the Big Ten Championship and who goes west to the Rose Bowl. Championships and Rose Bowls are a very important part of Big Ten football, but the real story is hidden behind closed doors, where two opposing coaches spend most of their free time throwing poison darts at each other's photograph. Of course, I'm talking about Woody Hayes and Bo Schembechler.

Bo Schembechler is the head coach at Michigan, but his career actually started at Ohio State. As head coach material there, he planned to sit back and wait for Woody to retire. It was a good plan and packed merit, but Woody had his retirement scheduled for sometime during the next century. When Bo realized that Woody might have a lifetime contract with OSU, his next plan was to blend his coaching philosophy into the old man's system.

Even though Schembechler was blessed with talent and had a future in coaching, Woody wasn't interested. Ohio State might have six practice fields, one dozen trainers, and 85,000 seats in the stadium, but there is only one head coach in Columbus. If Bo suggested a running play around the left end, Woody sent the offense to the right. If Bo got on the elevator and said "Up," Woody pressed the down button. It came to a point where if Bo had said there wasn't any Santa Claus, Woody would have insisted he believed in one.

At first, tones were quiet, but as their personalities clashed daily, everyone knew something was bound to happen... something serious. Before long Bo and Woody started spitting and punching at each other. One day at a meeting, Woody became so riled up over a few remarks Bo had made (not personal remarks, just coaching judgments) that Woody ended the meeting by throwing a metal chair at Schembechler.

Assistant Coach Schembechler was a pain in the neck for Woody Hayes, but Head Coach Bo Schembechler of Michigan moved that pain to a lower area of the old man's anatomy. It was one thing for Bo Schembechler to run all over the country recruiting high school stars for Woody; it was quite another story when the old man would stroll up to a prospect's door only to see the new head coach of Michigan sitting in the living room wearing an I-just-stuck-it-to-you smile on his face. That's when everything suddenly became serious. No one was permitted to use the word "Michigan" in Woody's presence. The big football game had just become a war.

I'm sure that Bo and Woody would have preferred to face each other in some alley behind the stadium and settle the issues once and for all, but school policies and NCAA rules frown on coaches punching each other in public. Much to Woody's and Bo's dismay, it's all settled on the football field with the football players.

I still think it would be more exciting to have Bo and Woody stand on the fifty yard line and let them explain their coaching philosophies to each other. That would prove more interesting than the football game. In 1977 ABC Sports must have had the same idea because they placed minicameras on the sidelines to watch the reactions of each coach. It wasn't the same as Woody and Bo trading insults and punches at mid-field, but it added color to an otherwise boring game.

During the season in Big Ten play, Michigan and Ohio State have the horses to beat up on the less talented schools by just blasting running backs up the middle for touchdown after touchdown. But when they play against each other, all their power and talent is neutralized and the game settles into a matter of few yards gained and fewer points scored. With each snap of the ball the offensive team inches forward into a virtually impenetrable defense and the ball carriers stumble over the arms and legs extending from the mountain of twisted bodies. It's a good sedative, but not much of a football game. Still, though, the coaches, who soon lose sight of the real objective (to score points and win), keep blasting away at the middle just as though they were standing at center ring slugging it out in the last round.

I was watching this particular game on television, and several friends stopped by to watch with me. Someone asked, "Hey, Tate, I'm startin' to notice a bad look in Woody's eyes. Any chance of him getting serious before the game is over?"

The situation was getting serious. Michigan, blasting and struggling most of the afternoon, had managed a 14-6 lead. Time was running out when Ohio State took over the ball deep in Michigan territory, but they needed a touchdown and a two-point conversion for Woody to go home with a tie.

I answered my friend, "I think Ohio State will screw up and lose the game. When that happens, Woody will punch the cameraman into the ground. I know the old man. He's been frustrated all after-noon and now he's just like a rattlesnake. Woody will strike at the first thing that comes near him."

The other coaches and players knew anything could happen and they knew Woody. They moved away. At the end, the only one standing near the old man was the cameraman. He obviously didn't know any better.

I started telling some stories about Mrs. Anne Hayes, Woody's wife, and how serious she was over the Michigan game. One time she wrote a letter to a friend who lives on Michigan Avenue in Chicago and she penciled on the envelope, "Ugh! Can't you change streets?"

Another time, when Woody's oldest son finished high school, Mrs. Hayes said, "Steve, I'll pack your bags and we'll send you to any college in the country except one. If you pick Michigan, I'll throw you out on the sidewalk and your bags after you."

I finished the stories just as Ohio State fumbled the ball and Michigan recovered. Michigan could sit on the ball for the next minute of play and then start making plans for the trip west.

The ABC camera caught Schembechler's reaction, a half-smile and a big sigh of relief. On the other side of the field it was different. When the cameraman zoomed in to get a close shot of Woody's face, I could see that his heart was shattered. The frustrations of the day, and the year, nearly brought him to tears, but only for a second. Then something terrible happened to Woody's face and he became a monster.

In a fit of rage Woody rushed the cameraman, swinging with wild lefts and rights. The cameraman was able to slip the punches but his camera was taking a terrific beating. I saw those big fists banging into the lens followed by distorted pictures of the crowd and sky. Then everything blacked out.

There was no excuse for a coach punching a camera or attacking a cameraman. ABC didn't have anything to do with Ohio State's fumble or Woody's loss but Woody repeatedly uses questionable tactics. There isn't any explanation that can justify his actions.

Without a doubt that was the darkest day in the tantrum-throwing career of Wayne Woodrow Hayes, but the darkest night was still to come and quite another story.

Nineteen-seventy-eight was a bad year for Woody and the Buckeyes. The season started off with a loss to Penn State, but Woody took everything in stride. He didn't punch any cameramen or cameras and I think he even may have congratulated Joe Paterno, the winning coach. I'm sure Woody's display of sportsmanship surprised a national television audience, but not me. Woody doesn't slug people or things when he honestly believes the best team won. Obviously, Penn State was the better team in Woody's estimation.

After the Penn State loss, the Bucks won a few games, lost another one, and were tied once. Naturally, Woody wasn't the happiest gentleman in the world, but it was still early in the season and there was the Big Ten title to consider. Although OSU had fielded the weakest defensive team in the history of the university, Woody managed to keep the title hopes alive, and once again it came down to the November showdown with the team from up north and Coach What's-His-Name.

But for the third time in three years, Coach Schembechler stuck it to Woody and Michigan packed for their annual trip west while the Bucks were scheduled for a December 29 date at the Gator Bowl. Woody didn't kick, punch, or spit at anyone, and in keeping with the spirit, he also didn't congratulate anyone. Deep down inside I'm sure he would have still liked to get that other coach by the neck and settle the Michigan-Ohio State issue once and for all, but the old man just sort of smoldered off the field.

In spite of a regrettable and preferably forgotten season, Woody had the Bucks sky-high for that Saturday night tilt with Clemson. After all, bowl games are usually considered the beginning of a new and fresh season and not the conclusion of a disastrous one. At least, that's what Woody believes and who would dare discuss that point with him?

From the opening kickoff, it was readily apparent that OSU was a stronger and more physical team than Clemson. The Buckeyes controlled the ball, had more first downs, more rushing yardage and more passing yardage. In fact, they led in every department except scoring. Late in the game the out-gunned Clemson Tigers were clinging tenaciously to a slim 17-15 lead but Woody's boys were pounding closer and closer to the goal line.

With two minutes to play, I opened my big mouth and told my friends (the same ones who watched Woody's bout with the camera), "I got a feelin' the Bucks are going to screw up, and look out for Woody when they do!"

Exactly three seconds after those very words fell from my lips, OSU's young quarterback, Art Schlicter, lifted a perfectly throw spiral into the waiting arms of Charlie Bauman. This was the beginning of a serious problem for OSU because Charlie was the middle guard for Clemson. That particular play sealed the Buckeyes' Gator Bowl defeat and the end of Woody's coaching career.

Actually, Bauman seemed to be one surprised dude when a football miraculously appeared in his arms, but after a split second of standing there looking dumbfounded, Charlie started running toward the Clemson goal line. Near the sidelines, he ran into a host of nasty Buckeyes and Charlie was blasted out of bounds.

What happened next actually surprised me. I've known Woody for many years and in that period of time, I have come to expect the unexpected from Woody. Woody is different and he does different things. Once you get to know Woody, he could show up for practice wearing ice skates in the middle of summer and it wouldn't shock or surprise you because you know that Woody is different. After the interception and collision near the sidelines, I actually expected Woody to punch or kick the hell out of Charlie Bauman. To my dismay, the old man bent down and helped the Clemson lad to his feet. I was shocked. I was amazed at Woody's display of sportsmanship and, quite frankly, I was speechless. It was so uncharacteristic of Woody, and for a second he really had me going. But then Woody became Woody. After helping Bauman to his feet, Woody sucker-punched him and followed up with two roundhouses from left field. The first one landed on Bauman's face mask, the second got him in the throat and the third bounced off his shoulder pads. From that point on, it got real nasty. Several of Woody's boys jumped in and tried to break up the scene but Woody turned on them. Normally, when a fight breaks out during a football game, it's one team against the other, but on this night, everyone jumped Woody and the old man held his own.

Keith Jackson and Ara Parsegian were broadcasting the game (they also did the Woody Hayes vs. ABC Camera fight) and they just played dumb. Everyone in the world who watched that game saw Woody Hayes slug Bauman after watching instant replay, but Keith and Ara started asking each other, "What happened?" What happened was that Woody Hayes lost to an inferior team and Charlie Bauman became the focal point of a season full of pent-up frustrations.

I realized at that moment that Woody was saying goodbye to coaching and Ohio State. He realized it, too, as he walked from the field surrounded by protecting players. Maybe I have made sport of the situation, and in a way it is funny, but in many more ways it is sad. An incident like that is shameful to Ohio State, the Big Ten and college football, but the one that carries the scar has got to be Woody. Because of that incident and other ones that started back in 1959, Woody Hayes will never be judged on the accomplishments of his football coaching career or his contributions to humanity. Woody Hayes is a great man, and few people will ever realize how great he is.

The next day it was official, and newspapers from coast to coast carried the headline, "Woody Hayes Fired!" Woody claimed he actually resigned before he was fired, but regardless, the man's coaching career was over. For the rest of his life, Woody Hayes will be a branded man.

It didn't take the press long to get into the thick of Woody's recent tantrum, but to my surprise some of the stories were positive. Once in a while some reporter had the guts to tell the whole truth, but for the most part, I'm sorry to say, Woody Hayes was all but strung up from the nearest tree.

About two months after the Gator Bowl, I was watching a boxing match on ABC with the volume turned all the way down. Howard Cosell was doing the fight and regardless of how exciting the action is, Howard has a way of putting me to sleep. Between rounds Howard interviewed Billy Martin, ex-Yankee manager. For some strange reason, Billy Martin has always reminded me of Woody Hayes. I can't figure it out, because they certainly don't look alike. Anyway, I turned the volume up and listened. Cosell asked about 1980 and the Yankee job and Billy answered with a "yes, maybe, I hope so." Then Cosell said, "Well, if you don't get the Yankee job, we'd like to schedule you and Woody Hayes for the heavyweight championship fight."

Billy Martin, being an intellectual and perceptive gentleman, replied, "Oh, I'd never fight with Woody, he's a great man." And Billy Martin was right, but Howard had to get in the last words. He said, "On the subject of Woody Hayes and Billy's remark ... I respectfully disagree."

Giving the man some credit, I will say that from time to time Cosell does have a genuine contribution to offer society. Though most of the time when I listen to him I get the feeling he thinks that maybe there was more than one perfect being that walked the face of this world and Cosell was the second one. People are entitled to their opinion, but national television isn't the place for anyone to smear Woody. I think everyone must realize that Woody is a human, an emotional human, and there isn't a soul in the world who feels worse about Woody's emotional actions than Woody. The man was wrong when he slugged Charlie Bauman; he was wrong when he punched Mike Friedman's ABC camera; he was wrong when he shredded the yardage markers; and he was wrong when he punched photographers and spit on fans. But you judge a man by his entire life and not by those emotional incidents when he gives in to pressures, loses control, and strays from socially acceptable behavior.

I realize that Howard Cosell is entitled to his opinion of Woody just like I am entitled to my opinion of Cosell. But rather than take a cheap shot at anyone and base my statements on pure opinion, I'll just pretend that Howard is a fine gentleman. However, on Woody Hayes and the questions surrounding his greatness, let me say this. Until you have suited up and worked as a player under Coach Hayes, you really don't have the right to judge the man or brand the man because of his emotional peaks during the heat of battle. I don't know Howard Cosell very well but I do know Woody Hayes. If I had to go into a battle and I needed someone loyal and courageous to cover my blind side, I know damn well Woody would be my man. I know, too, that God hasn't created a more generous, compassionate, or more understanding man than Woody Hayes. Sure, we all know Woody's bad side, his human side, because it's newsworthy. When a coach punches a reporter or a player, the press and public eagerly gobble it up. But when a man gives his blood and sweat to a cause, very few people will ever come to realize and understand that type of dedication.

In 1959 Woody Hayes slugged his first reporter and it was written in the newspapers from coast to coast. Only a select few know, however, that in 1978 he supported the family of an Ohio high school football coach dying of cancer. Sure we all know that he shredded the yardage markers during a football game but how many of us know that Woody Hayes sponsored a poor starving Vietnamese family emigrating to the United States of America? It's all too easy for us to throw dirt on the man's name for the seconds of his life when his does wrong but in so doing, must we bury over sixty years of self-sacrifice and accomplishment? I've seen Woody scream and slap some of his players for not paying attention but I've also seen him hug and brag about the same ones. It's often been said that Woody's players will not say anything bad about Woody. Maybe, just maybe, it's because we know Woody and we actually sometimes understand the man.

When I see Woody go berserk and punch or kick at someone or even something, I don't like those actions. But then, when I consider the total picture of Woody Hayes and what he represents to humanity and college football, I respect him and find myself very proud to have been a small part of his life. Woody is simply a competitor; the kind of man you want playing on your side and not against you. Woody is the type of man who will lead his troops into battle rather than sit back and tell them how to fight. Woody Hayes gives much more than he takes, and in my estimation that is the real test of a man.

I've said it more than once, "Woody is different." He can be softer than pudding or nastier than sin. Woody can read from the Good Book and sound like a hellfire-come-back-to-Jesus preacher one minute; the next minute he's foaming at the mouth and running around like a beast from the pit. The old man can be shocking or amazing; he can make you cry or he can make you laugh.

I remember getting suited up for practice on one occasion when the weather was horrible. There was lightning, heavy thunder, high winds and rain. No one gave a serious thought to actually going outdoors and practicing. No one except Woody.

Everyone was milling around the lockers going through the motions of getting ready while Woody stood by the window watching the clouds. Then Woody started waving him arms and screaming, "Hurry up! Hurry up!"

First reactions were, "The old man's been struck by lightning." Then we realized Woody was serious. He wanted us to get ready and go outdoors.

Woody said, "Hurry up and get ready! I'm gonna make it stop."

Instead of laughing in his face (this was Woody after all), we hit our faces inside our lockers and busted up. It was funny. I mean, the wind was rocking the building and the rain was coming down so heavily you couldn't see out the window. Then there was this lightning. And Woody was going to make it stop!

We suited up, and Phil Strickland said, "Okay, Coach, we're ready on our end. How you doing on your end with the weather?"

That did it. Everyone burst out screaming and laughing at Woody. The wind was lifting the building off the foundations, and Strick kept going, "Hey, Coach, I said we're ready. When's the good weather going to be ready?"

Our sides hurt from laughing but then an amazing thing happened. Woody opened the door and said, "Okay, Strickland, lead them out, but hurry up 'cause I don't know how long I can hold it off."

Strick looked outside. The wind and rain had stopped. The gray clouds were still up there swirling around but no rain or wind. Amazing.

Cautiously, we all stepped out of the locker room and followed Woody and Phil over to the practice field. Woody kept saying, "Hurry, hurry, hurry."

We practiced for more than an hour under threatening skies but it didn't rain one drop. After Woody had gone over everything, he said, "Okay, hurry back inside. I can't hold it off any longer."

Everyone looked for Strick to see what smart remark he was going to make, but much to our surprise, he and Woody were making tracks toward the locker room. Just then, lightning smacked near one of the goal posts and we took off running.

As Woody slammed the locker room door shut, it started again. Rain and hailstones the size of golf balls pelted the door, and we heard a loud roaring noise as someone screamed, "Tornado!" Everyone saw a huge whirling cloud dance right up the middle of the practice field and bounce back up into the clouds.

Most of us didn't know what to say, but Phil started praising Woody. Phil said, "Hey, Coach, that was great the way you held back that tornado! Real cool."

Woody sort of acknowledged Phil by tipping his cap as he turned to look out the window.

"Hey, Coach," Phil was shouting again, "you ever walk on water?"

Woody turned to Phil with a strange look and said, "Not recently."

From that day on, Phil Strickland and Woody Hayes started to hit it off. That was one of the strangest things I had ever seen because Phil didn't get along with anyone.

Strick was my roommate and he was strange. Some days he was easygoing; other times he wanted to fight and I never knew why. Anyway, one day I accommodated Phil and we went at it.

The fight started over his bed. Most people will fight over a lady or money or something serious, but not Phil. When he came into the room, I was sleeping on his bed. He jumped me and we started. After a few minutes of slugging it out in the room, we both agreed someone could get hurt. More serious yet, we might ruin the furniture and Woody would get mad. So we walked over to the elevator, went down into the lobby and walked outside.

Phil was the strangest guy I have ever fought. I'd drive my fist down his throat, pick him up, and throw him into the bushes, and he'd get up and say, "Tatum you ain't proved nothin' to me. You're gonna have to do that again."

I did it again, and again, and again, but Phil wouldn't quit. Later (it seemed like hours), we were both getting tired, so some of the guys watching broke it up and called it a tie. Two seconds later Phil was my buddy again.

Most of the time Phil was hard to understand. Maybe that's why he and Woody started to get along. It didn't make sense. For example, one time the offense was practicing a new play Woody had designed and the guards kept making mistakes. The old man started cussing and throwing his clipboard. It was a good bet that whoever screwed up next was going to get punched. Woody screamed at the guards,

"We've run this play five thousand times and five thousand times we've screwed it up. Is there anyone that can run the damn thing right?"

No one in his right mind would have volunteered, but Phil stuck up his hand and said, "I can run that play, Coach. I'll show 'em how to do it."

Phil sounded so confident that if I didn't know him, I'd have sworn that he was going to run the play right. But I, just like everyone else, knew Strick, and we all burst out laughing.

"What the hell's so funny?" Woody wanted to know.

"Yeah, what's so funny?" Phil wanted to know.

After Phil ran the play, both he and Woody found out what we had already known would happen. Just as expected, Phil ran the wrong way and trampled the quarterback into the ground.

The old man was mad. Screaming, he quickly turned toward Strick and drew back his fist. At that moment, Woody said, "If it's not you [meaning Strick] screwing up, then it's you [meaning one of the other guards]," and his punch sailed right on past Strick's head and landed on the other guard's jaw.

I figured that because Woody had one member of the team who honestly believed in him, he wasn't going to destroy Phil's dedication with a sucker-punch he could use on another, less dedicated guard. The old man had someone he could depend on, if you want to depend on Strick, and that was Woody's ace in the hole.

During our senior year, Phil Strickland proved beyond a doubt that he and Woody were pals to the end. The rumors started that some school official wanted artificial turf in the stadium, and the team rebelled. Anyone who has played on astro turf doesn't like it. It is a harder surface, and you can feel the game and the hitting in your body for days afterward. Not only that, the artificial surface doesn't give like grass and you can scrape and burn the skin on your knees and elbows.

Woody called a special team meeting and started to explain artificial turf. It was his way of brainwashing everyone into believing that fake turf would make us faster and better. Woody said, "Not only is it a faster modern surface, but think of the advantages during bad weather ... no more cold, muddy uniforms."

I was sitting next to Strick and he leaned over and whispered to me, "Hey, Tate, why doesn't Woody just make it stop raining on all game days? That's cheaper than gettin' fake grass."

After explaining the "advantages," Woody said, "I've talked long enough. You people have to play the games so it's all up to you. If you want to be modern, then vote for the new turf and you'll get it."

Sixty-six players quickly cast their votes against the turf; only one player was in favor of Woody's "modern" look. Afterward, Phil Strickland said, "Damn, Tate, I thought everyone was going to vote for the new grass. Didn't anyone hear what Woody said about making us faster?"

Strick was never noted for his logic, so someone pointed out, "Strick, the other team plays on the same field, too."

Woody had a democratic system at Ohio State, but just like Woody, his system was different. Woody was always the last man to vote. That way he only has to vote one time if there is a tie or as many times as he needs to win his point. At Ohio State all elections are close, but Woody always wins by one point. With Woody's sixty-six votes and Phil's one, Ohio State, by a narrow margin, went modern.

Woody Hayes is a dictator and the most stubborn man I have ever known. He goes rushing off the deep end and slugs photographers and cameras; he kicks fans, sucker-punches players and hates Michigan. But in spite of Woody's shortcomings, I, like my parents, believe in him. Woody is a human being and he makes mistakes, but he also goes to the extremes when it comes to hard work, fair play and honesty.

Sometimes I think that if Woody Hayes fell into a river and was drowning, I'd jump in and try to save him. Other times, I'd probably throw him some chains and say, "Grab hold, Coach."

Woody is the type of character who you can't love all the time or hate all the time. He's different.

Actually, the very first time I met Woody, I realized he was different. After all, most college coaches and scouts tried to recruit me, while Woody recruited my mother and she recruited me. That was just a normal type of different. It all started when I was just a freshman scrimmaging the varsity team. I came to OSU as a running back, but because Woody was different, I eventually asked to be switched to the defensive unit.

As a freshman, Woody expects you to be passive and let the upperclassmen knock the hell out of you. I guess we had a rebellious class because things just didn't work out the way Woody wanted.

Getting back to my first scrimmage against the varsity, Woody carefully instructed me to take the handoff from the quarterback and drive straight up the middle. Then he went over to the defensive unit and stacked everyone up on the line. He told them I was going to run the ball up the middle. I like contact, but Woody's idea of straight-ahead football wasn't setting very well with me and my classmates. I did as Woody instructed and took the handoff, and even went as far as to actually try the middle, but there was just no moving those eleven defensive bodies. So I did the obvious thing and broke outside for thirty yards and a touchdown. Scoring on the varsity really wasn't a big deal, because 1967 was a particularly terrible year for OSU. Everyone scored on the Bucks, even the freshman team. But I guess Woody was interested in building the morale of his varsity team, and getting beat by a brassy group of youngsters wasn't going to help that issue. Woody had tried to make the varsity look good against the freshman team, and quite frankly, that was one of his failures.

Jogging back to the huddle after scoring my touchdown, I heard Woody screaming at me. He said, "Tatum, what the hell did I tell you to do?"

"Run the ball, Coach," I answered.

"Run the ball where?" the old man questioned.

"Up the middle where there wasn't any hole."

Well, Woody didn't like my answer and he explained the difference between up the middle and outside. It wasn't important that I had scored, because Woody had ordered me to run the ball up the middle. Right there, I started thinking about my career at OSU. I came to college to play football and not to commit suicide. Woody's concept of freshman offensive football against varsity defense was silly.

I talked with the defensive coaches and let it be known that offensive football just wasn't my bag. I explained that playing defensive football had always been my childhood fantasy. I reasoned that Woody's style of offense called for a big, 230-pound "foolback," and my mother didn't raise no fool. After a few fumbles and a few no-gainers up the middle, Woody changed me to defense. That was the biggest mistake Woody ever made while trying to build the morale of the '67 team. As a running back I was getting hit, but as a linebacker, I was doing the hitting. Obviously, it hurts more to get hit than it does to hit, and before long, Woody's varsity running backs started running for the sidelines, slipping in the backfield, making those little mental errors, and even running the wrong way. Woody screamed and bitched at the varsity and called them everything from cowards to chickens, but at press conferences he talked quite differently and bragged about me to the sportswriters. Woody once said, "We have a freshman that hits so damn hard that our varsity running backs are scared to death of him. Jack Tatum is the hardest hitter I've ever coached or seen play the game of football, and next year people on our schedule will believe my words."

There it is: because Woody was different, I became a formidable defensive player. But that's still not the main reason I consider

Woody different.

I know for a fact that many universities have special bonus programs for star athletes. Of course, I'm talking about cash under the table and many other extras. But at OSU things were naturally different. An athletic scholarship at OSU abides by a strict interpretation of university and NCAA rules. Woody will not deviate from these rules one bit, and there is absolutely no payoff money. Woody's conformity is an honorable way of being different and a quality of his which I can deeply respect. I believe that if a coach breaks rules in recruiting an athlete, he will in all probability break rules in getting rid of an athlete who gets hurt, doesn't play up to expectations, or doesn't blend into the system. At OSU I knew because of Woody's principles that regardless of injury or whatever, my education was assured. Playing for and working with a coach who maintains that degree of honor is worth something, even if it's only peace of mind. I guess this all gets back to what I first said about Woody being everything from a prince to a monster.

As an athlete playing for Woody, you get to almost understand him. The upperclassmen usually school freshmen players about the "dos and don'ts" of Woody's philosophy, and by the time your senior year comes around, you come to realize that Woody is basically consistent in his philosophy and emotional responses, though still quite unpredictable in his actions. What I mean is that if Woody is losing to an inferior team, he's going to get mad. That is always a predictable emotional level that you know Woody is going to reach. However, one never knows whether he's simply going to kick, spit, punch, curse, or do something dramatically different. Woody likes to win, he wants to win, and will not accept any other alternative. Personally, I don't think there is anything wrong with developing a winning attitude, but the emotional level where Woody seems to peak is a point in deep space I have never reached.

Fortunately, most of my career with Woody Hayes was a winning effort. As a sophomore, I, along with sixteen other sophomores, started on offense and defense. A starting team consisting of so many second-year men was unheard of, and to be able to win with the youngsters was simply unthinkable. But because Woody Hayes made a tremendous coaching effort to that cause, we won and won.

That particular season, 1968, started off with a win over Southern Methodist University and ended on January 1, 1969, with a victory at the Rose Bowl. Although we were a young, inexperienced team, Woody pulled everything together, and we became the National Champions. Woody never let us know how good we were, and every week it took a greater effort on our part to learn more about Woody Hayes and winning.

After two wins in a row over SMU, 35-14, and Oregon, 21-6, we came to our biggest test of the season, Purdue. During the 1967 season Purdue had laid the wood to the Bucks and walked off the field laughing and pointing to the scoreboard, which read 41-6. Woody hadn't forgotten that score.

When you're young and inexperienced you sometimes believe everything you read in the newspapers. I know that although most of the players were eager to play against Purdue, they still felt that Purdue was practically unbeatable. After all, Purdue was the number-one team in the country; they had a great quarterback in Mike Phipps and an All-American running back who was one of the candidates for the Heisman Trophy, Leroy Keyes. It seemed like insurmountable odds for us to overcome. Adding to our feelings of inferiority was the fact that Woody had been quoted in the newspaper as saying, "Leroy Keyes is the best back in this country. No one can cover him one-on-one, and it's doubtful that any team can stop him."

Woody's statement was in the Sunday paper, and at practice on Monday he said, "Jack, we're putting in a special defense to stop Keyes. When he plays outside, you move out and cover him. When he's in the backfield, you move in and cover him."

"Coach," I said, "that sounds like you're putting me on Leroy man-for-man."

"Yes, Jack, that's what it sounds like and that's what it is," Woody informed me with a queer smile on his pudgy face.

"But, Coach, I read in the newspaper what you said about no one being able to cover Leroy, and ..."

Woody interrupted. "Jack, that doesn't apply to you. See, Leroy Keyes will read the newspaper, too. He'll believe what he reads, but the truth of the matter is that I know you can cover him one-on-one."

I wasn't sure Woody knew what he was talking about. Keyes was a tremendous running back and receiver. During a game the previous week, he had personally accounted for nearly four hundred yards, as Purdue blasted Wisconsin. But Woody had said, "Trust me," and I did.

As the week developed, I began to understand Woody's defensive philosophy against Purdue. It was quite simple. When Keyes lined up outside, he was a receiver and they threw the ball to him. When he lined up in the backfield, he was a running back and they gave the ball to him. All I had to do was stop him from gaining any yardage. All week long Woody kept on saying, "You see, Jack, how simple it's going to be?"

When Saturday came along, I believed that I could, and, quite frankly, would stop Keyes cold. More important, I knew we could win the game. I think it takes a great coach to completely change a team's attitude during the course of one week's time. When we started practice on Monday most of the players looked as though we were already beaten. But by Saturday it was a different story entirely. Even though Purdue was favored to win by thirteen points, we were certain that we were going to win the game. It wasn't just thinking that we could win, it was knowing that we were going to win. That was the big difference, and when Purdue stepped out onto the field, they could sense the difference, too.

When the smoke cleared, I had to give the so-called experts credit, for their thirteen point spread had been exactly correct, except that we had the thirteen points and Purdue had zero. During the game, I stuck with Keyes, and while I didn't exactly shut him out, I did manage to make things quite difficult for him. At day's end Leroy Keyes had rushed for nineteen yards, caught three passes for forty-six yards, and was all but carried off the field on a stretcher as I pounded and blasted him every chance I had. Now the newspapers carried another story, and it was about me and the fact that someone could stick with Keyes man-for-man. I felt a certain amount of pride because I had done my job. I knew Woody was thrilled, and that made it seem all the more important to me. I guess that's another indication that Woody is really a great man. When his players can take pride in their accomplishments and not be so blind as to miss noticing the old man's satisfaction with everything ... well, what I'm trying to say is that the major part of my pride came because Woody was proud of me. Even though the UPI Press voted me "Lineman of the Week," and AP voted me the "Back of the Week" (no one had ever had that happen before), my true reward still came back to Woody. I remembered he had asked, "Trust me," and because of that I had the faith and we won the game.

An undefeated season, Big Ten Championships, Rose Bowls, and a National Championship are but a small part of my experiences with Woody. Writers can record that particular type of history and still never begin to understand the deep and meaningful relationship between a coach and his players. I guess my experiences at Ohio State were better than those of some of the other players who came after me. During my career, we won with Woody and were also able to share losing games with the same man.

In three years we won many games, the exact number I really don't know. But during that same period of time, I clearly remember we lost twice. I remember the games we lost, I remember the scores; how, when, and where it all happened. I remember because it does hurt a little to lose, but maybe also because as a player I felt that somehow I had failed Woody. Maybe he failed us a little, too, but the end result is still the same — losing isn't much fun and you don't like to remember.

My junior year at OSU was a great example of failure. During the first eight games, we had been rated the number one team in the nation. Offensively, we were averaging slightly over forty-six points a game and defensively our first-string unit was virtually impenetrable. In all, we were awesome, and every team on our schedule was aware of that fact, but then it came down to the final game of the year against Michigan. Because of a Big Ten ruling which prohibited any team in our league from going to the Rose Bowl two consecutive years, regardless of what happened at Ann Arbor, we could not return to California that season. I don't look for any cheap excuses, but most of our incentive was taken away from the Michigan game by the Rose Bowl rule. Although Woody was sky high and he wanted to win in the worst way, the players were just flat. It was by no means a failure on Woody's part, just the wrong day, the wrong year, and the Buckeyes lost 24-12. I think about that game because of my performance. I wasn't sharp, and even though I kept telling myself, "I think we can win," I honestly didn't care. Afterwards, I didn't want to look at Woody because I knew that I was part of his feeling of failure. With Woody everything is built around winning and failure. Either you have won the game or you have failed. On that day we failed. That particular loss was most definitely the fault of the players.

Next season it was different. Once again we had little or no difficulty getting through the regular season and made it with a perfect 9-0 record. For the second time in three years I was going to play in the Rose Bowl, and once again the national championship was on the line. I honestly believe that every player on the team wanted to make that trip west and beat Stanford. For most of us it was the last game we would ever play in a Buckeye uniform, and no one wants to lose their last game. Also, national championships are hard to come by, and all we had to do to be number one was to beat Stanford. It certainly wouldn't take any special coaching philosophies to get us sky high for the Rose Bowl, but a mistake in coaching judgments could take away from what we already had.

Before the Michigan game Woody had promised that if we won, our stay in Southern California would be a very pleasant one. He told us that preparing for a Rose Bowl would take a certain amount of work, but he assured us that we would have plenty of time to relax and enjoy life in the sunshine. Actually, we didn't need that incentive to go out and beat Michigan but Woody wanted to be sure. We won, 20-9, and started packing for Los Angeles.

Somewhere between the pep talk for the Michigan game and the plane trip west, Woody forgot what he said about some R and R in the sunshine of California. It all started about ten minutes after our plane lifted from the snow-covered ground of Columbus. When I saw the trainers taking out their bags and the rolls of tape, I realized something was wrong. As the plane jetted west, the trainers taped everyone's ankles because Woody felt we needed a practice session on California soil. It couldn't wait until tomorrow; it couldn't even wait until we had landed and had something to eat. Woody expected us to step off the plane and go to our headquarters, break out the gear and practice. That was the beginning of the end. We practiced and practiced and practiced. Even though the game was weeks away, we practiced continually. While the Stanford players were on tours of Beverly Hills, the beaches and Disneyland, and still found time for light workouts, the Bucks practiced. "You know," Woody would exuberantly shout, "practice makes perfect!" and from somewhere in the crowd of players you could hear a low mumble, "Eat crap."

Most of us had played for Woody four years; some of the players liked him and some didn't. Still, all of us, without exception, respected Woody as a man of his word. For the first time in our college careers, Woody Hayes had backed down on a promise to us. He was anxious to cap an undefeated season with a Rose Bowl victory, and in his overzealousness, forgot the needs of his players. He felt that the formula for winning was: constant practice plus constant discipline equals victory. Hell, he even made us practice on Christmas Eve. It got to a point where everyone literally quit and Woody started getting serious. He began screaming and bitching at everyone thinking it would help. It didn't.

Sometimes, a coach can make a mistake. We didn't need hours of practice to beat Stanford. All we needed was a little understanding, a little fun, and a little work, but Woody wanted to be sure; he wanted another National Championship.

I don't think that Woody realized it then, and maybe he still doesn't understand, but we actually started losing the Rose Bowl and the National Championship on the plane trip west. Woody didn't have the confidence in us to realize that we wanted to win and he didn't need to take any special training and conditioning methods. When it came time for Woody to trust us with an important part of our lives, he didn't, and the results were a half-hearted effort that fell short of everyone's expectations. We lost the game, and this time our failure was Woody's fault.

I'm trying to say that Woody is only human. He has made mistakes because of his emotions and he has made mistakes when it comes to exercising good judgment in relatively unimportant situations. But then again, no coach is perfect all the time and no athlete plays all games at a 100 percent fever pitch. Coaches, like players, have many highs and lows; they win and they fail. But one must look at the whole scope of a man's career before making a final analysis of his performance. Coaching and playing are simply the blending of talents to chart a course of action that will ultimately lead to victory.

It may seem that I've been carried away on the subject of Wayne Woodrow Hayes, but the man has made a tremendous contribution to my life. I owe Woody one, and maybe this is may way of repaying a debt.

In talking with my publisher, I was informed that the style and sequence of this particular chapter was jumpy and confusing. Well, that's actually the way it should be. Woody Hayes is a jumpy confusing guy until you get to know him. My publisher felt I should have ended this chapter with Woody's exit from coaching and my personal testimony to the fact he was a straight shooter. But I don't want to remember Woody that way, and I don't consider him as being finished. Maybe it's because I know that only a part of the man was a football coach, while the rest was a great human being. Football coaches will retire and fade into the ranks of obscurity, while great men will continue to work and rise to unbelievable heights of accomplishment. Woody Hayes may never again strike at the ABC camera or spit on the fans, but he will continue to move through life in his strange way, with a genuine compassion for people and a special fondness for his boys.

6

Countdown to a
Super Bowl

An Oakland Raiders training camp is hardly a stalag of sweat and torture. Most of our practice sessions are held in a relaxed atmosphere. Some of the guys will take a break and sit down on their helmets and smoke. Others will clown around and have a laugh to ease the pressure. Some people think our system is questionable, but look at the game results. The Raiders win more games than any other team in professional football, and that is a fact.

Paul Zimmerman, a sportswriter for the *New York Post,* spent a day with the Raiders before Super Bowl XI. He walked away from that experience shaking his head and saying, "The Raiders may be the flakiest team in football. If they beat Minnesota in the Super Bowl, it might set reason and sanity back a few centuries."

We did beat Minnesota, but reason and sanity are still in the twentieth century. Zimmerman's feelings were understandable, though. The fact is that when you pull all the different talents and personalities of the Oakland Raiders together and have a training camp, *strange* things can start to happen.

A good example of what I'm talking about concerns our left cornerback, Skip Thomas. The first time I saw Skip play, I knew he was Raider material; he liked to beat people up. Skip considers himself a normal USC graduate with a few different ideas about life. Consider his nickname. Sometimes, Skip likes to be called "Dr. Death." He really isn't a doctor, but Skip had his nickname printed on both doors of his Corvette right under the skull and crossbones.

I don't know if it's bad or good for me, but when Skip came to the Raiders after college, they made him my roommate. I always seem to end up with special roommates.

Skip won't talk to reporters or let anyone take his picture. He says, "Gettin' your picture taken steals part of your soul." As for reporters, Skip doesn't like people, and of course reporters are people. One time a reporter came up to our room to interview *me.* Skip didn't like the questions I was being asked so he threw the reporter out the door.

"The Doctor" plays football from a different world. His body is on the field doing a job but his mind is off traveling to other planets and solar systems. The night before a game Skip will eat four or five full-course meals, drink a bottle of tequila, smoke two packs of cigarettes, and watch TV for hours after all the channels have signed off. Once, I stayed up and watched TV with Skip, but after ten minutes, I couldn't figure out what was happening. Now I just say, "Skip, I'm going to bed. Lower the TV 'cause I've seen that show before and I need my sleep."

Skip has a fascination for motorcycles and fast cars. When the motorcycle craze was going around, Skip had a dream of jumping the Golden Gate Bridge on a bike. He was going to build a ramp in the parking lot at our summer camp and practice by jumping over a couple of hundred cars. Al Davis put a stop to Skip's dream. I don't think Al was worried that Skip would hurt himself; it's just that the Raiders have a lot of expensive cars and Skip might damage one of the Rolls Royces or Caddies. Football players aren't poor.

Another time, Skip and Clarence Davis, one of our running backs, got into a debate about which was faster, a Corvette or a motorcycle. It was right back to the parking lot. C.D. was gunning the Corvette and Skip was on the bike. Al Davis didn't get there in time to stop the race and when they zoomed across the finish line, there wasn't enough parking lot left to stop the car or bike. C.D. banged off a few parked cars and slid into the practice field while Skip jumped off the bike and landed in a ditch. No one was hurt, but Al Davis sent the bike and car back to Oakland on a big truck. Al didn't understand that Skip and Clarence were just letting off a little steam. The car and bike were toys they played with, but they're really not alone. Other players bring toys to camp, too.

George Beuhler was our right guard. He stands 6 feet 2, weighs 275 pounds, and is probably the strongest man on the team. George is an All-Pro but he has a habit of losing interest in the game. Sometimes the other linemen have to slap him around in the huddle to bring him back. "He does have a tendency to drift a bit," Gene Upshaw, our left guard says. "Yelling at him doesn't always work. He seems to have his mind on one hundred different things other than the game. It takes a good slap to get him concentrating again."

Our fullback, Pete Banaszak, tells about a particular game when we were behind and driving for a last minute go-ahead touchdown.

Everyone was deadly serious as they listened to Kenny Stabler call the play. Then, all of a sudden, Beuhler started talking to Pete and asked, "Where'd you get those shoes? I've been thinking about changing mine and maybe I'll try a pair like yours. I like that fancy design."

We call George the "Mad Scientist" because he loves electronic gadgets. He made a little remote control tank that he sends out to pick up the mail every morning. Once, I was sleeping and heard "RRRrrRRRrrrRR" coming down the hall. I got up to investigate and saw this tank coming toward my room. At first it scared the hell out of me, but then I realized it was only George's toy.

George likes remote-controlled airplanes, too. He used to let some of the other guys fly them until Pete Banaszak crashed one into a building. Now he won't let anyone touch his toys. George says, "You guys don't know how to use the controls."

Unfortunately, George doesn't know how to use the control either. He brought a plane to practice one day. Everyone was in full gear preparing to scrimmage and George started flying his airplane around the field. The coaches told him to put the toy away but something was wrong with the controls. The plane started diving at us almost as though there were a nasty pilot flying it. Beuhler was punching the control box with his fist and cussing while everyone else was running around ducking and dodging. Finally, the gadget crashed into the goal post.

Someone screamed, "Beuhler, what the hell happened?"

He answered, "I lost contact!"

Skip and George are normal guys compared to Charley Philyaw. Charley's our 6-8 defensive end. We named him "King Kong." To say that Charley is sometimes a little slow catching on is an understatement. At practice, Charley hurt his hand and needed medical attention. He walked over to Pete Banaszak, holding his hand and asked, "Hey, man, what should I do?"

"Go see the doctor," Pete told him.

"The doctor?" Philyaw asked.

"Yeah, the doctor," Pete said.

Philyaw walked out into the middle of a pass defense drill and pulled Skip Thomas aside saying, "Man said I should show you this," and he stuck his bloody paw in Skip's face.

Coach Madden asked, "Philyaw, what are you doing?"

"Showing my hand to the doctor," Charley answered.

"Get that man the hell out of my sight!" Madden screamed.

Every morning the offense and defense go to separate film rooms and view game films. One morning, Philyaw was sitting in the offensive film room ten minutes before someone said, "Philyaw, you're in the wrong room."

Defensive coach Tom Dahms had a nice meeting going without Charley, and when someone said, "Coach, Philyaw isn't here," he answered, "Good!"

During a morning practice session, Philyaw sprained his ankle. He wasn't expected to practice for a couple of days, but that afternoon, like a good rookie, Philyaw was back on the field. Charley was wearing one shoe on his good foot and a sandal on the one he had sprained, but that wasn't all. Charley had on different colored socks, the wrong colored jersey, no belt, and his thigh pads were in upside down. Everyone stopped and stared in disbelief. This was a professional athlete? The coaches took Charley aside and started counting up the things wrong with his uniform. Philyaw set an NFL record. Ten things were wrong with his uniform.

There is, of course, a more serious side to our training camp. It's not all toys, mistakes and laughs. For example, the bar bowling and air hockey tournaments are serious to the point of almost being sacred rituals.

Phil Villapiano is our All-Pro linebacker, but his finest moment did not occur on the football field. Phil established the air hockey and bar bowling tournaments and even the rules and regulations the games are governed by. "Foo," that's Phil's nickname, is the commissioner of the tournament. The man responsible for Phil's nickname is Duane Benson, another linebacker, who got so drunk one night during the tournament games that he couldn't pronounce "Phil." He kept on slobbering out, "Hey, Foo, he's cheatin'."

"That's it," Foo shouted. "Everyone has to cheat! From now on cheating is the cardinal rule of all tournaments!"

Up to that point, we only had one rule, and that was that all contestants had to be drunk. Every so often someone would fake a drunk act and try to get in the tournament and win. But when Art Thomas threatened to start giving urine tests to everyone to make sure all contestants were equally drunk, everyone started tipping their glasses. Like I said, the tournament is serious.

When Foo added the cheating rule, all the air hockey players started wearing long winter coats. The people of Santa Rosa thought it was a little strange, us wearing heavy coats in the middle of summer with the temperature over 100 degrees, but the long sleeves were great for deflecting shots. Some of the air hockey games would go on for hours and no one would score.

During the last week of camp we hold our championship games, and the winners are driven through town in convertibles with a police escort. Foo sits in the first car and the champions follow behind. The throw candy out to the people who line the streets and make a parade out of it. The townspeople come out and wave and seem happy. I don't know if they're happy because of the parade or because our camp is just about over. The people of Santa Rosa really do act differently toward us when we are about to leave came than they do when we first arrive. I've noticed that when we first come up to Santa Rosa, the townsfolk seem a little jumpy and somewhat paranoid. I've seen mothers hide their young daughters behind their dresses when we passed by, and you see people peeking out of their homes from behind closed doors and windows. It all seems quite strange until I take a look at Skip's car, Buehler's tank, or Philyaw bumping his head on the same low-hanging branch year after year. Then I understand.

Really, the Raiders have never done anything serious enough to warrant people being jumpy around us. Unless ... well, there was this one time when the Coleco Company (they make the air hockey tables) decided to throw a party for the champions and the rest of the team. That was sort of a mistake on the management's part. Things were just fine when everyone was stuffing their faces with food, but then the management made their second mistake. Some Coleco Company official stood up, tapped his water glass with a fork, and said, "Gentlemen, may I have your attention?" I just shook my head because I knew it was bad timing. Nobody wanted to hear a speech. One of the guys threw a hot buttered roll at the man, hit him right smack in the head, and said, "Ah, shut up!"

Now that was funny. Someone else threw another roll and then another and another. It was getting hilarious. As the rolls began sailing all over the room, one of them hit the wife of a company vice president, and when she threw a dish of butter back at us, the war was on. Pies, green beans, paper cups, and drinks started flying around the room. Now, some people seemed to think all of that was uncalled-for behavior in a group of adults, but it was just what we expected at a banquet. After all, what's a banquet without a good fight? Still, though, the Coleco Company hasn't as yet had any more banquets for the Raiders.

I'm really starting to get ahead of myself. Here I am telling the story of the modern-day Raiders and I haven't given any history of the team. After all, the Oakland Raiders didn't wake up one morning and find themselves the type of organization they are presently. Just like anything worth having, it all started a long time ago and has taken countless hours of hard work.

For the trivia fans, the Raiders played their first game on a July night in 1960 against the Dallas Texans. With 4:27 left on the clock in the first quarter, a 190-pound running back named Buddy Allen broke off left and scored the Raiders' first touchdown. It seemed easy, but that was only the beginning of an uphill struggle that eighteen years later brought the Raiders their first and only Super Bowl Championship.

Although the Raiders went on to lose their first game, none of the 12,000 fans at Kezar Stadium could foresee that one of the most successful franchises in professional football had been born.

During their first three years the Raiders spent more time organizing and reorganizing the front office management than they did signing draft picks. Without quality athletes, game results did little to encourage team owners, and confidence within the locker room slipped to an all-time low. Everyone in the organization knew that something had to be done.

Before the start of the 1962 season, someone suggested "new blood" to restructure the organization. It was a great idea, and someone introduced the name of Al Davis, a then thirty-three-year-old, hippy-looking assistant on Sid Gillman's San Diego Chargers general staff. Davis had a genius for talking athletes away from the NFL and into signing with the Chargers. In a war between the two leagues, the AFL and NFL, Al Davis was the H-Bomb and commanded much respect.

Al Davis sounded like the man, although some thought he was a little too aggressive for the Oakland organization and his "do-anything-to-win" tactics might give the team a bad image. But when the owners reasoned everything out, the image of a "loser" seemed much worse than the image of a "do-anything-to-win winner."

Al Davis was hired as the coach and general manager and given complete control of the Raiders' future. His first day on the job was spent firing everyone from the ball boys to the ticket takers. His next actions concerned the football players themselves. The Raiders had a core of solid players to build around, but they needed new muscles in certain areas. Al weeded out every weak link and started to build anew.

AL Davis started training camp by saying, "Pride and poise! That's the answer! You're Oakland Raiders wherever you go; whatever you do. Anybody who is ashamed of that can get on a plane and leave right now. You're here to win! Win! Win!"

The door to the Oakland organization was swinging on new hinges, and the team started the season off with two home games in a row and two big wins. But when Al took the team east of the Mississippi, he ran into trouble. After three road games the Raiders were struggling along with a 2-3 record.

In every football game, and in every football season, there are points that can turn things either way. When the Raiders traveled to San Diego, few people gave them any chance of turning their losing ways around. After all, San Diego was the pride of the AFL and many people thought the Chargers could even beat any NFL team.

A capacity crowd filled Balboa Stadium, hoping that Oakland might field something that slightly resembled a professional football team – or, at the very least, the crowd hoped the Raiders would make a game of it, if only for a while.

The Raiders scored first, but the Chargers came back for a 10-7 lead at the end of the first quarter. In a matter of seconds, the Raiders were back on top, 14-10.

The San Diego fans started screaming for Raider blood and the Chargers responded with 13 unanswered points. The rout was on, or so it seemed.

When the fourth quarter of action started, however, the scoreboard read: San Diego 23, Raiders 28. The Raiders had managed to score two touchdowns on the Chargers in the third period; one on a lucky interception and the other on a long pass play. It didn't matter to San Diego, because the Chargers were getting real serious.

San Diego started off with a field goal, and three plays later they had the ball again. This time Keith Lincoln broke away for a 51-yard scamper and the Chargers led 33-28.

With a little over one minute to play in the game, some of the San Diego fans made their way toward the exits. But back inside the concrete structure, on the grass field of Balboa Stadium, the Raiders were about to answer their first real test of pressure. Much to the dismay of the remaining Charger fans, the Raiders did not shrivel up and disintegrate. Patiently they moved the ball closer to the San Diego goal line. Then, with just seconds left and using what seemed like an almost cocky display of talent and strategy, the Raiders worked halfback Glenn Shaw behind defenders for the touchdown pass that historically capped the Raiders' first come-from-behind win.

The Raiders were a growing organization, and Al Davis kept finding new ways to win. When Al started making personnel moves that bordered on brilliant, other teams suddenly became cautious of whom they traded to Oakland. Davis had a magical way of turning other teams' scrap into All-Pro players.

With Buffalo, Al traded away three promising players for a so-so Archie Matsos. The promising players were soon forgotten while Matsos went on to All-League status as a lineman.

Several teams in the league had a good laugh when Al seemed to lose all reason and sanity by making a trade for Clem Daniels, a defensive back who wasn't. Everyone knew that Daniels was big, strong and fast, but he didn't know how to cover receivers on pass patterns, and he didn't know how to tackle running backs. Al wiped the smirks off everyone's face by making Clem a running back who rushed for over one thousand yards during his first year.

If that wasn't enough, Al then went out and made a hilarious deal with Houston for their aging running back Billy Cannon. Rumor had it that Cannon was washed up, and why Al Davis wanted him was beyond anyone's ability to understand. As the season started, everyone found out what Al Davis had known all the time. Billy Cannon wasn't fast enough for a running back but his size and strength made him an excellent tight end.

Next came the deal for Denver's tight end Hewritt Dixon, who was not a great blocker, ran poor pass patterns and couldn't catch very well. Still, Al Davis made a deal for Dixon and turned the man into a fullback. Dixon became a tank that ran over defensive players. The essence of Al's success stemmed from the fact that he wasn't afraid to bring in washed-up players or so-called troublemakers. He was building a team, and judged a man solely by his talents and what he could do for the Raiders. As an Oakland Raider, I am given the flexibility to be myself. It's always been that way with the Raiders, and I like it. Nobody is ever prejudiced by the cut of his hair, color of his skin, or his weight. Everyone in the Oakland organization is treated as a professional until his abilities or lack of abilities dictate otherwise. Maybe that's why you can look down our roster and see the names of several men who were losers with other teams but became winners with the Raiders.

There I go again, getting carried away. Before I get into the modern-day Raiders, there are still a few stories worth mentioning about the history of the team.

Within a few years the Raiders had established themselves as a winning team that came from behind with miraculous finishes. But there was still another chapter of the Raider story to be written.

December 31, 1967, the Raiders hosted the Houston Oilers for the American Conference Championship. By now, Al Davis had given up his coaching duties to John Madden and was acting as the team's general manager. He still hired and fired the players, but Madden's job was to keep the Raiders winning. In 1964, when Madden took over, he started teaching something just a little different in the way of defensive football. Madden's style was aggressive and punishing. Slowly, the team started to develop this style, too, and in the championship game against Houston, the Raiders were blazing away with their big guns.

Although Gruesome Sunday started out innocently enough with the Raiders getting a 37-yard field goal from a Houston cast-off, George Blanda, everything seemed to pick up from that point. The home crowd sensed the hostility and started screaming for blood. Before long, the Raiders were chewing at the jugular veins of the Houston Oilers. This was the other part of the Raider image that I was talking about, the ability to become brutal and violent to the point of being almost indecent. Houston was being raped of pride and sacrificed to almost 50,000 Raider fans. The score totaled Raiders 40, Houston 7.

Then came Super Bowl II and the Green Bay Packers. Seasoned veterans such as Bart Starr, Jim Taylor, Henry Jordan, Fuzzy Thurston and the rest of the Packers knew their coach, Vince Lombardi, was going to retire after this game. They wanted to give him something special to remember. They did. The Raiders were handled rather easily, 33-14, but the game to them was more a direct violation of their motto, "Pride and Poise" than it was a disgrace. But even through the tears of disappointment, one thing was evident: The top was now in sight.

The next season the Raiders missed the Super Bowl. Joe Namath led the Jets down to Miami and beat the Colts 16-7 for the first AFL win ever. The Raiders had already earned a place in football history that particular year, however, by playing in the "Heidi Bowl."

Earlier in the season the New York Jets had come to Oakland for an important game, and NBC was there to televise the action, or at least part of the action. For some reason, the Raiders seemed to play their best in desperate situations, so they let the Jets get ahead 32-29 with only 1:05 left in the game. Everyone realized the Jets only had the lead and hadn't as yet won the game. It was going to be an exciting last minute of play, and football buffs from coast to coast settled down to watch.

Then, at 7:00 p.m. sharp, just as the Raiders took over the ball only seventy-nine yards from a touchdown, some wizard at the controls of NBC pressed a button and there was this little blonde girl prancing around a mountainside, picking flowers. This was Heidi, the little girl who lived with her grandfather at the foot of the Jungfrau and ate goat cheese.

While the Raiders were moving the ball down the field, Heidi was dancing in the forests, delighting the hearts of little children, while their fathers were melting NBC telephone lines with obscene calls. Even Julian Goodman, president of NBC, was on the phone trying to call the office and get the order in to restore the game. He was home watching the game, and even he wanted to see the ending. But all telephone lines coming into NBC were busy.

In the minute and five seconds it took Heidi to dance from her cottage to the fields of flowers, the Raiders had just scored and were about to kick off to Namath and the Jets. There was just about enough time for someone to score yet another touchdown. Heidi was about to catch a butterfly as the Raiders kicked off and eleven men clad in silver and black went rumbling after the football. The ball had taken a few strange bounces, hit a couple of Jets, and went on into the end zone, where it was covered by the Raiders for a touchdown. As Heidi sat in a field watching a buttercup grow, NBC flashed the final score across the screen: Raiders 42, Jets 32.

The Raiders had that flair for last-minute excitement and they were a physical team, but there was still the Super Bowl Championship that had never found its way to Oakland, California. I guess it all comes down to those fragile harmonies between players, coaches and general managers. I mean, that's what creates the outcome of most games, but the Super Bowl is something else. I'm sure that Al Davis had looked over his team's record, the best in professional football, and tried to figure out why the Raiders had never won the Super Bowl and had had only one chance even to play for the championship.

There really isn't any proven way to win the Super Bowl. When Green Bay won two Super Bowl championships, Lombardi was a coach who believed in the basic play book drilled to perfection. Dallas achieved success with a formula of complex strategy. Miami used a crunching running game and the zone defense, while the Steelers bulldozed their way to the top with a front four.

Every professional football camp starts with people taking aim on winning the Super Bowl. Any team that starts their season thinking only about surviving isn't worth much, and their record will reflect their very own shortcomings. I know that the two purposes of our Raiders' training camp are to get us ready for the coming season and to work toward the championship. But still, it all comes back to people, your people, beating someone else's people. I believe that winning year after year is a matter of pride and poise, or as the Raiders' institutional letterhead reads: "Commitment to Excellence."

Still, I am sorry to say, in my opinion getting to the Super Bowl and winning defy logic and come down to a matter of luck. Most winning teams have similar basics. Winners have quarterbacks who are true leaders and can handle the pressure. There are also several other important areas evident in all winners, such as good pass protection as a matter of pride and will, a front line that will put pressure on the quarterback, and a tenacious secondary with some-one just like me waiting to bust receivers. In addition, all winners have abusive running backs, speedy receivers, a solid kicking game, coaches who do not disintegrate under pressure, and management with vision.

When you get down to Super Bowl Sunday and you're playing for the championship, believe me, it's just a matter of luck. I'm not selling short the work and effort to get there, but when you have ten or twelve professional teams that start a season believing they can win, and they all go out and work toward a championship, it has to come down to a little luck. Luck can come your way in many different forms, and your good luck is usually the other team's bad luck. Say that one team has a great first-string quarterback and he gets hurt. That's bad luck for the quarterback and his team but good luck for the men standing on the other side of the field. So injuries are good luck and bad luck. Luck in football isn't based on injuries alone. Luck can be someone clipping your free safety and the official not seeing the play. Luck can be recovering a fumble that an official said was a dead ball or catching a pass that should have been called an incompletion. What I'm really trying to say is that because of the high level of competition, it takes luck to win the Super Bowl even though your every effort, dream and desire might tell you it was hard work paying off.

In 1972 our record was 10-3-1, and we ended the season with six impressive wins. Al Davis said, "This is the best Raider team in the history of the organization."

We had our sights on the Super Bowl, but in Pittsburgh we ran into a team with the same objective and working just as hard as the Raiders. The Steelers had won their first division championship ever and we felt that a 0-1 record in post-season play would be nice for our friends in Pittsburgh. The Steelers, however, had other ideas, and the game was a war with the final results resting on one second of playing time and luck.

Three Rivers Stadium was brand new, and the Steelers felt they should give the hometown fans something to cheer about. They came out for action in a surly mood, especially the defensive line with L.C. Greenwood, Joe Greene, Ernie Holmes and Dwight White taking turns smashing our quarterback, Daryle Lamonica, into the turf and batting his passes down his throat. The Steelers' defense was so nasty that Daryle was saying Hail Marys as the broke the huddle and thanking God for working a small miracle every time he completed a pass.

The game wasn't a runaway, because we also have a defensive team that can get nasty. And so, on that particularly warm December day in Pittsburgh, the air around the stadium exploded from the sonic booms of bone-shattering tackles. For fifty-seven minutes of playing time, the game was all defense, with the exception of two field goals by Pittsburgh's Roy Gerela. I believe the score might have ended 6-0 if it hadn't been for the last-minute heroics of our third-string quarterback, Kenny "Snake" Stabler, who was called into action with only a few minutes left to play and eighty yards between him and a touchdown.

The Snake was cool and answered the pressure of the partisan crowd and the Steelers by moving our team right down the field. With a first down and ten on the Steelers' thirty yard line, Snake dropped back to pass and noticed a safety blitz. He calmly tucked the ball under his arm and twisted and slithered his way down the side line and into the end zone, unmolested by Steelers. If the Steelers were wondering about Kenny's nickname, "Snake," before his thirty-yard run, they all knew why after he finished scoring. From his college playing days at Alabama, Kenny had been called "Snake." His college coach, Mr. Paul "Bear" Bryant, once said, "Why, Kenny's harder to get ahold of than a river snake."

Well, anyway, Blanda kicked the extra point and the good guys were on top. It seemed like another come-from-behind victory, but the Steelers had other ideas. When you get into a game with top-notch professionals and your team is only one point ahead, it's really not over. Sometimes, there is more football played in the last few minutes of desperation than in three quarters of blood, sweat, pain and punishment.

Only 1:13 remained in the game as quarterback Terry Bradshaw brought the Steelers up to the line. With the right play-calling, the Steelers could run eight, maybe ten, plays. I was hoping they would let Bradshaw call his own plays. That way the Steelers could only run one or two plays before the game was over. Bradshaw isn't known for his imagination.

Terry started off by flipping a nine-yard pass to Frenchy Fuqua and came back with a draw play to Franco Harris that covered another nine yards. I knew right then that someone was calling the plays from the sideline.

On the next two plays, Bradshaw tried passing in my area. The first pass was a good one and I was lucky to get my hand on the ball and deflect it away from the receiver. The second pass was a copy of a Daryle Lamonica Hail Mary attempt. Bradshaw was running around trying to avoid our people and he just put the ball in the air for anyone to grab. I nearly intercepted. With third and ten facing the Steelers, Bradshaw went up top again, and again I nearly intercepted. The Steelers had one more chance; it was do or die.

Bradshaw dropped back into a pocket and looked up in time to see our defensive line blotting out the sunlight with a tremendous pass rush. Without looking upfield, Bradshaw flung another prayer pass just as one ton of silver-and-black-clad bodies smashed him to the ground. By this time Frenchy Fuqua had broken into a little curl pattern over the middle. I dropped off a few steps and timed my hit to arrive in Frenchy's back just about the same time the ball was going to arrive in his hands. I wanted to smash one more Steeler before the final gun went off, and the Frenchman was my target. I didn't think Frenchy could catch my helmet in his back and still hang on to the ball, so I never gave a thought about going for the interception. I blasted into Frenchy with a full head of speed and the ball bounced off us and sailed twenty yards back downfield. George Atkinson and some of the other players came over to me and we were jumping around celebrating. They were all congratulating me for breaking up the pass, getting Frenchy to go limping off the field in a daze, and, of course, winning the game. That, we were all sure, was the Steelers' last gasp. But like I said, after I hit Frenchy, the ball sailed twenty yards back up the field. It just so happened that Franco Harris, outside the action, was heading over toward the sideline when the ball plopped into his hands. And what does Franco usually do when he gets the ball? He runs out of bounds if the defense is near him or he runs for the end zone if it's wide open. Hell, with the Raiders jumping all over each other because they won the game, it was a wide open freeway to the end zone, and Franco covered seventy yards like a '56 Buick with mudflaps and a coon tail hanging from the mirror.

Five seconds were still on the clock when Franco stepped into the end zone as hero but the screaming and cussing lasted longer, much longer. The Raiders' staff was screaming that the ball had hit Frenchy and it was an illegal play. On the other side of the field, the Steelers swore up and down that I hit the ball first and it was a legal play.

The ruling is that a ball cannot touch two consecutive offensive players and remain in play for the offense. If the ball even nicks a defensive man, and then the offensive man catches it, it is a legal play. The Raiders felt that the ball bounced off Frenchy into the waiting arms of Franco. The Steelers believed the ball hit me first and then Franco caught it. Me and Frenchy? Well, Frenchy wasn't in any condition to honestly judge who the ball hit or even what hit him. When the reporters asked Frenchy if the ball did hit him, all he could say was, "Damn, that sucker really hit me! I didn't know where the hell I was or even who I was, and you're asking me about the ball?" As for myself, I couldn't honestly say if the ball hit me. I wasn't worried about the ball at the time. I just wanted to lay some wood on Frenchy and I did.

The play was so close that even after we viewed the game films with stop action, nobody could tell who the ball hit on that moment of impact. But to this very day, because of my angle of attack and the position of Frenchy's body, I think it was an illegal play.

Referee Fred Swearingen was standing six or seven yards away from the play and he ruled it legal and signaled touchdown. Still, even he must have felt ill at ease over the quick decision and called for a time-out. The officials huddled together in the end zone and tried to figure out what happened, while both benches were screaming and cussing at each other. Swearingen then ran over to the dugout phone and called Art McNally, supervisor of officials, who happened to be sitting in the press box, and asked for a decision. Ten minutes later, after the home town crowd started getting a little restless, Swearingen ran back out onto the field and signaled touchdown for the second time in fifteen minutes.

There are advantages to the home field, and I'm sure the Steelers were enjoying theirs. If the game had been played in Oakland, that play would have gone down as an incompleted pass and we would have enjoyed our home-field advantage. So when all things are equal, you need a little luck to get you through to the Super Bowl and at that time and place, the Steelers had it going for them. Don't get the idea that I'm basing the success of professional football teams solely on luck because that's not true. I'm just saying that when teams have equal strengths, Lady Luck will usually decide the game results.

I know better than anyone that the Raiders have won their share of games on luck. For example, in 1973 and 1974 the Miami Dolphins won back-to-back Super Bowls. In 1975 the Dolphins didn't make it to the Super Bowl, because of the Raiders and one lucky play. On a last-second, falling-down pass play, Kenny Stabler got off a touchdown pass a split second before he was tackled.

In 1976 we got by New England and advanced in the playoffs, again with a last-second touchdown pass. That one pass play was the difference between us watching the Super Bowl and winning the Super Bowl. New England had us down 21-17, with less than a minute to go in the game. Stabler tried hitting Cliff Branch in the corner of the end zone, but the pass was high and it looked as though we were finished. That was our last play. Then one of the officials caught Sugar Bear Hamilton hitting Kenny after the play and we had new life. From there, it was a touchdown and a big win. The next week, we trampled the Steelers 24-7 and started looking forward to the Super Bowl and the Vikings.

I know that coaches and players alike believe in luck, and Al Davis, John Madden, and the Raiders are no exception to that rule. The only trouble is that the Raiders carry their luck charms and superstitions a little too far. I'm talking about Coach Madden and Al Davis for the most part because they really seem to sail off the deep end when it comes to mumbo-jumbo.

I guess the superstitious phases of Raider mania hit the hardest a few years back when fifteen or sixteen of the guys wanted to play in a golf tournament instead of practicing. Coach Madden understood, I guess, because the guys went golfing. Then, on Sunday, we smashed the New York Giants 42-0. That just happened to be the most points we scored all season and the only shutout the defense recorded. Now Coach Madden encourages the guys to go golfing and even started a special team golfing tournament.

The golfing tournament is simple compared to the many other superstitious beliefs the Raiders hold to. It's just like throwing salt over your left shoulder for good luck (Al Davis does that all the time) or the team not traveling on the thirteenth day of the month. Now, superstitions include eating the same pregame meal (if we won the last game), staying at the same hotel, and coaches wearing the same clothes. If we lose, then everything changes.

In Denver we always stayed at the Continental Hotel and we always beat Denver and we always won our division championship. I guess the Denver management also has some superstitious blood in them because they took over the Continental and moved us out. The team never really liked staying there anyway. It was an old, cinder block building, drafty and cold, and not my idea of upper-middle-class living. But Al Davis insisted that we beat Denver because we stayed at the Continental. This past season, when Denver took over the hotel, Al fought to keep us there, but the management of the place said we had to go. Last season Denver beat us twice and won the Division title for the first time in the history of their club. Al Davis went around scowling at everyone and saying, "I told you so!"

I didn't believe in that sort of witchcraft, but then we went to San Diego for a game. Strange things started to happen. In the past we stayed at the Star Dust Motel and the Chargers hadn't beaten us in sixteen games. As a matter of fact, San Diego couldn't muster enough points on the scoreboard to make the games respectable. But this past season, for some unknown reason, the Chargers' general staff decided to move their team into the Star Dust and they shifted us over to the Hylanda. I don't know if superstition spurred the move or not but we were quartered on the other side of town and San Diego had our winning motel.

Al Davis and John Madden were upset over the deal, but it didn't shake up any of the players. We still went on with a normal pregame night (five wild parties) and showed up at the stadium early Sunday afternoon in time for the kick-off. The game was simply unbelievable. The Chargers won, 12-10. After that experience, every member on the team started to avoid stepladders, black cats, and new hotels. Every pregame burp and sneeze became a new ritual.

Speaking of rituals, I've always let Skip tape my forearms before a game. It has nothing to do with good luck charms or superstitions. I hit people in the head with my forearms, and the tape provides me with some protection. Now the coaches come over to Skip and make sure he's going to tape my forearms.

Several years back, some of the coaches would frown on Skip screaming and cussing in the locker room before a game. Skip wasn't mad at anyone, he just likes to cuss. On one rare occasion, Skip didn't cuss and the locker room felt empty. We went out on the field and proceeded to get our heads beaten in by a funky Cleveland team, 7-3. Now everyone does his share, and it doesn't take much to keep Skip in the right frame of mind and cussing.

In spite of everything, the Raiders are the winningest club in professional football. I guess it comes down to Spirit. I'm not talking about ghosts or goblins. I'm referring to the camaraderie that develops among people working together as a team. I have built many friendships with my Raider teammates that I know will endure long after our football playing days are over. This is much more important to me than all the money I've made or the fame I have achieved. Unfortunately, however, friendships can sometimes lead to some very sticky, yet humorous, entanglements.

One time, we were playing in Pittsburgh and Clarence Davis came up to my room with a big smile on his face. He said, "Tate, I just gave an interview for you."

"Meaning what?" I asked.

Clarence started explaining with a smirk on his face, "You remember the time we went out to dinner in Oakland and you left me? Remember, Tate? Remember the time when you left with that big dude's lady friend?"

I remembered what C.D. was talking about. One time, when he and I went out to dinner, I noticed this nice-looking lady sitting across from us staring and smiling at me. Well, she got up to powder her nose and I just happened to get up to make a phone call or something, I just don't remember. Anyway, I talked with her in the lobby and we both decided to leave together. She left her boyfriend and I left C.D.

"Damn, C.D., I hope you didn't get upset about me sticking you with the check for dinner," I replied.

"Oh, no, Tate, I wasn't angry about the check I got stuck with. The lady's friend had a knife and he wanted to stick me with it. I was lucky to get away with my life so I decided to do you a favor. That's why I gave an interview for you."

C.D. was excited. I knew that he must have really stuck it to me, so I asked, "Okay, tell me about it."

"Well, Tate, I was down in the lobby just minding my own business when this man comes up to me and starts asking questions. It was strange, though, because he kept calling me 'Mr. Tatum.'"

I knew what had happened. A lot of times reporters and even fans mistake Clarence and me. Really, though, I can't see the resemblance. I'm much better looking.

The man who came up to C.D. was a reporter and he wanted to interview me. He asked C.D., "Tell me, Jack, what receiver of the Steelers do you fear the most?"

C.D. answered, "Steelers' receivers! Ain't none of them worth a damn."

Obviously, the reporter was startled at my arrogant display of verbal abusiveness, or, I should say, at C.D.'s. The man asked a second question, "Tell me, Jack, what do you think of the Steelers' running backs?"

"Chicken, all of them, chicken," C.D. replied.

The reporter was really taken in and he started firing questions at C.D.

Do you have any respect for anyone on the Steelers' club?" the reporter asked.

"Mister, if I told you the Steelers were gutless suckers, that would be a compliment. Ain't none of the Steelers worth a damn, and tomorrow, me, Mr. Jack Tatum, will personally beat them all over the stadium. You can quote me on that," Clarence told the man.

The man did quote him, and the Steelers read the story. Let me tell you, I had a hell of a time explaining everything to the few friends I did have on the Steelers' club.

Another time, I ended up with four armed bodyguards just because I was friends with George Atkinson. Some people say that George plays a little dirty; other people believe that George plays a little dirty; and still others don't like dirty football players. Because I play next to George, and we are good friends, the people who say nasty things about George believe the same about me. I'm really innocent but I'm considered guilty by association.

One time, this not-too-happy Pittsburgh Steeler fan thought George had roughed up Lynn Swann. That wasn't so very bad for me but when the same man started writing letters to the Raiders' front office mentioning my name right beside George's and also the fact that he was going to blow us off the face of the world, I became upset. Still though, I wasn't really worried until they caught the man planting a bomb in the Oakland bus station with "George and Jack" painted on it. The man knew we were leaving town to go east for a game with the Steelers and he figured he'd get us as we passed by the locker in the bus station. George and I both rationalized that the man was of low mentality, suffering from perverted and degenerate tendencies (obviously a Steeler fan), and certainly nothing to worry about. Raider management, however, felt it was serious and assigned four armed bodyguards for George and myself. We pleaded with Coach Madden, "The man was just a nut and you can't take him seriously. We don't even travel by bus, and if he was waiting for us at the bus station, he would have waited the rest of his life." It didn't do any good. For our trip to Pittsburgh, we had the company of armed bodyguards.

After it was all over, George and I talked about the man waiting at the bus station and why he would do such a dumb thing. We just couldn't figure it out, and then George said, "Maybe that's how the Steelers travel. Who knows?"

Sometimes, being a Raider can be rewarding, while other times it all becomes a serious problem and even embarrassing. A few years ago, we played in Washington, D.C., against the Redskins. It started off with a late flight into the nation's capitol and an evening meal. The team had made arrangements for us to eat at the hotel, and to start with, a salad bar was set up. Everyone was hungry after the flight except for Skip. He was hungry before the flight and during the flight; in fact, Skip is always hungry. But this time it was really bad. Skip was cussing and bitching before he got on the plane. The sandwiches he ate during the flight were not filling and he swore all the way across the country and into the hotel dining room. After all of that, Skip was going to eat. He walked up to the salad bar and started cussing at the top of his voice, "What the hell is this? Rabbit food? I'm a man and ain't gonna eat this damn rabbit food!"

Skip was screaming and people stopped eating. I could see lower jaws banging off china plates. We tried to pretend that Skip wasn't with us, that he just wandered in here by mistake. But sometimes you can't ignore Skip. I mean he has a way of using profanity that will capture your attention. Someone said, "Hey, Skip, keep it down!" That did it. Skip really started cussing. The hotel management rushed out with a couple of steaks and the rare meat managed to slow Skip down for a while.

After a light practice the next day, we decided to go on a tour of the White House. Actually Al Davis had made arrangements for us to see the White House and meet the President. Al made those plans honestly believing that Skip would refuse to go. But hell, Skip was all fired up and cussing to get going. He wanted to meet the President. Now we had a problem. How do you tell Skip he can't cuss in the White House and in front of the President? Well, Madden and Davis had a meeting with Skip before we left the hotel and Skip just wasn't Skip. All during the tour he stood there with his arms folded and bottom lip sticking out and didn't say a word. The only time Skip ever gets that quiet is when he watches TV after the channels have all signed off. It was a nice tour and when it was over, Skip finally spoke. He said, "HELL, if a man can't cuss, ain't hardly no sense to be alive."

I once, just once, went out to an expensive French restaurant with Skip. We had dinner at Robert's in San Francisco and it was different. When the waiter brought the wine, he poured Skip a little in a fancy crystal glass. Skip slid the glass my way and said, "I never drink from a glass," and took a slug right out of the bottle. Then he said, "Damn, that's good wine. Bring us each a bottle but no glasses."

Another time, I made a mistake and went out with Skip before a game in Pittsburgh. We went to a disco in the Parkway Pavilion and Skip started getting loud and he set up the bar a few times. As the evening went on, Skip set up the bar a few more times and pretty soon everyone was falling-down drunk. From that point on, it was just a matter of time before Skip had everyone laughing and cussing at the top of their voices. The people just went crazy and Skip was right there leading them in the howling and screaming and cussing. After a few more "drinks for everyone" and about one thousand cuss words (that's just one normal sentence for Skip), the owner of the Parkway asked Skip about the heavy bill he was running up. Skip said, "Don't worry, brother, I got it covered," and he went back to screaming and cussing. Then the owner asked him to slow down a little and Skip got uptight and left without paying the bill. Just about that time, the drunken crowd started turning a little mean and when everyone found out that Skip had split without paying the bill, they were all looking for someone, anyone, to punch around. When a big dude pointed at me and said, "He's one of them," I decided to find the exit.

It was a good thing that our attorney, Tony DeCello, lives in Pittsburgh and he knew the owner of the Parkway. Otherwise, Skip and I would have listened to the game from the Pittsburgh jailhouse.

When I think about Skip, Clarence, George and my other friends and teammates, I'm really proud to be a Raider. I know that most of the guys aren't playing with a full deck, but these guys are real. Any one of them would give you the shirt off his back or his last dollar bill. I guess that makes them better men than most of the phony people running around the streets today. So, when the summer comes along, I sort of look forward to going up to Santa Rosa and the start of camp.

In 1976, when I left Oakland for camp, I was looking forward to the season more than any other time in my career. I had a good feeling that this was the year the Raiders were going to do it. It was strange because everyone coming into camp honestly felt the same as I did even though nothing had really changed. The coaches were plotting secret plays and the players were rushing into new areas of foolishness but that is the way an Oakland Raider training camp always starts. Players can't get serious the first or second week of camp, and smart coaches realize that Super Bowl Champions are built over the course of a season.

When Foo (Villapiano) arrived in camp, he had a fantastic inspiration. He was going to find a Queen to reign over the Air Hockey Championships. Foo said, "But she's got to be ugly, ugly, ugly."

Foo came up with the lady after many hours of interviews and elimination contests. He sure can pick 'em. The lady accepted the honor of being our Queen and we held a special coronation. Kick-'em-in-the-head Hendricks, so named because of his favorite maneuver during a game, built a throne from old crates on the back of his pickup truck and drove Her Royal Majesty up and down the streets of Santa Rosa. If anyone had failed to notice before, then after Kick-'em was finished, the entire population of Santa Rosa knew for certain that the Raiders were back in town!

Meanwhile, back at the El Rancho Motel, our headquarters, Beuhler was busy with his erector set building a new tank, Philyaw was searching in vain for the doctor, and Skip was cussing. It seemed as though nothing had really changed. That was until someone came up with a new nickname for Beuhler: "Fog."

Nicknames are also an important part of Raider life. Getting your nickname is a sign that you've finally been accepted into the club. For example, most of the guys call Coach Madden "Big Red." Madden is a burly guy with red hair, but for some reason Skip calls him "Pinky."

Nobody is given a nickname; one must earn his title, even Skip. Most of the time we let ourselves go at training camp. We hardly shave and we never wear fancy clothes. After all, nobody is going to see us except the coaches and maybe the Queen. And who wants to look good for her? One day, Skip was walking over to the practice field looking the way he thought a Raider athlete should look. His appearance was bad even by Raider training-camp standards. Someone said that Skip looked as though he was coming back from one of his frequent trips to Mars and all points beyond. Bob Brown, a big offensive tackle, saw Skip coming up the path and jumped back ten steps and said, "Damn, Skip, you look like death warmed over, swallowed down whole and spit back out." Skip looked terrible, but the next day he looked even worse. After a week of letting himself go, Skip earned the name "Dr. Death."

Everyone who's been through the wars has a nickname. My friends call me "The Reverend," not "The Assassin." They know that I am a saintly person on the field, but George Atkinson is "The Weasel." George gets himself into impossible situations but has a knack for weaseling his way out.

Some of the guys like to use their mouths a lot. Gene Upshaw, our All-Pro guard, is the "Pelican Jaw." He fancies himself a politician and keeps his jaw moving talking about the issues. Dave Rowe likes to hear himself talk, too. We call him, "Radio Rowe."

All-Pro wide receiver Cliff Branch has run the hundred in 9.2 seconds. Naturally, Cliff is the "Rabbit."

Neal Colzie, our punt return specialist, thinks he's a ladies' man. We call him "Sweet Pea."

Dave Casper is the "Ghost." Dave is the whitest white person I've ever seen. At the opposite end of the color spectrum is "Black Angus." Football fans know him as Art Shell, All-Pro tackle. Mark Van Eeghen isn't black, but his kinky afro hair style started the rumor about his mother running off with a black man. Most of the time, we call Mark, "Black Blood," but if he doesn't crack a smile with that nickname, we come back with "Bundini Brown, Jr." Skip says that Bundini and Mark look alike.

Clarence Davis is another man with two nicknames. Most of the time, we refer to him as "C.D." but the bigger guys on the team call him the "Militant Midget." C.D. is only about 5 feet 9, and when people get on him about being short, he starts making threats about the little people taking over the world and shooting everyone over 5 feet 10.

If you're going to have a nickname, you must hit Al Davis with one, too. Everyone did call Al a variety of different names behind his back, but no one said anything to his face. As the general manager, Al is the man who handles contracts and the money. It's not that anyone treated Al like a special person, because he's really not, and doesn't put on any airs, but the players had this unwritten law to simply ignore the man. Treat him like he wasn't there until it was time for contract talks. But one night Skip forgot his wallet in the locker room and we drove back to pick it up. Al was in the weight room working out with his skinny arms. Skip started blasting on Al's physique and it was a heavy scene. Al rebutted with, "Skip, we're both the same size. You wear a size 44 suit and so do I." The next day at practice, to prove his point, Al came out dressed in a suit, size 44. Seeing how Al is more at home in a size 40, the jacket and pants fit a little loose. That's all Skip needed. Skip ran over and grabbed Al by the seat of the pants and started poking fun at the baggy suit. Skip was carrying on something terrible, and before long everyone was on the ground laughing, including Al. Finally, after Skip had nearly tugged Al's pants off, he blurted out "El Bago!" and now, even Al Davis has a nickname.

I admit that the Raiders do some strange things at a training camp, but there is also much time invested in serious work. The summers around Santa Rosa get blistering hot. I've seen the temperatures soar to over 100 degrees, and when you're wearing heavy equipment and undergoing physical stress, it really gets hot. I've tasted my own salty perspiration and worked my body until I couldn't move, but it's all part of the game and the price you pay. To win football games you have to be in top physical condition, and there is only one way to get in shape: work until you can't take another step and then run the last hundred yards full speed.

We practice about four hours a day. Some people might think a four hour day would be a snap, but those people would be dead wrong. When you get into the grueling work of summer training camp, you need nicknames, tanks and Philyaws just to keep your sanity.

Charles Philyaw is going to be one hell of a football player some-day. But even if Philyaw wasn't a great athlete, I think the Raiders would have kept him around for at least the summer training camp. Charles was good for the team.

On his way to practice, Philyaw stepped in a hole and sprained his ankle. He limped his way through the day and late that night came over to our room to see the doctor. Philyaw was standing in the hallway outside our room, all 6 feet 9 inches of him, explaining his problem to Skip. Philyaw was saying, "Trainer says to get the whirlpool from you."

"What you talkin' about, Dummy?" Skip screamed at Philyaw.

"Trainer said you have the whirlpool and I need it for my ankle," Philyaw explained as he started taking off his shoe to show Skip the swollen ankle.

Skip turned to me for help and asked, "Tate, what's this big dummy talkin' about?"

I just shrugged my shoulders and rolled over in bed. I wasn't about to get mixed up in any of Skip's and Philyaw's communication problems.

Skip slammed the door in Philyaw's face and stormed over to the phone. He called the trainer and cussed the man out. Skip wanted someone, anyone, to teach Philyaw the difference between the team's doctor and the team's cornerback. Skip didn't stop with a phone call to the trainer, either. He called Big Red, El Bago, Tom Dahms, and even one of the owners. Skip cussed and screamed for over an hour, but that was the last time Philyaw came after Skip for medical attention.

Every team has someone almost like Philyaw or "Fog" and even something similar to Skip. That only goes to prove that no team can base success or failure on reason and sanity. I agree in part with Paul Zimmerman, the Raiders are the flakiest team in professional football, but the Raiders are also the winningest team in professional football. To sit down and try to figure out the anatomy of a winner is impossible. There's really no way of getting inside the individuals and breaking everything down into easily understood terms. Football players defy logic, and the Raiders most of all. But one thing is for certain, when the official sets the ball for play and blows the whistle, something pulls all the talents, luck charms, superstitions and personalities into a working unit directing all energies at one purpose: Winning! That's the way we started out in 1976.

The 1976 season was highlighted by several key games. Our first encounter with the Steelers was important because it set the stage for the rest of the season. Although we lost the verbal battle with the Steelers, our 31-28 come-from-behind win put us at 1 and 0, while the Steelers' record was quite the opposite.

Early in the season, because of injuries to key personnel, we had some very close games but were sporting a 3 and 0 record when we arrived in New England. That day New England was hot and the outcome was a humiliating 48-17 beating. You don't lose a game 48-17 and start talking about the Super Bowl unless you're an Oakland Raider. Normal people after getting beaten so badly start thinking about picking up the pieces, but not us. The defeat marked the point when we got serious and decided to make a determined effort at the number one spot in professional football.

During the course of the season, it often works out that one Sunday a team can be your bitter enemy and the next week root for you to win. Well, that's exactly what happened with the Raider-Steeler rivalry. After losing to us, the Steelers started to look pathetic. After five games they had only managed one win, and the chance of their repeating as Super Bowl contestants was highly in doubt. The pure truth was that they needed a miracle finish to even make the playoffs. The season came down to this: Cincinnati had a one-game lead on the Steelers in their division. If the Bengals were to win the last two games, it wouldn't matter what Pittsburgh did, because Cincinnati would be the division champs. However, if the Bengals lost one of their remaining two games and Pittsburgh won both of their contests, then the Steelers, with a record identical to the Bengals', would be awarded the Central Division Championship by virtue of having beaten Cincinnati twice during the year. It was safe to assume the Bengals would beat their last opponent of the season, the Jets, but their other remaining game was against us. Because the Steelers had done a complete turnaround and were playing the best football in the NFL, some folks naturally assumed the Raiders would lay down, let the Bengals beat us, and prepare for the playoffs. That way the Pittsburgh Steelers would have been eliminated from any playoff hopes, making the road to Super Bowl XI much easier for us or any other team.

Once again the Oakland Raiders became the topic of many discussions in the Steel City, but this time it was, "Hooray for Oakland!" The Steelers, their fans, and all the news media in and around Pittsburgh tried everything from shame tactics to a praise-laden, positive thinking approach to get us in a winning mood for our forthcoming game with the Bengals. Some said that the Raiders were men and because of our pride we would go out and beat the Bengals. Some people accused us of being scared to death of the Steelers and predicted we would lay down and let Cincinnati beat us. People in the street, newspaper men and television reporters in Pittsburgh all had their own opinions of what might happen on the Monday night when ABC came to Oakland for the showdown game between the good guys and the Bengals.

If you were to look at everything on paper, the Raiders were a better team, but anything can happen during a football game. The Bengals came into town thinking about winning, I'm sure, and maybe even a few of them actually thought we were scared of the Steelers. Those who felt that way failed to realize that any winning organization is built on a deep-rooted pride, a pride that makes good teams great. Yes, the Steelers were playing excellent football and were quite possibly the best team in football. Then again, the Raiders hadn't exactly been playing shoddy football themselves. For anyone to assume we were scared of the Steelers was simply absurd. And for any coach, player, fan or reporter to think that we would lay down and let the Bengals win was ridiculous. It just so happens that I believe the Raiders are the best team in football, and I enjoy proving that point every Sunday or Monday night.

When you honestly believe you are the best in any profession, you do not shy away from a challenge; you seek out the best of the competition to test your talents against. Sure, Cincinnati had the potential to "get lucky" and beat us, but it would be a most difficult task. As Oakland Raiders, my teammates and I had no need of any of the Steeler psychology to get us ready us ready for the Bengals. To go on to win the Super Bowl without facing Pittsburgh again would have been a very shallow victory indeed. But to blast Cincinnati away and trample everyone who got in the way of our rush to become number one, well, that is what our motto, "Pride and Poise," is all about. It's all a part of becoming a man and being called a professional. To hide from any player or team is cowardice. If I had felt the Raiders were going to lay down, I would have asked to sit this one out. Maybe I would have even asked to be traded. Never in my career have I ever approached a football game or anything with the thought of letting the other team win. When Monday night came along, I am proud to say that every member on the Raider team and staff went out onto the field with a ruthless attitude toward the Bengals.

Simply winning the game was not our intention: We wanted something between slaughter and annihilation. It all came down to the fact that we believed the Steelers could offer us the best competition, and every member on the Raider team wanted to give the Steelers every chance in the world to back up their mouths with some playoff action. All year long we heard about "criminals" and "cheap-shot artists" and "lucky Raiders" coming from Pittsburgh, and for some strange reason we assumed those remarks were directed toward Oakland. A playoff game with Pittsburgh would be good for the teams, the league, the fans, and the reputation of foot-ball itself. With that special incentive, believe me, no one connected with the Raider organization even considered lying down for the Bengals.

I shouldn't say that Cincinnati was outclassed, but midway into the second period we were sporting a 21-0 lead and everyone started going for the throat. Although the final score ended up 34-21, the thirteen point spread was no indication of the real beating we gave Cincinnati. I don't know what the sports fans thought about us before the game, but I'm sure that even Pittsburgh fans across the country must have found a thread of respect to cling to when considering the type of men who wear the silver and black of Oakland.

When the season ended, because of our win over the Bengals, Pittsburgh was in the playoffs. Although both Pittsburgh and Oakland had different opponents for the semifinals of the American Conference, it was a good bet we would meet in Oakland for the championship. While we were busy with New England on Saturday afternoon, Pittsburgh was traveling to Baltimore for their Sunday encounter.

Our game with New England was highlighted with a typical Raider finish. We were losing 21-17 with less than one minute to play as Stabler began marching the silver and black machine down the field. As usual, Stabler moved the offensive unit into the end zone as the clock was ticking off the last few seconds. It was a 24-21 win for the Raiders.

On Sunday Pittsburgh proved they were one of the best teams in the NFL as they ran off 41 unanswered points. The Colts were never in the game.

After Pittsburgh's game the television cameras went inside the Steeler locker room for some interviews about the game and next week's affair in Oakland. Most of the Steelers expressed optimism about their chances against us, which was to be expected, but then they interviewed Franco. I was shocked to hear Franco say, "I can hardly wait for next week. I want to beat the hell out of those sons-of-bitches."

Obviously, he was referring to the Oakland Raiders, but I couldn't figure out how he was going to back up that rather stiff statement. I'm sure Steeler fans really felt Franco was their main man because of his brassy attitude toward the Raider menace, but saying something and backing it up are very different. Verbally, Franco was seriously threatening Cosell's crown, but there was always Sunday and the championship game for him to put his lip against my Hook. I was thinking, of course, about our past experiences with "Sideline Harris." He had not been what you might call a physical force to be reckoned with in any of those games, but maybe now, after all these years, he was wearing different colors. Sunday was to be a day where many questions would be answered.

As the drama began to unfold during the course of the week, it became obvious why Franco could make so daring a pre-game statement about the individuals in Oakland. It seems he hurt his ribs in the Baltimore game and wasn't even going to suit up for his "I-can-hardly-wait" encounter with the Raiders. We all know how disappointed Franco was, but he'll never realize just how sad it made the Raider defense feel when we learned he would no be in there slipping and sliding his way through eleven sons-of-bitches.

Later in the week Franco assured the press he would be ready for the game, but I knew those were only words in the wind. The reality of Sunday afternoon was that Pittsburgh would be without Franco and Rocky Bleier. Rocky had injured his foot during the Baltimore game, and although he wanted to play, it was simply a physical impossibility. I knew that without Rocky clearing a path to the side-lines for Franco, the Steelers were going to lose their punch in the running game, but they still had their great defense.

Before the game the press had worked over the cheap-shot angle and predicted the Steelers were going to get George and me, but that was only the press talking. It was also said that the game was going to be a grudge match because of the hatred that existed between the two teams, but that was only trash used to take up space in the news-papers. Both teams, I was sure, were going to get serious on Sunday, but I don't think that even Ray Mansfield was thinking about taking a cheap shot.

When everything was over, I was sorry the Steelers didn't offer us more competition. We won the game rather easily 24-7. I'm sure that injuries had taken something away from Pittsburgh, but even their defense wasn't tough. Our offensive team was able to run, pass and probably could even have walked over Pittsburgh. It just wasn't the type of championship game a fan wants to see or an athlete wants to be part of. But when it was over, I think everyone realized the Raiders at that particular time, even though the Super Bowl was weeks away, were the best team in football.

On Sunday, January 9, 1977, the Oakland Raiders met the Minnesota Vikings in Super Bowl XI. The Raiders were a physical team and the Vikings were a passive one. That was the first indication it wasn't going to be a great Super Bowl game. Also, the Vikings had several tendencies that could only hurt their chances against a team such as Oakland. For example, Tarkenton isn't a drop-back passer. Because of his size (he's only 5 feet 11), he rolls out slightly. This enables him to see the field of play better than if he stood back in a pocket while defensive giants blotted out the sunlight.

Tark's little roll-out would be ineffective against us because we could rush our ends from the outside in passing situations. Since our defensive ends range from 6 feet 5 to something near 6 feet 10, Tarkenton would still have a difficult time picking up receivers. Also, the Vikings are effective at throwing the ball to running backs. Our defense was to be a 3-4. This means that instead of the usual three linebackers covering running backs, we would have four active people in the same area. Offensively, it would be difficult for the Vikings to generate points against our defensive unit.

When Super Bowl Sunday broke, so did the sun. It had been raining in Southern California for several days, and weather reports indicated it could even be a wet Super Bowl. Although the clouds hung low toward the east and the mountains, the weather was perfect for football.

The game got off to a slow start as the first quarter of the game became no more than both teams exchanging punts. However, late in the first quarter the Vikings did something that no other team had ever accomplished. They blocked a Ray Guy punt and had the ball five yards away from the end zone.

This is a time when a defensive team either folds or goes out on the field and changes the momentum. The Vikings were thinking about a touchdown or, at the very least, a field goal and the lead. But the defensive team started thinking turnover. One play later, because of aggressive and violent play, we caused a fumble and owned the football. From that point on, the game was all Oakland.

The first score came in the second quarter of a twenty-four yard field goal by Errol Mann. After that the Viking offense started to look like a ballet with a one-two-three-kick routine. Our running backs were eating up chunks of real estate while our receivers were finding gaping holes in the Vikings' secondary. A Stabler pass to Dave Casper put us ahead 10-0, still in the second period. Before the half ended, Pete Banaszak blasted in from one yard out and we went into the intermission with sixteen points while the Vikings were still trying to figure out how they had fumbled the ball on their only scoring chance of the half.

Things didn't change much in the second half as we still had things our way. Mann kicked another field goal, this time from forty yards out, and we built our lead to nineteen points.

I'll admit that even though the Vikings were outclassed, they showed true signs of comeback ability. When our defense seemed to slack off a bit, Tarkenton found Sammy White open for an eight-yard touchdown pass. That play fired up the Vikings and they started making a game of it.

Momentum is a part of football that can change a game dramatically. Sometimes, one team will go flat while the other team grabs "Mo," and one of those easy football games can suddenly change into a life-and-death struggle. It was evident that the Vikings had caught fire and we had slipped. Our offensive team went out on the field after the Viking touchdown and looked anything but impressive. Three plays later, Ray Guy was in the team kicking the ball away.

Part of my job is to put out fires. The Vikings, as I said, were burning up, and I had to dig down for a special hit to cool everything off. Sammy White provided the exact opportunity I was looking for. Sammy was the Rookie of the Year and already an All-Pro receiver. He was great on long patterns and even better on a short one. Early in the game I had hit him with a fair shot as he attempted to catch a little turn-in pattern. It wasn't a good hit but Sammy knew I was there. As he was getting up, I said, "Don't come back here, boy, or you're liable to get hurt." Sammy smiled and walked back to the huddle. I knew the hit wasn't going to discourage Sammy from coming over the middle but I still tried to reach him verbally. Sometimes, a receiver or running back will take what you say to heart. They might get mad and say something foolish or they might worry about what you said. I was fairly certain that Sammy was too gutsy to get upset over mere words, so I knew that before the game was over he would come roaming into my area.

Just when everything looked as though the Vikings were going to come back, Sammy White ran a pattern over the middle without bothering to look for me. It was a delay pattern designed to clear me out by giving me a deep decoy to chase after and then bringing Sammy underneath into my area. I smelled the play and made a move backwards. Tarkenton glanced at me and thought I had taken the bait. Then he quickly started searching for White coming over the middle. That's exactly what I was looking for, too. I believe that Sammy must have thought I was going deep and the middle was open, because he came into my zone moving full speed.

In this situation I sit back and wait for the ball to be thrown. From there it's just a matter of building up a full head of steam and sticking the receiver just as the ball arrives in his hands. I admit that I actually did have several options to consider, but it comes back to my job and getting "Mo" back on our side. I realize that I might have intercepted the ball, or at least made an effort for the interception.

But, then again, Sammy might have been able to make the catch and take it on in for a score.

My hit on Sammy White may well be the best ever in the history of the Super Bowl. It was one of those collisions that defensive people dream about and offensive people have nightmares over. Both Sammy and I were moving full speed and it was head-on. During the impact White's helmet flew ten yards downfield, his chin strap shot twenty feet into the air, and some lady sitting near Al Davis screamed, "Oh, my God! He lost his head!"

Sammy was on the ground moaning about his eyes while I stood over him and issued another warning about coming into my area and getting hurt. I knew that Sammy was in no condition to hear my voice but his teammates were. That type of devastating hit has a tendency to discourage other receivers and running backs from trying anything over our middle. I had just wasted Sammy White. It was a knockout, and believe me, it slowed the Vikings down. When his teammates gathered around, I could hear Sammy ask, "Check my eyes! Are they still in my head? I can't see!"

After that hit, everything swung around. Banaszak scored again, Willie Brown intercepted a pass and returned it seventy-five yards, and the score was 32-7.

Late in the game I was surprised to see Sammy White back in the lineup. He's a great receiver and I respect him as a man and as an athlete. I was glad that Sammy was okay because I think he is a tremendous person.

The Vikings did manage to score again but it was over long before the final gun went off. The final score was 32-14, and for the first time ever, the Raiders were not only the winningest team in professional football but also "Number One."

7

Rating My Peers in the NFL

Quite often I run into people who actually believe the athlete of twenty or thirty years ago was better than our modern-day athlete. I realize it is ridiculous to even consider any comparison between yesterday's and today's products, but some individuals will argue the point that Louis could whip Ali or Thorpe was a stronger and faster running back than Campbell. When considering these points, I take a historical look at progress. The airplane, for example, is not faster than the jet, a buckboard does not compare to an automobile, and athletic progress is definitely part of the improving world.

Several years ago, an old-timer gave me quite a debate about the professional football teams of yesterday being able to compete against the teams of today. The old gentleman was emphatic when he stated that the Canton Bulldogs could have whipped the Oakland Raiders. "Canton," he said, "was a football team made of men and not sissies. Why, we never wore fancy equipment like face masks and helmets, and football was played more violently than it is today."

It was obvious the man had played professional football many years ago, and one look at his face confirmed his claim of never being permitted the luxury of a face mask or helmet. His nose was pushed all over his face and he had an ear where I have a mouth. But fancy equipment, I assured my friend, isn't a sign of weakness in an athlete. It simply is a mark of progress within the structure of the game. Furthermore, the athlete of today could never survive the brutal contact of today's wars without elaborate protective devices. But still, this old gentleman argued that he and his Canton Bulldogs would have whipped the Oakland Raiders.

Actually, there is no way we could prove to the old man that his Canton team of fifty years ago would get blitzed by many high school teams of today, and comparing them to even Tampa Bay on the professional level is absurd. But nonetheless, the old-timer stuck to his guns and will eventually go to his Creator believing the athlete of his day was better than our modern version. To satisfy my own curiosity I did a little research on the Ohio State teams of many years ago and compared them to the team on which I played. Of course, I could only arrive at a physical comparison and had no way of actually measuring the athletic potential, but the results of that investigation were amazing.

The first recorded instance of any OSU football activity took place in 1890. The football team was made up of fifteen men, seven of whom played rush line while the others filled the position of quarterback, two halfbacks, two fullbacks and even three substitutes. These football players were obviously men because their team picture indicated no fancy equipment – just slacks, jerseys and beanies. It was all very interesting reading but offered little in the way of comparison between the heights and weights of the two athletic groups.

In 1906 Ohio State started publishing the heights and weights of the football players on the team, and it was fascinating. That year OSU had a twenty-member team which won eight and lost one. Incidentally, their only loss way back then was Michigan, too. Anyway, the smallest member on the team was 5 feet 7 and weighed 153 pounds while the biggest member stood a towering 6 feet 2 and tipped the scales at 190 pounds. The average height of that team was 5 feet 11 and the average weight came out to a little over 170 pounds. Certainly, their size was not overwhelming. In fact, I'm sure that if our 1970 OSU football team were going to play against a twenty-man squad that averaged around 170 pounds, Woody would have hid the scouting report from us out of the fear that his squad might seriously injure themselves falling down laughing. Again, I say that we have no way of determining the athletes' abilities, but a 5 foot 7 running back carrying 153 pounds isn't going to frighten me or anyone else on the team. That running back would have to be damn swift or else he would be seriously injured once the beef caught up with him.

Now, the team I played on definitely had the size advantage. I'm not going to get into the size difference except to say that our running backs were forty pounds more than the biggest man on the 1906 football team. And if you want to consider big people, then our linemen were well over 260 pounds and they could move. In all, I don't believe an All-Star team of the college ranks in the year 1906 could have been within two hundred points of us if there were actually a way to play the game. So the athlete of today is the best this world has ever seen. When I play against a Lynn Swann or try to tackle an Earl Campbell, I am going against the best in the history of the game. Consider, if you can, what Earl Campbell would do to any tackler of the early 1900s. I believe that after tackling or attempting to tackle Earl, they would have rushed out and invented equipment or else they would have started playing checkers. It's just ridiculous to compare the athlete of yesterday to the athlete of today. I am making this point because in rating the best players in the NFL, the players I go against, I am, in fact, rating the best in the history of the sport. I admit that once in a while an exceptional athlete played in the NFL twenty or thirty years ago, but overall, the modern players are bigger, faster, stronger, and obviously better than any of yesterday's heroes.

In rating our modern football players, I'll begin with the quarterbacks. It is true that no one person can be responsible for a team winning or losing the game, but quarterbacks do have a dramatic control of eventual outcomes. After all, the quarterback calls most of the plays and handles the ball 90 percent of the time. More important, the quarterback's prime responsibility is moving the offensive team down the field into scoring position. Therefore, he is the number one man on the field.

The quarterback should be able to throw a football and make intelligent decisions, although there have been a few who lacked the mental capacity to become great. For now, let's just say it would help a quarterback's career if he could make intelligent decisions. That way, he can complement his physical abilities. Also, a quarterback must be fearless and display confidence and leadership qualities at all times. When the team believes in the quarterback, both the offensive and defensive units function better.

A good example of poor leadership by a quarterback happened with the Oakland Raiders during the early part of my professional career. Our quarterback was Daryle Lamonica. Although we won most of our games, and Daryle was given a lot of favorable ink in the newspapers, he actually hurt the Raider organization. There was much derogatory talk throughout the NFL about Lamonica being a coward, and he never did anything to dispel the rumors. It was said that all you had to do to beat the Raiders was smack Lamonica in the head, and many defensive linemen spent their Sunday afternoons with that as their objective. As I said earlier, no one person can be responsible for a team winning or losing the game, but quarterbacks do have a dramatic control of eventual outcomes. The truth was that Lamonica was gun-shy and in those physical games he was ineffective. Daryle did not possess confidence and leadership qualities, and his weaknesses reflected on the whole structure of the team. We lost a game to Cleveland 7-3. During that game, the defense was spectacular, but Lamonica, after getting roughed up a little, failed to move the offense. When a situation of that type occurs, the defensive unit has a tendency to let down. Under Lamonica's guidance the Raiders could never had made it to the Super Bowl Championship because he disintegrated under pressure. So when you analyze a quarterback, there are many things to be considered other than just how many touchdown passes he throws.

I guess the name of Joe Namath is synonymous with quarterbacking, and Joe offered the game many exciting moments. Joe was a fan's type of quarterback, a team man, and the type of guy the defense wanted to throw the ball. Joe had confidence, leadership qualities, and no one can ever doubt his courage, but I'd rather play against a Namath than a Stabler or Greise. Contrary to popular belief, Namath did not do a good job of reading the defensive coverages. Joe had a tendency to force the ball into the strength of a defense instead of looking for their weakness. When this happens, the end results are sometimes interceptions. Although Joe set a season passing record of more than 4,000 yards, he still was less than a 50 percent completion passer and was always near the highest in interceptions thrown. I've played against Namath, and sometimes his decisions defied all logic. Joe had the ability to set up quickly despite his bad knees and he had a quick strong release. But still, the man would force his passes into the teeth of a defensive team instead of looking for a secondary target. Maybe part of this was because of his bad knees and inability to move around, but it was a bad habit for any quarterback to develop. In spite of everything Joe did for the game of football, I would only rate him, at best, a fair quarterback.

If someone were to write down a formula of all the basics necessary to be a great quarterback from strictly an athletic point of view, the results would read Bert Jones of the Baltimore Colts. However, if Bert Jones played for the Oakland Raiders, I'd probably spit on him. Bert might have everything a quarterback should physically and mentally have, but he's only a little boy in a man's body. Bert, unfortunately, never grew up, and professional football is a mature game. One of the NFL rules concerns the very subject of maturity. A high school athlete cannot play in the NFL until he has sat out for five years or until his high school peers have graduated from college. This was done to protect young players who are blessed with athletic talent but still lack physical and mental maturity. Even though Bert spent his time in college and has physically matured into manhood, he shouldn't be permitted to play in the NFL because of his childish fantasies.

Bert Jones has a great arm and that ability to search out the open man. If all others fail, Bert still has enough to take off and run the ball, but professional football and quarterbacking require much more than all of those abilities. Bert Jones is the type of guy who wants to be out of the locker room first and he expects the people around him to bow whenever he passes through. Bert is the kind of man who will kick and scream and cuss at a receiver because the man dropped the ball and he will kick the ground, slap his helmet or cry when he has overthrown a receiver. Bert needs to learn that everyone who plays football is a human first. Receivers don't want to drop passes and quarterbacks don't want to miss wide-open targets. But somewhere along the line, Bert has developed the attitude that receivers should be perfect. If I was a receiver and Bert threw a pass that I dropped, and he screamed at me with fifty thousand people in the stands and several million at home watching on the tube, I would show the fans some real action. No one, not a quarterback, nor an owner of a team, has the right to subject a player to such embarrassment. In spite of all Bert Jones' abilities, Namath was a much better quarterback than young Mr. Jones can ever hope to be.

I think that a perfect quarterback would have Kenny Stabler's mind inside Terry Bradshaw's body. I'm not taking a slap at Bradshaw's mental capacity; it's just a fact that Stabler is a physical wreck. I admit, in a way, that I am also trying to say that Ken is a much better thinker than Bradshaw. While Bradshaw can succeed with overpowering physical abilities and the daring to make things happen, Stabler is a give-and-take kind of quarterback. Both men have the ability to produce the big play even though their styles differ, but for my money, I would feel better with Ken Stabler handling the ball in a pressure situation. Stabler is the type of quarterback who will look the situation over and remain cool through the heat. Bradshaw will make up his mind too quickly and sometimes be forced into mistakes. If I had written this book two years ago, Bradshaw would have received a lower rating than Jones, but Terry's leadership qualities have surfaced recently and I do believe the man is fast becoming one of the better quarterbacks in the NFL. But when I consider my reputation as a hitter and not an interceptor, the fact that I have only intercepted twenty-six passes during my career, and seven or eight of those interceptions have been gifts from Bradshaw, does indicate a major weakness in Terry's style. He has a tendency to rattle quickly and impulsively throw the ball up for grabs, or worse yet, take off running without any regard for his safety. But like I said, the man is trying and he is improving. Who knows, if Bradshaw can keep his body together and play for another twenty years, he may well become the greatest quarterback in the history of the game. But for now, Kenny Stabler is still my number-one man in the NFL.

I know that many fans are going to look at the Raiders' record last season and ask me to explain a nine and seven record and Stabler's thirty interceptions. First of all, eleven of Ken's interceptions were the result of pop-ups. Kenny threw perfect passes that hit the receivers in the hands or shoulder pads and simply popped up into the waiting arms of defenders. You don't fault the quarterback or the receiver for that kind of interception or incompletion. Those are just the breaks of the game. Also, the Raiders had a lot of new personnel on the offensive line, while at the same time, veterans Gene Upshaw and Art Shell are getting a little older and were not as effective in supplying pass protection as they had been in the past. Defensively, the Raiders also made numerous changes, and all of these different elements affected the entire season. Regardless of wins, losses or interceptions, Kenny Stabler is the best quarterback in the NFL. Stabler is the type of man who will take whatever the defense is willing to give. If we are moving by running the ball, then he will stay on the ground. If our rushing game is ineffective, then he will go up top. Even when passing, Stabler is still going to take whatever you are willing to give. If you double-cover our outside people, then he will look for the tight end. If you're playing a tough zone and the receivers are covered, he will start sending a running back into the pattern. Stabler lacks the physical status of some of the other quarterbacks in the league, but he has the experience and leadership qualities to gain my vote as the best in the NFL. Maybe next year Bradshaw will gain more composure and learn how to take whatever the defense is giving. If and when that happens, I would honestly say that Bradshaw is number one. But for now, it's still Kenny Stabler.

Receivers are a different breed of athletes. They must have speed and grace yet be strong and durable. They must maintain the quality of concentration and ability to catch the ball when they are under tremendous pressure. I have found receivers to be the biggest con artists in football, but it's all part of their job. They bolt off the line and give the defender a thousand false moves while trying to do something for real that will gain them that liberated step. In rating receivers, I look inside the man. Courage will make a mediocre receiver great in my estimation. Howard Twilley of the Miami Dolphins lasted many years in this league even though the experts said he wasn't going to make it. Howard wasn't big, he wasn't fast, and he had only adequate hands. But Howard had the biggest heart I have ever seen. We played a game in Miami and I spent a miserably frustrating afternoon trying to convince Howard that it hurt to run patterns over the middle. He was good at running a short pattern over the middle, and Miami was picking up the yardage on that particular play.

I hit Howard with a few good shots, and on one occasion, he was assisted from the field. But every time I looked around, Howard was back in the game courageously running his short patterns. When a receiver cannot be intimidated, he will be effective against any type of coverage or any of the assassins in the league. Howard was paid to catch the football whether in traffic or on the open field. Even though the so-called experts in the game never rated Howard very highly, I did. He never had the natural ability to become a great receiver, but he had the courage to be very effective.

There are good receivers in the league and several who boarder on greatness. But because a receiver's job is basically suicidal, it becomes very difficult to find the individual who will go out and play the game without being intimidated. I don't know what made Howard Twilley run but I know he was special. If all receivers played the game with his style, my job would be frightening, frustrating and virtually impossible. Fortunately for me, most receivers can be intimidated, and that gives me the edge.

In rating the receivers whom I have played against, several do stand out. Intelligence plays an important part in a receiver's effectiveness. The receiver knows that he must catch the ball, and he understands that the ball will attract some undesirable people. The secret is to be smart enough to run a safe pattern, make the catch, and then start worrying about defensive backs trying to stick their headgears through your rib cage. Fred Biletnikoff is a fantastic receiver. Fred never had the blazing speed to go long, but he was deceptively quick on his patterns. Also, Fred was highly intelligent and never overstepped the physical limits of his body. Fred had little or no fear on patterns across the middle but was intelligent and experienced enough to pick his spots. Most of the time he would curl into the middle rather than run a reckless, full-speed pattern into the teeth of the defensive unit. Above all, Fred's first concern was to catch the ball and then worry about the defenders. One bad habit many receivers get into is looking for defenders and not fully concentrating on the ball. Believe me, even if you're looking for the defensive man and you're lucky enough to see him coming, it's still going to be too late to react to anything except the hit. Most of the time, under these conditions, the receiver is going to drop the ball. Why pay the price of getting blasted if you're going to miss the pass? Biletnikoff always caught the ball and then started taking the necessary steps to protect his body. On my personal list of great receivers, Fred ranks as third.

My number one man is Paul Warfield. Paul has the speed, quickness, and ability to catch the ball under any conditions. He was a big play man and could do more than any receiver in the game. I only saw Warfield look at the defender one time before he caught the ball, while other times he was simply fearless in that way. I think Paul Warfield was a physical copy of Lynn Swann, but he had more courage. Warfield, in my estimation, is most definitely number one on my list of all-time great receivers.

When I think about the best receiver in the NFL, I consider all the aspects of the game. Twilley had the courage but lacked the speed and quickness, while Warfield had all the natural abilities but lacked blazing speed. Warfield had very good speed and was quick, but blazing speed is faster than quick. Warfield, I am told, ran the hundred in 9.7, an exceptionally fast time, but blazing speed is much faster. Speed defies coverage. It makes sense that if the wide receiver is faster than the defenders, he is usually going to be open. Blazing speed requires double coverage and special assignments, and Cliff Branch of the Oakland Raiders possesses that ability. Cliff has run the hundred in 9.2 and looked as though he was coasting. Once Cliff gets a step on the defender, the gap quickly widens to ten yards and Cliff is on his way to six points. But Cliff has more than blazing speed. When you consider the everyday basics of catching the football, running sharp patterns and having courage plus intelligence, Cliff is overwhelming. He runs a smart pattern over the middle while concentrating on the ball. After making the catch, he has the ability to quickly spot the defenders and avoid those serious head-on shots that cripple receivers. Most important, Cliff is dangerous from any spot on the field. He has the ability to turn a five-yard reception into a ninety yard gain. The Raiders have a very effective passing game because Cliff Branch requires double coverage all the time. When a receiver can beat the double coverage either short or long, the man is great. Cliff is not a record-setter, only a steady All-Pro who can beat you in many ways. In 1976 he made 46 catches for 1,111 yards. That's a little better than 24 yards per catch. When you consider than an offensive team only needs to pick up ten yards for a first down, it's no wonder that the Raiders are usually one of the highest-scoring teams in professional football.

I realize that some people might think I overlooked Lynn Swann for personal reasons. After all, he did write some nasty letters to Pete Rozelle in my behalf and has sounded off to the press about my tackling style. But Lynn Swann has not been overlooked. I believe that Lynn is truly a superb athlete. He is graceful, has quickness and speed, and he can catch the ball like few, if any, other receivers can. Lynn Swann could be the best if it were not for his one major weakness. There have been several times when I sincerely believe that Swann has been intimidated. Sure, he has played some great games, unbelievably great games, but I have often been on the field when Lynn has actually quit. His concussion during the 1976 game at Oakland was questionable. I know that he went to the hospital, but I remember seeing him running up and down on the sidelines after Atkinson had blasted him. He seemed okay to me then, but when I got Stallworth and Lynn Swann was asked to go back into the game, he suddenly fainted on the sidelines. Maybe he was actually injured; I really don't know. It's just hard for me to believe that George's "semi-Hook" was that devastating. I've watched the films of that action and in my estimation the hit did not look that awesome. Quite frankly, since that incident, Lynn Swann has continually been ineffective against the Raiders. In fact, one hardly realizes he is in the game with us. I know most teams take special precautions when defending the Steelers' wide receivers, but we don't. If Lynn Swann was truly a great receiver, we would be extremely cautious when playing against him. Instead, we concentrate more on Stallworth and Cunningham because they have a tendency to stick their noses in the action, whereas Lynn will not.

I give Swann all the credit in the world and sincerely understand that self-preservation is a very important part of football. Maybe if I were the receiver and he The Assassin, my reasoning would be the same as his. Maybe! But at the same time, I rather doubt it. You see, I realize that football is a contact sport and people must get hit. I'm sure Lynn Swann also realizes this, but at the same time, he is trying to play the game without actually getting involved in the serious contact. Lynn will probably continue to hide from the contact and survive playing in the NFL for many years to come. He will play many more great games and pile up his statistics against the passive teams, but he will cause little concern for the physical teams.

The tight ends are a cross between the wide receivers and a runaway freight train. Most of the tight ends have the speed to beat you on long pass patterns and the physical makeup to run through the most aggressive tacklers. Tights ends start at about 6 feet 4 inches and weigh upwards of 240 pounds. They block, catch passes and run safeties over. Every team in the NFL has a big tight end, but the three that stand out in my mind are Dave Casper, Raymond Chester and Russ Francis. Casper and Chester are Oakland Raiders. I am glad of that. But Russ Francis plays for New England. Russ Francis is the best tight end in football. That happens to be my opinion, and it also just happens to be almost everyone's opinion. Even the so-called experts, if you can believe they are actually right for once, agree that Russ Francis is the number-one tight end. Russ Francis has the size and speed to kill you; he has intelligence, and he can catch the ball. I can believe that quarterbacks love to see a target that size running down the field. It certainly makes their job easier.

If there wasn't a Russ Francis in the league, then Dave Casper would be the number-one tight end. Dave and Russ are similar in size, but Russ has a tremendous edge in speed. But what more can a tight end do than what Dave Casper does every game? He blocks the biggest linemen, flattens linebackers, catches clutch touchdown passes, runs over free safeties and has the courage of a lion. Again, Casper could be the best, but Russ Francis can do it all, and in addition, Francis has far more speed.

Raymond Chester is another great tight end. During the 1977 playoff game with the Baltimore Colts, Raymond Chester could have been the difference in winning or losing, but the Raiders won and Raymond's team lost. That year Raymond wore a Baltimore uniform and was the tight end for the Colts. I'm not sure of the reason, but he and Bert Jones never got along. Anyway, because of their mutual disregard, Raymond was wide open on several plays but Bert wouldn't throw the ball to him. After all, if you're not going to bend down and kiss Bert's feet, then he isn't going to throw you any touchdown passes. Throughout the entire game, Bert ignored Raymond, and we won the game by six points in overtime. From his seat near the press box, Al Davis decided he needed another tight end and Raymond Chester was the man. As I said before, nearly every team in the NFL has a big tight end, but the Raiders are more fortunate than most teams; we have two of the great ones in our lineup.

Receivers are my favorite people, and next to them I like running backs. Receivers and running backs provide me with more thrills and more action than anyone else on the offensive team. On nearly every play, I have to go against a receiver in one way or another, and every so often a running back will break our first line of defense and I introduce myself to the man. There were times when the man introduced himself to me, so to speak, and those were shocking experiences. Larry Csonka, of the Dolphins wasn't what you would call a great running back but he certainly earned the respect of every defensive back in the league. Larry was the type of guy who would go out of his way to try to run you over. His size, adequate speed and bull-like charge were more than most defensive backs wanted.

You learn early in your career that a big man will run you into the ground if you try to make a high tackle. Larry Csonka is a big man. I would venture a guess that will equipment and all, Larry Csonka probably played at 260 pounds. That is a big man, and like I said, you don't try to tackle him high. Early in my career I mistakenly jumped on big men, who carried me down the field like I was a sack of flour. After a few incidents like that, I learned to hit the big man at the angles and drive through him. But Larry Csonka was a different type of big man. Larry ran low to the ground and used his elbows to ward off tacklers. It was practically impossible to get a good solid hit on him. I can truthfully say that he was the only man who repeatedly stung me with his abusive running style, and worse, I was never able to sting him. Larry Csonka was a very effective running back with the Miami Dolphins because of their personnel and particular style of football. The Dolphins had a good line, and they had two other excellent backs in Jim Kiick and "Mercury" Morris. During their reign, they were able to control the tempo of the game. In this type of offense, Csonka was, as I said, very effective. However, if he had played on a team that didn't have excellent offensive personnel to complement Larry's style, he naturally would have lost some of his effectiveness. Csonka was a good back, but not a great one. In looking for that special quality that makes a running back great, I would have to look at his overall contribution to the team and try to determine whether or not he has game-breaking abilities. Csonka was quite effective with a very good team, but would have had great difficulty running the ball had he played for Buffalo. O.J. Simpson, on the other hand, had the ability to make even the weakest team a serious offensive threat. When O.J. played for Buffalo, one did not beat the Bills' offensive team; they simply scored forty or fifty points on the defensive team. O.J. Simpson had the ability to make the Buffalo offense go. Regardless of their record, the Bills did score points. With a Larry Csonka in the backfield instead of the Juice, the Bills' offensive production would have been seriously impaired. O.J. had the ability, and I do say "had," to break a game open from any point on the field. He had exceptional speed, balance and power. Several years ago O.J. was the number-one running back in the league, but not any more. Time and injuries have a way of catching up with the swiftest of running backs, and then there is the ever-present reality of the ultramodern athlete, Earl Campbell.

I would advise those of you who have never tried to tackle an Earl Campbell to be careful should the opportunity arise. Actually, I have always believed in seizing opportunity and I used to look forward to meeting Earl on the field of battle. Now, I believe it is sometimes better to surround opportunity rather than try to seize it. Earl Campbell has the size of a Csonka but more drive and power in the legs – if that's possible. Also, Earl has as much balance and speed as O.J. Simpson. He can be overpoweringly abusive or he can be very elusive. Earl was only a rookie in 1978 and he hasn't fully developed mentally or physically. I think Earl will get stronger as his career develops and he will learn the little intricate techniques of being a great running back. First, he will learn that being abusive is good, but one must first hold onto the ball. I don't care how big the running back is or how fast he can run; he will not score a single point without the football. Earl Campbell has a tendency to give up the football, and that can be very costly. In 1978 we played Houston and were in serious trouble. The Oilers were winning by six points and threatening to score another touchdown: They had the ball first down and goal to go on the three yard line. On the very next play, Campbell took the ball and tried the left side of the Raiders' line. He wasn't protecting the ball, and someone knocked it loose. Ten seconds later our strong safety, Charles Phillips, was standing in the other end zone with the ball and six points on our side of the scoreboard. That ninety-seven yard fumble recovery was eventually the difference in the game, and we won.

I guess what I am trying to say is that if Earl Campbell stays healthy and learns something new every day of his career, he will go on to become the number-one running back in the NFL. But the man must first learn that all the size, power and speed isn't worth very much unless he remembers to take the ball.

For now, I believe the number-one running back in the NFL is Walter Payton. Walter isn't what you would call a big running back because he's only slightly over the 200-pound mark, but he runs with big-man authority. The first time I hit Walter head-on I received a jolt. Usually, when I zero in on a ball carrier and I get him with a good straight-on shot, the man is going to fall backwards. My first experience with Payton resulted in a stalemate as we both toppled over sideways. I just couldn't believe that he ran with that much power, because he didn't have the overwhelming size. But after tackling the man a few times, I realized that he was a strong and powerful running back. Payton has the power to beat you for hard-to-get yardage up the middle and has the speed to score from any point on the field. I think he is stronger than O.J. Simpson and a more daring type of runner. For the most part, O.J. would try to finesse a defender first, and only if that didn't work would he attempt to power you. Payton is a straight-ahead type of guy who can literally explode through would-be tacklers by lowering his head and ramming straight on. Payton also has great speed, and once he gets a step on the defender, it's just God and green grass between him and a touchdown. Walter Payton does have all the physical abilities that make for a great running back, but the difference between him and the other gifted athletes laying claim to number-one status is simply courage. Where Payton is a small man with a big heart, some of the other running backs in the league are big men with small hearts.

Chuck Foreman of the Minnesota Vikings is another great back who can do anything. I rate Foreman very high because of his daring and overall ability. He isn't a Walter Payton, but Foreman is a great back who makes the most of his ability. I can respect that in any athlete. Foreman doesn't have the power of a Payton or the speed of a Simpson, but he makes things happen. He has good size and plays an intelligent game. A running back like Foreman makes my position all the more challenging because I know he is a quality athlete with that blend of courage.

Whenever I think about the most gifted athlete in the NFL, Franco Harris' name comes to mind. Franco is a big back with great power and breakaway speed. But I have never seen a more imposing physical specimen of an athlete with less drive than Franco. I am aware of Franco's achievements in professional football, and they are fantastic. But at the same time, I cannot help thinking what records he could have set had Franco Harris played football with heart. Many football fans will disagree with my remarks about Franco, and I realize the impact of these statements. But to prove my judgment, I ask all football fans, even Steeler fans, to objectively observe Franco Harris in any football game. If Franco doesn't run for the sidelines, slip and fall, or cake out before anyone gets near him, then believe me, someone else is wearing his game jersey.

In 1974 we played the Steelers in Pittsburgh, and that was the first time I realized Franco wasn't an overpowering running back. The Steelers had the ball on our four yard line with a first down and goal. At that time it was a close game; I think we were ahead 7-0. In this situation, I felt certain they would give the ball to Franco on some straight-ahead play. Well, Franco got the ball and his offensive line opened a big hole. All Franco had to do was lower his shoulder and bull ahead over the Raiders' free safety for six points. In other words, all Franco had to do was run me over and he would have scored. But instead of running like a man who weighed 235 pounds against a man weighing 205, Franco ran like a real chump and I buried him. I saw Mike Webster, the Steelers' All-Pro center, look at Franco in shock. Mike was trying to figure out what had happened. The Steelers ran that same play again and again I creamed Franco with a one-on-one tackle. It was like running into soft butter, and Franco went down again. By this time, I started thinking that either

I was the most vicious tackler in the universe, or Franco was holding back. After a third attempt and a third burial, the Steelers gave up on Franco and tried another back in another direction. I know that Mike Webster tried to figure out what had happened, and maybe now he really knows the truth. I am a pretty fair tackler, but any old lady in the stands could have run the ball in that situation and shown more class than Franco.

Since I mentioned Mike Webster, the All-Pro center for the Steelers, I may as well get into the great linemen for the game of football. The linemen are rarely mentioned and seldom given credit for their tremendous contribution to the game. Take the center, for example. Here is a man who snaps every ball back to the quarterback and then opens holes for the running backs or protects the passers. If I had a football team, I would want Mike Webster to be my center. Mike has the size, intelligence and raw strength to ward off any defensive lineman in the league. Mike's only problem is that he plays for Pittsburgh; and if a center is going to get pushed out of the lime-light on any team, it will be Pittsburgh. With the great personnel on the Steelers, it's a wonder anyone knows that Mike Webster is alive. But I'm sure the people who play against him know that he is for real.

When anyone mentions great linemen, the names of Art Shell and Gene Upshaw become synonymous with excellent line play. For many years now the Oakland Raiders have had an All-Pro line with Art, Gene and Dave Casper at tight end. I think that Art and Gene are two very good reasons why the Raiders have an effective passing game. Whenever a quarterback is given three seconds to throw the football, the results are going to be good. But when a quarterback is given five, six, seven, or more seconds to throw the football, the results are going to be overwhelming. As a quarterback, Ken Stabler can tell you that Gene and Art are in a league all their own.

I believe that O.J. Simpson's record-breaking 2,003 yards in a season was made possible by two excellent guards, Joe DeLameilleure and Reggie McKenzie. They had the ability to open holes up front and the speed to get outside. A successful running game depends on intelligence and quick guards. I think that Larry Little of Miami is also that type of guard. When you look into any great rushing team, you will find some great individuals on the line. During Miami's reign, Larry Little was instrumental in keeping defensive people away from Dolphin running backs.

In rating the defensive people, I like to start with the middle line-backers. Actually, the middle linebacker is really the quarterback of the defensive team. He is the man who makes things happen. He calls the defensive signals and is responsible for keeping the defenders in an aggressive frame of mind. Although the middle linebacker could, as Dr. Arnold Mandall said in his book, *Nightmare Season*, "be the class president," he can also be a Jack the Ripper. The middle linebackers are most unusual characters.

I believe the best middle linebacker in the history of the game was Willie Lanier. Willie had tremendous intelligence, a nose for the ball, was great on pass coverage, and he could hit. When you consider his size, speed, and the number of years he played in the league, you come to realize why the man was, and still is, great. I have learned something new every year in the NFL. I realize that maybe I have slowed down a little, but my experience is invaluable. Well, Willie Lanier played more than ten years, and he knew the game inside and out. Just when the offensive team figured they had Willie out of position, he would show up on the spot with an animal-like hit on some unsuspecting running back or jump up and make an interception.

Now Bill Bergey of the Eagles is the best middle linebacker in the game. Bill has everything it takes to fill that position, and he could play for any team in the NFL. There isn't a better middle linebacker in the business. However, if Willie Lanier decided to play another season, I think he would still be number one.

Steeler fans are no doubt asking about Jack Lambert. Well, Jack Lambert is a fair linebacker, but he certainly isn't in the same company with a Lanier or Bergey. Lambert is great because he plays for Pittsburgh and they have the best defensive line in professional football. With the talent Pittsburgh has on their front line, they hardly need a linebacker at all. In fact, Franco Harris could play that position and look good. Lambert is fair on pass coverage but is quite weak against the running game if a team can semi-handle the front four. In 1976 during the championship game against the Steelers, we felt our offensive line could neutralize their front four. That way, our tight end, Dave Casper, would be free to block down on Lambert. I don't have to say that Lambert was ineffective, because the score, 24-7 in favor of the Raiders, gives a good indication of the quality of Lambert's performance. Also, Lambert has trouble against teams that can get a running back through the front four on any type of straight-ahead play. If all the running backs in the world were sideline-to-sideline Francos, then Lambert would look good all the time. But, unfortunately, some running backs actually do run straight ahead, and once in a while, they even get past the Steelers' front four. Then, I'm sorry to say, Lambert is usually quite useless.

So that Steeler fans will not get the idea that I don't respect any of the men wearing the gold and black, let me give my opinion about their outside linebacker, Jack Ham. Jack Ham is truly a great professional. He has the ability to do everything an outside linebacker should do and much more. Ham can tackle, cover the pass, and find the ball in any situation. Again, Ham, like Lambert, is playing behind the greatest defensive line in the game, but I sincerely believe that Jack Ham could play great football with the Giants, Jets or the Pottstown Firebirds; whereas Lambert would only be effective with the Steelers.

Another great linebacker is Randy Gradishar. When Denver drafted Randy, they drafted a perennial All-Pro. Gradishar is just a shade below Jack Ham and Bergey. He's one of those players who seem to be completely out of the play until you look around to see who made the tackle or the interception. I have watched him play for the last several years, and he is amazing. His range and movements are fantastic.

Considering the defensive line and the great ones in those positions, I simply think of the Pittsburgh Steelers of 1975. I don't think any team in the history of football has had four more talented athletes playing on the defensive line than Pittsburgh. I'll even go so far as to say that I doubt whether any team in the future will ever have a better defensive line than the Pittsburgh Steelers. I know that might sound like a contradiction, but let me explain. During the glory years of the Steelers, and they are still actually enjoying those years, Chuck Noll assembled the greatest defensive line in football. What happened was that Pittsburgh ended up with an All-Pro defensive line the likes of L.C. Greenwood, Ernie Holmes, Joe Greene and Dwight White. They were simply awesome. I realize that athletes will continue to improve, so the younger members of Pittsburgh's front four will improve as the older ones decline, but it will take some doing to again place four such athletes on the same team on the field at the same time. The Steelers did it in 1975, and I doubt if it can ever be repeated.

Another great defensive lineman worth mentioning is Louis Kelcher of San Diego. Louie looks like a refrigerator; one of those twenty-five-cubic-feet ones. Louis is big. I don't mean just big in a tall sense; I mean big all over. The first time I saw him all I could think of was a refrigerator. At first, I didn't think that anyone built like a refrigerator could move well enough to play football, but when he started flattening our people, everyone began asking, "Who the hell was that?" Then you would hear the San Diego fans start chanting, "Looou, Looou, Looou." It was frightening, and "Looooou" went crazy knocking the hell out of everyone.

There are many excellent defensive linebackers and linemen in the NFL, but I have just mentioned a few of the ones who come to mind; the ones I consider far above average. Now, that leaves only the defensive backs to rate.

Anytime I hear the term "defensive back," I immediately think of our cornerback, Willie Brown. I guess that's because I first heard about Willie when I was playing high school football, and then again when I played in college, and ever since I've played in the NFL. Willie admits to thirty-eight or thirty-nine years, but sometimes I think he's much older. That's when I see him walking around town slowly or telling some young receiver to take it easy on him. Then, there are times when Willie swings into action and I think he is younger than he admits to being. Willie is one of those remarkable athletes who time seems to forget about, or at least it passes a little slower for them. Willie is remarkable because he is always expected to retire and yet comes out for the team every year and contributes. I think that now it has become a matter of experience rather than quickness, but still Willie Brown can stay with the youngest and quickest receivers. Not only that, in Super Bowl XI, Willie picked off a Fran Tarkenton pass and returned it seventy-five yards for a touchdown. In my estimation, Willie is one of the real experts at cornerback.

Other experts include Mel Blount of Pittsburgh and Mike Haynes of New England. Both these defenders are a rare cross between a push-and-shove, man-for-man defender and a slashing assassin in their zone. Both are excellent at pass coverage and both possess knockout power in tackling.

I guess my rating system should also include coaches. Actually, a fielded football team is nothing more than an extension of its coach. If a coach is passive, his team will reflect that style; if the coach is aggressive, his team will be aggressive, too. Coaches do not go out and battle on the field like the players, but they are part of the war and part of the system. For coaches and players alike, the system is simply to produce or you're gone.

George Allen is a well-traveled coach. Several years ago he left the Rams for Washington. Later he left Washington for the Rams, and then he left football for good. Actually, he was booted out of football because he didn't produce. Allen's theory was that you win with old vets who have the experience. Now I admit that experience is a very important part of football, but so are youth and new blood. When I was in college, I had the ability to run forty yards in 4.3 seconds. But as my experience increased, so did my time in running the forty-yard dash. Experience, I'm afraid to say, is a luxury enjoyed only by the older football players. Time is the price one pays to gain experience, and with age one will lose that quickness and speed of his daring youth. George Allen failed to realize that and developed his teams around football's old-timers. To a degree, experience can be a tremendous asset, but over the long run the old man is going to wear down, and all the experience in the world isn't going to pay off if he's falling down wheezing and gasping for a breath of air. Experience will push you, but the old body won't carry you to the point of accomplishment. While Allen was with the Rams, he had some excellent players with the needed experience. But again, he lacked the new blood. In Washington, George Allen again gave up his draft picks for veterans and almost won football games. When he made his triumphant return to Los Angeles, he followed the same pattern – trade the draft choices for experience and almost win.

Coaches have their individual styles, and they all differ. Some of them stand out in a crowd, and so do their teams, while others seem to fade into a background of colorless expression and neither suffer much nor enjoy much. Who's the coach for the Saints, Atlanta, the Redskins, the Giants, or just about any of the eighteen or nineteen teams that lack the luster of championship form? What I'm trying to say is that most football fans can only associate with a winner. Talk about football teams and the average fan will start with Pittsburgh and Noll or Landry and Dallas, and move on to names like Lombardi, Madden, Brown and Ewbank. Winning is the only thing that counts, whether you're a player, a coach or the water boy. And I believe it all starts with the man at the controls – the head coach. A perfect coach is one who doesn't disintegrate under pressure and has the intelligence to look into tomorrow. He must also be fair, have compassion and understanding for his players, and burn with the desire to win.

I'm going to start out by talking about my ex-coach, John Madden. John was forced into retirement by ulcers and nothing else. I know the rumor had it John was asked to step down because of the bleak 9 and 7 season the Raiders went through in 1978, but that's not true. For health reasons alone, John was unable to continue coaching. Believe me, if he had been fired, and the health factor hadn't been the sole reason for his early retirement, John would have accepted a job at any one of the six or seven teams that called him. But the pressures of the battle and that consistent grind to win finally caught up with the man, and he has gone back into a more serene life of simply being a fan.

When I look at the man, John Madden, I see something special. He could deal with people on any level, and the Raiders' success and development of their personnel offer proof of that statement. Look down our roster to see what I mean. Many of the Raiders were a band of misfits, rogues and ruffians who couldn't get along with their own mothers until Madden took over. Some of our guys have been in more football camps than they can remember, and because of their attitudes, were branded as undesirables. But Madden had a way of taking the undesirables and turning them into a functioning machine that gave him the highest winning percentage of all the coaches in the NFL. There have been coaches who have won more total games than John but none have a win-loss ratio as impressive as his.

A coach has to be able to understand his players. John had the ability to communicate with anyone on the team, even Skip Thomas. I don't mean to slight Skip. It's just that Skip had different ideas, but John was able to understand and love the man. Skip is a tremendous athlete, but most teams would have given up on him a long time ago. John took everything in stride, though at times it was tough. For example, we were once in Houston getting ready for an important game and John received a phone call about Skip. At that time, Skip was on the injured list and in a hospital in Los Angeles. The hospital administrator was cussing out John because Skip brought his motorcycle into his hospital room. Well, John pacified the administrator and then called Skip. Most guys would have gone berserk, but John calmly asked Skip what the trouble was. Skip said, "I don't want some nigger stealin' my bike!"

If you know Skip and understand about his bike and his car, you realize it was a serious problem to the man. I know it sounds crazy but Skip really cares about his bike and doesn't want anyone touching it, much less stealing it. It wouldn't be a problem for most people, but John realized what it meant to Skip. He took time from his busy schedule and made arrangements for the bike to be taken out of the hospital and put in a safe place.

What I'm trying to say is that John understood people and could talk to and get along with anyone. Because of John we had a relaxed atmosphere in our camp, but that didn't mean the conditioning and working aspects of professional football were lacking. John believed that we were men first and professional athletes second. His style of conditioning was to let us do it on our own. If we cared enough about our bodies and our jobs, then he cared, too. If we didn't care about getting into shape, that simply meant we didn't care much about our job, and from there it was a quick trip to the exit gates.

Madden knew football inside and out, and his teams reflected his personal desire to be the best coach in football. When a coach has pride and wants to win, his players will develop that same attitude.

Madden was a great coach and a great man, but there have been others in the business, too. Vince Lombardi was a forceful type of coach. He believed in a tough conditioning program and a simple play book drilled to perfection. He was a hard-working and extremely aggressive man with an appetite for winning. His players rallied around Vince and would fight to the last second of every football game. That deep-rooted relationship between players and coach developed because it all started on a man-to-man basis. Lombardi would say, "I'll treat you like a man until you prove yourself otherwise." When a coach respects his players, the players will respect their coach. Lombardi was a credit to the game, God rest his soul.

I think Chuck Noll is another great coach, and his most fantastic asset is vision. Noll has a great ability to look into the future and picture what a young athlete is going to look like years from now. I believe that while Chuck Noll is coaching right now, his vision is three or four years ahead of the present action. Noll took what was once the worst team in the history of football and made a complete turnabout. He used his draft picks wisely and also developed previously unheard-of athletes into All-Pros. The Steelers are two and three deep in every position and every year they seem to land two or three more blue chippers. This is because of Noll's vision and constant planning for the future. In all his years of coaching, Chuck Noll has made only one mistake, and we need not cover the running backs again.

Coaches, as I have said, all have different styles. Don Shula, for example, is a very serious individual who seems distant to me. I don't know the man personally but from talking with some of his players, I get the feeling that Shula keeps a distinct line between the players and coaches, whereas other winning coaches try to develop a feeling of camaraderie between the players and the coaching staff. Shula is successful in his environment but I doubt that such a man could keep the Raiders under control. In my estimation, straitlaced coaches like Shula, and possibly Landry, would have a tendency to make things a little sticky. I'm not saying that they are not successful people in their jobs; it's just that they win with a different type of athlete. I personally like a coach who will jump up and down once in a while or show a little enthusiasm toward players who are doing a good job or making that great play. Landry, Shula and Bud Grant of the Vikings always have that uncommitted expression on their faces. I don't need a coach hugging me or showering me with affection, but I like the idea of a man saying, "Well done, great play," or "Get 'em next time." Still, though, one cannot argue with success, and Shula, Landry and Grant have had their special moments, and I respect that accomplishment.

There are two coaches, no longer in the game and quite opposite in style, whom I think about quite often. The first man is Weeb Ewbank and the second is Hank Stram. Ewbank is the only coach to win championships in both leagues. Weeb won a championship with the Colts and then again with the Jets in the Super Bowl of 1969 that proved to the world that the American Conference had arrived. I think Weeb was effective in his days because he had the vision to try something new. But if Ewbank were coaching today, his system would be totally ineffective. In studying Ewbank's teams, one can see a trend slanted toward the smaller, quicker type of player. Weeb believed in speed and quickness first and size second. As a result, he found the speed and quickness he desired in an athlete in men of questionable size. It wasn't so very many years ago that a professional lineman could get by if he weighed only 220 or 230 pounds. But not anymore. Because of weight and strength techniques and better diets, the professional football players have grown in both size and speed. Weeb stressed speed and quickness and seemed unaware of the fact that a good big man is going to beat the hell out of a good small man. Speed and quickness have a place in football, but so do size and strength. Successful teams have that combination of good overall quickness and speed blended with size and strength. In selecting an ideal lineman, Weeb would end up with a defensive end who could run the forty in 4.7 but had the body of a 200-pound defensive back. Other teams would go after the defensive end who ran a 4.75 forty and stood 6 feet 5 and weighed 270 pounds. Which man is going to win the battle?

In 1971 Weeb's theory built on yesterday's vision was shattered by today's realities. The small quick man was out and the bigger and increasingly quicker man was in. Weeb's New York Jets spent more time in hospitals than they did on the playing field.

Hank Stram, however, believed in the biggest players he could find. Hank's idea was to first find the giants and then teach them to develop speed and quickness. Well, speed and quickness can be developed to a degree, but you don't take a lumbering 6 feet 10 tight end and make him capable of 4.5 speed. Stram was a great coach and a very successful man, but I feel that his teams needed a little more balance. Stram had some great players and won a Super Bowl, but I believe he could have improved by looking for a little more overall team speed and quickness. I can't help but think what a combination Ewbank and Stram would have made. Weeb would have been looking for the speed and quickness in players and Hank would have been in search of the giants. Finding the player with that blend of size and quickness would be finding an All-Pro.

I think Paul Brown was a pretty fair coach, too. He had the ability to size up ballplayers and develop weak areas on a team. But more important than all of that, Paul had that innovative flair for the unexpected. I remember playing against the Bengals early in my career, when Paul took us by surprise. We were holding on to a slim three-point lead with the time running down. The Bengals had the ball and could at best run one or two more plays. It was one of those situations that called for a pass and a prayer, but Brown sent his fullback up the middle on a draw play. It was an absurd call, but the man went seventy yards for a score.

Now, there are bums coaching professional football teams and then there is a Bum Phillips. I'm not going to get into the bums, but I am going to mention Bum Phillips and Houston. Bum Phillips looks like a reject from the rodeo, with his cowboy garb, but the man is something special to his boys. You see, Bum is the type of guy who loves his players and they love him. It's a style that some individuals can use effectively to get players to go that extra mile. At heart Bum is a winner with his own personal touch of class. The players can associate with him and by blending the talents of players and knowledge of coaching into a workable system, Bum has accomplished great things with the Houston Oilers.

Maybe some readers will feel that I have been particularly hard on their favorite superstar, but I've only tried to be open and honest. I tell it the way I see it and the way I know it happens. Actually, you don't have to play free safety for a professional team to pick up on the true character and abilities around the league. Just watch any NFL game and you'll see what I mean. The great ones will be great regardless of the situation, while the phonies will show their true colors.

In 1978 I was watching ABC's "Monday Night Football" and Bert Jones gave one of his most unforgettable performances. Bert was coming off a serious shoulder injury and seemed to be having great difficulty throwing the ball on the sidelines. ABC had a sideline camera zeroed in on Jones and every time he lifted his arm to throw the ball, the expression of pain registered on his face. It was dramatic and touching. Howard Cosell went on and on about Bert's great courage and what a man he was to play under those painful conditions. It was so touching that I almost had tears in my eyes watching Bert's show and listening to Cosell's words of praise to the king. Bert would throw a weak and wobbly pass, grimace with pain, and let his right arm dangle loosely at his side. My, but it was touching. Then the game started and Bert struggled out on to the field with his right arm dangling as though it were broken in fifty or sixty places. What an effort! What a show!

"If only Hollywood were watching," I thought, "then Bert would surely be in the movies come tomorrow."

Everything seemed blown up to me. I've seen players with their arms pulled out of the sockets and they looked better at the time of the accident than Bert did 95 percent recovered. But it was Bert Jones and his dramatic return to professional football, so I anxiously watched.

Then it happened. With tearful eyes, the brave Mr. Jones dropped back for his first pass of the evening and uncorked an eighty-yard incompletion. His arm hurt and he doubled over in pain, but still he tried again. Next he fired a bullet pass over the middle for a completion. This time his arm didn't hurt. Throw an interception or incompletion and the pain in the right shoulder was unbearable, but throw a completion and it didn't hurt? Right then, Bert received my nomination for the Academy Awards, and with that I turned off the television.

I know by now everyone is asking, "What does Jack Tatum think of Jack Tatum?" and I will answer that question. First of all, my college coach was once asked in my presence, "Woody, who was the best athlete you ever coached?"

"Well," Woody answered, staring out of his window at St. John's Arena, "it wasn't Jack Tatum. Jack was one of the best, but I think Archie Griffin was the greatest ever."

Then Woody was asked, "Who was the best pass defender you ever coached?"

Woody answered, "Well, it wasn't Jack. I think maybe Tim Fox."

Then the same person asked, "Woody, who was the best hitter you ever coached?"

Woody, without a second of hesitation, said, "That was Jack Tatum! Without a doubt, Jack Tatum was the hardest hitter I ever coached or saw play the game of football. Why our own people were scared to death to go out and even practice against him."

Well, I don't think I'm exceptional when it comes to interceptions, but in a way, that really isn't my job. What's more, I never really found intercepting passes all that exciting. I believe my game is built around contact. I am paid to hit, so I hit. There are safeties in the NFL who are better than me at playing the ball, but when it comes to making a tackle, I like to believe most receivers and running backs wish I didn't exist.

8

Me, An Assassin?

After eight or nine years in the NFL, you have a tendency to start counting your stitches, bumps and bruises and looking at a future day when your body will start to slow down a little and physical exercise will not be a necessary way of life. When that happens, I know that arthritis and bursitis will settle into my bones and joints and yesterday's hits on wide receivers will become tender and stiff areas of my body. Humans were just not built with the contact of professional football in mind. And regardless of all the conditioning a football player does, there is still the chance of serious injury and still a price that will be paid during old age. Even now, it gets more difficult for me to get out of bed for days after a game. I know that is simply a combination of the aging process and football's minor injuries catching up with me. Still, though, it's the type of work I have chosen and the price I must pay, and , hopefully, when my NFL career is over, I'll still be able to stand upright and walk like a human being.

I have really been lucky during my career. In high school I was never seriously injured. During my college days I was hit from the blind side just once; knocked senseless for a few minutes; and then I went back into action. I had only received some minor bumps and twists through my scholastic career. In professional football my luck has thus far continued. I've only had but a few injuries compared to some of the athletes in the NFL.

Whenever I consider my personal injuries, I only count the injuries that prevented me from playing in a game. Under game conditions I know that I will bleed and bruise. I can't remember the number of times my head or face has been stitched up during a game or afterwards, but that's to be expected in the NFL. Sometimes a finger gets past your face mask and into you eyes or a part of equipment scrapes against your body. Those are little injuries, areas of pain with which you still play the game. I even split my head open during brutal contact and still went back into the game. That type of injury requires only a towel to wipe the blood from your eyes and a few stitches to return you back to the action.

The injuries that add up and really hurt are, as I said, injuries that prevented me from playing in or finishing a game. My knee injuries have been of this type. I have twice undergone operations for knee problems. That usually requires a week or more in the hospital and six solid weeks of rehabilitation. Sometimes a person doesn't come back after knee surgery with the full range of motion he had previously. Other times the knee joint is never normal again and requires more surgery and much more time in rehabilitation. There are many players in the NFL who have had their knees operated on six, seven and eight times. I know that Joe Namath and his four knee operations have been well-publicized, but few people know that our All-Pro center, Jim Otto, has had at least ten knee operations that he can remember. At least Namath can walk without the aid of special knee braces. Jim Otto can't. Before he gets out of bed in the morning, Jim straps braces on his knees to keep them from collapsing. Jim Otto played NFL football and paid the price during his career with hard physical work and dedication to a job. But now, and for the rest of his life, Jim Otto will carry the scars of his NFL career and continue to pay for his achievements with pain. He wasn't as lucky as I.

Although I have been lucky, I still have had more injuries than just a few to the knees. One time, during a game with the Steelers, I tore all the muscles in my groin. I've also had a slight shoulder separation, neck injuries, and my hands look as though a cable car in San Francisco parked on them for a night. After my career is over, I'm going to get my hands and fingers operated on. I want my fingers to be straightened out a little to make them look at least halfway normal, and I'd like to be able to someday move all my fingers. Who knows, maybe someday I might want to learn how to play the piano or guitar.

In all, I would say that during my career I have only missed, on the average, two or three games per season. In the NFL that is a remarkable record. I know there are those who have never missed a game because of injuries, but most of those guys give less than 100 percent. For the most part, when playing in the NFL, one accepts the fact that he will be injured. Every player who goes into battle understands that at any second, on any play, his career could come to an abrupt and tragic conclusion.

August 12, 1978, I was involved in a terrible accident with Darryl Stingley, a wide receiver who played for New England. On a typical passing play, Darryl ran a rather dangerous pattern across the middle of our zone defense. It was one of those pass plays where I could not possibly have intercepted, so because of what the owners expect of me when they give me my paycheck, I automatically reacted to the situation by going for an intimidating hit. It was a fairly good hit, but nothing exceptional, and I got up and started back toward our huddle. But Darryl didn't get up and walk away from the collision. That particular play was the end of Darryl Stingley's career in the NFL. His neck was broken in two places and there was serious damage to his spinal cord. Darryl Stingley will never run a pass pattern in the NFL again, and it may well be that he will never stand up and walk across a room. For weeks Darryl lay paralyzed in a hospital and there were times when, because of complications after surgery, he nearly lost his life.

I want to be tough and I want to work at playing the game hard, but within the structure of the rules. Still, though, there are times when I wonder about myself and the structure of NFL football. I am tough, but I'm not a brutal animal. I think it's possible for a football player to be proficient in his job and still possess sentiment. I want to do my job, and the contact of the sport doesn't bother me, but I certainly don't want to hospitalize Lynn Swann and I wasn't thinking about killing Riley Odoms.

When the reality of Stingley's injury hit me with its full impact, I was shattered. To think that my tackle broke another man's neck and killed his future ... well, I know it hurts Darryl, but it hurts me, too.

One week later we had an exhibition game against the Rams. The Stingley incident was still troubling me. I didn't know if I wanted to play in the game against the Rams. In fact, I didn't know if I could ever play football again. During the week I had spent some very trying hours talking with the doctors about Darryl's condition. That was constantly on my mind and tearing at my insides. My head was a ball of throbbing pain and my body felt like a hollow shell that no longer belonged to me. And then, too, I couldn't help but think about negotiating for a new contract this past season and how Al Davis had handled everything. Davis, I know, is nothing more than a company man, and if you wanted to play for nothing, and the NFL accepted that contract, it would be fine with Al. If you want a million dollars for three years, Al will try to get you a hundred thousand. I don't fault the man for doing his job, but he does make it difficult for an athlete when it comes time to talk about new contracts.

In 1977 I had played out my option and was looking for more money with the next contract. To be perfectly honest, I did have some loyalty to the Oakland Raiders, but I couldn't pay my bills and completely establish myself for the future with that loyalty. I wanted money ... more money.

Al Davis started our contract talks by trying to cut my pay. When it came time to explain his reasons, he had thousands, and if I had given him the time, I'm sure Al would have come up with a million reasons why he wanted to cut my pay. But the crux of the matter was that I intended to end up making more money and whichever color uniform I put on really didn't matter. To me, my future in the NFL was a matter of green and nothing else. Al still cited incidents during games when I missed a tackle or failed to knock someone out. He started with a game several years ago when we were beating the hell out of Cincinnati, and late in the game, Archie Griffin got by me and scored. At the time, I was a little tired, and a little lazy, too. That touchdown had no bearing on the game, but Al still thought I should have blasted Archie. From there he verbally replayed almost every game of my career and pointed out situations in which I had not done the job the Oakland Raiders were paying me to do. The whole thrust of the contract talks with Al centered around the notion that I was not hitting like I did earlier in my career. Al Davis was telling me that I was paid to be a warhead, and anyone who came near me should get knocked into hell. Al left me with the impression that my only marketable talents in professional football were those of an intimidator. My job with the Raiders was that of a paid assassin. Well, so be it.

Again, one expects this kind of situation whenever it comes time for a new contract. The management will point out your failures while you bargain from strong points. It's only good business. But now, after the Stingley incident, it all began to trouble me. I started thinking that the Raiders actually did want me in their secondary for the express purpose of intimidating receivers, running backs or any opponent, as the press had indicated.

It was a week of soul-searching. I have always believed in working hard for the things I want out of life. In a way, I was accomplishing all my objectives, but when the safety of another man's life is the cost for personal or team goals, I wondered if my objectives really meant all that much to me. Yes, I want to do my job, and that requires hitting and intimidating opponents, but breaking someone's neck, or even worse, shouldn't be the price anyone must pay.

I though about our first exhibition game of the year and how I had played. Actually, I was only in for one quarter, but because of my hits two members of the Chicago Bears were carried off the field. The Raiders' front office told my attorney that I was playing the best football of my career. That was a strange statement coming from the Raiders, because in May Al Davis had tried to convince me that I was over the hill and a pay cut was in my future. Then I go out in our first exhibition game, knock two receivers cold, and once again I'm a great ballplayer. I was wondering if the Raiders would think I was worth a million dollars because of my last performance.

It might sound wrong for me to knock the Raider organization and how they arrive at the dollar and cent value a player is worth, but in professional football a passive free safety isn't paid as much as one who has the physical ability to inflict fear and damage on opponents. The Raiders don't exactly tell me that I must knock out receivers and running backs, but everything about the game encourages hard and violent play, and the more violently I play, the more the Raiders appreciate me. My life and career sounds like a contradiction, and maybe it really is. After hitting Darryl Stingley, I started thinking about professional football and the safety of all the players, including myself. I don't want my neck broken. I don't like to think about receiving a serious injury any more than I relish the idea of being guilty of inflicting that same type of suffering on someone else. But at the same time, I have a job to do, and what if I slack off?

I did play in the game against the Rams. I shouldn't even have dressed for it. My mind wasn't on the field and my heart was back at the hospital bed where Darryl Stingley was fighting for his life. For the first time in my career I played a game with a passive attitude, and it hurt me. It wasn't a physical pain that I received, but my pride was wounded. On what started out as a normal running play, I zeroed in on the Rams' Wendell Tyler. It was one of those head-on shots that I usually win by knocking the back into the stands, but this time it was different. I came up and met the play flat-footed and passive. I wasn't moving with any velocity and was just hoping to get ahold of Tyler and bring him down. Seconds later I was flat on my back as Wendell ran me over. It was a shocking and very embarrassing situation.

Even had I knocked Tyler out with one of my bone-jarring tackles, it wouldn't have proved anything. I think that now I look at professional football in a more mature way, and say there must be a happy medium and a better way of controlling the game. From my own point of view, if I sit back passively, every running back in the NFL will make tracks over my fallen body, and before long the Raiders will have a just cause to ship me out. I like the game of football, and contact doesn't scare me in the least. But at the same time, I do care very much about myself and the opponents I tackle. Football is a contact game, and we must never forget that, but there should be a line drawn somewhere to separate hard contact from animal brutality. As a free safety, I must hit hard and be intimidating, but a measure of protection can be added by simply changing the rules of the game.

Every year the NFL meets with the owners and goes into rule changes, but it amounts to a waste of time and money. In the last few years, what rules have actually been changed to ensure the safety of the players? When you consider the rule changes that have been made, they all have been designed to make the game more exciting, and believe me, excitement in professional football means higher risks for the players. A good example of a rule change to generate more excitement has made the most dangerous play in all of professional football occur much more frequently. I'm talking, of course, about the kick-off. Several years ago the ball was kicked from the forty yard line. With strong legs, the modern kicking stars were booting the ball out of the end zone most of the time. The ball would be spotted on the twenty yard line, since the run back had been eliminated. That wasn't a terrible thing, but some ranking official in the NFL decided that the fans were being cheated out of the excitement of the kick return, so the rules committee moved the kicker back to the thirty-five yard line. Thus, you have the excitement of twenty-two bodies building up full heads of speed and slamming into each other. The very first injury I ever sustained came on the kick-off team. Returning kick-offs is dangerous, and covering kick-offs is dangerous, but because the kick-off is exciting, some whiz who sits behind a desk in an office decides to move the kicking team back five yards to ensure the kick return. If someone wants to start changing some of the rules to make the game safer, then start by putting the ball back on the forty yard line and let those strong legs boot the ball the hell out of the end zone.

It seems that few of the rule changes are channeled into the area of safety. I know that the owners of the NFL teams, the players and the league officials often talk about how to protect the athletes, but little is ever really done to satisfy the players' complaints. I want to play football by the rules, and I don't want to see any more necks broken. When I stop and look back over my career, I can say in all honesty that cheap shots have never been part of my game plan. But at the same time, I admit to using the rules to my advantage. Sure, I could just make tackles without really trying to blast through the man, but I am expected to, and the rules are designed in my favor because people want the excitement of violent play.

The Raiders play a zone for the most part, and as I have said before, I really don't have a specific responsibility except to seek out the ball and blast into opponents. A zone coverage is dangerous for receivers and running back who attempt any patterns over the middle. Running a pass route through a zone defense is similar to running full speed through a woods in the middle of the night. The offensive man simply cannot see the defenders like he can in a man-to-man defense. And all teams play a zone defense. The zone is designed so that linebackers and safety personnel have areas to cover, rather than people. In my position I just sit back, watch the quarterback for any indication about where he is going to throw the ball, and then, wham! A receiver is looking for, and concentrating on, the ball while running a pattern full speed across the middle, and the free safety acts like a missile homing in on the man's rib cage, head, or knees. It's got to hurt the receiver, and after a few hits the man's will to win is warped. I wouldn't want to be a receiver. In fact, with the rules structure as it now stands, I wouldn't play football in the NFL if I was a receiver. Playing wide receiver and running patterns over the middle against any team, passive or otherwise, is the most insane thing anyone could ever do. I realize this and can truly understand why some receivers get gun-shy on crossing patterns. Okay, do I let the receiver have the edge and give him the chance to make catches around me because I'm a sensitive guy or do I do what I am paid to do? The answer is obvious, and my career bears testimony to whether or not I earn my money. But nonetheless, something must be done to give receivers a chance, and it comes back to the rules.

The owners and the NFL officials should make player safety their number-one priority when it comes time for their annual meeting. It wouldn't be that difficult to change the ruling in favor of the receiver, and I would not resent it. Just outlaw zone coverages and move every team to a five-man defensive line. With man-for-man coverage, the game becomes more of push-and-shove, bump-and-run game. When I have to cover on a man-for-man situation, I must run with, or chase after receivers. There isn't any camping in the middle of the field and looking for those head-on shots that can render a man unconscious or break his neck. The purpose of the five-man line would also be a step in the offensive team's favor. This way, most team would probably go with two linebackers instead of three or four, but still have four safeties. Without a group of surly linebackers mopping up on short-range passes, those areas would be more vulnerable to short passes. This type of rule would also give added protection to the running back and open up the offensive aspect of football tremendously.

Another valid point to consider is doing away with the dangerous quick slant. A quick-slant pattern is designed for a six or seven yard gain or an incompletion. The receiver bolts off the line and fakes to the outside, then quickly slants in toward the middle. The defender has no chance at the ball, and the quarterback will either complete the pass or it will fall incomplete. This is a risky pattern because the defensive secondary must target the receiver and forget about the ball. You must hit the receiver and forget about the fumble or at least make him wary of your presence on the next attempt.

In that now-tragic game, New England was good for at least five quick slants, and we took the necessary steps to protect against that particular play. Unfortunately, Darryl Stingley paid the price with a broken neck. I remember that moment too well. Once again, for the safety of the player, they absolutely should outlaw the quick slant.

We have talked about protecting the quarterback, and believe it or not, there are rules designed to offer protection. It is illegal to hit a quarterback after he has thrown the ball, but many times this is a judgment call that requires all the officials to use the same judgment. Again we are back in the area of officials lacking consistency. I believe that particular rule should be enforced in favor of the quarterback even if the play is close. I'm sure if the officials started calling these plays a little closer the defensive lineman would be careful of late hits. At least, I believe they would consider the possibility of a flag and fifteen yards going against the defense. But at the same time, a little balance is needed. I mean, this league is filled with smart-ass quarterbacks who will take off on a fifteen yard run and then slide into second base when the defenders close in. Several years ago, Steve Grogan took off on a little boot-leg play and when I moved in for a tackle, he fell down. Because of the rules, I simply downed him and the officials threw a flag. Damn it! A player isn't considered tackled and downed until a defender has made contact with him. I was doing my job and still received a fifteen yarder. Another thing is the quarterback pump-faking. That is simply a quarterback ploy to slow down the defender or fake the man off his feet into the nickel stands. Let the quarterback drop back to pass or even roll out, and let's give him the protection of flagging the close calls. But no more pump-faking and no more slides into second base. While the quarterback is in the motion of passing the ball and he gets hit, then call the play. And if the quarterback takes off and crosses the line of scrimmage then let him pay the price. This way the quarterback will be offered a little more protection from the rules, while at the same time defenders won't feel cheated.

A new rule has been added this year that experts claim will "offer the quarterback more protection." I think the rule is a waste of time and bunk. This season, when a quarterback is in the clutches of a defender the official will blow the play dead. I don't believe that is going to offer the quarterback any more protection and that particular rule will take away from the game. Quite often, quarterbacks have the ability to break free and complete the pass or run for extra yardage. Actually, this type of rule is putting professional football on a touch football plain. I'm all for giving the quarterback protection with the rules, but let's keep some balance within the structure. Let's not jump from one end of the spectrum to the other.

Another ruling that should be changed would offer the quarterback a little protection.

When several sportswriters asked the question about special consideration for quarterbacks, Steeler lineman Jack Lambert said, "Give 'em dresses!" Obviously that statement was a weak attempt at humor over a serious problem. Quarterback injuries are a serious threat to the success of any team so you would think the owners would push for this change. They don't. Like Lambert, they think only of blitzing the other team's quarterback and knocking him out of the game. I wonder what Lambert thinks about when it's his own quarterback writhing in pain because he took a split second too long in releasing the ball. I've seen Bradshaw wobble to the sidelines wondering where he was after taking a shot in the head by an overzealous lineman or linebacker. Naturally, it all becomes a different situation to Mr. Lambert and the Steelers when it's their quarterback asking, "Who am I?"

Quarterbacks should be protected! Quarterbacks must be protected, and I'm not talking about better-blocking linemen. I think special consideration should be given to a man who drops back in a pocket to pass the football. A quarterback can't fight back, and in a passing position I believe he is the most vulnerable to a serious injury of any man on the field. A quarterback stands there looking down the field, concentrating on the type of coverage, and searching for that opening. The big defensive linemen and linebackers start coming after him at full speed and he knows he will get clobbered whether or not he gets the pass off. It takes a brave individual to still stand in there, deliver the ball, and take a hit.

Many changes in the rules can offer more protection to the quarterbacks. First of all, blitzing could be eliminated. In every All-Star or All-Pro game, there is a no-blitzing ruling. This is a step at protecting the quarterback. Blitzes create weakness in the pass protection and usually are designed to give one defender a free route to the quarterback's head. If the people who set up the rules outlaw the blitz during All-Star games, why not exercise that same reason and sanity for the regular season? I'm not saying they should put dresses on the quarterbacks, because that would be an absurd solution to a serious problem. But let's give the quarterback a special consideration. I wonder what type of courage Lambert would exhibit if he was asked to play quarterback for a game. I don't think I would have made NFL football my career if I had to earn my money playing quarterback.

Changing the rules to protect the athletes isn't a sign of weakness or cowardice. I've gone nose-to-nose with the biggest running backs in the NFL and fought with the strongest linemen. They know for a fact that I am fearless, and no one has ever questioned my appetite for contact. But there comes a time when reason and sanity must take hold. I, for one, am not interested in answering doorbells that never rang, and the knowledge of nearly killing a wide receiver doesn't set easily on my mind. What I am trying to say is that I don't want to get injured before my scheduled retirement and I certainly don't want to send any more receivers to their early retirement. But until the rules are changed, I will continue to play the game according to the rules. My position and style of play dictate the terms with which I meet the receiver and running back. Because of the zone, it is to my advantage to sit back and wait. If I tackle at half-speed, then I only increase the chance of serious injury to myself or the probability of getting burned by some receiver. The rules can be changed to take away the high-risk areas of football and still maintain that degree of hard-hitting action the fans love. As the rules now stand, there are some areas of football that bury the human side of football players and bring out the animal. For a receiver to run those patterns across the middle against the zone defense is suicide, because until the rules are changed, those assassins will be waiting in the secondary.

The rules and officiating have been a complaint of mine since my early days in the NFL, but until recently, I never gave it much thought. I always figured there was little or nothing that could be done to change the structure of NFL football. Yet now, after I have had some serious time for thinking about the problems in the structure of professional football, I see many avenues which the owners and league officials could explore. I've mentioned a few rule changes that could eliminate many of those murderous head-on tackles that break the concentration of the best receivers and strike fear into the most courageous running backs. And I have mentioned the advantages a quarterback would have with a no-blitzing rule. Obviously, these changes would give the fans more offense and offer the players a greater degree of safety. But all the rule changes in the world aren't worth a damn unless the men in the striped uniforms develop some sort of consistency with their calls. One time, I slap a running back on the head to down him and they call a fifteen yard penalty against me for unnecessary roughness. Then, during that same game, I make a tackle on a receiver and he jumps up, slugs me in the face and wants to fight. The official just breaks up the mess. I'm talking about a game with the Steelers when I made a tackle on Lynn Swann and his emotionalism got the best of him. He missed the pass, and I guess as a reaction to this frustration, he started kicking me and jumped up and slugged me. An official was right on the spot, but instead of throwing a flag, he just pulled Swann away from me.

I have been part of the NFL since 1971 and the only consistent thing I have ever seen in the officiating was the ability to be inconsistent. Some of the officials' mistakes can be passed off as human error, and I can overlook and sympathize with those personal misjudgments. However, when individual bias is injected into the officiating, I am greatly disturbed. Swann could jump up and take a swing at me because everyone in the world knows that I could physically break him apart. Therefore, Swann is the good guy and I am the villain. So go ahead and kick the villain in the testicles, spit on him, slug him, call him dirty names and the official will only break up the scene. But if the villain slaps a running back on the head or fights back, it becomes a situation requiring penalties and fines. To me, that is all a bunch of crap and I don't like the idea of being considered the villain. I am simply an athlete who is paid to hit. Lynn Swann is an athlete who is paid to catch passes and score touchdowns. Just because our missions during the football game are in conflict doesn't give anyone the right to label one of us a saint and the other a sinner. It all comes back to the point I'm trying to make about the inconsistency of the officiating. If it's wrong for me to slug anyone during the course of a game, then it's wrong for Swann or any other player in the NFL to take that type of action. The first rule in officiating must be consistency. An official should be able to act in total fairness and treat all infractions of the rules in such a manner that each type of infraction constantly carries the same penalty. When we arrive at a fair and consistent enforcement of the rules, the safety conditions and the game itself will greatly improve.

Boxing offers a good example of the type of consistent rule enforcement that is lacking in football. Professional boxing, or boxing at any level, is brutal. The purpose of a boxing match is for each opponent to make an attempt at beating the other man's head in. Yet in boxing the rules do not favor one fighter over the other. It's illegal for both fighters to hit low; neither man can butt, elbow, hit on the breaks, backhand, rabbit punch, etc. The rules apply to both contestants. In football some players, because of their position or size, can get away with infractions of the rules, while others are penalized. Professional football needs the same type of rule enforcement found in boxing.

Still, the officials, like all mortals, are subject to errors. I strongly believe in using one judge who sits up in the press box and has the power to veto any questionable calls. Since TV cameras cover everything from the antics of the fans to the cheerleaders' legs, I believe that a system could be set up that would eliminate the human factor in close calls. There are arguments from owners and league officials, who claim a camera system covering all the angles of a football game would be impossible. At the last meeting of the owners and NFL officials, they completely ruled out the use of such devices. I think they made a grave mistake. I sat at home and watched Michigan lose the Rose Bowl because of an officiating error. On a goal-line play an official signaled a touchdown for Southern California, even though a Michigan defender stopped the play two yards from the end zone and caused a fumble — a fumble that Michigan recovered. The Michigan people were upset, but the official assured everyone that the back had crossed the goal line and was in the end zone before the fumble occurred. The official obviously needed to see his optometrist, because the instant replay clearly showed the back was two yards short of the goal line and he actually did fumble. Southern California ended up winning the game by exactly seven points.

In 1977 we played Denver for the American Conference Championship. The winner of the game would go on to the Super Bowl and the loser would stay home and watch it on television. During a goal line stand I got a good hit on running back Rob Lytle, and he fumbled. We recovered the ball, and our defensive team was leaving the field along with the Denver offensive team. It was a fumble, and everyone in the world who was watching the game realized it. Denver knew it was a fumble, Rob Lytle certainly knew it, I knew it, and most of the fans knew it. But somehow, and I still can't figure it out, one of the officials who must have been looking up at the blimp or something, signaled no fumble and gave the ball to Denver. They scored and won the game 21-17. Of course, after the official viewed the instant replay, he knew what the world knew when the play actually happened — it was a fumble. Like a good guy he wrote the Oakland Raiders a letter apologizing for the error. Even the Commissioner's office wrote us a nice "we're sorry" letter, too. That might have been a million-dollar mistake for the Raiders to eat, because that's just about what the team and players would have split up had we gone on to win the Super Bowl. But I couldn't very well take a letter, or, should I say, two letters of apology to my bank.

I could fill a book on the bad calls made by the officials last season alone, bad calls which could have been corrected if the NFL had an official sitting in the press box watching the action. But the owners and the NFL office think it would be too difficult to set up that type of equipment. Hell, I'll lend them my television, or better yet, I'll buy them a TV, if it would help to clean up the sloppy officiating. I know that type of setup can work both ways. The Raiders have won some questionable games and lost some, but in fairness to the sport and the athletes who participate in the game, let's get a system that will improve these cloudy areas of professional football. Then "may the best team win" will be an expression with a much higher probability of coming true.

I think a replay system would also help clean up a lot of dirty action. How many times during the course of a game have you seen your favorite player get knocked out with a cheap shot the official missed? As I write, I can almost hear Pittsburgh fans screaming, "the time Atkinson hit Swann," and I'm thinking, "the time Mansfield speared me." How can a referee really be expected to call something that happens so fast only a slow-motion camera could prove it? In that type of situation, the league official could be sitting up in the press box watching several angles of replays. If he spots something cheap, he could press a little buzzer, tell the head linesman about the incident, and let the boys on the field pass judgment. That type of action would make several players around the league think before they acted. The penalty should include special fines and suspensions against the real cheap-shot artists, in addition to lost yardage at the time of the infraction.

When the camera catches someone hitting the quarterback late, or maybe a linebacker kicking a receiver in the head, the first action should be a fine. But how effective are fines? I was fined twice, and the money really didn't hurt my pocketbook one bit. Even if it is rather stiff, like the $5,000 fine Joe Greene received for his right hook to a lineman's gut, the owners of the team will sometimes sympathize with the athlete and pay the fine themselves. Then, too, even $5,000 isn't going to sting all that much when you consider some of the players' salaries. It might make you stop and think for a second, but it's still not the complete answer to the problem.

Step two in any of these criminal activities during a football game must be a severe suspension. I know that a twisted knee doesn't really start hurting until I am sitting in the stands watching my team play the game. What I'm saying is that any athlete, starting or otherwise, wants to play in the game because he loves the game. Sure, we make big money in the NFL, but for most of us professional football is a great love affair that gives us Sunday thrills. It hurts to sit out a game. More important than hurting the athlete who has committed the infraction, it also hurts the team and the team's owners. When anyone plays in the NFL, he is damn good, but there are first-string goods and second-string goods. When any member of our starting defensive unit is out with an injury, we are not totally effective.

It's that way with any team. When you have starters sitting on the bench, you're in trouble. So if the league officials took this action against cheap-shot artists, the problem of dirty play would almost disappear. Every team wants to go into battle operating at 100 percent effectiveness. If players risk suspension because of serious infractions of the rules, then everyone from the athletes to the coaches, and even the owners, will handle this situation with extreme caution.

Needless to say, this type of operation must also have a high degree of consistency, and a judge must be fair. I guess what I am trying to say is there must be professionalism attached to all aspects of football if the game is to remain civilized. Otherwise, the violence and brutality is going to increase and the life expectancy of professional football players will be measured in games instead of years.

I think about Darryl Stingley and the exciting moments he'll never be able to give to the fans. I think about Gayle Sayers and how injuries ended his career before it was actually started. Even Joe Namath played as half a football player. In my estimation, Gayle Sayers was a great running back, and I enjoyed watching him play football. But he had to quit because of knee injuries, and that cheated Gayle and football fans out of years of exciting games and great runs. You simply don't replace a Gayle Sayers. Joe Namath was the most talked-about, most publicized quarterback in the history of the NFL. When you consider the man was crippled because of football injuries and he played every game of his career under extremely difficult conditions, he must have been one tremendous athlete. A crippled Joe Namath placed his name in the record book, but I wonder what a healthy Joe Namath would have been like.

When we watch a football game visions of touchdowns and tackles are in our mind, but the ever-present reality of football is injuries. Any athlete who has participated in a football game knows that it requires top physical condition, the best equipment and a great deal of good luck to escape the crippling pain and punishment the years have a way of collecting within your body. And then again, for the athlete who has tasted the thrill of scoring a touchdown and making a solid tackle, there aren't any words that can describe the feeling. It's a good feeling, a great feeling, to be able to compete on a professional level and beat the best team in football or provide that game-saving play. It takes a special courage to dare to play football, but once you're hooked, it becomes a habit that can never be fully satisfied. True, I play football because I like the money, but I also love my job. When any man can arrive at that point in his life where he actually loves his work, then he is indeed a successful man. I guess it's because I love the game, and in a way I even love with a great respect the other guys who go up against me. I have one bad memory, and I don't want another. Darryl Stingley will never play football again, and maybe never walk. I can't undo yesterday's misfortune, but I might be able to prevent some of tomorrow's pain. Professional football must make that decision to change some of the rules or we are all doomed to a retirement of nursing broken bones, stiff joints and knees that collapse. The point is to clean up football and make it safe on all levels, because with better coaching techniques and bigger and faster athletes coming into the game, people are going to start killing each other during the battle. Look into the high schools across this country of ours and see the training programs coaches have these young athletes on. Weight training, flexibility drills, diets, vitamins and a thousand other little gimmicks and gadgets are designed to make everyone stronger, faster and more violent. I love kids too much to see one of them share a memory similar to mine or one that might be worse. Therefore, something must be done to change the game, something that protects the safety of the athletes.

My suggested rule changes are not the answer to all the problems in football, but these changes would take the animal out of a brutal game. Football would still be a contact sport, and that part we could never change. What's more, I would never want to change the contact, because to me that is the essence of the game. But there are those areas I mentioned that could provide a greater safety factor for the athletes themselves and still offer the fans the excitement of contact, scoring and competition.

Unfortunately, they have hardly changed the rules of football, and I have this season to consider. I could play the game passively and let all the Wendell Tylers in the league run me over, but I have a deep-rooted pride that would never allow that to happen. Also, in all probability, the Raiders would never let their free safety remain passive. Either I would do the job or they would get someone else to cover my position. My job is to first of all consider the rules and regulations and then to use everything in the structure of the NFL to intimidate and discourage receivers and running backs. Since there have been few rule changes to the contrary, I can still sit back in my zone and wait for unsuspecting people to come into view. When that happens, because of what I'm paid to do, I must be The Assassin. If and when they really do change the rules, I believe that I am enough of an athlete to change my techniques. But the way everything is structured, a push-and-shove free safety may just as well play his football in a "touchy" league and not the NFL. I care about the other athletes in the league, but I also care about me. I am not going into any more games with only half a heart.

9

And For Tomorrow

A writer once wrote, "The name of one John David Tatum has not been included into the Professional Football Hall of Fame ... yet. But his day shall come and when that event happens, the caption under his name will read, 'The Assassin.'"

When I think about my career, I hope that my achievements are not overshadowed by the title, "Assassin." In reality, I am not an assassin, but rather a human being with a deep compassion for little children, young people and my fellow athletes of the NFL. I have always resented anyone comparing me to some cheap-shot artist, because, as I have tried to explain in this book, I am only an athlete who has a job to do.

Several years ago I was visiting in Niles, Ohio, and stopped at a restaurant called Alberini's. It's a fantastic place with excellent food. I had gone there with a friend who introduced me to the manager, Ray Iezzi. Ray is a football nut and one very funny guy. He's a practical joker and the type of person who can make you laugh until your sides hurt. Ray had known me for approximately two minutes when he asked, "Jack, can I have some fun and introduce you to a guy who loves football?"

I had no objections, so Ray called one of his bartenders over and asked, "Art, the three of us have been having a terrible argument and I want you to settle the issue once and for all. Tell us who you think is the meanest, dirtiest, hardest-hitting, rottenest bastard who ever played the game of football. Think about it, Art; a no-good bastard who hits like a ton of bricks."

Obviously, Art didn't know who I was. He stood there for only a second thinking about his answer and then blurted out, "Hell, that's got to be Jack Tatum of the Oakland Raiders. I saw him nearly kill Lynn Swann down in Pittsburgh."

"Art," Ray said with a peculiar grin on his face, "meet Jack Tatum."

Art's lower jaw dropped to the floor and with an embarrassed look, he tried to explain, "I don't mean you're a dirty player; you just hit."

I knew what the man meant, and the incident was funny. Art was a man who knew football and football players. He honestly didn't mean that I was a cheap-shot artist; it's just that I do hit. Maybe now, after reading my book, more fans will understand that I am only a human being and not some villainous character you want to hate. I realize that getting my name in the record book as only an athlete and not as an assassin will, in all probability, be an uphill battle. But my real battle is out there in the world, and that's the fight I want to win. I'm talking, of course, about the young people; the people who live in a ghetto or spend their days looking out into the world from a hospital bed; the people who have lost hope and faith; the people for whom yesterday is a bitter memory and tomorrow offers only more pain and suffering. I know that I'll never be able to change the course this world is traveling, but I will be able to do my small part.

Every year I go back to Passaic for business and just to visit old friends and make new ones. I have a scholarship fund going in Passaic, and each year they have a banquet. It's a good cause, and I know that because of my name and a little effort, some kid in the ghetto is going to get a chance at college and the opportunity to move out into the world. Still, there are more reasons for my trip to Passaic than just my scholarship fund. I always go back into the ghetto and talk with the young people there. I tell them about being tough and what it takes to become a man. Sometimes the kids listen, while other times they don't. I explain to them that being tough isn't buying or selling drugs, nor is it taking part in knife fights or robberies or murders. Tough is rising above all the adversity and going out into the world and actually making everything work. Anybody who feels sorry for himself because he was born and raised in a ghetto is going to die in the ghetto. To me, the ghetto was a blessing, because no I can appreciate my life and can share everything I have learned throughout the years. No one can tell me that I don't understand their side of life, because I was there and I lived it. But more important, I had a plan, a dream, and I worked it to the best of my ability. Now I play football in the NFL and my financial security is assured. Maybe I was lucky, but then again, maybe a man earns his own luck in this world.

I feel for the kids in the ghetto, but they do have young bodies and minds than can, if they are properly used, overcome adversity. The little kids who live in hospital beds and are deprived of good health are the ones my heart goes out to more than anyone else. I find it rewarding to spend time visiting these youngsters in the hospital, and I try to give them hope. That's all I can really do for those little people, but the young man in the ghetto can get up and walk into a better life on his own — if he has the fortitude.

I know it is tough for those kids from underprivileged homes to have hope, but when I sit on the edge of some little kid's hospital bed and see his skinny legs and braces, it makes me want to cry. I know this little man will never have the chance to run and play or even stand up and walk, and then I think about what tough really is. I had the courage to dare to be different while growing up in the ghetto, and I have the toughness to play professional football, but at the same time I realize how much more strong-willed some of those little children in hospitals across our land must be just to accept a yesterday, today and tomorrow of the same painful memories and same limited hope. My life is a fantastic adventure. I have the ability to move about and see the world, but there are some who are handicapped by physical and mental restrictions, and for them, my heart cries. I really care about people and what happens to this world, but from my exposure in professional football, I have been dubbed an assassin without morals and ethics. Well, surprise, football players are human, too.

If anyone spent a day with me, they might be astonished. At heart, I'm just a homebody, or more accurately, I'm still that little country boy who loved to sit and listen to his grandfather's stories. I don't go in for wild parties, heavy drinking, or running with fifty or sixty different ladies. I enjoy privacy, a quiet life, and the company of just a few good lady friends. I know the stability of some of my football buddies might be questionable, but the fans should understand that football is one thing, while life is quite another. Skip Thomas, Clarence Davis, and George Atkinson might be characters on the field of battle, but most of the time they are quite different in real life. Clarence, George and I enjoy chess and a quiet game of pool. I'm not talking about barroom pool. George and Clarence have pool tables at their homes and we have some serious games. Even Skip is different in real life, most of the time, at least.

Several years ago we played in San Diego, and the night before the game Skip was having problems. He had refused to talk with reporters, told the front desk "no calls," and just wanted to be off alone with himself. Then a friend of mine stopped by our room with his little boy. Skip was under the covers and had four of five pillows over his face. He didn't want to be disturbed until he heard the little kid's voice. That was it, and before I knew what happened Skip was up and talking to the little dude about professional football, life, Corvettes and motorcycles.

Football is a strange game and does strange things to the athletes. There are mental pressures, physical pressures and the overall uncertainties of your future. One day I could be the most aggressive tackler in the NFL and the next day I could be lying flat on my back in a hospital bed with a broken neck.

Darryl Stingley will probably never walk again and that really tears at me. I don't like to pass off the incident as "just part of the game," because it sounds callused and hard, but during contact, serious injuries can, and often do, occur. I realize it is impossible to undo what happened to Darryl, but at the same time I can think about his tomorrow. Right now, I'd like to start a special fund-raising program to help with his medical bills and give his family the things he worked for during his time in the NFL. Football is a brutal game, but there is still room for sentiment. Like I said, I care.

In planning for my tomorrow, I know that my NFL days are numbered, and when my time is over I must be able to accept the fact and move into something else. Physically, I feel good, but now it requires a lot more work to get the body into shape, and it takes a little longer to shake the bumps of a game. Maybe two more years, or possibly three, I don't really know, but it's just a matter of time before I have to retire. Hopefully, I won't be like the fighter who goes one round too many. Hopefully, I'll have the intelligence to recognize the signs and be able to walk away from my NFL career. I believe that I will have the wisdom to do the right thing, because that's the way my life has always been slanted.

When I hang up the cleats, I think I'll become a farmer or rancher. I like the outdoors and have my eyes on some land in Southern California. Right now that's my dream, but my reality is still the NFL. Another season is upon me and the press has started writing about the villainous character wearing the silver and black. Maybe because of my style of play I am The Assassin, but at heart I'm a friendly assassin who honestly cares about people and the world.

THEY STILL CALL ME

ASSASSIN

HERE WE GO AGAIN

by Jack Tatum with Bill Kushner

Original © 1989

*Football's infamous
assassin is back, but this time
he's hitting on the
hypocrites and hierarchy
of the game.*

Contents

1

Clint, What's Good for Rope Burns?

My first book, *They Call Me Assassin*, was released January 7, 1980, and twenty-four hours later I was a best-selling author. Actually, I became a best-selling author the same day the book was released, but my publisher didn't make it official until the next day.

I was told that it takes a sale of about 50,000 hard cover books to make the best-seller list and according to my publisher we sold 80,000 copies — the first day. I figured that made me a best-selling author and then some.

The thought of my accomplishment was astounding. Me ... a best-selling author, and with my simple little story about football. I couldn't believe it, Jack Tatum, the country bumpkin from Crouse, North Carolina, a best-selling author.

I never realized that writing was such an easy and lucrative profession. Most of the stories I heard about writers were of incredible hardships, struggling against overwhelming odds, and sometimes even practically dying of starvation before the first sale. Since I'm a guy who likes to see quick results, and I have this habit of eating three meals a day, being a writer just didn't appeal to me. But, what the heck! I decided to give it a try anyway and all of a sudden my book was on the charts. I had arrived, so to speak.

If my quick rise to literary stardom wasn't in record-setting time, then my fall from NFL grace certainly was ... but I'm getting ahead of myself. Let me retreat a little.

For the next day or so, I enjoyed the status of being a literary genius. I didn't run off and buy and ascot or a pipe but I did consider getting one of those fancy sports coats with the leather patches over the elbows. Hey, what the hell! Since I was a pro of prose, I might as well look the part.

The first indication of trouble or that maybe I really wasn't cut out to be a writer appeared in the *Boston Herald American* on

January 11, 1980. Originally, I though my book was concise and rather well-written. But while staring at the headlines of that particular newspaper, my suspicions were that I should have used more words or perhaps less syllables in writing the story. As I scanned the article, it became obvious that a few individuals had already missed the entire theme of my work.

Joe Fitzgerald, a pretty fair Boston sports journalist, stepped down from his most-of-the-time professional ranks just long enough to do a little surgery on my book. As I read the headline "NFL's Rozelle on Jack Tatum's book: 'That's asking for it,'" I had a sneaking suspicion that Commissioner Pete Rozelle wasn't exactly thrilled that I had penned my autobiography.

I later discovered that Joe Fitzgerald hadn't, as yet, even read the book, but he did see several excerpts from the publisher. From a little sampling of text Mr. Joe Fitzgerald was able to deduce the entire thrust of my story and thereby give his reading audience exactly what they wanted: a paper lynching of another villain. Writers with the *National Enquirer* have that same instinctive ability, too.

Fitzgerald began his assault of yours truly with, "There's an old saying which maintains that if you give some people enough rope, they'll hang themselves, and the suspicion here is that Oakland Raider defensive back Jack Tatum may have done just that in publishing his inflammatory autobiography, *They Call Me Assassin.*"

Those were pretty strong words coming from a dude who, like I said, didn't even take the time to read the entire book. Needless to say, Fitzgerald's opening paragraph sort of grabbed my attention, but I couldn't understand what he meant by my publishing an "inflammatory autobiography."

I knew what "inflammatory" meant, but I couldn't understand why that word was being associated with my story. Read on, I told myself. Read on, and perhaps you will discover the gist of his words.

Following that advice I read on and learned that Fitzgerald actually interviewed, by telephone, NFL Commissioner Mr. Peter Rozelle. Naturally, their topic of discussion was my inflammatory autobiography, and naturally, Commissioner Rozelle was typical vintage Pete.

It wasn't so much what Pete said about the book, because he always had a tendency to say things that didn't make a lot of sense. But the mere fact that he would even make a comment on my autobiography totally bewildered me.

Pete hadn't read the book, and making this situation more bizarre was the fact that he hadn't even seen any excerpt from the publisher. Nevertheless, Pete Rozelle was already pointing his you've-been-a-bad-boy-again finger in my direction.

Thus began my fall from NFL grace, but it wasn't quite as dramatic as tumbling off a high mountain. It was more like walking along a level stretch of road.

The fact is that if Pete Rozelle had his rathers, he'd rather that I had been a baseball player somewhere in Hiroshima on August 6, 1945. I'd been sent to the office a number of times and to say that Pete and I didn't always see eye-to-eye might be understating it a tad. But I've never been one to hold a grudge, even if Pete won't admit being wrong.

"Oh, boy!" Pete was quoted as having said. "There's always something, isn't there? But that's asking for it. Unbelievable."

Asking for what? Clue me in, because I really don't understand. Asking for what? I quizzed myself over and over again and couldn't come up with an answer.

Well, I figured the intelligent thing to do was to stay cool and not jump to any conclusion before I finished reading Fitzgerald's entire article. "Read every word," I told myself, "know what you're talking about instead of going off half-cocked and sounding like a complete ass ..." That's what I told myself and it was pretty good advice — advice more people should follow.

Continuing on, Fitzgerald quoted me as I described my Super Bowl XI collision with Viking receiver Sammy White. The article seemed to indicate that the commissioner was upset because of that particular hit and my vocal comments directed at an incoherent Sammy White.

I paused for a moment and thought about the hit. Damn! Both of our bodies traveling in opposite directions at full speed! What a hit! I can still picture it all. Sammy's body went one direction, his helmet another, his chin strap straight up in the air. The next thing I knew he was flapping around on the turf like a wounded duck crying for his "Mama." Then he rolled over and asked the trainer, "Check my eyes ... are my eyes still in my head?"

"Yes!!!" the trainer answered.

"But I can't see! I can't see!" mumbled a dazed Sammy White.

Then I saw something that was nearly impossible to believe. Sammy not only caught the ball, but on impact he didn't fumble it, either. He was there, down on the turf, asking about his eyes and still holding onto the ball as if his life depended on it. Not the official or the trainer or anyone else could get the ball away from Sammy. Damn!!! What a receiver!!! Get hit like that and still make the catch!!!

Sammy was going to open those sleepy eyelids and realize his eyeballs were in their sockets and that he could still see. After that, I figured he'd put all the pieces together and before long, Sammy White would be back in my zone trying to catch another pass.

A great athlete like Sammy White was tough to discourage, and given enough unmolested opportunities, sooner or later, he'd burn someone in our secondary. If possible, I wanted to own Sammy — physically and mentally. I followed the hit with a verbal assault. I stood over Sammy and said that I'd be waiting to punish him if he came back into my zone. For good measure, I also threw in a couple of heavy cuss words.

Perhaps the next time he came running over the middle like a free spirit, maybe, just maybe, Sammy would think about the Assassin and pain instead of concentrating on catching the football. A defensive back has to use every mental and physical trick to break the receiver's concentration, and I was trying my best during Super Bowl Sunday.

The truth is, it didn't matter what I said to Sammy under those conditions. With loud bells ringing in his head he probably never heard my seemingly whispered words of warning. And damn, if that hit wasn't enough to discourage him, then nothing was.

Pete Rozelle couldn't possibly be upset because Fitzgerald wrote that I "boasted" of "wasting Sammy White." Naw. Impossible. Pete couldn't be upset with that. I told myself that Pete's being upset couldn't have had anything to do with my hit on Sammy White or even my verbal assault. Or could it?

I gave everything a serious moment of thought. First of all, it was a clean and legal hit. Secondly, many coaches, players and fans thought it was the best hit in the history of the Super Bowl. Even Sammy White had to agree. It was a great hit.

The hit and verbiage that followed was simply a part of football. Don't be too shocked, but after all, hitting and mouthing off have always been synonymous with football games on any level of competition — at least in all the games I've played.

Of course, I realize the officials can flag you for taunting. But at the time, no flag was thrown in my direction for the hit or the one-sided conversation that followed. There was an official right on the spot. He heard what I said. It wasn't enough for the man wearing the striped shirt to even think of reaching for the flag.

Now, for anyone, especially Commissioner Rozelle, to think that athletes of the NFL never do any "wasting" and "boasting" and verbal jousting during the heat of the battle is ... well, let's just say it's silly and leave it at that. I don't want to get into any trouble with this book so I plan to be very careful about my choice of words.

At any rate, I think I've introduced enough evidence on the

Sammy White incident to pacify most of my critics. Of course, some individuals, such as the now-retired hierarchy of the National Football League's front office and the noble sports journalists, will still disagree while forever maintaining that I hit Sammy too hard.

I'm sorry, but during my entire football career I never had a coach who taught me how to make a polite tackle. Believe it or not, all of my coaches, from my high school days and Coach John Federici to college and Coach Woody Hayes, and even Coach John Madden of the Raiders, always insisted that I run faster, be more aggressive and hit harder. Contrary to what some individuals might claim, hard hitting is not detrimental to the integrity of professional football, or for that matter, football on any level of competition.

At Ohio State, Woody Hayes even had a theory on aggressive and hard tackling. He was always talking about mass times velocity. Coach Hayes wanted me to increase my body speed at impact so that I was doing the hitting instead of getting hit. He always said that I would never feel the impact of a good, solid tackle if I applied his theory during contact. Well, Coach Hayes' theory must have worked to perfection with Sammy White because I didn't feel a damn thing.

There is another theory that most football players subscribe to and that is that many injuries occur when athletes let up or are caught standing still.

I hurt my knee when I relaxed in a game against Cincinnati. There were only seven seconds left in the first half and I was the safety on a kickoff. I was thinking more about halftime instead of the game. While jogging up the field, not paying attention, I was clipped. Because of a few half-hearted seconds of football, I missed parts of the next two seasons nursing a gimpy knee.

There were other times when I was caught out of character. It hurt the team and it hurt me. I remember playing the Los Angeles Rams. It was only an exhibition game and when I saw running back Wendell Tyler break through the line, I stood flat-footed and waited for him to come to me instead of attacking. Wendell left cleat marks on the front of my jersey and the number on my back was obliterated from the mud and grass stains.

There were other contributing reasons why a small running back like Wendell Tyler got the best of me on that night and I will explain it a little later on. But for now, my point is that no offensive or defensive player can go into a game and come out in one piece unless he is aggressive. And even when you're aggressive, injuries can happen, but standing around only compounds the problem.

Deacon Jones once played for the Los Angeles Rams. He was part of a front four called the "Fearsome Foursome." Deacon played an entire football career from high school, college and through the pros, without getting so much as a scratch. His approach to the game was, "Attack, attack, attack!!!"

To be perfectly honest, I've never seen a limp-wrist, slap-happy tackler make anyone's highlight film or draw rave reviews from the coaching staff. The fact is, that if a dude prances around the field attempting to make wimpy tackles he's not long for the NFL. That kind of individual would quickly become the Rodney Dangerfield of football — he'll get no respect.

I think, and please correct me if I'm wrong, that Mr. George Halas, the founder of the National Football League once said, "Pro football will always be a game of hitting."

I assume that Mr. Halas meant hard hitting and not polite hitting. Then again, it could be that Papa Bear Halas was talking about old-time football when he made that rather profound statement. I guess in order for me to understand the modern spirit of contact, I'd have to hear about football from a first-class, top-notch individual of today's game.

Bill Walsh, recently retired head coach of the San Francisco 49ers, ranked as one of the most intelligent men in modern football. Bill Walsh once articulated, "Well … the critical part of football is hitting the other man before he's ready for it."

If that's too difficult for some folks to understand then let's try Denver Bronco coach Dan Reeves' theory on playing modern-day football successfully. Coach Reeves believes, "It's better to be the hitter than the hittee."

Patriot Coach Raymond Berry once stated, "If you lose the battle of hitting, I'm not sure you can win the other battles."

Don Shula, head coach of the Miami Dolphins, feels that when a team is going into a football game where all things are equal, "winning is usually decided by the team that hits the hardest."

Of Super Bowl XI it could be said that the Raiders hit the hardest and were the more physical team. I think Sammy White and the other Vikings would attest to that and I'm sure football fans throughout the country agree. The Raiders won the game 32 to 14 and Super Bowl XI was history.

It's that same history and literature that makes the Fitzgerald article and Rozelle's reaction to my writing about Sammy White seem all the more inconceivable and ridiculous. It wasn't that my published story of Sammy White and Super Bowl XI arrived on a bolt of lightning in the form of an earth-shattering revelation. And it certainly wasn't a question of my having seen the light and suddenly I'm rushing forth with the cleansing confessions of an assassin.

I'm trying to emphasize my point that my hit on Sammy wasn't the guarded secret of someone pulling off the perfect crime. I mean, what the hell! There was more evidence as to whodunit to Sammy than a smudged fingerprint. Damn, the imprint of my helmet was embedded into Sammy's chest; my cleat marks ran up and down his ass, and a television audience of one hundred million football fans saw me do the "wasting." What did everyone think I said while standing over him? Believe me, I wasn't inviting him to a Mac-attack at McDonald's after the game.

I find it strange that no one in the world criticized my hit on Sammy White or had anything to say about the taunting when everything happened. Oh, Sammy's family might have thought I hit him too hard, but even they didn't complain.

I can't be positive, but I'm fairly sure Pete Rozelle saw the hit and my antics afterwards. He was somewhere in the stadium during the game and, believe me, he wasn't working in the peanut concessions. If I was "asking for it," or if my scene with Sammy White was "unbelievable," then why didn't the commissioner come down on me right then and there?

My hit on Sammy and the antics afterwards were part of that particular Super Bowl Sunday and viewed by the sports journalists from the smallest, one-horse town to the greatest cities of this country. Strange, but I never saw a single printed word of complaint in any newspaper or scandal sheet — including the *Boston Herald American*.

Then, a couple of years later, I write the book and all of a sudden someone is giving me "enough rope" with the suspicion that I'm about to hang myself. Give me a break … please.

I was only a few paragraphs into Fitzgerald's article and it was already smelling like the stockyards after the filming of a Merrill Lynch commercial. The stench was getting to me, but I bravely continued reading. Once again, I cautioned myself to read every word because only a real dork would form opinions from hearsay and excerpts.

Joe Fitzgerald again quoted me, and accurately I might add, "I never make a tackle just to bring someone down. I want to punish the man I'm going after and I want him to know that it's going to hurt every time he comes my way … I like to believe that my best hits border on felonious assault."

Pete Rozelle quickly answered my self-incriminating felonious assault statement by saying, "Jesus! I'm just trying to think of what would be a sensible thing to say in light of litigation and everything."

Strange, but after reading Pete's comments I too was trying to think of what would be a sensible thing to say.

"Litigation and everything?" Was he serious?

Once again I didn't understand what the heck was going on. Why was Pete so upset? This was the commissioner of the NFL and I couldn't believe he didn't know that the premeditated contact of professional football doesn't border on felonious assault, it is felonious assault. Surely, Pete Rozelle must have some vague notion that the marketing potential of the NFL was built on the foundation of legal mayhem and not the ballpark hot dogs they serve.

Just because we call it a "game" and have a set of hypocritical rules that separate felonious stadium action from real life conduct doesn't alter the true facts. I knew what was legal on the football field, and I know a little about the laws of society. After all, I've been in both arenas. I've been a part-time warrior and a part-time fan, but I've been honest about my involvement in both worlds.

Football is no different from boxing or hockey, or any of the other violent contact sports. Athletes are given the green light and expected to do things on the field, in the ring and on the rink that differ from the laws of society. So why would anyone get uptight or be surprised because I honestly believe and accurately wrote that my best hits bordered on felonious assault?

I was beginning to feel as though I were in one of those damned if you do, damned if you don't situations. I mean, had I written, "my best hits bordered on a misdemeanor," people would have laughed at me and the title of Assassin would have had little or no impact.

Concerning my wasting of Sammy White, I could have made up some yarn about trying to avoid full-speed or head-on contact and that I accidentally ran into him. Then I could have written that I was apologizing instead of taunting. With that, I would have been branded a liar, sounded like a fool, never made the headlines in the *Boston Herald American*, and the title of my first book would have been *They Call Me Hypocrite*.

That particular book wouldn't have been all that controversial and we all know what sells books. Here I go again, asking for more rope. But since I've touched upon the words "sells books," I realize that some enterprising journalist or critic is no doubt going to mention royalties and that usually brings up the subject of dirty old money. I've heard it said that the only reason I wrote the book was for the money. Now how does one even begin to answer a brilliant statement like that?

Hold onto your chairs because I'm going to try to answer those critics and everyone will be surprised as to my reason for writing the book and even why I risked serious injury playing football all of those years. I'm probably the only individual in the world with this philosophy and, call it greed if you so desire, but I did write the book for the money. That's why I played football. Oh, sure, there were other reasons for doing both, but ranking right at the top of my list was money. And money was probably the second, third and fourth reasons, too.

My problem is that I have all of these bad habits such as eating, needing a roof over my head and the other basics of supporting myself in a decent and honorable fashion. I discovered that making money the old-fashioned way seemed to satisfy my physical and mental needs. So I've earned my living through the hard work of professional football and the honest words of a book. I feel pretty good about my accomplishments in both worlds, too.

I'm sure that everyone else is different and I'm probably the only individual in the world motivated by money. It's not that I don't get involved in other things, but money definitely seems to be one of the priorities in my life.

It's like I said, I'm different, and I have a hard time believing that tale about money being the root of all evil. I like to think that money can be good and money can be bad — it's good to have money and bad when you don't.

For some strange reason I feel good when I'm honestly earning money. It gives me the feeling of a security blanket, but it also enables me to do other things. Money gives me the opportunity to share with charities, to work with young people, and to have a scholarship fund set up in my name so that some deserving high school kids can get a college education. There's more, but it's not that important to our story because I'm not attempting to convince anyone that I am a saint. I'm only a human being.

Okay, so what if I did write the book for money? Or so what if I did write the book because I had a story to tell? So what if I'm writing another book because of money? Or so what if I have something else to say? The point is that I've been honest from the wasting of Sammy White to the writing of the story, and the hierarchy of the NFL along with journalists simply haven't recognized that fact. But I know, I know … I'm sensationalizing and capitalizing on the painful, dark side of football. The NFL knows that side of the sport exists. I know it exists. Everyone knows it exists, but no one is supposed to turn a profit from pain and punishment.

This is going to come as a real surprise to Pete Rozelle and my other critics, but when Pete was commissioner, there was a company turning a profit from the violence of professional football. *Sports Illustrated*, in conjunction with NFL Films, Inc., has a video on the market called *Crunch Course*. *Sports Illustrated* and NFL Films, Inc., unannounced, I'm sure, to the league office, have taken films of the hardest, most violent hits in the history of professional football and marketed a video tape.

Did I say, "hardest, most violent hits in the history of the NFL and marketed a video tape?"

I did, and for some reason I'm reminded about "an old saying which maintains that if you give some people enough rope, they'll hang themselves."

If my published story about Sammy White was "asking for it," then the *Crunch Course* video is worthy of Joe Fitzgerald and Pete Rozelle forming the lynch mob. For openers, the *Crunch Course* video comes in this attractive little box featuring a mugging of Dallas Cowboy running back, Hershel Walker. Two Denver Bronco defenders are physically holding up Hershel as a big defensive lineman is honing in on his midsection. It's a technique the Denver fans boast about calling the "Orange Crush."

If an oily journalist ever got wind of the cover of that video, good Lord, there's no telling where it would end up. Why I might see an article that reads: There's an old cliché which maintains that a picture is worth a thousand words, and the suspicion here is that NFL Films has published a home video depicting atrocities worse than the unimaginable horrors of Auschwitz.

"Golly," the head honcho might say when informed of this video, "Does that kind of stuff really happen? Gee whiz!"

Sprinkling a little aviation fuel around the office of the head honcho, the enterprising journalist would twist his shining black mustache and read the billing on the cover of this inflammatory video. "Forty-two hard-hitting minutes of the NFL's outstanding defenders, past and present, who have elevated the art of punishing ball carriers into a science."

"My goodness," the head honcho would say while sitting up rigidly, "should I use the red phone and call the president? Should we nuke 'em? … By the way, who's behind NFL Films, Inc.?"

The oily journalist would smirk and answer, "You figure it out." Then, casually lighting his cigar, he flips the match in the direction of the bewildered head honcho and exits stage left.

Well, they can't blame that one on Jack Tatum, but give me some more rope because here I go again.

Crunch is brutal and violent, and much more. Jeff Kaye, the narrator of the film, says of the officials and players, "But the men who wore stripes on the field were no match for men who behaved like they should have been wearing stripes off the field." Damn, it sounds like a prison movie to me.

Don Paul, a soft-spoken linebacker with the Rams during the '50s tells the audience, "I could do things on the field that I enjoyed doing that I would probably be put in a pokey for if I weren't on the field. Not that I'm a flat criminal … it was a way of expressing myself."

Leo Nomellini, a defensive tackle with the 49ers said of his peers, "If they could kill you, they'd kill you honestly. Okay? But nothin' dirty. Nothin' wrong with drawin' a little blood here and there …"

Kill you honestly?

Don't get excited, Pete, but Leo doesn't mean kill as in death by murder. When Leo uses the word kill, it was a form of simple football jargon acceptable to most folks. It's similar to "wasting" a receiver.

I know what Pete Rozelle is thinking right about now, and, yes, there's a Commandment that clearly states, "Thou shalt not kill."

It's difficult to explain, Pete, but Leo means a different kind of kill.

If a person can't understand my "wasting" of Sammy White, or the "kill you honestly" of Leo Nomellini, then I could be here the rest of my life attempting to explain the meaning of smashed, peeled, a pasting, beat, stick 'em, crushed, hammered, stuff 'em, stomped, kick 'em, pounded, punished, blasted, jam it down their throats, etc. … and those are only a sample of the printable words. If Pete Rozelle, during his thirty years at the helm of the NFL, ever came down on the field and heard those guttural sounding words of a football game, he would have quickly retreated to the men's room in need of clean underwear.

I don't know why, but every time I hear the word, "commissioner," I'm reminded of a chief inspector and I keep seeing this Pink Panther in my imagination.

The next time CBS, ABC, NBC and ESPN cover an NFL game and a commentator uses one of those inflammatory words to describe a particular play, Pete Rozelle and Joe Fitzgerald should collaborate on a sequel to their silly article on my book.

If there were one thousand people in a room, a journalist and an ex-commissioner included, I'd be willing to bet that exactly 998 of those individuals would know what Leo meant when he said "kill." With odds like that, why even waste the time explaining turf talk to those who will never understand or to those who do understand but are more than willing to exploit and capitalize on the situation?

Perhaps I am about to slip the noose around my own neck, but here goes anyway. I've been extremely kind in quoting the players who appear in *Crunch Course* interviews. There is enough conversation on that tape to make my "felonious assault" remark sound like kid stuff. There is talk about cheap shots, getting even, punching, gouging, killing. You can hear a little cussing and a whole lot of BLEEPS. If you're into sadism, get a copy of the tape and listen for yourself, because the best conversation of all is with a respected and celebrated Hall of Fame linebacker talking about his favorite movie — "I got kind of a charge out of that scene when this head comes rolling down the stairs." He said, "I tried to project those kind of things happening out on the field ... ah, not to me."

Hold onto your chair because here I go. I believe *Crunch Course* is a quality video. It's about football, football players, and everything else that *Sports Illustrated* claims, "Forty-two hard-hitting minutes of the NFL's outstanding defenders, past and present, who have elevated the art of punishing ball carriers into a science."

Seriously, I'd support that video even if I wasn't part of those "outstanding defenders, past and present, who have elevated the art of punishing ball carriers into a science." And I mean that.

I'd tell all of my friends to subscribe to *Sports Illustrated* and get a copy of that video even if my collision with running back Earl Campbell wasn't included in those "forty-two hard-hitting minutes."

I'm serious. I would support the NFL Films' *Crunch Course* video no matter what ... even if they had not used the film of "my wasting Sammy White."

But they did and now there goes that Pink Panther again!

By now Joe Fitzgerald's motivation for fanning the spark was rather obvious. Hey, there's nothing wrong with sensationalizing and capitalizing on a story that will sell newspapers. But I was wondering if Joe could actually pull everything off. I know it was looking pretty good for him right about now; but most of the time, when a person gets involved in a two-sided controversy, he usually walks away having made a friend and a bitter enemy.

I didn't think that Joe and I would ever become friends because, as a rule, I don't get along with journalists. Then again, at the time, it didn't seem as though we were going to part as enemies, either. I wanted to sell books and the more controversy the better. But some people didn't want me to sell books and the less controversy the better. Someone was going to win and someone was going to lose, and it wasn't a telephone I heard ringing. It was cash registers at B. Daltons's, Waldenbooks and Crown's Books.

To make it all work, Fitzgerald needed to convince someone that my hit during Super Bowl XI was the now-solved crime of the century. That same someone had to be convinced that justice could only be served through a lynchin'.

The first step of the plan was to write an article about old sayings, and plant the thought of enough rope. The second phrase would be to subtly mention hanging and, in the same paragraph, use the words "inflammatory autobiography."

That was the easy part of the scheme, and now came the easiest step of all: finding that one naïve individual, that only person in a world of four-and-a-half billion people who would be gullible enough to believe everything to the point of coming after the villain.

If it took Joe Fitzgerald a minute to write the first paragraph of the article, it only took him several seconds to search throughout the ranks of humankind to find his boob to bait. From that point in time, it became a matter of telling the secretary, "Get me the commissioner on the telephone while I wash my hands."

I knew that Fitzgerald got Pete all riled up and that the league office was planning some sort of a necktie party. But since I'm more of a casual dresser, I wasn't about to let anyone put a tie, or anything for that matter, around my neck.

Joe Fitzgerald was slick enough to know that Pete would take the bait and come after me through the press and other avenues. I'd venture a guess Joe also figured that because he broke the story to the league office, the *Boston Herald American* wasn't going to be just another newspaper hounding the commissioner for the follow-up stories. From now on, Joe Fitzgerald was going to be one of Pete's boys. At least Pete would read it that way, but only Joe Fitzgerald would know the real truth as to who was standing up doing the coaching and who was bending over playing receiver.

Joe Fitzgerald was going to have the best of two worlds — three worlds if you count the points he scored with his boss. He knew the league office and all of the high-powered attorneys in the world couldn't do anything about my writing an honest book, but he would fuel the controversy anyway. It was good for business — his business of selling newspapers and my business of selling books. I couldn't get mad about that, and … so what if Pete Rozelle was dumb enough to fall for the ploy and still think Joe was a straight shooter.

Far be it from me to criticize or pass judgment on a man capable of playing both sides against the middle and actually getting away with it. Me? I'd rather take a firm stand and ply hard at one facet of the game instead of trying to walk along both sidelines at the same time. Doing it that way, sometimes I lose the game, but it's those times when I win that really make me feel good about being me.

Most journalists are involved in that game, but rarely do they pull it off. That's why we hear stories about phony journalists being booted from locker rooms by the coaches, or the stories about players taking offense at slanderous write-ups and wanting to come after the wimp who wrote the crap.

Journalists are protected by the law. It's called freedom of speech. First Amendment rights protect the sports journalists when they write sleazy articles about athletes, but in the eyes of the commissioner the same law shouldn't apply to athletes writing honest books about the establishment. Because of this freedom of speech amendment, the journalists know the athletes' hands are tied and most of them are smart enough to stay away from the sidelines during the game. Every so often it happens though, the athlete gets ahold of one of those skinny-necked turkeys and does a feather dusting of four walls, a ceiling and a floor. It's fun for a while, but everything usually ends up in litigation.

Al Capone would occasionally slap a copper back in line but never a reporter. Even Big Al knew the pen was mightier than the machine gun, and if he couldn't fight it, no one can. That's why I just roll with the cheap shots most journalists have taken at me. That's why I just mind my own business. After all, sticks and stones will break my bones, but words will never hurt them.

I can understand why some people thought that I was upset with the way Joe Fitzgerald handled everything. But I wasn't. He did me a favor by not reading the book before he started piping off. Why, he might have read the book and discovered that I wasn't such a bad guy. Then where would I be?

In one sense, Joe did me a best-selling favor. I sold a lot of books and made plenty of dirty old money. I was happy and Pete Rozelle seemed happy, too. For what? Who knows. Maybe Joe Fitzgerald patted Pete on the back and said, "You done good, Pete. You done good."

Seriously, I can't get upset because Joe Fitzgerald was clever enough to dupe Pete Rozelle into believing the published story of Sammy White's Super Bowl mugging was my stepping forth from the closet and confessing to a perfect crime. I can't get upset if Joe tricked Pete into taking offense at my using the words, "wasting, punishing ... and I want him (the receiver) to know that it's going to hurt every time he comes my way."

The fact is that all defensive and offensive players have, in football vernacular, wasted and punished and hurt a few people during the course of their careers. I think it's silly for Pete Rozelle, or anyone, to stand up in public and insist that NFL hits do not border on felonious assaults. But that is Pete's image problem and not mine.

All the same though, I gotta hand it to Joe Fitzgerald for pulling everything off. It takes a unique individual to instigate a fight and walk away with everyone thinking you did him a favor. Joe Fitzgerald did exactly that, and hopefully he'll get involved again. This time I'll even send him the excerpts. I'll even pay for the telephone calls to our retired commissioner, wherever he might be hanging out these days.

The next time I want Joe Fitzgerald to be a little more careful about hammering my character and public image. I want to make money, but I'd like to be able to go out in public and spend it without the fear of people trying to lynch me. I found out that many people actually believe what they read in the newspaper. Sometimes a shoddy bit of journalism can really hurt a person, but I wasn't complaining … yet.

If the first part of Fitzgerald's article had me counting the gold bars at Fort Knox, the second phase of the story sounded more like a burglar alarm warning the guards that someone had illegally entered the vault.

Joe Fitzgerald figured that since he put a word in for me at the league office, he might as well go the extra mile. Telephoning the Raider's organization, he reached Al LoCassale, an executive assistant to owner and managing partner, Al Davis.

Here we go again. Al LoCassale hadn't read the book either, but nonetheless, he thought I was being "exploited" by the publisher. It seemed those excerpts had arrived on his desk before the book, and Al was making a case out of that "best hits border on felonious assaults" statement of mine.

Al LoCassale wasn't damning or condemning me, like some people. He was investigating the situation with a more open mind. Unlike someone from the league office, and I won't mention Pete's last name, Al had a more professional and intelligent approach to everything. He wasn't going to get bowled over by a couple of excerpts or the city slicker talking on the phone from Boston. Al wasn't having trouble with the fact that NFL hits border on felonious assault, but he was having a problem with me writing those words.

"Knowing Jack, and you're talking about a nice kid here," Al was quoted by Fitzgerald, "I can't picture him using the word 'felonious' or the term 'felonious assault.' That's not Jack Tatum."

I appreciate Al LoCassale coming to my defense, but I would and could and did use the word felonious. The Raider organization, management and players included, are close and share a legitimate sense of loyalty toward each other. It begins at the top with Al Davis and runs down through the ranks. Joe Fitzgerald had an easy time with his "Let's hang Tatum" scheme on the east coast, but the movement was met with resistance in the west.

"Felonious assault" wasn't an expression I often used, but I knew what it meant and wouldn't change it in the book even if I could. Felonious assault … I started thinking about those words and for some reason my memory started working.

I was actually seeing the words "felonious assault" on a page of a book and suddenly I realized it wasn't titled *They Call Me Assassin*.

At that exact moment another word bounced around inside of my mind, and to coin an old Al LoCassale expression, "I can't picture him actually using the word plagiarize as in plagiarizing."

That was when the alarm sounded and I stopped counting the gold. It was getting a little scary so I got out of the vault.

Steve Cassidy had written a book titled *The Good Guys*. It was a story about the history of the Raiders' organization and was a favorite of management and players alike. We helped Steve promote his book and I did some work with him on a few other projects.

By now, everything was crystal clear — the words of Steve's book, that is. He did a little section in the book about the Raiders hiring a "warhead for their dormant missile." This dude was "the Assassin that no winning team is without." In fact, this dude tackled so hard that his "best hits bordered on felonious assault."

All of a sudden Pete's statement about "litigation and everything" was making a little sense. But hell, to my knowledge, Pete didn't know Steve Cassidy. When *The Good Guys* was published, no one in the league office had anything to say about the book, good or bad.

"Naw," I told myself. "Don't be givin' Pete too much credit. His 'litigation and everything' remark was still spontaneously stupid."

Let's see here … I never charged Steve for my pictures in any of his books. I was always an accommodating gentleman in helping him to promote his work. I think he's a marvelous writer, and I have no plans to sue for all those slanderous remarks about me being "a warhead" for a dormant missile or an "Assassin that no winning team is without" or even that character-tarnishing remark about my best hits "bordering on felonious assault."

After glancing at copyright laws, I decided the best defense wasn't a good offense. I was hoping that "out of sight, out of mind" would apply with Steve Cassidy, and I spent the next several months doing just that — hiding out.

Then one day, as fate would have it, we bumped into each other. I was doing everything possible to avoid any conversation on my book, but all of a sudden Steve blurts out, "By the way, Jack, did you know that you used some quotes of mine in your book?"

"Really?" I was trying to look surprised, like I didn't know what he was talking about.

Then with a wry grin Steve tells me he has another book coming out … and, well, he knows how busy I am and everything, but he wants me to help him promote it. And only because I'm a nice guy, I did.

Finally, I got around to talking with Steve Cassidy about the book — mine. He thought it was a fantastic job and then some. Most of the people who read the book had a similar opinion. Even

Al LoCassale.

Al stopped worrying about the felonious assault statement long enough to read, and I might add, enjoy the book. Not that he agreed with everything I wrote, because he didn't. For some reason he would occasionally bring up the "felonious assault" issue almost believing I would finally say that it wasn't me. But Al LoCassale never questioned my rights or motives for doing the book. He never said that I was boasting, or that my tackles didn't border on felonious assaults, or that I did it for the money. Amen.

The commissioner made a lot to do about nothing, but I enjoy a good laugh as much as the next man. However, there was still the last half of Joe Fitzgerald's article and that wasn't a joking matter.

I've mentioned cheap-shot journalism and there's not much a person can really do. The reporter quotes you out of context, adds a little inference along with a few choice words and all of a sudden you're sounding more like a terrorist driving a battered old Mercedes filled with dynamite than a professional athlete. It's not just me or athletes in general, it's everyone and anyone in the public's eye.

I have a friend who worked on a movie with Priscilla Presley in Thailand and the Bahamas. He got to know Priscilla fairly well and even met her daughter Lisa Marie. I was curious as to what kind of a lady she was behind the scenes and away from the camera. It's a stupid thing for me to say, but reading about her and Lisa Marie in the newspapers and tabloids, I had formed a negative opinion. I had this notion that they were both a couple of snooty rich bitches always fighting like a cat and dog.

My friend said, "Don't believe that garbage you read in the news-papers and tabloids about Priscilla and Lisa Marie. Damn, Jack, you of all people should understand better than anyone. You know that most of the time reporters are nothing but a bunch of liars and cons."

He went on to tell me that Priscilla was a hard-working person. She was determined to become a good actress, and her talent had nothing to do with a last name. Then he said, "She's a good lady, and what's more, she's a damn good mother, too."

Reporters come with the turf and are part of the occupational hazards anytime a person steps into the limelight, or in my case, places their head in the noose. I may be using the title, but believe me, most journalists are the real assassins.

I'm thinking about once-upon-a-time presidential hopeful Gary Hart. I guess that old saying of "enough rope" really applied in his case.

The journalists were out to get him and they did exactly that. Of course, they had to hide in garbage cans, sleep in dumpsters, waddle in gutters and when Gary sat down on the toilet he probably heard voices coming from the pipes below. But go ahead and flush because it was worth it. They got their man.

Hey, so what if there was a little "monkey business" involved. And so what if a lady came to his place in the middle of the night. I'm not passing judgment on what happened either way, because I don't know. And does anyone writing the story actually know the truth?

My point is that journalists will stoop to any depth to get you, and once the rope is around your neck, right or wrong, it's over. To hell with your wife, children, family, friends and any hint of respectability thereafter. When they get you, they've got you, and it's over.

I know! I know! It's their job. Doing a job is one thing, but the fact is that most journalists have no scruples. Right or wrong is never a prerequisite to duty, and therefore, most journalists usually create distorted images of real people in the spotlight.

I can't say if the journalists were right or wrong in their assessment of Gary Hart's situation with Donna Rice, but I have a friend who knows the real Priscilla Presley, and I know Jack Tatum better than anyone.

I've been pretty honest with myself as to how I lived my life and how I played the game of football. In life I've always had a laid-back style, but I played football the only way it can be played — hard and aggressively.

Make no mistake about it, I was an intimidating assassin. I didn't want my peers to like me when I was on the football field. I wanted them to respect me. Every football player who is honest with himself will tell you exactly the same thing — respect, you've gotta earn their respect. Putting aside big salaries and championship rings, football comes down to a game of respect — they've gotta earn my respect and I've gotta earn theirs.

On the football field, I didn't like Walter Payton. He ran too hard, played too aggressively and much too violently; but I surely respected him.

On the football field, I didn't like Miami receiver Paul Warfield. He was quick and fast, caught just about everything thrown in his direction, and he couldn't be intimidated, but I respected him.

During Super Bowl XI when I saw Sammy White coming over the middle, I didn't like him. But when he got up and returned to the game, I sure as hell respected him.

It's ironic, but nearly every sports journalist in the country criticized my writing about "wasting Sammy White," but not one person ever mentioned my last words on the subject.

"Late in the game I was surprised to see Sammy White back in the lineup. He's a great receiver and I respect him as a man and as an athlete. I was glad that Sammy was okay because I think he is a tremendous person." —Jack Tatum, *They Call Me Assassin.*

To quote me on that published fact would be an indication that perhaps I did have a degree of sensitivity or that maybe there was a decent streak to my character after all. But hey, I understand. If you're going to hang a guy, you want to make sure it's a tight knot and that no one watching the execution is going to have second thoughts about him being a miserable SOB.

George Atkinson, a former teammate and good friend, and I went to watch a cowboy movie. The movie started off where a group of ranchers spotted a dude on the range with a bunch of cattle.

It turns out that the ranchers are looking for a cattle rustler and this dude had all of these cattle. They called it "insurmountable evidence, an airtight case. Guilty! Hang the bastard!"

One of the ranchers throws a rope over the limb of a nearby tree. It's looking real bad for the dude with the cows.

"But just wait a second here," the dude with the cows says. He's getting a little pissed off. George and I can see it in his eyes. "I gotta bill of sale for these cattle."

George and I both know that these ranchers are not going to waste a lot of time reading a stupid bill of sale. Who knows, maybe they can't even read.

Quicker than we can say "Pete Rozelle," they string up the dude and ride off.

Now the movie starts … it turns out the dude swinging from the limb with this rope stretching his neck is Clint Eastwood. I hope to tell you that when he gets loose, and he does get loose, the ranchers are going to have one riled-up cowpuncher on their hands. And what's more, Clint doesn't take prisoners.

The ranchers had to be complete fools because everyone should know that, if you're going to lynch a dude, make sure he's thoroughly lynched before you ride off. Think about that one for a moment…

Most people come to a point in life when they stop and look back at where they've been. It's no different for me; and naturally, I'm often asked if there is anything I would change if I had it to do over again.

That's an interesting and difficult question to answer, but I'll try. Now, if it were possible to change a little bit of history, I would aim a little lower; but the velocity and intent would still be the same.

My answer probably doesn't make much sense right now, but trust me and it will.

In October of 1988, the L.A. Raiders came up to San Francisco for a game with the 49ers. This event prompted the newspaper article, "Mortality in the Secondary."

Lowell Cohn writes for the *San Francisco Chronicle* and his story featured hard hitting and 49er defensive backs Ronnie Lott and Eric Wright.

In the article, Ronnie Lott told Cohn that meeting yours truly was the biggest thrill of his life.

Surprised? Don't be. I still have a few friends, you know.

Lott said, "I enjoy Jack's physicalness. Gosh, for a DB to hit with that authority. I couldn't see myself not wanting to hit like him. When I watch films and see good hits, I get tingles. It's an unbelievable rush."

Cohn, a professional, was working on a legitimate article and so he quickly pointed out to his reading audience: "It's not that Lott is a sadist — far from it."

About that time I started thinking that someone should warn Ronnie Lott about Pete Rozelle and journalists in general. It's not a good idea for Ronnie to make statements such as, "I enjoyed Jack's physicalness — hit with that authority — couldn't see myself not wanting to hit like him…" And Ronnie, to think that you are a Jack Tatum fan is one thing, but to have the balls to mention it in public is, in the words of Pete, "asking for it."

Ronnie Lott continued to explain a little more about hitting. He mentioned that the 49ers' defensive unit can't stand any teammate who's afraid to hit. The article reads: "If a guy comes out for the team and he doesn't really blast people, the other DBs stay away from him. At first, they had their doubts about DB Tim McKyer." It seemed that Tim McKyer wasn't hitting up to 49er standards. It wasn't until he started launching his body into the opposition that the other defensive players accepted him.

Then, Cohn got around to asking Ronnie Lott about Raider All-Pro running back, Marcus Allen. Ronnie and Marcus were teammates at USC. Cohn wanted to know how Lott played against his friend. Did he hit Marcus Allen hard considering they were teammates and are still close friends?

"No question," Lott replied. "I've taken some of the best shots of my career at him. If I didn't, he'd lose respect for me."

Cohn then asked him, "What would happen if you hit Allen so hard you broke his neck?"

Lott replied, "It would be the worst feeling of my life."

"What if you hurt him badly, and then you could turn back time. Would you hit him as hard all over again?" Cohn asked.

Lott answered, "If life was like a tape recording and I could run it backward, I'd try to do something different. I'd drop an inch lower.

I'd still have the same velocity, the same intent."

Cohn then turned to Eric Wright, another 49er defensive back. He began the same line of questioning. Cohn wrote, "Wright is friendly and decent, and he couldn't understand why he should be merciful."

"If I ever feel bad after hitting someone, that's the time for me to quit," Eric said. "When I see the ball coming, I lick my chops. Here comes a big hit I would love to have. You lay for the big hits."

I was hoping, for Eric's sake, that Pete Rozelle wasn't reading this article ... or worse yet, that Joe Fitzgerald wasn't reading it.

Continuing on, Cohn wrote, "I asked what he would do if he permanently disabled someone, but then had the chance to turn back time and do the play again."

Eric answered, "I wouldn't do anything different."

After a moment of thought, Eric Wright said, "I hope to get a really good hit on a guy. Unconsciously, I think he's going to jump right back up. If he didn't, God, I would hate to be in that situation."

Ronnie Lott is right — it is the worst feeling of my life. It's like Eric said: "God, I hate to be in this situation. If we could run the tape recorder backward and do it over, I too, would aim an inch lower, but the velocity and the intent would still be the same."

I'm sorry that I can't change events, sorry that it happened, sorry that he didn't jump up, sorry that nothing I ever do or say will make it better.

I realized long ago that journalists would never again write my name without mentioning Darryl Stingley. For those of you who don't remember or never heard the story, let me explain. August 12, 1978, during an exhibition game against the New England Patriots, I tackled wide receiver Darryl Stingley. It wasn't a hard hit, but Darryl never walked again. To this day, Darryl Stingley is paralyzed from the neck down.

Of course, with excerpts from my book in hand, Joe Fitzgerald was on the telephone to Darryl's attorney, Jack Sands. And, of course, with a little inference and quoting me out of context my portrait was beginning to resemble a bloodthirsty savage, void of sensitivity or compassion for my peers. After all, with my "boasting" about wasting Sammy White, it wasn't difficult to build a case against me. What is it they say? Guilty until proven innocent ... isn't that how it goes?

I've heard it said that I deliberately tried to injure Darryl, that I could have stopped before hitting him, that I didn't have to hit so hard. WRONG!

I've heard every expert and critic tell what they would have done in that split second of time before two bodies collided in what is football's most horrible tragedy. Perhaps the experts and critics, if they were in my shoes on that particular night, would have had a premonition and never made the tackle in the first place. Or perhaps the experts and critics would have had the ability to change direction just prior to impact or maybe stop in the instant the ball fell incomplete.

Maybe there is a superman playing football who can react in a split second of time, but I change my clothes in the locker room and not in a phone booth. Maybe there are psychics who see tomorrow, but I was paid to make tackles and not read Tarot cards.

The critics make noise after the fact and some people begin to believe that the accident could have been avoided. But there were two athletes and neither man was able to react in a split second of time. Who's right? Who's wrong? Well ... if there wasn't a real life villain to point the finger at, maybe football and the rules of the game would be the main culprit.

I'm not trying to blame football or indict the NFL and I make no claim of being an angel. What happened was within the confines of the rules and part of the game. Writing that kind of statement doesn't mean that I have no remorse or sensitivity. It simply means that if two athletes are playing within the structure of the rules and one of them ends up disabled for life, then maybe it's time to rethink our priorities. Maybe it is time for the NFL to give some serious thought to the game, the players and their safety.

Most of the sporting world believes I wrote *They Call Me Assassin* to capitalize on Darryl Stingley's tragedy. WRONG! I was working on the book long before the accident. The true motivation behind my doing a book wasn't to "boast" about wasting people. There was more to my story than hitting and hurting; but, in order to discover the essence of the book, one would have to read the book.

Naturally, I wanted to tell my life story, but I also wanted it to be a football book about football players. Professional football is a violent game and it takes a rare breed of athlete to play it. I didn't see anything wrong with an account of war and its warriors.

I was honest and accurate about the violence, but there was the other side of my story that got lost. Few individuals know the truth, but I had a chapter on rule changes that I believed, and still believe, would make the game safer. Sure, I was an assassin, but I was also a crusader.

Many journalists and critics are going to find that last statement hard to believe, but then again, many journalists and critics didn't read the book before trying to lynch me.

I find it incredible that no one, at least to my knowledge, ever quoted me concerning my thoughts on the safety of the players and changing rules to eliminate some of the violence and mayhem. Don't take my word for it, get a copy of the book and read it.

I suggested rule changes to protect the quarterbacks. The commissioner should get a copy of *They Call Me Assassin* and pay particular attention to that section ... but then again, keeping NFL quarterbacks healthy has never been much of a problem. Only a couple of dozen quarterbacks went down in 1988.

I suggested outlawing zone coverage and going with strictly man-to-man defenses. That way, it would become a game of push and shove, bump and run. It would surely save a lot of wear and tear on receivers and defensive backs, but I guess that wouldn't work because even though we'd reduce injuries, we'd be eliminating some of those head-on collisions. Fans don't want to see football players running around the field playing tag. Football is bodies crashing into bodies — full speed, head-on and with no regard for safety. That's what the fans pay for: a football game where a receiver thinks it was man-to-man coverage only to wake up the next day realizing that an assassin was sitting back in a zone just waiting to make the highlight tape of the NFL's *Crunch Course.*

Ask Sammy White. He saw man-to-man coverage, and our corner-back, Skip Thomas, was playing him man-to-man. Guess what? I wasn't!

If there was a man-to-man rule I wouldn't have been there waiting for him to take the bait. I would have been off somewhere chasing another receiver and Sammy wouldn't have stopped running until he reached the goal line. But what would the fans rather see, Sammy in the end zone dancing, or Jack taunting a receiver who can't find his eyeballs? Sorry, Sammy, nothing personal ... I was just playing by the rules.

If the league didn't like changing the rule to a straight man-to-man coverage in the secondary, then I suggested eliminating the receivers running quick slants. The way it reads now, a receiver bolts off the line, runs a quick slant and the defender doesn't have a chance to play the ball even if he wanted. It's a situation where the defender can only come after the receiver in a physical way. It's macho football where the defender has to get after the receiver — strictly physical, punishment, pain and worse.

It's ironic, but I was writing about that particular rule change in June of 1978 ... just before I left for training camp ... just before the exhibition season ... just before August 12th. I thought it was a dangerous situation — that quick slant. Strange, but I'm still thinking it's a dangerous situation.

Maybe I did have a premonition or was a little psychic because I always believed that someone was going to get seriously hurt while he was running or defending the quick slant.

An athlete wearing a different colored uniform ran a quick slant against the Raiders' secondary on a warm balmy night in Oakland, California, on August 12, 1978. I reacted to the play like always — quick, aggressive, and with a mean intent. They teach the technique in high school, work on it in college and perfect it in the pros. You've got to play the man and you've got to be physical.

It wasn't a particularly hard hit. It was a good hit, but nothing that would awe the crowd. Just another play.

I remember thinking, damn … I wish the hell they wouldn't keep running that slant. They had run that play two or three times already.

I turned and began walking back to our huddle, then I realized the other man was still down. I saw the trainers coming out onto the field … then I saw Darryl. I expected him to get up … he never did!

The quick slant is similar to a dangerous intersection without a red light. It was a rural road intersecting a four-lane highway. There were a lot of accidents at that intersection, and people were always getting hurt. But the Department of Highways never did anything.

Then one day a couple of teenage girls were on their way to a basketball game. They pulled up to the stop sign and saw a truck coming. The driver thought she could make it, but a vehicle passing the truck was coming too fast…

There's a light at that intersection now … and not more than a hundred yards up the road, just off to the right, is a cemetery.

I think about that intersection every so often and the fact that two lives had to be lost before changes were made. I also think about combination defenses, slant patterns, violent hits and I wonder what it's going to take for those changes to be made.

All of a sudden the status of being a best-selling author wasn't an enjoyable experience. I had written a book … hard-hitting, yes, but there was also that plea for rule changes and a genuine concern for the safety of the players. Yet, in light of the controversy, my crusade was overlooked and simply ignored.

Darryl's attorney, Jack Sands, drafted a letter to Pete Rozelle asking that I be suspended immediately. He also launched a campaign to have the book banned. And attorneys are supposed to be educated people.

The book wasn't banned. I never thought it would be. I wasn't suspended; even Pete Rozelle had better sense than that. But the spark once fanned by Joe Fitzgerald had become a flame, the flame a fire, the fire an inferno. Let it burn itself out … because I'm tired of fighting.

In October of 1988, Ed Glavin, an associate producer with *The Morton Downey, Jr., Show* telephoned me. They were going to do a program on violence in sports and Mort wanted me to be on his show. Boy, I didn't know about that…

For the past decade I hadn't been into giving interviews, much less guest appearances on television. It had to do with asshole journalists and for some reason Mort Downey, Jr., reminded me of old newspapers covering the floor of a dog kennel. I still gave the matter some thought because maybe some good could come out of it all. Then I realized the timing conflicted with another commitment.

Just for the record, Ohio State was having a reunion honoring the 1969 National Championship Team. I was a member of that team and there were several other things on my schedule. I couldn't make the program and canceled.

I guess I was expected to drop all of my plans and run because *The Morton Downey, Jr., Show* had called. When I didn't, Mort became upset with me. At least that's what I've been told.

It turned out that Darryl Stingley was scheduled to be on that same show. It's a well-publicized fact that I haven't seen or talked with Darryl since the incident. But I'll get into all of that in a later chapter.

The program was aired. I didn't see it. Then again, Morton Downey, Jr., isn't something I usually stay up to watch. I did, however, hear about the program from a number of close friends.

Mort, I understand, did a telephone interview with Darryl. I guess I wasn't the only no-show. I also understand that Mort said Darryl was a "helluva guy." Even Morton Downey, Jr., can be right once in a while.

Then came the assault of Jack Tatum. It was reported to me that Mort said I was gutless for not showing up, and that I was a "sleaze-bucket." Or was it a "bucket of sleaze?"

I am told that Mort really did a number on me. He thought it was sinful for anyone to deliberately injure another human being and then write a book bragging about it.

Conrad Dobler was one of Mort's guests for that show. Conrad, while playing offensive line for the St. Louis Cardinals, had developed a reputation as a dirty player. After retiring, he wrote a book titled, *They Call Me Dirty*.

I wonder where he got that title? Knowing Conrad the way I know Conrad, I'll bet he wrote the book for many reasons … but money was probably right up on top of the list.

Anyway, back to Morton Downey. I guess Conrad stuck up for

me and made a statement that no one in professional football plans to hurt another guy and then pulls it off. He told Mort that my hit on Darryl wasn't a cheap shot, that it couldn't have been avoided, and that it was part of the game.

I wonder why Conrad would even bother defending me. Oh, it's not that I didn't appreciate it, because I did. But after so long, I've learned to live with it. You see, there's a million Morton Downey, Jrs., out in the world … you know, big mouths who never have the facts and yet they're always piping off about one cause today, and tomorrow finds them charging forth representing the other side. Sort of like journalists.

To be sure I had my facts in line, I had a friend call *The Morton Downey, Jr., Show* and talk with Ed Glavin. I wanted to be sure that Mort did call me those names, and I wanted to be sure that he did have his facts all screwed up. He did call me some names … big deal, and he did have all of his facts screwed up, but I figure that's par for the course.

We made another call to Ed Glavin to let him know that I was willing to come on the show and meet with Darryl Stingley and Morton Downey, Jr. I told them to bring in the press, the films of the hit, the commissioner; and face-to-face, eye-to-eye, Darryl Stingley and Jack Tatum could each tell his side of the story. This way, once and for all, the world could see what happened and everyone could hear how we each honestly feel about the other and about the accident. I got the feeling that when Darryl and I did meet, a lot of people would be surprised at how we feel.

"Great!" Glavin said, but then he never called back.

Why?

Well, it's only speculation on my part and I don't want to sound like a journalist; but maybe after everyone thought the situation over, they decided to leave well enough alone. This way there's always going to be a good guy and a bad guy, and no one will ever have to put a red light at that dangerous intersection where the defender meets the receiver running the quick slant.

This is a strange world that we live in. I write a book titled *They Call Me Assassin.* It's about me, my life and football. It states that I played aggressively but within the structure of the rules. I even go as far as to suggest legitimate rules changes to help protect the athletes. The next thing I know, I'm swinging from the limb of a tree right beside Clint.

Conrad Dobler writes a book titled *They Call Me Dirty.* He admits to bending, stretching, occasionally breaking the rules and people laugh and think it's a joke.

I'm not getting down on Conrad, because I read and endorsed his manuscript prior to publication. It's a good book, an honest book about football and the players. Now, maybe some players didn't like Conrad when he was out on the field, but they damn well respected him.

I was finding my situation incredible, unbelievable and I couldn't figure out what went wrong!

A friend of mine, a real philosopher, said, "It has to do with opinions, Tate. Haven't you ever heard it said that opinions are like assholes? Everybody has one."

"Yeah, I understand that," I tell him. "But my problem is trying to figure out why assholes have opinions."

Just because I've mentioned a few buttholes in this first chapter, don't get the notion that this book is going to be a study of proctology. It isn't.

First of all, this book is going to be for all the Conrad Doblers who have defended me over the past ten years. These individuals know the real Jack Tatum, while the public in general still sees a blurred image of a football character called the Assassin. With this book, I'm simply going to bring everything into focus. This way, the would-be fans, and perhaps even some critics, will understand how everything happened and why. In the end, they may not agree with me; but along the way, I promise a few good laughs. And who knows where it's going to end — maybe at the movies where I finally do get lynched?

Also, I don't think I could write this book without putting the establishment under the microscope for a real close examination. There's a lot to football, and I'm checking out everything from the fans right through to the owners. There are problems between the players and the union, the union and the management, and with the rules and the drug scene … and that's a bad scene.

At the same time, there's a bright side to the game of football because there are quality people doing good things in big ways. So, I'm taking aim on a complete football book and my literary style isn't going to be any different than how I played the game — aggressively, hard-hitting, honest and strictly by the rules. But in journalism I learned the hard way, there ain't no rules.

I heard that *They Call Me Assassin* gave Pete Rozelle and a few other people mild indigestion. If that was true, then I can promise that *They Still Call Me Assassin* is going to choke them. If you have one of those weak stomachs, then don't read this book.

Here we go again.

2

Trust Me Jack, 'Cause I'm Gonna Make You Famous

I had only been in the best-seller's arena less than a week, but already it was proving more volatile than a bad day in Beirut. I'm only kidding, of course. It wasn't all that bad.

The ban the book and banish Jack Tatum movement was in full swing but going nowhere. I have to admit that Darryl Stingley's attorney, Jack Sands, was trying his best to eradicate me and the book from ever having existed, but he seemed to be stumbling over a little-known and obscure twist in the law called the First Amendment. Even if Jack Sands found a way to get around my rights to freedom of speech, I know a little about attorneys and how long it took to get any results. Hopefully, Darryl wasn't paying his attorney by the hour. I dismissed the Jack Sands crusade as a waste of his time even though I spent many nights thinking about Darryl.

To say that my reputation and the excerpts of the book weren't coming under a serious siege would be an understatement. CBS's *Sixty Minutes* had taken a pretty good shot at me; but once again, it was obvious that only excerpts were involved in their research and not the actual reading of the book. I never wrote the book believing that everyone was going to agree with my views, but I did have some thoughts that people were at least going to read the damn thing before criticizing me. Perhaps I was expecting too much. Then again, the book was selling so I was at least hopeful that someone would eventually get around to reading it.

If Joe Fitzgerald was the first journalist to write about my felonious assault confession, he certainly wasn't going to be the last. By now every sleaze-ball reporter in the country had gotten wind of a lynching and most of them were waiting for me by the old oak tree with typewriter and dictionary in hand. Amazingly enough some of these reporters had already learned to look up the spelling of Jack, and a few of them, with a little help, could even do the Tatum part of my name. Suddenly every journalist in the country was writing about the Assassin.

With all the hype I figured it would just be a matter of time before Pete Rozelle would call me into the office. I heard some stories about Pete hiring a group of Philadelphia attorneys to actually read the book and then he was going to come down on me. I guess that Pete was positive he wasn't going to like the book. Well, whatever course of action Pete chose to pursue, I would be ready.

In literary circles, true success is measured by that first appearance on the *Tonight Show*. To reach the exclusive summit of the writing profession, I would have to sit down with Johnny Carson and discuss the book. Then, and only then, could I truly say that I was a successful writer.

Two out of three wasn't bad and to this very day I tell all of my friends that I almost reached the pinnacle. The book made the *Tonight Show* and Johnny was there for one of his rare appearances, but for some reason I wasn't invited. I think someone must have felt that I might show up and start taking shots at the staff, cameramen, Johnny, and maybe even Ed and Fred.

It was a pretty good program because Joe Namath filled in for me. Even though Joe was a retired quarterback, he wasn't a bad guy. He knew a little about the game of football and the politics. It wasn't long before Johnny and Joe began discussing the book. Interestingly enough, Joe Namath was actually the first person I heard making sense on the subject. Joe made a few comments on the articles he had seen, but he also mentioned the fact that he hadn't read the book. Therefore, he couldn't offer much of an opinion either way.

I think Joe understood my situation, because of his playing day battle with the press and the commissioner. It was an interesting war story because Joe was supposed to have lost all the battles, but in the end, he somehow won the war. Pete Rozelle, on the other hand, claimed to have won all the battles and yet, he somehow managed to lose the war. Damn, whenever Pete Rozelle got involved, it became confusing.

I was in college at Ohio State when Joe had his serious run-in with the press and the front office of the NFL. I think everyone in the sporting world had followed that story. At least my Buckeye teammates and I found the entire saga to be simply astounding. For those who don't remember the shootout at the Bachelor's III nightclub, let me tell you the story.

Joe Namath was a seasoned veteran, not only on the field but off the field as well. The players around the NFL and fans respected Joe for his courage, toughness, winning ways and flamboyant style; but most of the press didn't like him because he had a reputation for telling journalists to screw off with a capital F. Joe didn't like reporters misquoting him and prying into his private life. But the more touchdown passes he threw, the more money he made, and from that point in time, Joe Namath was newsworthy twenty-four hours a day.

Joe became so popular that he didn't have to say anything to be quoted. The journalists just made up Joe Namath quotes and stories, and most of the time he wasn't even around. *Life* magazine kicked some dirt on Joe when they wrote about his New York City nightclub, the Bachelor's III, being a "hoodlum-haunted" dive. Then, there were some published stories in *Newsweek* about all-night crap games in Joe's New York apartment during January and February of 1969.

I often heard stories about Joe Willie Namath really getting around, but those all-night gambling parties in New York during January must have cut into his practice time in Fort Lauderdale. In January of 1969, Joe and the New York Jets were in Florida preparing for the Super Bowl. Then, after winning the Super Bowl, Joe spent some time in Okinawa and Hawaii visiting army hospitals before he returned to his home in Florida.

The journalists weren't interested in writing about Joe's charitable work because that might add a little luster to the image they had been working overtime to smudge. The press kept after Joe and, when all else failed, they would simply sit down and make up Joe Namath stories. Hey, what the hell, it sold newspapers and magazines.

In the spring of 1969, Pete Rozelle must have heard some of the rumors and probably read an excerpt or two from the magazine articles. That was the beginning of the end for Joe Namath's involvement in the nightclub business ... well ... almost the end. It's a long and complicated story, but Pete was on the scene so one would normally expect the issue to become somewhat clouded by stupidity.

Pete was busy unearthing a ton of incriminating evidence to use against Joe. It turned out that some of the customers frequenting the Bachelor's III actually had names ending in vowels. A number of these people even had Vegas suntans all year round, and we all know what that means. We're talking about undesirables, individuals who ate spaghetti and worse.

Growing up in Passaic, New Jersey, I learned never to trust anyone from New York who had a year-round suntan, especially if his name ended in a vowel. Maybe Pete was really onto something.

Naturally, the commissioner knew that Joe Namath was operating his private life and business in a way that was "detrimental to the integrity of professional football." In Joe's case, it wasn't just some excerpts from a book that got Pete all riled up, it was that ever-growing mountain of insurmountable evidence. If the Italians coming into the Bachelor's III weren't bad enough, then Pete soon discovered that Joe's people were serving drinks laced with booze. It was bigger than Pete could ever have imagined and getting bigger all the time.

Pete's spies soon learned that there were ladies going into the Bachelor's III, and guys, too. Then there was the music and dancing and people having a good time along with a few spaghetti dinners blatantly served right out in the open. Hell, Joe Namath was actually seen taking a shot or two of Johnny Walker Red. He had conversations with ladies and was even seen going from table to table patronizing customers.

If that wasn't enough evidence for the NFL to indict Joe, then there were the persistent magazine rumors of gambling and even the inference that he had thrown a couple of games. Joe had two outings where he was intercepted five times and the press said he threw those games. Damn, even I knew if a quarterback was going to throw a football game, there were less conspicuous ways to do it.

With rumors and inference flying about, Namath was guilty all right. Of that there could be no doubt. With the verdict in before the jurors were selected, the commissioner was ready to hand down the sentence. Pete Rozelle was going to make an example of Joe Namath, and for this historical announcement, he called a press conference. That way, for whatever it was worth, everyone could see and hear that the commissioner was on the job. And so, with the world looking on, Pete Rozelle gave Mr. Joe "their names end in vowels" Namath an ultimatum: either sell out his interest in the nightclub or get the hell out of football.

It's like I said, I was still only a young and innocent college student when Pete Rozelle sat down to play the game with Joe Namath, but even I knew who had all the picture cards. However, if Pete's objective was to show how absolutely stupid he could be, then his plan was incredibly brilliant. My teammates and I simply couldn't understand Pete's motivation.

What the hell was Pete Rozelle trying to do anyway, commit suicide? The entire scenario was ridiculous. Joe Namath had the right to own a nightclub and so what if Italians or even Russians were coming into the place? I always felt that First Amendment rights applied to football players, too, even quarterbacks.

Since Joe Namath was what you call a man of principle, he elected not to sell the night club and started making plans to leave football. At that moment, Pete Rozelle should have quickly called another press conference and said that he was just kidding around with his "sell or get out of football" ultimatum. Then, Pete should have immediately dropped to his knees, kissed Joe's Super Bowl ring, and made a solemn vow to come in on weekends and serve the spaghetti dinners at the Bachelor's III. But, stupid or stubborn or both, Pete stuck to his guns and they were empty guns at best. I just couldn't believe that Pete Rozelle was that stupid or that he had masochistic tendencies. It was obvious to everyone in the sporting world, and even a bunch of college kids at OSU, that Pete Rozelle was walking into a serious ass-kicking.

It turned out that a lot of people were a little more than casually upset with Pete. Some folks, such as team owners involved in a football merger, thought that Joe Namath was the most marketable sports figure in the world and his early retirement wouldn't be in the best and most profitable interests of the game. And then a group of marketing experts who just happened to own the NFL television rights believed that Joe Namath would send ratings soaring, and without him it would be a difficult sell. And what about those hardworking fans who paid for season tickets to see Namath play, but wouldn't get to if he retired?

Pete Rozelle was the man in charge of developing the TV potential of the NFL. He also had to work with the owners and had a responsibility to the fans. But it all seemed that getting Joe Namath was more important to Pete than anything else. I was totally baffled back then and I'm still baffled. I've heard journalists and several NFL franchise owners singing praise to Pete for securing the TV contract that has grossed four billion dollars since 1961. From my point of view, if Joe Namath would have left football, then Pete Rozelle would have been responsible for jeopardizing that contract. Football was coming to television with or without Namath, but he was the big carrot, and not Pete Rozelle's salesmanship.

Forgive me, but for some reason I have to laugh whenever I hear stories about Pete going out and bringing television to the NFL. Let's face reality and tell it like it is. Fred Flintstone could have secured a television contract at that time and it still would have grossed four billion dollars, perhaps even more. Football was ready for prime time television and prime time television wanted football. Believe me, football was a marketable product and the NFL securing a television contract had nothing to do with Pete Rozelle.

It's like I said, football was television-bound, but Pete still had the Namath situation to resolve. By now Pete had all the facts. But what were the facts? Sure, he heard the rumors and had seen the write-ups in the papers and the magazines, but what else? And sure, Pete's spies had seen sleazy characters hanging around the Bachelor's III, but those were only journalists, reporters, and various types of press people. Everyone knew that Joe wasn't too keen on them to begin with. I could not understand how the very integrity of football was at stake when Joe hadn't done anything wrong. But Pete wasn't going to let Joe get away with this one.

There were plenty of meetings between attorneys and the front office of the NFL, and even Weeb Ewbank, head coach of the Jets, became involved. But little or nothing was accomplished and it seemed as though Joe Namath's career had come to a premature end because of Rozelle's dictatorial policies.

The entire situation was absolutely ridiculous. Even after admitting that Joe hadn't done anything wrong, Pete Rozelle still insisted that Joe sell his interest in the Bachelor's III.

Finally, on July 13, 1969, Joe's attorney, Jimmy Walsh, gave Pete a graceful way out. Jimmy proposed that Joe would sell his interest in the Bachelor's III and the commissioner would give Joe permission to open other Bachelor's IIIs. If Pete Rozelle agreed to this, it meant that Joe could go out and open a Bachelor's III nightclub in Tuscaloosa, or Birmingham, or Fort Lauderdale, or even in New York City, right next door to the one he would sell.

Honest to God, and cross my heart and hope to die if I'm not telling the truth, but Joe Namath didn't retire after all. The great difference between Joe Namath and myself is that I would have made the deal and then opened up a Bachelor's III right next door to the one I just sold. It would have been a matter of principle, but Joe never was one to run up the score.

Joe Namath did go out and open up two or three nightclubs in different locations around the country, and he used the name, Bachelor's III. Why shouldn't he capitalize on the millions of dollars of free publicity?

Everything worked out just fine for Joe Namath and business couldn't have been better. My problem was understanding what Pete thought he had gained or why he got involved in the first place. Oh sure, he wasted a lot of time and NFL money; but outside of that, Pete really didn't accomplish a damn thing. To start a hassle over the Bachelor's III was stupidity, but for Pete to agree to the compromise defied reason and logic. No one in the world was that dumb, or did Pete Rozelle just want everyone to think he was?

That's when everything suddenly dawned on me. Joe Namath would have had to pay a first-class public relations company some big money to come up with that kind of a publicity stunt and there would be no guarantees. But with Pete Rozelle involved and crusading against his "hoodlum-haunted" dive, Joe got a ton of free publicity. I figured the only was for all of this to make any sense was that Pete had, in reality, come up with an absolutely brilliant publicity scheme, and Joe was actually paying him under the table.

Before Pete Rozelle started on the Bachelor's III, it was just another nightclub. But when Pete was finished with the publicity campaign, everyone in the world was coming to the Bachelor's III, and Joe ended up building a whole chain of successful nightclubs. If I worked from the premise that Pete was only acting stupid, then the Bachelor's III incident was ingenious. But one thing still troubled me. I just couldn't see Joe and Pete in some back room of the Bachelor's III jumping up and down slapping high fives. Joe wouldn't do something like that, but still, Pete couldn't have been so stupid that he'd walked away with nothing.

I figured that unbeknown to Joe Namath, Pete Rozelle was somehow raking profits from the Bachelor's III. For the longest time I truly believed that Pete Rozelle was one of the sharpest guys in the world pretending to be the dumbest. Then my college days were over and suddenly I was part of the NFL. In the fall of 1976, I finally got to meet the commissioner and I discovered the truth for myself.

My trip to New York and my first meeting with Pete came about through a football game. September 5, 1976, the Raiders opened the season with the Pittsburgh Steelers. Even though we got together and partied with some of the Steelers the night before, everyone knew that come Sunday afternoon it was going to be war.

The game itself started exactly the way I figured: violent and brutal. When playing against the Steelers or any of the physical teams, I always expect solid contact and flaring tempers, but somehow this game immediately started getting out of hand.

Early in the game our wide receiver, Cliff Branch, caught a short turn-in pass and was quickly scooped up by Steeler defensive back, Mel Blount. Cliff wasn't a very physical receiver, and when Mel had him shackled, that should have been the end of the play. Unfortunately, it wasn't. Instead of just making the tackle, Mel grabbed Cliff, turned him upside down, and then tried to pile-drive his head into the ground. It was obviously a deliberate attempt to hurt the man and it got some of our defensive people talking about getting the Steelers' receivers. Personally, I don't believe in the big brother routine, but I never liked to see another player deliberately try to hurt anyone. Sometimes things like that happen and it sort of sets the tone for the rest of the game. I knew it was going to be an all-out war and when that happens no one takes prisoners. It was just one of those games where everyone gets uptight and goes after it extra hard.

A few minutes later our defense was on the field and the Steelers ran a simple dive play. Tight end Randy Grossman hit me after the whistle. I defended myself by throwing Grossman to the ground and punching him. He took a shot at me and I took a shot back. Naturally, I ended up on the short end of a penalty flag because that's the way it usually went. It was wrong for Grossman to come after me like that and I resented the shot, but two wrongs don't make a right.

Later in the game Steeler running back Franco Harris took the ball off left tackle and headed toward the sidelines. I had the angle and Franco was going to get blasted into next week. Before I could hit Franco, he saw me coming and simply went down. I thought about spearing him or stepping all over his head; but instead I downed him with a light slap on his helmet. I barely hit him and the next thing I see is the penalty flag landing on the ground. The official thought it was unnecessary roughness and I thought it was bullshit.

After that, another Steeler running back, Rocky Bleier, circled over the middle and hit me in the knees. I was sensitive about getting hit like that and I told Rocky what I thought. Later in the game I saw Rocky trying the same play again and this time put it in high gear and went after him. When Rocky saw me coming he tried to stop, but I didn't. I drove my fist and forearm up under his mask and dropped him. It was a pretty good shot and while I stood over him I said, "I don't like people getting into my knees."

Rocky got up and said, "No problem." He returned to the Steeler huddle as I checked to see if there were any flags. This time, I probably should have been flagged, but the officials missed one.

There were some other flags thrown, a few cheap shots, plenty of good hits, and a come-from-behind 31-28 victory for the Raiders. When the game was over, most of us shook hands and said wait until next time.

Then early Monday morning it really started. Steeler coach Chuck Noll was mouthing off to the Pittsburgh press about "criminal elements" in the game of football and he was pointing the finger at me and our strong safety, George Atkinson. I wasn't going to lose sleep over anything written about me in the Pittsburgh newspapers because Chuck Noll had always been a poor loser. Besides, if Chuck was talking about criminal elements, he should take a hard look at

Mel Blount's body slam of Cliff Branch or Grossman hitting me after the whistle. But I understood. Chuck thought he had the game won and before the final gun went off, he lost. Time heals all wounds and Chuck would eventually forget about this one.

A few days later, George and I received word from the commissioner's office that we had been fined for unnecessary roughness, or was it unprofessional conduct, or was it conduct unbecoming a professional? Pete Rozelle wasn't sure of the charges, but all the same was hitting me with a $1,500 fine, and George was ticketed $2,500 for putting Steeler receiver Lynn Swann in the hospital with a concussion. I want to be perfectly clear on the Lynn Swann incident. George Atkinson got Lynn and not me. People are always blaming me for that hit or giving me the credit and it belongs to George.

We made plans to debate the issue with Pete Rozelle. In the back of my mind I figured this was going to be another of the commissioner's brilliant publicity stunts. I hadn't forgotten the way he'd helped out Joe Namath with the Bachelor's III, and, naturally, I thought he was up to his old tricks again. I didn't understand how everything was going to work or why he had selected George and me; but hell, Joe Namath was probably in the dark when the commissioner pretended to kick him out of football. I told George to go with the flow because Pete Rozelle was a PR genius. Somehow, all of the publicity was going to pay dividends. I could hardly wait until I got to the Big Apple and met my main man, Pete Rozelle.

We scheduled our New York trip on a Monday following a late season game in New England. George was still pretty uptight about everything, but I was cool. I kept telling George that Pete Rozelle had to be one of the sharpest dudes in the world, and George kept insisting that Pete was a racist and he wanted to put us in jail or worse. It took some doing, but George started coming around to my way of thinking.

In Boston we boarded a 747 for the flight to New York. It seemed a little spooky, a wide-body jet for the short hop to New York and me and George as the only two passengers. George started talking about the possibility of the captain pointing the jet out to sea and then bailing out. The next thing I know, he's cussing Pete Rozelle for trying to get rid of us. With that thought growing in his mind, George tried to get off the plane and put in a call to our coach, John Madden, for the Greyhound schedule to New York. John Madden always felt that if God had intended for him to fly he'd have feathers and a couple of wings. It was always difficult getting Coach Madden on a plane and equally as tough keeping George on this one.

The captain and a couple of good-looking flight attendants finally calmed George long enough to explain that, because of fog in Atlanta and a few other Southern cities, several connecting flights had been canceled. The captain assured George that he was a Raider fan and our flight to New York City was still on. George and I were then given a first-class green light ticket. It turned out to be an enjoyable experience and I felt we were merely setting the tone for the coming meeting with Pete.

Monday morning arrived and I finally met the genius behind the National Football League. Pete Rozelle came into the conference room, shook my attorney's hand, shook George's attorney's hand, and the NFL's attorney's hand — everyone's hand ... except mine. He looked at me but never said a word. I didn't understand.

Pete was different with George. Not only didn't he shake George's hand, but Pete looked right through the man. It was almost like he was pretending George wasn't even in the room. I thought it was a rather cold reception and getting colder by the moment.

Suddenly I realized Pete was sporting a year-around Las Vegas suntan. It was like I said before. When I grew up in Passaic, we never trusted anyone from New York City with a year-around suntan ... especially if his last name ended with a vowel. Admittedly, things were looking bad; but I still had the feeling that, even if I didn't understand what was going on, Pete did and it would all work out. After all, I spent several years of my life believing that Pete Rozelle, behind closed doors, had cut some kind of a deal to help promote the Bachelor's III nightclub. I was still working from the premise that no one in his right mind would get involved in that kind of a lose-lose situation unless there was some intricate, under-the-table deal going on. To an outsider it might look as though I was in some hot water, but this was the same Pete Rozelle who pulled off the great Bachelor's III caper. This guy had to be as sharp and slick as they come ... unless??? I didn't even want to think about those implications so I put all of the negatives out of my mind. I told myself that Pete was a genius and before the day was over I would see the real man in action.

We had been going back and forth about the reasons I was being fined, and for the most part, the NFL's attorney, Jay Moyer, was doing all the talking. We had looked at the films of the game in questions and it was obvious that Randy Grossman had hit me after the play was over and I impulsively retaliated. For the official to flag me because of my hit on Franco Harris was ridiculous and everyone agreed there was no foul on my part. Next came Rocky Bleier. The films showed that Rocky did get into my knees with a cheap shot.

Next time around, the films showed that I went after him with my fist and forearm. I was wrong and Rocky was wrong, but fine me and they would have to fine him. Everything seemed cut and dried and then Pete opened his mouth. The master was about to speak and the grasshopper was eager to learn.

"Jack," Pete said, "I personally think you hit too hard."

Pete obviously had a sense of humor, so I wanted for the punch line. He stammered a bit and then said, "I'm quite serious, I think you hit too hard for football."

He was serious, but I didn't understand. Naturally, I tried to keep a straight face even though I was chuckling a little inside. I wasn't going to come right out and laugh in Pete's face. After all, he was the commissioner of the NFL, and there was the Bachelor's III campaign that he engineered to consider. All the same, Pete was beginning to look and sound like a big dummy. Still, maybe there was something to Pete's statement.

Pete thought I hit too hard, but I always felt that O.J. Simpson ran too fast. Then there was Larry Csonka. He was too big and powerful to be a running back, and Earl Campbell was an incredible combination of speed, size and power. If the commissioner could control O.J.'s speed, Larry's size and do something about Earl, I'd certainly think about toning down my hits although it might be difficult. I'm only joking, of course, because by now the statement of my hitting too hard was idiotic.

I just sort of cleared my throat and looked around the room at the others to see their reaction. Maybe Pete was telling a joke and I was the odd man out, the one who didn't get it. No one was laughing, at least not out loud, but it was obvious that everyone was attempting to wipe a smile off his face.

Finally I asked, "Mr. Commissioner, Earl Campbell weighs 235 pounds. He runs a 9.6 hundred, each one of his thighs is 34 inches of thick hard muscle ... ah, really, I don't want to be a wise guy, but how would you tackle him easy?"

I heard a muffled laugh or two as a dumb expression settled over Pete's face. He thought about my question for several moments and then turned to his attorney, Jay Moyer, as if to ask, "Well?"

Jay Moyer didn't have an answer either and, about that time, I began to see the light. Pete was a real boob. For seven years I believed that Pete Rozelle was to football what Einstein was to physics and P.T. Barnum was to the circus. For seven years I believed that Pete was a promotional genius, and now, in the space of seven minutes, I discovered that he was to football what the Stooges were to serious drama.

Giving Pete the benefit of the doubt, we continued our debate over hard hitting and fines. We went back and forth on everything and it was fast becoming apparent that Pete had made up his mind on the issue and there was no sense confusing him with the facts. Evidently Pete had checked out all the game films of my career because to fortify his "I hit too hard," statement he mentioned an incident that took place in 1972 during a game with the Steelers. He was talking about my hit on Lynn Swann and I remembered the play and what followed. I got Lynn with a real good shot as he was coming over the middle. It was a clean and legal hit, but Lynn ended up in the hospital with a concussion. Later in the game, one of the Steelers had fumbled and I was going after the ball. All of a sudden, Steeler center Ray Mansfield speared me with a cheap shot and injured my knee. After the game Ray piped off to the press that he was trying to get me. He admitted and has always maintained, that he wanted to break my legs because I got Lynn. I've talked to Ray about that incident many times. Once we were invited to the same sports banquet and he even told the audience that he tried to break my legs because he thought my hit on Lynn Swann was uncalled for. Ray knows the difference between my hit on Lynn and his spearing me. It's a big joke now but it wasn't that way when it all happened.

Pete agreed that my hit on Lynn Swann was legal and Mansfield's attacking me was a cheap shot. Pete also agreed that Ray should never have told the press he was trying to break my legs. There was no question that I hit Swann with a legal shot and no question that Ray's retaliation was a premeditated cheap shot. Since we were talking about fines and cheap shots I asked Pete why Mansfield wasn't fined for hitting me.

Pete's answer defied logic. He said, "If I fined Ray for hitting you, I'd have to fine you for hitting Lynn Swann. So I couldn't fine Ray without fining you."

I didn't understand his reasoning, but I thought it would be an interesting question if I asked about my recent fines. I was being fined for hitting Grossman, but he took a cheap shot at me and the same with Rocky Bleier. I wanted to know why they weren't being fined. Did all of this mean that my fines were being canceled, and what about my expenses coming in here for this waste of time?

The fines were not canceled even though the films clearly indicated that I had a valid defense. Pete did lower my fines from $1,500 down to $750, and promised to pay my expenses home. I was what you call partially guilty, almost guilty, not quite innocent. It was illegal for me to use my fists during a football game even in self-defense. According to Pete's way of thinking I should have just let the

Steelers take cheap shots at my knees. More important, I should learn to tackle easier.

I didn't like the almost guilty implications so I gave Pete a compromise. I told Pete to call it a "washout." I'd pay my own expenses for the flight home and my attorney's fees if he'd drop the fines and the ridiculous charges. Pete said he couldn't and he gave me reasons such as ethics, principle and integrity. I figured that meant a certain coach and several players expected him to fine me.

Okay, I would agree to pay the $750 fine and Pete promised the NFL would pay $500 for my ticket home and expenses. The deal had the odor of a dead skunk because everyone behind those closed doors saw the films and knew why I had taken certain actions against Grossman and Bleier. I knew the truth and so did Pete, as well as most of the players in the league, but the fans never did. From that day on, I was forever more the bad guy.

I paid the fines and waited for Mr. Pete Rozelle to live up to his word and reimburse me the five hundred dollars for my ticket home. I never received my five hundred dollars from the NFL, and I've made a point of mentioning it quite often. It's not an issue of money. It is however, a matter of ethics, principle and the integrity of the man who represented the NFL for nearly thirty years that I, to this very day, question. Looking back on my first experience with Pete Rozelle I can almost excuse the fact that he was and still is a boob and a bigot, but I don't like a liar.

After my trip to New York, I felt I should burn my clothes and wash with old-fashioned lye soap to get rid of the stench. The sour taste stayed with me for a long time afterwards. Pete Rozelle's system of justice might be acceptable in Cuba, Libya, Panama and a host of other countries where democracy is spelled dictatorship.

From that day on I always believed that Pete Rozelle was going to test the authority of his throne against someone who had the time and money to prove that democracy still works even within the kingdom called the National Football League. That someone turned out to be Mr. Al Davis of the Oakland "they can't move to Los Angeles" Raiders. In another chapter I am going to tell all about that Pete Rozelle blunder because it is a classic multi-million dollar court-room drama. But for now, there was still me and my book. If rumor had any substance, then Pete Rozelle was making plans to come down hard on the Assassin.

Granted, my situation was a little more complex than a nightclub frequented by people who were sporting year-around suntans and who had names ending in vowels. After all, Pete couldn't order me to sell out of books because that was already happening. My suspicions were that he would try to hit me with some kind of a fine and perhaps a suspension. Regardless of what avenue Pete chose to pursue, I felt they all led to a courtroom. Maybe Pete didn't understand, but it's a long hard fall from dictator to defendant.

It goes without saying that I was actually looking forward to the commissioner calling me in and questioning me about the book. First of all I was going to look Pete in the eye and ask him about my five hundred dollars. Then, I was honestly hoping that he would come up with a real innovative blunder involving my career or the book because I was serious about pursuing the issue through a higher court than Rozelle's conference room. But knowing the real Pete Rozelle and his past record and style of Bonzo logic, I couldn't even begin to imagine what plan of attack he was going to follow.

In the meantime I guess there wasn't enough publicity to suit my publishers because they came up with the brainstorm that Joe Fitzgerald and I should meet face-to-face. That way I could spill my guts and maybe say something dumb and be quoted in the *Boston Herald American*. I'm sure the consensus of opinion was that I would, at the very least, say something "inflammatory" and help keep that fire burning under Pete Rozelle.

I figured if I did grant Fitzgerald an interview, he'd have enough ammunition for about three months of "that's asking for it" quotes from the commissioner's office. On the other hand, even if I didn't grant the interview, Fitzgerald would have enough ammunition for about three months of "that's asking for it" quotes. Or, if I did grant the interview and just sat there and said nothing, Joe Fitzgerald would still have enough ammunition for about three months of "that's asking for it" quotes.

In reality I had said just about everything I could say in the book. I wrote about coaches, teams, some of the owners, a number of players, rule changes, and even the bad and ugly of the game, Pete Rozelle. Sooner or later someone was going to read the book and discover this wealth of Jack Tatum quotes. So, why not sit down with my old buddy Joe Fitzgerald and point him in the right direction?

Of all the exotic and wonderful places in the world to meet Joe Fitzgerald, my publisher selected the city of Pittsburgh. Pittsburgh wasn't a favorite of mine and I wasn't a favorite of Pittsburgh. Mutual feelings like that wouldn't be bad except for the fact I understood the mentality of Pittsburgh football fans. If word got out that the Assassin was in Pittsburgh, it wouldn't be out of the question for some of the Steeler loyalists to hide out on the rooftops of buildings with high powered rifles. Heaven help all the good-looking "brothers" in the city when that happened. You know, "we" all really do look alike.

I sneaked into town under the cover of darkness and met quietly with Fitzgerald. It wasn't much of a meeting or an interview for that matter. Fitzgerald spent most of the time trying to convince me that he was my pal and that Pete Rozelle was out to get me. Hey, as far as I was concerned, Joe Fitzgerald and I had no axe to grind. After all, Joe and I were sort of partners. I was helping him sell newspapers and he was helping me promote the book. And with the book selling, I still believed that before long people were going to start reading it and would discover the truth for themselves. I wasn't an insensitive thug deliberately trying to hurt people. I was an athlete playing by the rules and some of those very rules needed to be changed for the safety and longevity of athletes.

Somewhere along the line Pete was going to learn the truth: about journalists, about football being a contact sport, and about letting his stupidity help push my book over the top. Maybe Pete was going to realize that he couldn't believe everything he read in the newspapers; but, as Joe Namath no doubt appreciated Pete's involvement in the Bachelor's III matter, I certainly wasn't going to be the one to slow down Pete's blossoming friendship with Mr. Joe Fitzgerald and the *Boston Herald American.*

Not much came out of my Pittsburgh meeting with Fitzgerald, but I was hopeful my next stop would prove more interesting. Finally, I was on my way to see the commissioner and I had my attorney with me. We were both primed and ready for a courtroom drama.

Pete hadn't changed since I last saw him. He was still sporting a suntan and he went the same route by shaking everyone's hand except mine. This time it didn't bother me because I had no intention of shaking his hand.

Just before we all sat down and got started on the subject of the book, I asked Pete about my five hundred dollars. Pete didn't have an answer. Actually, he just pretended not to hear the question. I asked the question once more and once more Pete pretended he didn't hear. What would I expect from a dude who has a Las Vegas suntan all year round. I understood, and with that, we began.

For the first several minutes there wasn't any zest or excitement to the meeting because Pete just sat there and kept looking through his notes, or I should say, my quotes. Jay Moyer, attorney for the NFL, asked the opening question. He wanted to know about the "knockout competition" George Atkinson and I had and whether I stood by the statements I made in the book.

I smiled while remembering the story I wrote in *They Call Me*

Assassin about knockouts and limp-offs. During my second year with the Raiders, George suggested that he and I start a contest for who would get the most knockouts over the course of the season. It sounded like a good idea and we came up with a set of rules. First of all, neither of us wanted to get into a penalty competition so we agreed our hits must be clean shots and legal. Next, the man you hit would have to be down for an official injury time-out and he had to be helped off the field and couldn't return to the game. That would be considered a "knockout" and worth two points. Sometimes, one of us would hit a man and he'd take the injury time-out but would limp off the field under his own power. We called that a "limp-off" and it was worth one point.

Sure I stood by what I had written, but it was simply a locker room story covering a paragraph in a book for football fans. It was similar to the NFL's *Crunch Course* video's narration about "knockouts" and "cheap shots" and "blood" and violence in general ... only not near as graphically worded. I continued explaining to Jay Moyer that there's plenty of talk like that before games, during games, and even after games. Football language is a part of the sport as I've already explained, and not to be taken seriously. No one had ever questioned it before, but I write a book and all of a sudden it became a major issue with the office of the commissioner. Damn, I couldn't believe these turkeys.

So what if George and I had conversations about hard hits. What did it matter if we kept our own statistics when it came to knockouts and limp-offs? Big deal! Every defensive player in the NFL goes for the hardest hit he can make and most of them will brag about it, too. Hard hitting isn't against the rules, and it wasn't against the rules for me to write a locker room story in the book. It wasn't as if George and I were obsessed with trying to knock out opponents. We rarely mentioned it, and during a game you're not out there planning a knockout or limp-off. You take your best shot at receivers or running backs and if a knockout happens, it happens. And sure, the truth was that when I got a clean hit, the receiver or running back would probably take the count; but, if I wasn't that kind of a hitter then I would have never made it into the NFL. That is a football fact.

I was still trying to explain my point when Pete looked up from his notes and bogarted into the discussion. He felt that I was the only NFL player who tried to hit hard. What a dope. How incredible! "One Track Pete" was expounding on his theory of easy tackling and I was picturing him personally demonstrating the technique on Earl Campbell. If Pete spent more time watching football games up close instead of going to the tanning salon, he would understand the basics of contact and perhaps be in a position to critique my style. I shook my head in disbelief. If Pete didn't know by now that football was a contact sport, he would never understand. I asked Moyer for another question.

Jay Moyer had several pages of my quotes he wanted to discuss and I think he knew we were about one more of Pete's silly interruptions away from calling the meeting off. He tried to settle Pete down because I think Jay realized that we didn't have to be there in the first place. I was tired of it all and certainly wasn't interested in wasting any more of my time debating football with a man who thought a right guard was a can of deodorant.

Jay asked another question and Pete looked up from his notes and interrupted again. Pete wanted to know what I meant when I wrote that he was always "mouthing off." A good question and I had the answer; but before I could speak, Pete "mouthed off" again. He wanted to know why I referred to his system of justice as a "kangaroo court." And again, before I could answer, he was back to a ludicrous claim that no other player in the NFL went out on the field and tried to hit hard.

I was ready to let it all out so I started. But my attorney felt that enough was enough and he told Jay Moyer that if Pete and the NFL would like to ask any more questions, they could pursue the matter through the courts. We would be most happy to oblige. Pete was still mumbling and asking what I meant by "kangaroo court" when my attorney and I got up and left.

I was a little disappointed that Pete and I didn't get together in a courtroom, but maybe it was for the best. I never had anything against Jay Moyer or the NFL. The problem was the man at the controls. But that was the NFL's problem, and my dilemma was bridging the credibility gap between the real me and the distorted image the Assassin brought to everyone's mind.

I wrote a book and found myself at the mercy of a few key journalists and Pete Rozelle. Add a couple of excerpts, an accident on the playing field and suddenly I'm forever branded football's bad boy. To comprehend the entire scenario, one must understand where and how it all began. I'm talking about writing the book because, if I wasn't a best-selling author, I would probably be enjoying retirement instead of continually defending myself. I guess it all goes with the turf and I'm really not crying, just trying to explain the facts.

Although ten years have passed I can still vividly see him saying, "Trust me Jack, 'cause I'm gonna make you famous." I'm not talking about the commissioner, either.

In all honesty I can truthfully say that he did alter the course of my rather mundane life, but I'm not quite sure about this newly acquired status of so-called fame that seems to have immersed my character in a cesspool of controversy. Perhaps the problem is that my original expectations of being famous differ from the reality I am now waddling through. Then again, perhaps he said something other than "famous."

I guess I should explain that my first book was actually his idea. I'm talking about my old buddy, my faithful pal, the collaborating writer. Giving credit where credit is due, he was the literary giant who "helped" pen the book that made me famous.

Forgive me, but for some reason I have a difficult time saying or even writing his name, and believe me, it has nothing to do with sour grapes. It's just that every time I mention his name, he shows up on my doorstep and all kinds of things start to happen — strange things.

The first time he came around my dog didn't even bark. Now, that's unusual because my dog always barks. My dog barks at white people, black people, Indians, Orientals, good people, bad people ... hell, my dog barks at me when I come out to feed him. But when "he" came around, the dog just stood there. If I didn't know better, I'd say the dog was confused. When the dog couldn't get a reading on the man, no one could, and I should have been suspicious.

Anyway, he took my uneventful life and developed everything into a best seller. With great diligence he restructured the actual story and modified my character so that the final product would, in his words, "be slightly controversial but extremely commercial." Then, leaving nothing to chance, he read Steve Cassidy's book, *The Good Guys,* and gave me the nom de plume, The Assassin. Suddenly I'm a best-selling author and I find myself being trashed in newspapers and taking on the league office. I get all choked up just thinking about it.

The really nice thing about my deal with him was that we were only partners on the royalties. He told me up front and early on, "The glamour and glitter synonymous with being a best-selling author is strictly yours, Jack. You can take all the credit for this book ... in fact, please don't even mention my name." He forgot to mention that I could take all the flak, too. But what are friends for?

I have to admit that he did have a way with words. He was also a complex character and I never knew what to expect. Sometimes he would go off into the corner of the room and quietly write a sentence or two. Here, I could almost see a little of Shakespeare within his written words. Then he would speak and sometimes I'd swear he was possessed by Mike Tyson's old trainer, Kevin Rooney.

"Yeah, I saw younse playin' up in Michigan," he said as we were discussing the Ohio State-Michigan rivalry.

Younse? I thought while trying to remember the dude. The name sounded Hungarian, but I couldn't remember any Hungarians on the team during my Ohio State days.

"What position did he play?" I wanted to know.

"Who?" he asked with a quizzical gawk.

"Younse," I answered, still trying to place the dude.

Shaking his head back and forth he explained, "Damn, Tate, don't you know nothin' ... younse can be anything from two persons up to a whole bunch a peoples."

Needless to say, we had a slight communication gap but nothing that a little patience couldn't bridge. After awhile it got to where we could understand each other. I did most of the talking and he did all the listening. That way, things never got confusing and we developed a good working relationship. To this day we are still friends.

I remember telling him my thoughts on Lynn Swann, an All-Pro wide receiver with the Pittsburgh Steelers. I always felt that when facing zone coverage, Lynn was tentative about coming over the middle on a pass route. Expounding on the difference between man-to-man coverage and the zone defense, I explained that a receiver would have to be a complete idiot to run full-speed into zone coverage without looking for the defenders. Man-to-man coverage means that receivers are being chased all over the field by the defensive backs. Zone defense is like a dude running up the sidewalk in the middle of a dark night all of a sudden, WHAM! a fire hydrant gets his attention! Simply stated, Lynn Swann was not an idiot.

The writer considered my analysis of wide receiver Lynn Swann for several moments and then casually explained that he would take my thoughts and translate everything into words the general public would understand. He assured me that, although my spoken words would look slightly different written on the pages of a book, they would mean exactly the same thing. He concluded by saying, "But don't worry 'bout anything. Just trust me, Jack, 'cause I'm gonna make you famous."

We continued on the subject of the Pittsburgh Steelers. All-Pro running back Franco Harris was mentioned. Franco was a great running back but he had a tendency to use the sidelines. Instead of taking the defenders head-on and trying to pick up a few extra yards, Franco would usually skip out of bounds just before contact. I never agreed with that particular style of running the football. But then again, Franco was rarely injured and he had some great games.

When *They Call Me Assassin* was published, it was exactly as the writer had said ... my words did look slightly different on the pages of a book.

I realize that in verbalizing my opinions of Lynn Swann there was the inference that I questioned his courage. In reading my published words the issue seemed rather concise. Yet even to this day, I believe those written words, "Lynn Swann is gutless," differ from my original dialogue.

The same holds true for my statements about Franco Harris. Even to this day, I truly believe that if Franco had lowered his head and gone for extra yardage, he would have surpassed Jim Brown on the NFL's all-time rushing list. However, "Franco's a chickenshit," wasn't exactly what I had in mind when I told the story to the writer.

To this very day the writer is claiming that, as a result of his dedication and hard work, my book, *They Call Me Assassin*, has become a literary masterpiece and I'm famous. But damn, I'm still trying to figure out if my old pal is saying "famous" but meaning infamous?

Basically though, it's a pretty accurate account of what I told my old pal even though some of his personality and philosophy crept into the theme every so often. But that's okay, too, because he was telling the truth from his point of view and believed he was doing me a favor. Remember? He was gonna make me famous.

I'm not looking to blame my day of infamy on anyone in particular. I'm simply trying to figure out what went wrong. Sure, from my telling the story to the actual writing, I realize that some of my words lost meaning or perhaps gained a little imaginative edge. But so what? Even by taking into consideration the negatives: a certain attorney trying to have me banned from football, journalists trying to sell newspapers, and a commissioner auditioning for the part of an idiot, there was still no legitimate reason for the general public to treat me as though I was the predicted coming of the antichrist, or worse.

When *They Call Me Assassin* first hit the stands I couldn't believe the negative reaction. Naturally, I had my little circle of family and friends patting me on the back while saying it was a great book. My buddy, the writer, was there too. But Pete and Joe, and a few others, didn't agree and probably still don't agree. After all, I admitted to having hit Sammy White and that locker room talk about knockouts and everything just didn't set well with some folks.

If I was a hypocrite my first book would have been different. I would have gone out of my way to make a bunch of phony friends instead of enemies. I could have sprinkled rose petals in and around my stories of football and written that everyone within the structure of the NFL was a marvelous, outstanding, intelligent, courageous and compassionate individual. I could have gone on to write that no one ever farted in locker rooms, that there was no bad breath in the huddles, no drugs behind the scene, no violence on the field and all football players, coaches, management and owners were practicing saints. All I had to do was begin the book "Once upon a time," and end it with "they lived happily ever after," and I would have been at peace with the critics and the establishment. And then, with my nose getting longer by the minute, Walt Disney Studios would have hired me for some work in motion pictures. Under those conditions I don't think I would have liked myself very much because Hollywood always seemed plastic to me. Looking in the mirror and seeing the Assassin is one thing, but seeing a phony would make me puke. So, if I was going to write a book, I was going to do it the only way I could — it had to be honest.

They Call Me Assassin, like I've already mentioned, had some overtones of the collaborating writer's style, but it was an honest account of how I played the game. It was also an honest appraisal of football and the truth about many characters I've met during my career. Truth and honesty got a lot of people pissed off. At the same time, there were a few people who, although they may not have agreed with everything I wrote, still respected my opinions and admired me for telling the truth without pulling any punches.

Woody Hayes, God rest his soul, was my coach at Ohio State. I did an entire chapter on Woody in my first book, and I have mentioned him in this one — he deserves more. Although every word I wrote about Woody was my honest opinion and from the heart, the stories were not always complimentary.

I sent Woody a copy of the book and he read it, every word. Then, in the early part of March, I went back to Columbus, Ohio, for some promotional work. I was in a department store selling books and signing autographs when Woody came strolling in and sat down beside me. I'd sign a book and then Woody would sign it. The old man caused quite a commotion. He usually did. Before long people were fighting to get a copy of the book. They wanted Woody's autograph in my book.

I leaned over and whispered to Woody, "Thanks."

He looked surprised and asked, "For what?"

"For coming in here and backing me and the book," I answered.

"I should be thanking you," the old man smiled. "Hell, you're a famous writer and I'm proud to be part of it all."

Woody hung in there for a good hour and finally the store sold out. After that, we got away for a little while and discussed the book and had a laugh about all the hype. "To hell with the journalists," Woody said. "You've written a damn good book and I respect you for it. It's funny, pretty damn honest, and fairly accurate."

Woody's "fairly accurate" statement meant there was something I wrote about that he disagreed with. Actually, Woody's only beef came down to one little area. I wrote that Woody Hayes we the reason we lost in the Rose Bowl against Stanford my senior year. Woody made the team a promise that if we beat Michigan and won the Big Ten title, we would go to California, work hard in preparation for the game, but still have a good time visiting all the places most of us only read about.

We beat Michigan 20-9; but on the flight to California, the trainers started taping everyone. One hour after the plane landed we were on the practice field. We didn't do any sight-seeing and we didn't have a good time. In fact, it was practice, practice and more practice. We even practiced on Christmas Eve, and the old man was running around screaming and bitching, acting like anything but Santa Claus. It was obvious that Woody had forgotten his promise or pretended to forget, but we didn't, and by game time everyone was fed up with football. We just wanted to go back home and sleep in our own beds. To hell with it all!

Woody told me that I had the right to believe whatever I wanted to believe and I had the right to put it all in a book, but he still disagreed with me. Then he smiled and said, "You really do believe that's the reason we lost to Stanford, don't you?" Yes, I did, and I still do.

It was a great conversation and I enjoyed the time because he was vintage Woody. I had called him everything from a "prince" to a "prick," and he was, but Woody only took exception to my blaming him for a Rose Bowl loss. I wrote about Woody's antics, his temper, his compassion, his punching photographers, his working with the poor. I told it all and, make no mistake about it, Woody was a part-time prick, but most of the time he was a prince and I loved him like family. He was family.

It's sad because most people hear the name Woody Hayes and talk about the negatives. They never met Woody and never understood the compassion and sensitivity that were the major parts of his character. It all comes back to the journalists and what sells newspapers: punching a photographer is news, feeding a starving refugee family isn't. With me, I disliked a few of the things Woody did, and yet, I loved and respected him because of the good that was within the man I called Coach.

I understand a little bit more about myself and my situation because of Woody Hayes and the things that happened to him in his lifetime. My friends know the real Jack Tatum and so do some of my fans. But the average person on the street wouldn't know me if I walked on by, and yet, if you mention my name, the reaction isn't going to be positive. "Sleaze bucket," I think is what Morton Downey, Jr., called me and some folks wouldn't be so tempered in their assessment.

There was a time when I didn't care what fans thought about me, good or bad. Off the field, I got along with most of the players throughout the NFL and I had my own circle of close friends. Naturally, I signed my share of autographs and at the same time I received my share of hate mail. Either way it was okay.

Then I came to a point in time where I wanted people to know the real me. I simply grew tired of journalists forever taking their cheap shots and television personalities turning up their noses when my name was mentioned. I don't want big mouths like Morton Downey, Jr., telling lies and distorting truth about my accomplishments as a football player and my feeling toward my fellow man, and how I live my life or why I wrote the book. I know how I played the game of football and I know about my life and to hell with all the bullshit and the bullshitters. It's time the legitimate fans knew the truth, and from that perhaps they will draw a more positive conclusion about me and my career. At least with all the evidence they'll have a chance to check out the facts and discover the truth.

I was in a restaurant in downtown Pittsburgh one Saturday night having a quiet dinner when a dude staggered up to my table. He obviously had a few too many as he said in a slurred but surly tone, "I recognize you ... you're one of the damn Raiders."

Most of the people having dinner were dressed up. This man seemed a little out of place with his jeans and Steeler jacket, but I had seen die-hard fans in Pittsburgh before.

I didn't have a chance to answer because he continued slobbering and babbling, "You're a Raider. Clarence Davis, ain't you?"

I told the man to sit down and I'd buy him a drink. I had the feeling he didn't like Raiders and instead of causing a scene, I'd distract him with a drink — coffee, sober him up a little and then maybe we could talk.

He sat down at my table and started by telling me, "Look here, Davis. I oughtta take you outside and kick your ass. Matter of fact, I'm gonna take you outside and kick your ass."

"But why?" I asked.

"Why?" he blew his breath in my face and spit all over my meal. "WHY?" he shouted so that everyone was now looking at us. "I'll tell you why ... because that rotten bastard Tatum got Swanie last year and you're a Raider. That's why. I'm tired of the Raiders taking cheap shots and the refs never calling it."

For several moments I didn't know what to do or say. I had been in these kinds of situations before and never could win. It wasn't that I was afraid of this dude giving me an ass-whippin' because I figured he would have to be at least a tenth degree black belt or else he would have to grow about eight inches and gain seventy-five pounds before he could take me outside and even hope to keep his promise. He was a little dork and stumbling-down drunk. The problem with these kinds of people is that their minds are made up and they have all the answers. Drunk or stone cold sober, I knew this little fan wasn't going to change his opinion or let reality and the facts confuse him. To this little man, football was an illusion. He saw what he wanted to see and believed what he thought he saw.

"Tatum's a cheap-shot artist, a rotten, back-stabbin' prick and they should run him out of football," he said.

I decided to have some fun and answered, "I gotta agree with you. That's why the Raiders traded him today."

He looked a little perplexed as everything slowly registered. "No shit," he said. "I didn't know that."

"Yeah, it's true," I told him while nodding my head up and down. "He'll be in a new uniform tomorrow and we'll be playin' against him."

Suddenly everything hit home as the little Steeler fan replied, "But you guys are playin' the Steelers tomorrow."

"Right. Steelers traded Swanie for Tatum," I said.

"Swanie for Tatum," the words choked in his throat. Then there was a long period of silence as he stared at the table shaking his head slowly back and forth in disbelief. A moment later he responded, "That's just what the hell the Steelers need, a hammer like Tatum in that secondary poundin' the shit outta receivers." Then he looked at me and said, "On second thought, I'm not gonna kick your ass 'cause Tatum will get you tomorrow."

The point here is that I'm not writing this book for the die-hard football fans who would only accept Jack Tatum if he had played on their team. I'd like the legitimate fans to read this one because only they have the sense to understand and appreciate a good play or great game regardless of which team wins. Legitimate fans realize that winning and losing are part of the game and they don't sit around making silly excuses for losing. Diehards will blame the loss on officials making bad calls, bitch about cheap shots by the opponents, stupid coaching, dumb quarterbacking or a host of other excuses. They never consider the possibility that the competition was, for the day, simply the better team. It's like I said, diehards see illusion; legitimate fans, for the most part, understand the reality of the game.

The human mind is complex and, because of that, every once in a while even a legitimate fan gets a distorted image of what was really there. I was told a story by a very reliable source and, if it's true, it helps to illustrate the point that even legitimate fans once in a while get a fuzzy image of reality.

The story goes that a lady was on vacation in Los Angeles and staying in a very exclusive hotel. One evening she was on her way up to her room and pressed the button for the elevator. As the elevator doors opened, she was greeted by four large men, black men, standing toward the back of the elevator.

The white lady stood there for a moment undecided as to what she should do. The large black men were not getting off the elevator and she was apprehensive about getting on. Finally, the lady slowly stepped into the elevator compartment praying that she wouldn't be robbed or raped or perhaps even murdered by these blacks. She turned and faced the lobby, the doors of the elevator were still opened, and now she had second thoughts.

Suddenly a voice from behind her said, "Hit the floor, lady."

Instantly, the lady dropped to the floor, face down, spread eagle. From behind her came a chorus of polite chuckles and giggles followed by one of the black men saying, "No, lady, I meant hit your floor button. That way the elevator doors will close."

The lady, now a red-faced lady, got to her feet, hit the floor button and went up to her room without looking back. Oh, she could hear the muffled giggles of the black men who were trying to control themselves, but she knew this was certainly the most embarrassing moment of her life.

Several days later the lady went to check out. Upon doing so, management presented her with two dozen red roses, a note, and said that her bill had been paid. Opening the note she read, "Thanks for the most enjoyable elevator ride I've ever had ... Best wishes, Lionel Ritchie."

The lady had always been a Lionel Ritchie fan, but on that particular night, when she stood only a foot away from him and his bodyguards, she saw someone else. Sometimes you gotta open your mind before you can see.

3

Hit 'Em Again!
Harder! Harder!
Hit 'Em Again!

The cheerleaders were screaming, "Hit 'em again! Harder! Harder! Hit 'em again! Harder! Harder!" Then the fans started screaming, "Hit 'em again! Harder! Harder! Hit 'em again! Harder! Harder!" So, I did! And I did it again, and again, and before long, I had the reputation of being the hardest hitter ever to play high school football. I don't know if I was the hardest hitter or not, but I did become a high school All-American.

After high school, several hundred colleges offered me scholarships and coaches from all over the country tried to recruit me. I selected Ohio State and was a three-year defensive starter. In college I never scored a touchdown and I only intercepted four passes. Yet, I was twice selected as a first-team All-American; I was in the balloting for the Heisman Trophy; and, recently, I saw a program on ESPN where they rated the four greatest defensive backs in the history of college football: Mel Renfro, Kenny Easily, Ronnie Lott and Jack Tatum. I'll let the football fans figure out what we had in common.

My college coach said that I was the hardest hitter ever to play the game of football. Maybe I was … maybe I wasn't, but after the first few games during my sophomore year, everyone began to avoid me. For the rest of my college career, I had to go out of my way to find any action.

In spite of collegiate touchdown deficiencies and my lack of interceptions, I was still drafted, and in the first round by the Oakland Raiders. I had become a member of the NFL and I'll let my critics explain the reason why.

During my football career there was always a dichotomy in my character that swung from benevolence to belligerence without any stops in between. For most of the week I was kind of an easygoing couch potato but, on game day, I'd become a nasty hunk of muscle and bone looking to kick some butt. From experience I found it to be that way with most of my peers. Football players usually have a passive attitude and image away from the stadium but during a football game there just isn't any room for Mr. Rogers or Captain Kangaroo.

When I played free safety for the Oakland Raiders my football-season-Sunday-afternoon-best-behavior was a modern version of Mr. Hyde with a little of Jack the Ripper thrown in for good measure. Make no mistake about it, on the football field, I had a reputation as a big hitter and did everything I could to maintain that image. At the same time, I managed to play by the rules and wasn't overly flagged. Legally aggressive was my style in high school, college, and ten years in the NFL, including my three All-Pro seasons. It wasn't a secret and everyone knew that I played aggressively and hit hard all the time. Strange, but no one had a beef until I wrote an honest book about hitting and hitters.

It might be difficult for some people to understand but football is a hitter's game. The harder a defensive player can hit, the better his chances are of playing in the NFL. Anyone who doesn't understand that concept doesn't understand football.

Sure, football has its traps and powers, stunts and blitzes, rubs and streaks, overs and unders, but the winning edge is found in demoralizing your opponent through intimidation. Although few coaches and players would openly admit it, intimidation is the name of the game. The fact is that during the course of contact, one team will usually lose its appetite for aggression and the more physical team will go on to victory. I was an intimidating factor throughout my career and that is the only reason for my having made all-everything. I'm not bragging, just stating a simple fact.

The intimidators in football are a special breed and not everyone can make it work, even in the NFL. Intimidation is a matter of size, speed, quickness, strength, position and courage. A physical and intimidating style is not solely a defensive exclusive, either. However, playing offense is somewhat restricting. Offense is not a hitters' game. For example, offensive linemen are not intimidating because of their position, lack of quickness and overall speed. The offensive linemen play in cramped quarters and rarely get to build up a full head of steam before impact. Without speed there isn't much velocity and intimidation is measured by energy at impact.

Quarterbacks are never intimidating because of the position and physical impossibility. It doesn't matter what you've heard about tough quarterbacks because they all break easily, and if you don't believe me check the weekly injury charts.

Wide receivers, on rare occasions, are physical, but never intimidators. I'm reminded about an incident that took place during the 1988 football season in a game between Denver and Seattle. In an early season meeting, Denver's defensive back, Mike Harden, caught Seattle receiver Steve Largent coming over the middle. It was a questionable forearm to the head and the hit put Largent in the hospital with a concussion. It also destroyed Largent's face mask, broke some facial bones and loosened several teeth. The incident cost Harden some cold hard cash in the way of a stiff fine and there was some talk about retaliation.

When Denver and Seattle got together for the second meeting of the 1988 season, it was payback time, but Steve Largent fought his own battle. Mike Harden intercepted a pass and started working his way to the end zone. Suddenly, a Seahawk blasted Harden to the turf. I mean to say it was a good hit, not a "knockout" or even a "limp-off" but a good hit. I thought maybe a guard or tackle had built up a full head of steam and delivered the blow that knocked Harden airborne for about a five yard ride. To Harden's surprise, and everyone watching the game, it was Steve Largent. The hit wasn't something that would intimidate Mike Harden, but it served to warn that Steve Largent had the ability to be physical. All the same, it's a long way from physical to intimidation.

Tight ends can be physical and on occasion are intimidating, but the position is restricting. Most of the time a tight end is concentrating on his pattern or catching the ball. Defenders anticipate a tight end's moves and usually gain the advantage. Most of the time the tight end is getting hit instead of hitting.

Offensively, the only real opportunity to be an intimidator is found in the position of running back. Most of the time, the average running back will dance around looking for the openings. But I played against Earl Campbell, Larry Csonka and Walter Payton and they were not your average running backs. They did their dancing on the bodies of would-be defenders.

Earl Campbell was quick, fast, and weighed about 235 pounds. He had a low center of gravity, powerful legs and thighs, and incredible balance. He would make an effort to get around the defenders, but if he couldn't, then it was time to buckle up your chin strap because he sure as hell was going to try to run you over. Earl was an intimidator and a defender had to be extremely careful when coming after him.

I had several run-ins with Earl and, to tell you the truth, sometimes I don't know who won. There was one time when I got a pretty good shot at him on a goal line stand. I hit him in the chest and tried to project myself through his body. On impact I started thinking knockout or at least a limp-off. To my astonishment, somehow Earl staggered into the end zone. Scoring the touchdown was bad enough, but watching Earl get up and walk over to the sidelines as though nothing had happened tormented me for the longest time.

Several years later I talked to Earl about the hit. I explained that I couldn't believe the power and the balance he had. He had taken one of my better shots, but got up and walked back to the sidelines under his own power. It was like I hadn't even been there. I figured that either I was getting old or Earl Campbell wasn't human.

Earl tilted his head back and smiled as he said, "After that hit, I didn't know who I was or where I was ... I woke up on the sidelines wondering what happened."

Larry Csonka wasn't as quick and fast as Earl Campbell, few people were, but he was probably twenty-five pounds heavier. Larry had good speed but the frightening thing about him was that he played football like a cornered rat, mean and vicious. Larry would get low and smash the defender into the ground with his helmet and shoulder pads. At the same time he would be punching and blasting away with his forearm, but most frightening was the fact that he actually went out of his way to hit defenders. Csonka, as the intimidator, was a lot like the creatures in the movies "Predator" and "The Terminator": they never asked for any mercy, nor did they show any.

If Csonka wasn't intimidating enough, then Walter Payton was. They called him "Sweetness," but don't let the name fool you. Tackling Sweetness always left a bitter taste in my mouth. Sweetness was a nice guy off the field, but during the game he was like a rattlesnake. If you left him alone he was okay, but try to hold him down and he'd bite you. Sweetness was actually an illusive runner until there wasn't any room left to be illusive. That's when he'd turn and strike like a damn snake. He was quick and, if you weren't prepared, he'd get you.

Walter Payton wasn't quite six feet tall and only weighed about two hundred pounds. Sure, he had speed, quickness and strength, but his courage enabled him to play like a man twice his size. Walter never looked for the easy way out. He never accidentally tripped or ran for the safety of the sidelines. He fought for every inch of real estate and earned his reputation as an intimidating running back. Every defender in the league knew that if they hit Walter, Walter was going to hit back.

I hit Walter one time, head-on, helmet to helmet and both of us were moving with a pretty good head of steam. They tell me the impact shook the stadium, but I didn't hear a damn thing. Everything was silent for a second or two as Walter toppled over to one side and I stumbled over the other way. Then I began to hear a strange noise. The strange noise was me. My body was humming like a tuning fork. I struggled to my feet, and to my surprise, so did Walter. We just glanced at each other and went back to our own huddles. Damn, what a collision, I thought. Walter had taken a pretty good shot, and he returned the favor. It ended up a tie, but don't believe that crap about a tie being the same thing as kissing your sister. Fighting Walter Payton to a tie was like Armageddon and the feeling that followed was hell.

Walter was an intimidating running back, but I had a reputation, too. If I couldn't get the man with one good shot, I'd try again and the next time I'd look for a better angle or anything to give me the edge. But sometimes intimidation didn't work and it was that way with Walter Payton. No matter how hard the hit, he couldn't be intimidated. Then again, neither could I, and that's when football became hell.

Most football fans don't understand intimidation and the hitters of the game. They think they do, but the average fan doesn't have the vaguest notion of speed, velocity and the numbing pain of intimidation. Pure intimidation can be a "limp-off" or a "knockout" or the sound of air rushing out of lungs or sometimes the dull snap of breaking bone. Intimidation is a painful and frightening experience and sometimes it can even take the heart out of a champion.

A good example of an intimidator is heavyweight champion Mike Tyson in his recent fight with Michael Spinks. Michael Spinks believed he could win because he knew his own abilities. He was a champion. He was tough, and helping to build his confidence level was the fact that many journalists, and even some boxing fans, claimed that Mike Tyson built a reputation beating up bums. Even if someone had told Michael Spinks he didn't have a chance against Tyson, he wouldn't have believed it. He might have said that he and Tyson put on their pants the same way or uttered something ridiculous about "conceive, believe, achieve." I've read those "self-help, positive-attitude" books, too, but W. Clement Stone and Norman Vincent Peale were writing about financial matters and not testing some mind over muscle theory in the ring against Mike Tyson.

Sitting in his dressing room there was a degree of confidence in Michael's eyes. The only problem was that eventually he would have to leave the security of those four walls and climb into the ring. That's when Michael Spinks would learn about intimidation. I figured that Michael was a real bright guy and it wouldn't take him very long to catch on. It didn't.

I don't think Michael saw the first punch coming in the first minute of the first and only round. It was a quick and painfully decisive shot to the ribs. Michael seemed a little confused. I'm sure that, somewhere in the deep chambers of his mind, he was aware of burning ribs, but that was strange because he couldn't remember being invited to a barbecue. Equally strange was the blurred image of a man wearing a bow tie shouting numbers. And what the hell was that other "Thing" in the hazy background?

Suddenly it dawned on Michael. It wasn't the aroma of a barbecue that was tantalizing his brain, it was the god-awful burning pain of his own crushed ribs. Reality had a sobering effect on Michael. He had been mugged and punched to the canvas, and that "Thing" in the far corner, patiently waiting for him to get up, was Mike Tyson. Oh, my God, no, not even for fifteen million dollars!

The competitive spark in the eyes of Michael Spinks had been extinguished by one intimidating punch. I could see it and so could the whole world. Courage would lift him to his feet, but intimidation already had him looking for a softer spot to fall. It usually happens that way whenever intimidators land a solid shot. Intimidators is only a word, but believe me when I say it can snatch the heart of a champion, too.

Once in a while I talk to football fans about hitting and intimidation and someone will usually mention the name of Dick Butkus. People actually think he was an intimidator and a big hitter. That kind of thinking goes to prove that most football fans don't know a damn thing about the basics of hitting and intimidation.

Get ready for this: Butkus wasn't a hitter. I watched the highlight films of Dick's career and he was aggressive, but he wasn't a hard hitter. As a middle linebacker, Dick had a pretty good position for launching the attack and he had courage and size, but he didn't have speed. He lumbered around the field as a mauler, but that's not hitting. Even when Butkus got a good shot at a ball carrier, he never had velocity behind the hit. Now, I'm not saying Dick Butkus wasn't a solid player because he had a great career. There's just a difference between his mauling style of play and my idea of pure intimidation.

Dick Butkus, by his own admission, made it perfectly clear that he couldn't hit. Dick once said, "Whenever I get a clear shot at the ball carrier, I don't want him turning around to see who did the hitting. I want him to know without looking it was Dick Butkus." I'm sorry, but if you hit someone with your best shot and he's still able to think, then you're not a big hitter.

Pete Rozelle is going to get upset with me again. He did the first time I wrote this, but I still believe that if you hit a man with your best shot then he should wake up on the sidelines with train whistles blowing in his head wondering what hit him and not thinking about who hit him. Whenever I hit someone with my best shot, they usually woke up without the vaguest clue as to what happened. That's the difference between mauling and hitting.

It might seem like I'm picking on Dick Butkus, but really I'm not. I'm being honest, and indirectly Butkus is helping to illustrate my overall picture of football, football players and myself, both as an athlete and a human being. I'm the first to admit that Butkus is a true legend of the game. As a football hero, people think he's bigger than life. But that's okay because I'm only looking for a little respect and nothing more. I'm tired of being the Rodney Dangerfield of football and it's time to set the record straight.

NFL Films has a feature on Dick Butkus. During the film, the narrator said that Butkus "played the game in a bloody rage." Deacon Jones said, "Butkus was so mean that he'd follow players up into the stands or follow them into the tunnel … just to get 'em … and I saw him do it." And Monty Stickles, an end with the 49ers from 1960 to 1967, said of Butkus, "He tried to hit you so hard that your helmet and your head would fly off … he damn well tried to knock your head off on every play."

I don't know if Dick Butkus played in a bloody rage or if he chased opponents up into the stands or if he honestly tried to knock their heads off on every play, but I never did — chase opponents up into the stands, that is.

I think about Dick's favorite movie, *Hush, Hush, Sweet Charlotte*, and that part "where the head comes rollin' down the stairs." My goodness, did Butkus really think about hitting a guy so hard that his head would come off, or was that simply football talk and not to be taken seriously?

I'm just being sarcastically facetious, of course, because we all realize that Dick and his fans were engaging in a humorous monologue of locker room stories. No one runs around the football field believing he can knock off heads… and I mean, no one. Only a complete imbecile would think that Butkus and his friends were serious.

I've mentioned the word imbecile and suddenly I am reminded of the treatment I received from Pete Rozelle and several sports journalists when I wrote about knocking off heads in my infamous book. They gave me a lot of flak because I wrote about my style of headhunting even though it was mild compared to Dick's horror stories of football. Then again, I wasn't a famous linebacker so I should be condemned for telling those kinds of stories when others are not. Right? I guess my situation only makes sense when you understand the word hypocrisy and realize that Pete Rozelle and most sports journalists are hypocrites.

In the first book, I explained a legal technique that George Atkinson and I referred to as the "Hook." The Hook was simply flexing your biceps and trying to catch the receiver's head in the joint between the forearm and upper arm. It's like hitting with the biceps by using a headlock type of action. The purpose of the Hook was to strip the receiver of the ball, his helmet, his courage and his head. Of course, I only used the Hook in full-speed contact and it was most effective from the blind side. The Hook caused fumbles, knocked off helmets, and one application was, usually, enough to snatch the courage out of just about anyone's heart ... anyone except Sweetness and a few others who believe the cheer, "Hit 'em again, Harder! Harder!" was for the benefit of the offensive team.

One time George and I were working out a heavy tackling bag practicing the Hook. Defensive coach Bob Zeman watched us for several minutes. The next day, he had all the defensive backs practicing the Hook. Why not? It wasn't illegal, but to listen to my critics, it was.

Now, even though I mentioned using the Hook for the purpose of decapitation, I never got a head and I never expected to achieve that kind of a result. Sure, I wrote about trying to knock off a head or two, but it was a figure of speech, a funny line, locker room talk, simply the kind of story that Dick Butkus often tells. Most of my fans got a good laugh out of it. Butkus probably did too, but some imbeciles took me literally.

George Atkinson and I had merely taken the standard NFL "Clothesline Tackle," souped it up with a little speed, modernized the technique and called it the Hook. During the early part of my career the Hook wasn't just legal but an important weapon in a good hitter's arsenal. I always felt the Hook was the best intimidator in the game; but, when the rules were changed, I stopped using it. I truly believe that, because of my perfecting the Hook, the NFL had to change one of its rule and the game was made a little safer. Shots to the head were once legal, but then I started using the Hook and everything changed for the better.

The Hook was no different than some of the other once-legal but now-illegal techniques of the game. In fact, the Hook was mild in comparison to a few routines employed by the early men of the NFL. In the old days, leg whipping was legal and players would tape magazines around their shins. The magazines protected the shin but they also turned legs into rock-hard, lethal weapons. Today the leg whip is outlawed and the same goes for grabbing the face mask. But it wasn't always that way. When the "face bar" was first invented for protection, it wasn't illegal to grab it and make a tackle. It doesn't make a lot of sense to invent something to protect the face then let the players use it to break necks, but it's true. Early on, defensive people had a theory that wherever the face mask went, the helmet, and maybe the head, would follow. The old-timers made a science out of grabbing the face mask and twisting. It was an easy way for the defensive man to bring down the ball carrier. What the hell, all a player needed was a strong hand and a quick wrist. What could be easier than that?

It finally dawned on someone that the face mask was connected to the helmet and the helmet was sort of connected to the head bone and the head bone was definitely connected to the neck bone. The technique could prove hazardous to the player's health and thus grabbing the face mask was banned.

I think when a problem crops up that becomes a major threat to the safety of the players, they will make an attempt to change the rules. But overall, football still remains a hitter's game, and a person doesn't have to be a Yale grad to figure out why. Big hits, hitters, intimidation and violence are among the marketing gemstones of football and everyone knows it. I'm positive the league office would never openly admit to anything like that, but give fans and television advertisers the choice of spending their dollars on a high-scoring affair between the Dolphins and the Cardinals or a blood bath between the Bears and Vikings and see who plays on the tube.

Until the NFL perfects the old Pete Rozelle theory on easy tackling, and then changes the rules, and convinces television marketing people that the fans want to see two-hand touchy, I'm afraid it's going to be a hitter's game with hitter's rules. So don't cry or complain when people get hurt.

I guess that's part of my problem, and I'm not talking about hard hitting. Some individuals will never realize that life and football are played in separate arenas and each has a different set of rules. I've always made an effort to go by the rules; but at the same time, I believe a person has to make a one hundred percent effort regardless of where he lives or works or plays the game. Anything less and he'll come up a loser.

When it came to football, I was hard-hitting and tough. Even the most aggressively violent hitmen and assassins of the NFL have the ability to be quality human beings making contributions to real life.

The fact that just because they played football as football was meant to be played doesn't make them less sensitive to life and the people they've met over the years. That is true of me because there just isn't an easy way to play football, and that's a fact. But Pete Rozelle and some sports journalists still put out cookies and warm milk for Santa.

Reggie White, defensive lineman for the Philadelphia Eagles, is one of the toughest, meanest, nastiest players in the NFL. During the strike-shortened 12-game season of 1987, Reggie had 22 quarterback sacks, one short of the sixteen game record. As a football player, Reggie's objective is to smash, trample and flatten the opposition, especially quarterbacks. When he's on the football field, people try to avoid him. It's the intelligent thing to do. Seriously, out on the football field, it's like Reggie has contracted a contagious disease, or maybe he has an extremely serious case of bad breath. Whatever, it's obvious that everyone is trying to avoid Reggie White the assassin.

However, Reggie White the human being is another story. Away from the stadium and in real life people want to be around him. Reggie is one of the friendliest and most compassionate men alive. He's an example of living a clean life, doing the right thing because it is the right thing to do, and, also, he is a true believer in the Bible. Reggie White is an ordained preacher, a good man traveling between two worlds. As an assassin, he's feared; as a human being, he is admired. And that's they way it should be because football and real life are played in separate arenas with a different set of rules.

Lee Williams, an All-Pro and apprentice assassin for the San Diego Chargers, is another example of a dual personality. I realize that San Diego is just about the last place one would expect to find an apprentice assassin, but I really think the Chargers' philosophy of scoring fifty points a game in order to win by one is becoming a fading echo against the reality of always being pretenders to the title instead of contenders.

Several years ago, the yachting competition of San Diego was more physical than Charger football. I'm serious. Dennis "The Skipper" Conners, and Michael "Gilligan" Fay did more hitting at press conferences than the Chargers did at the stadium. When jibing around an obstacle course off Point Loma in quest of The America's Cup took precedence over any claim to the Lombardi Trophy, it was time for the Chargers to do something about the Gilligan's Island image.

On September 29, 1988, the *San Diego Union* had sports page headlines that read: "Williams' mission is to punish quarterbacks." It was a good thing that Pete Rozelle didn't hear about that write-up because some heads would have rolled.

I had to read the article because the *San Diego Union* was one of the many newspapers that blasted me on my first book. Even though I wrote about playing within the confines of the rules, it was my confessions of aggressive play that caught the eye of *Union* sports journalists and thus began the negative barrage of insulting write-ups about the Raider Assassin.

The *San Diego Union*, as I remember, was particularly hard on me because I wrote things like, "football is a violent game." Also I wrote, "I try to punish my opponent," and, "there's nothing illegal about my style, but I want my hits to intimidate." For the obvious reason, this article on Lee Williams really caught my attention. Knowing how the *San Diego Union* handled the confessions of a Raider Assassin, I was interested in seeing how they would handle the antics of Charger apprentice assassin, Mr. Lee Williams.

Since I'm dedicating an entire chapter of this book to the art of journalistic hypocrisy, I'm going to skip the lecture and direct my attention toward Lee Williams and this particular write-up. *Union* staff writer T.J. Simers wrote of Williams, "He looks intimidating in uniform, sometimes talks like 'Rambo' and does what's necessary to run down quarterbacks like 'Dirty Harry' guns down bad guys."

Lee Williams states, "Personally, I try to put my helmet square into the middle of the quarterback's chin, pick him up off the ground and then punish him into the turf."

Lee then mentions what would be deemed unmentionable in some NFL cities: "Football is a violent game. You don't really know what's going on in the trenches; it's not a pretty sight."

When he was asked about delivering an injury causing blow to Seattle quarterback Dave Krieg (a shoulder separation that sidelined Krieg for eight weeks), Lee Williams said, "I have no remorse."

Lee explained that Seattle offensive linemen, and NFL offensive linemen in general, were always trying to hurt him intentionally, and were picking on him, so to speak. That may or may not be true. I really don't know, but I do know that Lee has learned the first rule of being an assassin: ask no mercy and give none. You play by the rules, of course. You use the rules, stretch the rules, and once in a while break the rules, but you don't show any mercy and you don't expect any in return. It all sounds brutal and violent, and it is. But it's a hitter's game and there's nothing illegal about Lee's disposing of quarterbacks.

Lee Williams is fast becoming a legend with Charger ticket holders at Jack Murphy Stadium and before long people are going to start keeping score. One point for the "limp-off" and two points for the "knock-off." Maybe Lee will even get a head or two, and why not ...

he's one helluva hitter. Lee is really busting up the opposition with his style of San Andreas football, but damn it, football is a hitter's game.

I realize that hard-nose football might seem cruel and insensitive to folks in other areas of the country, but in defense of Charger players, fans, coaches and even sports journalists, I'll intervene. This is going to sound callous, but quarterback bashing and hitting the opposition hard is perfectly legal and simply part of the game. Six weeks into the 1988 football season, 19 starting quarterbacks were successfully bashed and I haven't the vaguest idea of how many other injuries occurred because of hard hits.

September 26, 1988, Al Michaels of ABC's *Monday Night Football* in doing the Cleveland Browns–Indianapolis Colts football game made a jovial statement concerning a successful bash. Early on, Colt quarterback Jack Trudeau was semi-bashed and had to leave the game with some bruised ribs. He later returned only to discover that Carl Hairston, a 6-2, 270 pound lineman for the Browns was waiting patiently for his turn at the ever-popular quarterback bash. Trudeau dropped back to pass, and Carl Hairston quickly slipped by the offensive lineman assigned to prevent any bashing. A second later, Trudeau was rolling around the ground in pain clutching his knee and pointing to his hip. Make no mistake about it, Jack Trudeau was bashed and in pain. While looking at the slow-motion relay I was thinking that maybe he broke a hip or blew out a knee, or both.

Al Michaels, adding a little *Monday Night Football* humor to the slow-motion replay of agony in progress said in jocular fashion from the safety of the press box, "This time, Carl Hairston effectively removed Jack Trudeau from the game."

Originally, when my book first came under siege, I started thinking that maybe I was in the wrong. Maybe I didn't use proper words or maybe I told the wrong kind of stories. Then I took a closer look at the NFL, and I listened to the great ones as they expounded upon their careers and the game itself. But, of course, it was different back then, so I had to study a rising star, a gladiator whose "mission is to punish quarterbacks."

If it wasn't for the word "hypocrisy," I'd never understand the reason for my condemnation. Perhaps justice will one day be served, perhaps not. But like I said, I've always believed a person has to give 100 percent regardless of where he lives or works or plays the game. And that goes double for writing a book.

"Hit 'em again! Harder! Harder! Hit 'em again!" They did, and I did, and they still do, because it's a hitter's game.

4

What's a "No-Huddle, Quick-Snap Offense," Ollie?

On Sunday, January 8, 1989, as the Cincinnati Bengals and Buffalo Bills were getting ready to go out onto the field and play the AFC Championship game, Pete Rozelle was at it again. I hate to keep picking on the guy, but he just doesn't quit. This time my Pete Rozelle story has to do with a last-minute rule change that had the Bengals roaring and me laughing. Let me back up and tell the entire story because it is a classic.

For about three or four years the Bengals occasionally used a no-huddle, quick-snap offense. This was designed to prevent a defensive team from running their various specialists in and out of the game. In short yardage, for example, the defensive team will load up with linemen and some linebackers to stop the run. However, in passing situations, a team might use five or maybe six defensive backs and a good pass rusher. With a no-huddle, quick-snap offense, the Bengals or any other team choosing to use the tactic could make it difficult on the opposition when it came to changing defensive personnel. The Bengals were getting pretty good with the system and sometimes they even caught their opponents with extra players on the field when the ball was snapped. That was part of the strategy because extra players on the field are illegal, but a no-huddle, quick-snap offense isn't ... or, I should say, wasn't. To be precise, a no-huddle, quick-snap offense wasn't illegal until 11:33 a.m., January 8, 1989, or thereabouts. I figure that's probably when the Bengals' head coach, Sam Wyche, was notified that the NFL had changed the rule on him.

Prior to the sudden rule change an offensive team could go directly to the line of scrimmage, set for only one second and then begin the play. I don't want to infer that Sam and his boys couldn't line up on the ball, because I think Pete was saying it was just illegal to go on a quick-snap count. In other words, they had to give the Buffalo Bills time to make all their defensive changes and then the ball could be snapped. I never was quite sure how the new rule read and I don't think anyone was. It was a bit confusing especially when you consider the ruling was handed down just before kick-off. But the fact remained that if the Bengals used a no-huddle, quick-snap offense, they would be penalized for unsportsmanlike conduct.

I could picture Sam checking the calendar to see if he had been asleep for the past three months. Was it actually April 1 … already? It wasn't April Fool's Day, so Sam had to be thinking that the sudden rule change was some kind of joke, or perhaps a mistake. Hell, everyone knows that you don't change a rule just minutes before the kick-off. No one is that dumb. Rule changes are made during the off-season and are supposed to be done by a vote of 28 team representatives.

I wonder how many shades of red Sam Wyche turned when informed that this particular rule change was an impulsive, unilateral decision made by Pete Rozelle. First of all, there's the embarrassing shade of red a person turns when the implication is that he's been cheating. Sure, Cincinnati used this tactic for seventeen games during the past season, and they've been doing it for three years or longer. Why not? It was a legal maneuver and in the past nothing had ever been said about changing the rule. Then suddenly, most dramatically, and just prior to the AFC Championship game, the commissioner changed the rule and was now pointing his familiar, "you've-been-a-bad-boy" finger in the Bengals' face. Sam Wyche and his Bengals were not cheaters, of course not, but for the commissioner to take such a drastic action it certainly indicated wrong-doing on their part. After the game, and a hard-fought 21-10 Bengal victory, Sam told the press, "It's tough to finish an emotional game and evaluate the rightness or wrongness of a ruling and come out looking good. You look bad; let's face it, I'm going to look bad."

The Bengals had only spent a week preparing for the game, but it was probably some of the most important time they, as athletes, would ever spend. The winner of this Sunday's encounter would go on to the Super Bowl and perhaps reap the rewards of a championship season. With everything at stake, I would have to believe that a fair amount of practice time was dedicated to an offensive game plan that involved the no-huddle offense whereby Sam Wyche and his boys could take advantage of certain Buffalo defensive personnel. Changing the rule unilaterally was totally in error, but the midnight hour timing was extremely unfair to the Bengals and their fans.

Angry red, and rightly so, was the next coloration of Sam's face. He couldn't understand that if an action against the Bengals' no-huddle, quick-snap offense was forthcoming, why Pete waited until the last minute to spring the trap. Normally, that would be a logical question, but if logic has anything to do with it, Pete Rozelle will never ride on the bridge of the *Starship Enterprise* as its first officer. Logically speaking, there was no answer to Sam's legitimate questions. However, if you take into consideration Pete's mastery of bad timing and poor judgments, the sudden rule change was merely par for the course.

Sam made the statement, "I think it's one of the biggest mistakes our top (NFL) management has made." Sam was angry and under that type of emotional stress a person will say things without even thinking. If Coach Wyche sat down and really thought about Pete's ability to pull off major league blunders, then his present dilemma would grow pale by comparison. Sometimes I believe that "Big Mistakes" is Pete's middle name.

Sam was enraged by the league action and claimed that he was losing sleep over it all. He probably was and I truly felt for him. But I had to disagree when he tried to blame the conspiracy on Buffalo head coach, Marv Levy. During the week, Marv did make a number of complaints about the Bengal's no-huddle, quick-snap offense to the press and, for that matter, anyone stupid enough to listen. But who in his right mind would ever have thought that a little bitching could bring about an overnight rule change?

Larry, Curly and Moe would have had the good sense to leave the situation alone, but the commissioner isn't a stooge. Pete was simply exercising his authority as Commissioner of the National Football League and he deserved a little respect for being on the job early Sunday morning. He probably thought it was Monday morning, but at least he was trying.

As for Marv Levy, I think Sam Wyche and the other coaches of the league should congratulate the man for pioneering a new frontier of coaching strategies. In successfully petitioning the commissioner for a Sunday-morning, last-minute rule change, I think Marv Levy has laid the groundwork for an extremely promising and potentially innovative 1989 football season. Dwell on that for a moment.

During the 1989 NFC Championship game, I remember the Chicago Bears had a tough time with San Francisco wide receiver, Jerry Rice. Under the new system, Bears' coach Mike Ditka, could have petitioned the commissioner, just prior to kick-off, and got a new ruling to eliminate Jerry Rice from making those fantastic catches and long, fast touchdown runs. A little rule change and Jerry

Rice is taken out of the game.

And what about the trash the Redskins ran at Denver in Super Bowl XXII. The Redskins used a load and heavy load formation and ran some type of a counter gap that Denver couldn't stop. Under the new system, Denver could have called a time-out and petitioned the commissioner for a new ruling preventing the Redskins from using "illegal formations and running plays." Presto! Pete changes the rule and we have a competitive Super Bowl XXII and not some turn-off-the-TV-at-halftime blowout. It would have made for a better game.

We've all heard about the NFL's instant replay, so why not try the instant rule system and see what happens. Think of all the possibilities. Steelers' coach Chuck Noll doesn't like Oilers' coach Jerry Glanville. So under the Rozelle instant rule system, Chuck simply petitions the commissioner to make up a new ruling that would ban anyone named Jerry Glanville from ever coaching in the NFL. Ditka could use the same ruling against any wise guy named Ryan, but only if he coached in Philadelphia and, perhaps, some guy called Buddy coaching in Philadelphia could get a ruling about hard asses called Mike, but only if he was born in Aliquippa, Pennsylvania. Think of the potential we'd have with this new system. We could get rid of all the Mikes, Jerrys and Buddys coaching in the game today and bring in some new names like Porky, Donald and Daffy. Who knows, with Pete spending most of his time working on rule changes, maybe the NFL would need a new commissioner. Let's call him Elmer, as in Fudd.

Whenever I had dealings with Pete, I'd get the feeling that every day was April 1st, but he always forgot to say, "April Fool." Pete would say or do something dumb, and just sort of leave me hanging on the edge, waiting for him to finish with a big punch line. I'd wait and wait and wait only to discover there was no joke. It was probably that way with Sam Wyche when he first heard about the sudden rule change. He waited and waited for the punch line, but gradually realized there was none. Welcome to the club, Sam, and for what it's worth, you're not alone.

Sam Wyche hasn't had much experience in dealing with Pete, so he's bound to get uptight over a little thing like a rule change or two. I understood completely, because I used to feel much the same way after Pete would come down on me for nothing. But after a while you learn to roll with the whims and woes of the suntanned man pressing the wrong buttons in the New York office. It comes with experience and I've probably had more experience in dealing with Pete than most.

For a while, Pete and I had a weekly thing going. Every Monday morning, just like clockwork, Pete would fine me $150. The reason for the fine was that I wore special arthritic braces to keep my knees warm during games. Sitting around on the sidelines, my knees would stiffen up and hurt. I discovered that a rubber arthritic brace would keep the heat in and prevent the pain and stiff joints. The only trouble was that you could see the black braces around my knees and the NFL has a strict dress code. It's an important issue, of course, or Pete wouldn't sit around the office checking out game films to make sure that the players' jerseys are neatly tucked in, that socks are pulled up to NFL specifications, and that no arthritic knee braces are visible regardless of the reason.

I explained my position to the league office and there was no argument over the fact that the braces did keep in the heat and prevent the stiffening pain in my joints. But ... I was breaking the law, and once a week, I was hit with a $150 fine. I wasn't going to take off the braces, and after a while it became obvious that the league was equally stubborn. I had a legitimate reason for my stubbornness, but the league didn't. Unless they considered stupidity reason enough.

Finally it was decided that I could wear the braces, but only if I got a note from a doctor. That could easily be arranged since one of my best friends was a "doctor," so to speak. Pete seemed to enjoy playing games and I started thinking about joining in and having some fun of my own.

My roommate during training camp was a doctor. He wasn't an orthopedic specialist, but he was, nonetheless, by Raider standards, a doctor. Instead of practicing medicine, he played cornerback and his name was Skip Thomas. I was positive Skip, I mean the doctor, would send a note to the commissioner on my behalf. That could prove interesting but only when you understand Skip, if understanding Skip is possible.

Skip Thomas always considered himself a normal USC graduate with a few different ideas about life. For openers, Skip wouldn't talk to reporters or let anyone take his picture. He used to say, "Getting your picture taken steals part of your soul." As for reporters, Skip didn't like people and, of course, reporters fell into the category of people. One time a reporter came up to our room to interview me. Skip didn't like the questions I was being asked so he threw the reporter out the door.

Skip played football from a different world. His body would be on the field doing a job but his mind would travel off to other planets and solar systems. Don't misunderstand me. Skip was a great athlete. He had so much ability that during practice and sometimes during the games he would become bored. I've never seen anyone defend against the pass quite like Skip. He could run full speed with the receiver, watch the quarterback throw the pass, and at the last second knock the ball away. Most defensive backs have a similar technique, but at practice Skip never just 'batted' the ball away, he would jump up and 'kick' it away. I've seen Skip jump four and five feet off the ground and kick the ball out of mid-air just as the receiver was reaching for a catch. Skip has a style all his own, a strange style at that.

The night before a game, Skip would eat four or five full-course meals, drink a bottle of tequila, smoke two packs of cigarettes and watch TV for hours after all the channels had signed off. Skip Thomas didn't actually study medicine in college, but he earned the title of "doctor" during the Raiders' training camp his rookie year. Earning that title in a Raider training camp was more difficult than any medical school in the world. That's why I figured Skip would be qualified to write my doctor's excuse to the commissioner.

Most of the time, we, as Raiders in good standings, would let ourselves go at training camp. We would hardly shave and never wore fancy clothes. I mean to say, after a week or so, everyone was really scuzzed-up. One day, Skip was walking over to the practice field looking the way he thought a Raider athlete should look. His appearance was bad even by Raider training camp standards. Someone said Skip looked as though he was coming back from one of his frequent trips to Mars and all points beyond. Bob Brown, a big offensive tackle, saw Skip coming up the path and jumped back ten steps and said, "Damn, Skip, you look like death warmed over, swallowed down whole and spit back out." Skip looked terrible, but the next day he looked even worse. After a week of letting himself go, Skip earned the nickname "Doctor Death."

The name caught on and it got to where Skip liked to be called "Doctor Death." He even painted the name "Doctor Death" on both doors of his Corvette, right under the skull and crossbones. Before long everyone called him "Doc," even the trainers and coaches. By Raider standards Doctor Death was board certified to practice medicine, but no one in camp ever considered asking him for a cough drop let alone a serious medical question. Then, the Raiders drafted Charles Philyaw and all of that changed. The "Doc" was in business.

Philyaw was a 6-8 defensive lineman. Charles would have been a helluva defensive player if he could put everything together at the same time. But that was the problem, he couldn't put it together at the same time. If he wasn't getting mixed up putting on his uniform, then he was confused as to which meeting to attend. Philyaw showed up at practice one day with two different colored socks, the wrong colored jersey, no belt, his thigh pads were in upside down, and instead of football shoes, he was wearing sandals. Everyone stopped and stared in disbelief. This was a professional athlete? The coaches took Charles aside and started counting up the things wrong with his uniform. Philyaw set an NFL record that will never be broken. Ten things were wrong with his uniform and that's hard to do when you consider there are only eleven items in the uniform category. He got one point for having his helmet on and in the proper position. Some of the guys thought he was just lucky and there were some bets that he couldn't put his helmet on in the proper way three times in a row. Fooled everyone when he did.

Every morning the offensive and defensive teams would go to separate rooms and view game films. One morning Philyaw went to the offensive section by mistake. Now I could understand walking into a dark room by mistake, but sitting there with the wrong people and watching the wrong game films would be an indication that something wasn't exactly right. But it never dawned on Philyaw and he sat there in the offensive room until someone explained the situation to him.

In the meantime, defensive coach Tom Dahms had a nice meeting going without Philyaw, and when someone said, "Coach, Philyaw isn't here," he answered, "Good!"

To say that Charles Philyaw was a little slow in catching on was an understatement. At practice, Charles hurt his hand and needed medical attention. He walked over to Pete Banaszak, holding his hand and asked, "Hey, man, what should I do?"

"Go see the doctor," Pete said.

Philyaw promptly walked out into the middle of a pass defense drill and pulled Skip Thomas aside saying, "Man said I should show you this," and he stuck his bloody paw in Skip's face.

Well, the Doc knows more cuss words than a barroom filled with drunken merchant marines and he let fly with some choice dialog. Coach Madden came running over, settled Skip down and tried to explain the situation to Philyaw. After five minutes or so, Philyaw got the picture and went off looking for one of the trainers.

About a week later, Skip and I were in our room taking a nap. Suddenly, there came a knock at the door. Skip got up to answer. He always did, even when I was expecting company. Opening the door, Skip found himself looking into the face of Philyaw. Skip cussed a little and asked, "Whatta you want, you big dummy?"

Philyaw started explaining about his sprained ankle and said that someone told him to see the "Doctor" about getting a whirlpool. Philyaw had forgotten that Skip wasn't a doctor, and knowing Philyaw, that was understandable. After Al Davis explained everything to Philyaw, Skip never had that particular problem again.

I figured that if Philyaw made two trips to see Skip before he understood the facts, then I could get away with one note to the commissioner signed by that same doctor. I knew Skip would gladly write the note, and I was equally positive that if Pete was the only one to read a medical report signed by "Doctor Death," everything would be just fine. I'd probably be given the green light to wear the braces, and only the Raiders would know that the infamous Doctor Death had, for only a day, practiced medicine.

I later reconsidered. Word of that medical document could get out and some loyal secretary would, sooner or later, explain to Pete why everyone in the office laughed whenever he came into the room. I didn't want to risk Pete getting upset with the Doctor or with my sense of humor because that would probably lead to rule changes and more fines. After going back and forth on the matter for quite a while, the Raiders finally had a real doctor send a note to the league office and I was given permission to wear the braces.

With a little experience it's not that difficult to understand the man in charge of the league office. If everyone were to stop and consider Pete's record and his tendencies, then a last-minute rule change is a matter of consistency. To a casual observer it doesn't make much sense and I can understand that. After all, we're talking about the NFL, wealthy and powerful franchise owners, millions of dollars of revenue, NBC, CBS, ABC, ESPN, HBO television markets, the greatest athletes in the world and all of sudden we hear this little voice ask, "What's a 'no-huddle, quick-snap offense,' Ollie?"

The classic answer to that particular question was witnessed by 130 million people, and a certain NFL commissioner during Super Bowl XXIII. With 3:20 left to play in the game and the San Francisco 49ers trailing Sam Wyche's Bengals by three points, football fans throughout the world saw what is now commonly referred to as 'The Drive.' Gathering his troops at their own eight-yard line, 49er quarterback Joe Montana began chiseling out a place in Super Bowl history as he took the 49ers the length of the field for the go-ahead touchdown and a 20-16 Super Bowl win.

The interesting thing about The Drive was that most of the plays were called at the line of scrimmage, without a huddle, and the ball was snapped on a quick count. Time was of the essence, and with only 34 seconds left in the game, Joe Montana hit receiver John Taylor with a 10-yard scoring flip, thus giving the 49ers their third

Lombardi Trophy.

I realize that a number of football fans are wondering how the 49ers got away with the infamous no-huddle, quick-snap offense when that tactic was branded illegal on January 8, 1989. Well, if the Super Bowl had been played two weeks earlier and in Cincinnati, Ohio, the no-huddle, quick-snap offense would have been illegal. But somewhere between the AFC Championship game and Super Bowl Sunday, the rule was changed again and the no-huddle, quick-snap offense wasn't illegal. That's right, someone had changed the rule back to the way it used to be. I know it doesn't make a lot of sense, but remember, these things usually end up in Trivial Pursuit. So, if you're ever playing the game and you get a ridiculously stupid and confusing question about the NFL rule changes, you should know the name of the boob behind the blunder.

It goes without saying that Pete has made a career out of jumping back and forth between the frying pan and the flames, but some guys like it hot. I saw the commissioners of baseball, hockey, basketball and Pete on a CNN program in December of 1988. It was the same old Pete, playing with matches and on national television.

The CNN host was asking a variety of questions and three out of four answers actually made sense. I think we can all take a wild guess as to what I'm actually saying. It was obvious to even a casual observer that one of these commissioners didn't hit the high note with any of his answers. Questions about drugs in professional sports were asked and three of the commissioners gave logical answers. Then came a question about the use of steroids within the NFL. The host mentioned specifics and asked about a published report that indicated the exact percentage of NFL players who were allegedly involved in the use of steroids. Pete seemed a little foggy on the issues and answered, "I don't know." He hadn't heard anything about percentages of football players using steroids, and I'm not quite sure that he knew what steroids were.

The host glanced at Pete is a peculiar way, then sort of cleared his throat and went on to another question. This time he asked about the status of the litigation between the NFL and Raiders' owner Al Davis. Pete answered, "I don't know." The attorneys were handling everything and Pete didn't know exactly what was going on.

Next, the host asked Pete about the players' strike of 1987, and if there was any progress between management and the players' union. Pete stammered a little and then answered. Once again his answer was vague, something along the line that he didn't know what was going on, or that he wasn't quite sure what was going on. After all of that, he probably didn't even remember the question.

From my experience it's always been that way with Pete. I've asked him legitimate questions and never received anything that even resembled an honest answer. Other times he came out of the woodwork with fines or made bizarre statements about my tackling too hard. But a last-minute rule change? Damn, that's really pulling one out of the twilight zone.

If Pete was really doing his job, he would have made a move the week before the championship game because that's when the no-huddle offense caused a stench and the odor wasn't coming from the Bengals' players or coaches. The Bengals were playing Seattle and trying to use their no-huddle, quick-snap offense. But every time the Bengals would line up for a quick snap, Seahawk defensive lineman Joe Nash would fall down with a leg injury. The officials would call an injury time-out. A moment later Joe Nash would get to his feet and walk off the field. In the meantime, the Seahawks would change their defensive people. Joe Nash probably set a record for injury time-outs, and even the TV people were questioning the tactic. If a player is injured, that's one thing, but if he is faking an injury in order to get the time-out, that's cheating and against the rules. The officials should have warned Seahawk coach Chuck Knox that they suspected fakery, and if it continued they should have thrown the flag and stepped off a big one for unsportsmanlike conduct. Even if the officials didn't have the guts to do what was right, then Pete Rozelle should have been on the telephone to Cincinnati Riverfront Stadium making sure the game was played under existing rules. But Pete's style was better served by taking a pre-game cheap shot and changing the rules on a team running a legal offense. It's not the biggest blunder of Pete's career, but it's not bad for a spur-of-the-moment, Sunday-morning whim. What can I say? Simply a day's work in the life of the commissioner.

5

The Real Dogs Eat
Gravy Train

April 1, 1980, and I'm serious about the date, I watched the mailman coming up to my front door with a rather large, awkward looking box. I was suspicious of this incoming mail only because of the date and the kind of people I hang around with. Most of my friends have a strange sense of humor and they would finish a practical joke with more than a punch line. Naturally, I was doubly prepared for anything, even a surprise from Pete.

The package was from my publisher and had nothing to do with a practical joke. However, a closer examination of the contents would point me in the direction of some "fools," but don't start thinking this is going to be another Pete Rozelle story. That particular trend of thought would only be partially true.

Actually, one of the publicity girls working for my publisher was saving "Assassin" articles that appeared in the national newspapers. She had collected enough to fill up a box and thought I would enjoy the reading. She also included a little note. It read: "Dear Jack, I'm targeting the arrival of this package for April 1st as I believe it to be the most appropriate time for reading some of these articles. Be forewarned that as fools can only write foolish things, there are, nonetheless, a growing number of quality journalists who have read the book and are reporting the facts."

Sitting down on the floor I began glancing over the articles collected from major newspapers and magazines alike. Most of the ink was favorable as a number of sports journalists had read the book. No one was rushing out to form a Jack Tatum fan club, but most of the journalists recognized my honesty and they knew the truth about football. It's a violent game and I was a big hitter.

The *Oakland Tribune* had a couple of articles on me written by Ron Bergman. He did a thorough job that included reading the book, interviewing me and even my old buddy, the collaborating writer. In his articles, Ron wrote things like, "Tatum's problem — he tells the truth," and "Reaction to quotes overblown," and "Society creates a monster."

I read on as Bergman mentioned the Stingley incident: "This wasn't a real hard Tatum lick, but unfortunately, Stingley's head and neck were bent in such a position at impact that he sustained a permanent disability.

"The collision couldn't compare to what Tatum applied to Houston running back Earl Campbell the past season. Campbell staggered and fell like a steer who's had his head cut off in ritual slaughter, but he wobbled across the goal line for a touchdown.

"It's nonsense to become agitated at Jack Tatum for the way he plays football. He very rarely is called for penalties and he plays the game the way it's supposed to be played. If he played it any other way, he would be out of a job, quickly."

If I read ten clippings, seven of them were honest accounts of my book. Not that everyone was calling me a literary genius or even suggesting that I played your average run-of-the-mill football, because it wasn't that way at all. Some of the write-ups suggested that I went the extra mile trying to punish opponents. I don't know how true that was, but I rarely hit a man simply to bring him down. I played 100 percent all the time and I was always up for the big game. But damn it, football is a tough profession and there's not much room for sentiment when it comes to hitting.

I glanced at another article. This one was by Dick Young, of the *New York Daily*, and titled, "Tatum's Confession Draws Overreaction."

"Tatum's sadistic self-portrait," Young wrote, "reminds me of a movie character from an old Bela Lugosi movie. This beauty used to eat flies, but not until he had plucked their wings off, one at a time. He surely was an ancestor of Jack Tatum."

I don't know if I had any ancestors like that, but I understood ... it was simply Dick Young's style. For the time being he was only entertaining, but I had the feeling there was going to be more to this than a few chuckles.

I read on: "Nothing that Tatum confesses is much of a surprise. What is surprising is the furor it seems to have created. People in my business are horrified. People in the football business profess shock. The fans are indignant.

"C'mon fellows. Jack Tatum has been doing this, right in the open, for years. He has been leveling receivers with hooked arms around the neck, blind-siding them with a torpedo helmet, crunching their kidneys and then standing over them to enjoy the convulsions.

And he has been bragging about it all the while, enjoying the image, inviting newsmen to write about it so that his reputation as a destroyer would discourage pass-catchers from invading his turf.

"The actions have been recorded in journals across the land. A visit to most any newspaper morgue will verify it. His boss, Al Davis, will verify it. 'I didn't draft Tatum to defend against passes,' Davis has said more than once. 'I picked him to tackle ball carriers.' This tells you that Tatum was a savage worthy of attention even in college.

"Why then this belated outcry? Is it because he has finally put it all between the covers of a book with the charming title, *They Call Me Assassin?* Is it the concentration of his violent deeds in one tome that inspires outrage? Surely nobody thought of him as Saint John."

Dick Young was pulling no punches. He read the book, and what's more, he understood what he was reading. The man had my attention and I continued on.

"Football players," he wrote, "on the defensive unit are a special breed of animal, especially those in the secondary. They get their kicks from hitting, flattening, hearing the other guy groan. It seems perfectly natural. They don't score touchdowns. They don't get the glory the point-getters do. Their payoff is the hit — and the appreciative oooooooh! of the crowd.

"The crowd long ago glamorized the belters of the defensive unit. That's where the chant originated, 'Dee-fense! Dee-fense!' It was the days of Sam Huff's world. They did the first TV documentary on it: 'The Violent World of Sam Huff,' linebacker, New York Giants. Nobody in the NFL office, to my knowledge, was ashamed of it. They were proud of it. They were a success."

Except for the names and a few of the places, Dick Young was writing about the NFL that I knew and not a distant fairy tale land some people would lead you to believe exists.

Dick passed away several years ago. I'm kind of sorry that he's not going to be around to write a line or two about this book. But I'm sure there'll be enough publicity on this one and some of it will be in the style and tradition of a Dick Young. Others will still miss the point.

I found it interesting that a group of people could read the same story and get a totally different view. Dick Young, while reading the book, saw the cold, dark side of football. Whereas Mike Antonucci, a reporter with the *San Jose Mercury*, read the same book and saw the lighter side of football. Who's right? Both of them. I wrote about the humor, the warmth, and human side of the game because that exists, too.

Mike Antonucci's headlines read: "Tatum's critics guilty of

headhunting." I liked the article already.

Mike started off by writing, "Everybody sit down, grab the sides of the chair and hold on. Jack Tatum is a victim, not a villain as far as his book is concerned.

"Tatum's reward for writing a courageously frank, hilariously funny and intensely personal book has been a spate of outraged reviews focusing only on the sections which can be used like a well-padded forearm against the Oakland Raider defensive back.

"There is no denying the disturbing aspects of the book, menacingly entitled, *They Call Me Assassin.* There are sections which are horrifying because of the brutality Tatum admits to practicing with meticulous devotion. There are sections Tatum must have known would bring his enemies out head hunting in force.

"There are also section which reveal an uncommonly sharp insight into human nature. In discussing former Ohio State coach Woody Hayes and former teammate Skip Thomas, for instance, Tatum is dealing with a pair of personalities so unusual as to border on the eerie. Yet as strange as they are, Tatum manages to give them warmth which anyone even skimming the book should have felt.

"Why are those softer, lighter sections being ignored? Tatum hoped the book would restore some balance to his reputation. Instead, it is being quoted as selectively and prejudicially as possible. Reporters are proving themselves guilty of everything Tatum ever accused them of when he began to worry about his image.

"Let's give Tatum a chance to get a laugh, too."

A form of justice was obviously running its course. Journalists were reading the book and coming to realize that I wasn't an insensitive thug bragging about mugging a bunch of old ladies. The articles were getting justifiably positive. Yet, my situation served to remind me of the man who wasn't even at the scene of a drug deal, but someone 'thought' it was he. The authorities came, kicked the man's door in, handcuffed him, dragged him out of his home with all the neighbors watching, threw him in the police car and took him off to jail. Finally the man was judged innocent, but only through a lack of evidence. He was free to go back home and resume his life. But what was left? The system said he was innocent until proven guilty, but it was more like guilty until proven innocent. Sure, he was exonerated by the system, but the system didn't live next door or across the street or work at the office. There was always going to be that little element of doubt, and because of doubt, he was always going to look a little guilty. The damage had already been done. I wondered if that was true with me. I had a mountain of evidence to prove that I wasn't a primitive savage masquerading as a professional athlete, but maybe there was always going to be that element of doubt.

I remembered a game we played against Green Bay, when, according to Coach Bart Starr, I was guilty of the most horrible cheap shot in the history of football. Green Bay ran a receiver up the field and cleared out our cornerback. Terdell Middleton, a Packer running back, waited a count, then swung toward the sidelines and trailed the receiver up the field. I knew they had the play and was just laying back waiting. It was going to be one of those sideline slaughters every defensive back would just love to have: full speed ahead, blind-side and take no prisoners. Terdell didn't realize it but the Sandman cometh.

A day later, Bart Starr went public and started blasting me in the newspapers. All the wire services carried the story where Bart Starr explained the situation and said, "It was an unforgivable cheap shot. That sort of butchery has no place here."

First of all, the commissioner should have fined Bart Starr for taking the issue directly to the press and not the league office. Pete didn't, but I understood. This, of course, was Bart Starr and according to him, I was guilty of a repulsive act against a fellow human being.

Several days later, Bart Starr viewed the films of the "unforgivable cheap shot," and the "butchery" of Terdell Middleton. He saw what actually happened, that Terdell glanced up and saw me coming. Just as I was about to whisper "good night," Terdell dropped to the turf, and I mean an abrupt drop. He was so low to the ground that the blades of a lawn mower wouldn't have hit him, let alone a defender aiming at his ribs. I missed Terdell by two feet and that was the cheap shot of the century that Bart Starr had so vehemently complained against.

Bart sent a telegram to the Raiders' office apologizing for the statement but never said anything directly to me. The follow-up story was so inconspicuously placed in the newspapers that Sherlock Holmes would have missed it. Even to this day I still hear fans occasionally complain about my "cheap shot" on Terdell Middleton. After all, Bart Starr called it "butchery" and butchery forever it remains.

I wrote the book actually thinking things would be different. I believed that even my critics would eventually read it and discover that only five percent of the story was about hitting. I've covered a lot of ground during the course of my life and it wasn't all confined to pounding receivers on the stadium turf.

Mike Antonucci thought there were disturbing aspects of the book, but he also found the warmth and humor. Dick Young, after reading the book, felt that some of my ancestors ate flies, but he also left no doubt as to the fact that I had accurately described the game of football. As different as the styles and opinions of Dick and Mike were, it all came down to the same thing. "Why this belated outcry? Why not give Tatum a chance to get a laugh, too?" In spite of their hitting on my ancestors and those "disturbing aspects of the book," I gained a lot of respect for Dick and Mike. They were pros. I believe they understood a little about my work on the field and what I had accomplished off the field with a typewriter.

I knew going in that everyone in the country wasn't going to praise each word and page of the book. I figured there would be questions concerning my "meticulous devotion" to the art of hitting opponents. I figured that some reporters and fans would say that I wasn't that great a hitter, and others would call me a cheap shot artist. I expected a lot of flak, but my error was in assuming that every sports fan, journalist and the commissioner knew that football was a violent, contact game. Obviously I assumed too much.

I'm beginning to sound like a broken record, but as a football player, I was paid to hit. I did my job and like to believe I was as proficient as anyone in the game. During my playing days there weren't many arguments or complaints either way. I wasn't the only hitter in the game, but I was the only one to sit down and write a book, a real book, an honest book about a job in the NFL. It was a book any number of defensive people could have written, a story that plays in part during every NFL game and on every highlight film. Take a close look at the next game and tell me there aren't hits that border on felonious assault. Check out the NFL highlight films, watch the action, listen to the commentary, and then tell me I was a minority of one. I wasn't alone when it came to playing the game and making the big hits, but I was when it came to writing the true story.

January 13, 1989, I was watching the *Arsenio Hall Show.* I had to because the "Boz" was on. Brian Bosworth plays football for the Seattle Seahawks. He's a defensive player with somewhat of a reputation. What's more, he wrote what journalists refer to as a "controversial book," simply entitled, *The Boz.* I never read the book, never saw any Joe Fitzgerald articles on the subject or heard any Pete Rozelle statements denouncing the Boz. It probably wasn't about the violence in pro football, but listening to the Boz talk about the game, I knew that if Pete was tuned in, then someone was "asking for it."

The Boz talked about hitting and hurting quarterbacks. He said that whenever he hits a quarterback and sees him on the ground moaning in pain, he always goes over and apologetically asks, "Are you hurt?" When the quarterback moans, "Yeah," Boz answers, "Good!" The audience laughed and laughed and laughed.

Arsenio and Boz talked about sex and the night before a game. Boz said that was a no-no. He's an aggressive guy and feels that love-making takes the edge off his game. Since Boz's ultimate highs come from hitting and hurting people, he's not going to burn up his energy rolling around in a bed the night before a game. The night after was another story.

Boz then mentioned violence in the NFL. His story would surprise and shock some of my critics, maybe. And if Pete was listening, well, who knows what Pete would have said, and then again, who really cares? I don't, and I have a feeling the Boz doesn't give a damn, either.

If I had it to do over, write the book, that is, how would I describe some of the action during my career? How would Dick Butkus describe some of his hits? What would Mike Singletary, linebacker for the Bears, write about his style of making a tackle? Or Ronnie Lott of the 49ers? How would these people describe their big hits?

There's only one problem though, they weren't writing a book. I was, but how could I make my audience understand the speed, velocity and impact of professional football? Or how could I ever hope to put into words my Super Bowl hit on Sammy White? I could have written that my tackle was a good 'rap,' but rap sounds too much like 'tap,' and tap is limp-wristed. When I thought about it, a good slap had more velocity than rap and tap combined. I needed another descriptive word. Maybe it was a 'bump,' or a 'thump?' No, not 'thump' because that reminded me of rabbits. A friend of mine had a rabbit named Thumper, and believe me, I didn't thump Sammy White. Besides, no one would buy a book titled, *They Call Me Thumper.*

Next, I tried a combination of words. "My Super Bowl hit on Sammy White was a jolly good show." Ugh! Pete Rozelle would have loved that line, but the world would have laughed. The hit wasn't a jolly good show because it damn well knocked a grown man back to the days when "Mama" could protect a young boy from the boogyman. The truth is that my hit on Sammy was something more than a rap, tap, bump, thump or just another tackle. It was a 'motherfuckinmassacre,' but that's a football word that only football players will understand. I didn't use football terminology in describing my hit on Sammy, but I must have done something right. An estimated 100 million people saw the hit, Rozelle and journalists included, and to borrow a word from Dick Young, the only thing anyone could say was, "oooooooh!" Then I wrote a book describing the incident and, just like Dick Young, I was wondering, "Why the belated outcry?"

It was that way with several of my violent stories in the book. They were simply accounts of football witnessed by thousands of people and, at the time, few complaints worth mentioning ever came my way. Perhaps I was a more graphic writer than a devastating hitter.

That's strange because I always believed in the old saying that "a picture is worth a thousand words." I thought my hits were as strongly a worded statement as anyone could make, but evidently I was wrong. As Pete might say, "Unbelievable."

There were many favorable articles even though no one considered me a saint. I was, for the most, reading the work of professional journalists. Paul Hersh, *The Chicago Sun-Times*; Russell Schneider, *The Plain Dealer*; Joe Gergen, *Newsday*; Bob Cordasco, *New York Post*; Jerry Izenberg, *New York Post*; Dave Anderson, *New York Times*; Chuck Heaton and Hal Lebovitz, *The Plain Dealer* (Cleveland, Ohio), had hit the issues, and hit hard, but they didn't develop their stories from cheap shot controversy. Some of these sportswriters insisted on calling me "Assassin," others said that I was 'brutal,' and even to a degree 'violent,' but not one of them ever said that football was a passive game played by passive people. Not one of them ever suggested that I should be ousted from the game, condemned to the gallows, or that I was a cheap-shot artist looking to deliberately hurt people. They knew the essence of football was hitting and understood perfectly that I was counted among the big hitters of the game.

I even found a letter to the editor written by a fan, Kevin Kubiak. He wrote: "Jack Tatum should be admired for his actions, not persecuted. Part of the game of football is physical contact. People hate Tatum because he's a hard-nosed player. How about guys like Dick Butkus and Bubba Smith? If the Browns had a few players like Tatum they might have been in the Super Bowl."

Fans were discovering the truth, as were some journalists, but there still existed that rebellious element seeking to have me booted from the game. Bob Rubin, of the *Miami Herald*, blasted me from one end of the Sunday sports page to the other in his article of January 10, 1980, entitled, "'They Call Me Assassin' — No Room in NFL for this Animal." Rubin claimed that I tried to hurt people and was attempting to capitalize by bragging about it in a book. He called it blood money, but I considered his style of journalism strictly "Bow Wow." Rubin really tried to dog me. If Dick Young felt that some of my ancestors plucked wings from flies before they ate them, I'm sure he would have written about Rubin's relatives barking at the moon and sniffing fire hydrants.

Rubin took a couple of shots at George Atkinson, too. He referred to George as a "Raider thug" and really took exception to our "knockout" and "limp-off" contest. It was the same old trash: a journalist reading excerpts but not the book. Rubin wrote that "Legitimate football players rely on skill and hard hitting, not felonious assault.

"Assassins have no place in football. Assassins belong in jail.

"NFL Commissioner Pete Rozelle should give Tatum and his book the Hook, as Stingley's lawyer had demanded."

Now, that was an interesting thought. George would be more than willing to teach Pete the Hook, but I had a feeling it would have been one of those learn-by-experience lessons. I could just picture George saying, "You stand here, Pete, hold the football and pretend you're looking down the field toward the end zone," and WHAM! "No, no, Pete," George would say while helping the commissioner to his feet and brushing him off, "That wasn't quite right. Here, let me show you again." WHAM!

Then it would be my turn to play professor. I would demonstrate, on Bob Rubin, of course, how legitimate football players relying on skill and hard hitting can generate a velocity that borders on felonious assault.

It goes to prove that I should have explained everything in detail because some people are dense and never quite grasp your meaning or intent. Just like now, some people will shriek in horror, actually believing I said that George Atkinson hit Pete Rozelle with the Hook. Well, for all the Bob Rubins the world, I was just kidding. George wouldn't hook Pete any more than I would waste my time explaining the difference between the rules of football and the laws of society to a certain Miami journalist.

Interestingly enough, the very next article I picked up was written by a (Cleveland) *Plain Dealer* reporter, Hal Lebovitz. Hal wrote, "Tatum happens to be better at hard hitting than most. On the streets, such violence would land him in jail."

Hal Lebovitz understood my "felonious assault" statement, but then again, he was a pro. He made a living writing words and had the common sense to understand statements made by other people. Not everyone in the field of journalism could say the same.

I glanced over several more articles and two other Florida-based journalists were writing about the "Assassin." Steve Hummer and Bernie Lincicome, both of the *Fort Lauderdale News/Sun-Sentinel* did a couple of articles.

Lincicome wrote, "Tatum believes what he says about his job as a defensive back for the Oakland Raiders, which seems to be to knock the courage out of anyone who comes across his path.

"That is, after all, a basic precept of football. Kids are taught to hit harder than the guy hitting them. Violence is rewarded with admiration from coaches and fans. Finesse is insulted."

Isn't that what I've been saying all along? Isn't it the truth? If so, why the uproar?

Lincicome continued, "We all forget, from our living room seats in front of a television that miniaturizes the game, that football is a sport played in rage. Huge men get incredibly angry at each other every 30 seconds. You can't play football any other way.

"Professional football is a result of weeding out the guys who have no stomach for bashing another human being as hard as they can.

"Give yourself a quick test. What is the most admirable thing about Larry Csonka? His delicacy? His graceful style of running? Csonka is the most popular Miami Dolphin of all time because he 'pounds' people.

"I think what upsets most players about Tatum's book is that in it he breaks the faith. Privately, or within the playing community, it is okay to admit that your 'best hits border on felonious assault,' or that Franco Harris has 'no heart.' But don't share those opinions with the civilians.

"And, of course, what scares the hell out of the NFL is that the public will believe that Tatum represents football. The NFL would like us all to believe that football is pure escapism, a delightful encounter among tough sportsmen who might play hard but are compassionate, feeling human beings just like the rest of us.

"The truth is, they aren't and neither are we.

"I really don't think Tatum's philosophy, taken at its cruelest, will turn one fan away from the game. You take violence out of football and you take the fruit from the nut.

"Football gives us what we want. It caters to the same base instinct that makes us stare at auto accidents and pick our scabs until they bleed.

"Until we want something different, the Jack Tatums of the league will prosper."

That type of an article wasn't one hundred percent flattering, but I could accept it because the basic fact of football was there. Bernie understood it was a game of hard hitting and the harder they hit, the better. I simply couldn't understand why so many reporters failed to comprehend the violent and basic fact of the game. Football players hit, boxers punch, track stars run and jump ... damn, it's not that difficult to understand the objective or facts of any sport.

Mark Twain once said, "Get your facts first, and then you can distort them as you please." I once believed all journalists actually worked that way. But lately I was learning it was more of a case of isolated stupidity than a deliberate distortion of facts. There were times when I would consent to an interview, answer all the questions, and several days later some incredible story would show up in the newspaper that didn't even vaguely resemble anything I had told the reporter. It got to a point where I rarely gave out interviews or answered questions. Interviews only got me in trouble, and most reporters asked single digit IQ questions and were intellectually lost if I gave a simple, double-digit answer such as "yes" or "no." I'm serious! Even though I was discovering that a number of sportswriters were professionals, many were not.

After Super Bowl XXIII I watched a television reporter from Los Angeles interview San Francisco 49er, All-Pro center Randy Cross. Damn, I couldn't believe the questions I was hearing and neither could Randy. Earlier, Randy had announced his retirement and said that, win or lose, Super Bowl XXIII was going to be his last game. Randy is a terrific human being, and was a great player for thirteen years. During his career he had been through it all, and on this night he was going out a winner, a champion. One would think there would have been a wealth of questions to choose from, but what did this TV personality ask? He wanted to know how Randy would have felt if his bad snap on a missed field goal had cost the 49ers the game? Randy sort of apologized, but he was probably trying to figure out how he got into this live TV interview in the first place. Well, if that question wasn't dumb enough, then the TV reported reminded Randy that he had a critical penalty called against him during the 49ers' last drive. The implication was that if the 49ers had not scored, then Randy would have been the "goat" of Super Bowl XXIII.

I realize that kind of stupidity goes with the turf, but hell, there were a hundred legitimate questions to ask Randy and it didn't take a scholar to come up with at least one or two. There were questions about Cincinnati nose tackle Tim Krumrie. One of the Super Bowl match-ups was Krumrie and Cross: two All-Pros going at it for the championship. But early in the first quarter, Krumrie broke his leg. I would have asked Randy about the incident, if he knew how it happened, or what it was like to prepare for Krumrie and then have to face David Grant? Maybe I would have congratulated Randy and the 49ers' offensive line for doing a great job or simply told the man 'thanks' for thirteen great years. But then again, I'm not a journalist.

The Randy Cross interview was just average run-of-the-mill stupidity, but sometimes a reporter can take stupidity to the outer limits. Prior to Super Bowl XXII, a pencil-necked journalist asked Redskin quarterback Doug Williams, "Doug, how long have you been a black quarterback?" Considering that Doug has been black for all of his life and a quarterback for all of his football career, it was a tough question to answer. When an athlete is asked one of those questions and doesn't come up with a quick answer, the reporters start writing that he isn't real bright.

I knew a lot of athletes had similar problems with the press, but now I was beginning to understand that even in journalism there were, so to speak, thoroughbreds, and there were mongrels. It was refreshing to see that a number of pros were reading my book and doing justice to the story, but it was a case of too little too late.

My fall from NFL grace was actually due to a number of things and I certainly can't place the blame entirely on a bunch of 'mongrels' barking at the excerpts of a book. Shoddy journalism got the wagon rolling down hill to where even the pros of prose couldn't stop it when they tried ... and they didn't try all that hard. Sure, there would always been the Darryl Stingley incident hanging over me. The title of the book didn't help that issue, either. Then I played for the Raiders; they wore black, won football games, and had a reputation. If I had played for Tampa Bay or some other team wearing a pastel colored uniform and with a reputation to match, things would have been different. I still would have played like a Raider, but another colored game jersey would have made a difference. Bad guys wear black ... don't they?

I realize now, that everything got off to a bad start when Joe Fitzgerald broke my story in the *Boston Herald American*. Joe only reported bits and pieces of the story, but his crafty and yet flamboyant style captured the commissioner's attention. Joe Fitzgerald was helping me sell books and that's what writing a book is all about. But with Pete Rozelle mumbling his quotable, "That's asking for it," and some real Rin Tin Tin journalism, my reputation as a football player and human being was beginning to look like something less than immaculate. The damage had been done and, regardless of the avalanche of positive publicity, most people figured they knew everything about Jack Tatum and preferred not to confuse the issue with facts.

I glanced over a few more of the articles and came across one that read like the sounds of an empty tin tray being licked around the floor of the dog kennels. If there ever was a Gravy Train Award for journalism, Steve Bisheff from San Diego would get my vote. His article was inferior, by comparison, to the other barkers making a living with words. But what set Steve Bisheff's article apart from the other dogs in the kennel was that he and my collaborating buddy, the "Writer," became entangled in a war of words in which they used one of the San Diego newspapers as their platform.

Debating anything with my buddy the "writer" was, is and will always be a waste of anyone's time and energy. I know because I've tried. There were times, while engaging in a dialog with the man, that I was positive I was winning the discussion. But when everything was said and done, I would walk away believing I had won my points, but know that I, somehow, lost the debate. He has a knack for convincing a person he is right even when they know he isn't. You have to understand the man before he makes any sense. Bear with me because I will explain, but first things first.

Bisheff took a cheap shot at me in one of his articles, and my faithful pal didn't like it. Bill, that's my writing partner's name, got on the telephone to San Diego and verbally went after Bisheff. Why Bill chose to debate the book with a "ham & egger" like Bisheff only makes sense when you understand Bill. The fact is, that if I had not had experience with Doctor Death, Charles Philyaw, Woody Hayes, and some other similar characters who travel in and out of my life, then I would still be trying to figure out the man. He's different. But stick with me and you'll understand, too.

Bisheff hadn't read the book, which didn't surprise me. Therefore, Bill insisted that he first read the book and then, "perhaps" they could carry on an "intelligent" conversation. Bisheff took the advice, read the book, interviewed Bill, and then wrote another article, "Assassin's Defense." In the article Bill explained that 100 words out of 80,000 were the cause of all the commotion. "Locker room talk," Bill told Bisheff. The article continued in Bisheff's amateurish but seemingly positive style. Bill explained all the details of the book including my concern over several bad rules of football. Everything seemed under control and then Bill started piping off about Pete Rozelle not having "a leg to stand on." The next thing I read was a wild quote from Bill where it almost sounds as though he is daring thinking that a courtroom scene between the NFL and me would be great for business. Talk about a loyal friend … the man had me all choked up.

The Gravy Train Award for journalism came when Steve Bisheff wrote his final lines, "The author tried hard in our conversation. He made some good points. But, I'm sorry, after reading the entire book, my overall opinion hasn't changed. Jack Tatum's philosophy of football still sickens and disgusts me."

I could understand Steve Bisheff writing that trash before reading the book, and before his debate with Bill, but not afterwards. Bill wins arguments even when he's wrong. This was probably the first time in Bill's life that he argued in defense of an issue where he was 100 percent right and he ended up 100 percent wrong. It didn't make any sense, and that's why I had to give Bisheff the Gravy Train Award. Not knowing the facts is one thing, but having been spoon-fed the information and still blowing the article is "Bow-Wow" journalism.

6

But Don't Drink the Water
or Breathe the Air

After about three months of headlines, the book was finally on its way to becoming old news. I was positive the brain trust behind the NFL wasn't going to spark the fire again by pursuing the issue in a court of law, even though Pete Rozelle was still making his public statement, "the NFL totally rejects that philosophy." By now, I was certain that if anyone had asked Pete what philosophy he was talking about, he probably wouldn't have remembered why he was saying those words.

Further confirmation that all the hoopla was over and my sudden rise to literary stardom was already on the down side, showed up on the pages of *Pro Football Weekly* late in March. Ed Stone, a writer with *Pro Football Weekly*, hung around the kennels long enough to do 'Simply Ban Tatum.' Damn, I knew my story was slipping, but finding Stone's article on page 10 of *PFW* told me I only had a few gasps left as an author. Then it would be back to being fined by the NFL, proving my innocence in Pete's kangaroo court and paying the fines. And I'm serious about that last statement. I actually believed that Pete sat around his office, simply pulled names and numbers out of a hat and issued the fines. Obviously he was fascinated by my name and number.

I remember a game against Seattle when I had a chance to really sedate a young receiver, but for some reason that I never could explain, I pulled the throttle back a notch and just made an average tackle. The official was standing on the spot and when I got up he said, "Congratulations."

"For what?" I asked.

The official smiled and replied, "You had a chance to really cream that guy and you didn't. It's gotta be a first for you. You must be getting old, Jack." I laughed and went back to the huddle, but on Monday morning, I got word that Pete was fining me for the incident.

Seriously.

Under normal conditions the NFL's system of justice was strange, but now that I had written an inflammatory book, I could only imagine what was going to happen to me during the coming season. I'd probably get fined for everything from no starch in my jock strap to putting my pants on before my jersey.

I scanned Stone's article and, all of a sudden, I burst out laughing. Here it was, the end of March, and I couldn't believe what I was reading. "At this writing, Commissioner Pete Rozelle had made no decision because he still hadn't read the book. But based on excerpts, he said, 'the NFL totally rejects that philosophy.'"

What the hell was Pete doing with his time for the last three months? Okay, so he had to present the Lombardi Trophy to the winning team at the Super Bowl, but that only took about ten seconds. And since this was the off season, Pete wasn't involved in analyzing game films and checking for improprieties such as jerseys not properly tucked or socks that weren't pulled up to NFL regulations. So, what the hell was Pete doing with all of his time? Even if Pete spent fifteen or twenty hours a week working on his tan, he still should have had enough time to read my book. After all, the very integrity of the game had come under siege. That's what everyone was inferring and I'd have to believe that the commissioner would make a priority out of resolving the issue. That would be the intelligent and logical thing to do. Even though I've already touched upon a certain person's inability to make decisions through the simple application of logic, I certainly have no intention of calling the man an illiterate. I'll simply state the facts and let everyone draw his own conclusions.

I put Ed Stone's article in the proper place, on the floor of my dog's house, and resigned myself to the fact that, unless something dramatic happened, my days as a celebrated author were numbered. Then I received a telephone call from a friend of mine in Cleveland. He informed me that a radical dude was on local TV, hyping the book. "Was this radical dude," I asked, "by any chance, named Bill?"

Yes, his name was Bill. My old buddy the collaborating writer was still out there promoting the book. This time he and Thom Darden, a defensive back with the Browns, did a local program about football, yours truly and the book. I guess Bill got Thom all riled up and both of them were sounding off about hypocrisy within the NFL, a need for rule changes, shoddy journalists, Pete Rozelle, and everything and anything. "Jack," my friend informed me, "this dude should be playing for the Raiders and not writing about them. He's as wacky as all your other friends out in Oakland."

A day later I received a call from another friend. Bill was now in my favorite western Pennsylvania city defending me and the book. He did a number of radio programs and even took time to put in a appearance on television, in my behalf, of course. Damn, Pittsburgh was the wrong place to be saying negative things about the Steelers, but that's what my main man was doing. Bill informed me he was only boosting sales, but I thought it was more like committing suicide. I warned him about the Pittsburgh fans and cautioned him to be careful. He said, "Don't worry, Tate, I only got on a dozen or so of the Steelers, but damn, I did a number on Pete ... just for you."

With Bill running around the country defending me and the book, so to speak, I started giving serious thought to the possibility of the NFL pursuing litigation. If Pete were to take some type of courtroom action against me, did that mean Bill would be involved, too? After all, he helped pen the book that made me famous. Furthermore, he was the one going around the country daring Pete to press the issue, not me.

Of course, I spent a little time going around the country protecting my backside by telling everyone that I wrote the good stuff, but Bill wrote all the negative crap. I continually maintained that I gave Bill a story about my life and career and, after my final approval of the manuscripts, Bill took it upon himself to make several changes. Hey, don't laugh, it always worked, especially when people knew Bill. One time that little ploy even saved my life.

Shortly after the book was published, Bill asked if I would be the guest speaker at a high school banquet back in his hometown, Brookfield, Ohio. Since it was for the high school football program and the athletes, I accepted the invitation.

Driving to the banquet hall with Bill, I couldn't believe all the traffic. When you figure there are about ten cars in all of Brookfield Township, and half of them don't run, I thought a traffic jam was strange. Stranger yet was the overflowing crowd at the banquet hall. There were several thousand people outside of the place, some of the top radio personalities from Brookfield, and even TV people from Youngstown.

Bill and I worked our way through the crowd and moved indoors. Inside the banquet hall a man came up to me and said, "Like match sticks ... he's gonna break 'em like match sticks." The man walked away, but now, everyone in the place was looking at me. I turned toward Bill and asked, "What's goin' on?" At that moment, I saw Pittsburgh Steeler center Ray Mansfield standing in the crowd glaring at me. Ray didn't like the way I treated Lynn Swann and, other Steeler receivers, for that matter. During the course of our careers, Ray tried to break my legs several times. Actually, every time

I played against the Steelers, Ray tried to break my legs. In fact, Ray openly admitted in public that he wanted to break my legs and I heard that he had taken a blood vow promising that one day he would do it.

With Ray staring intently at my legs, I asked Bill, "What the hell is Ray Mansfield doing here?"

With a dead-serious expression Bill answered, "He's here to break your legs." He paused, then laughed and said, "Don't worry, Tate, Ray don't really hate you ... all that stuff about him wanting to break your legs is just a wild rumor."

"Wild rumor!" I whispered to Bill. "That wild rumor speared my knees the last time I played in Pittsburgh. I spent a week at the doctor's office getting fluid drained from my knees because of that wild rumor standing over there."

"Ray told me all about it," Bill said. "But, Tate, you shouldn't have kicked him in the face. You drew blood and that really upset Ray. Every time he looks in the mirror and sees that jagged scar between his eyes he gets pissed off."

I tried to explain that Ray hit me first and then I kicked him in the face. But like I said, debating anything with Bill was, and still is, a waste of time. I should have known that coming to Brookfield wouldn't be an easy trip. It never was. But tonight might well be the most difficult time of all.

"By the way," I asked, "who the hell invited Ray?"

"I did," he answered without hesitation. "I played against Ray in a golfing tournament in Florida and we got to talking about you. I thought you two guys would like to talk over old times."

Not only did Bill invite his golfing buddy Ray Mansfield to the banquet, but he also invited two other Steeler linemen, Jon Kolb and Mike Webster. Bill, being the kind of guy who would never let opportunity slip through his grasp, informed the press that the Steelers were in town for a question and answer session with the infamous Assassin. Remember? Someone wrote that Franco Harris and Lynn Swann were gutless and chicken. With those statements as a matter of record, it didn't take much to figure out why every fight fan in the tri-state area was attending a high school football banquet in Brookfield, Ohio, and talking about someone's legs getting broken like "match sticks."

Ray started making his way toward me, and Bill, the buddy that he was, excused himself. The crowd backed up and gave us some room as Ray moseyed up to me and said, "Jack."

"Ray," I acknowledged.

Just about then I saw Jon Kolb and Mike Webster coming toward me. Damn, I was looking at about nine hundred pounds of the Steelers' offensive line. I never realized just how big Ray, Mike and Jon actually were. Not only were they big, but they were some of the meanest, toughest offensive people to ever have played in a football game and I wasn't getting the feeling they were exactly overwhelmed to see me. Kolb stared at me for a moment and then said, "Jack."

I replied, "Jon."

Then Mike Webster said, "Jack."

And I said, "Mike."

When the formalities of the introductions were over, the conversation seemed to bog down. Actually I never wrote anything bad about Mike Webster or Jon Kolb, so I could not see why they would be uptight. I wrote that Mike was the best center in the league, and right now I suddenly remembered that he was the strongest and probably the toughest, too. And then I glanced at Kolb. Damn, was he big. Just about then, Ray started fingering that scar of his, the one right between his eyes, and I was trying to come up with something witty to say. It didn't look good; but just then, a couple of giggling ladies bogarted into our conversation and started asking for autographs.

The first rule of being a good writer is always having a pen and note pad. I gave Ray my ink pen and even offered the note pad. In fact, I insisted that Ray keep the pen and pad. With the Steelers busy tending to their fans, I quietly excused myself.

I started moving around the banquet hall looking for a certain writer. I've heard of people losing themselves in a crowd, but this was ridiculous. Everyone I talked with had just seen Bill, but I still couldn't find him. It was almost like he was trying to avoid me, but I knew that wasn't true … not my buddy, Bill.

Finally the master of ceremonies, Doctor Len Pleban, went to the podium and began directing the audience to their seats. Doctor Pleban told me that Bill made the seating arrangements and, once again, my old buddy was looking out for me. Ray Mansfield sat to my right and Mike Webster to my left. Bill being a rather shy and modest man insisted on sitting in the audience. Earlier, he told Dr. Pleban, "This is Jack's night … I'll let him have the spotlight."

For some reason I had lost my appetite, but the food didn't go to waste. During the thirty seconds it took Ray to eat his meal, we didn't carry on much of a conversation. When he finished licking his plate he looked over at me and asked, "What's the matter, you don't like food?"

I made up some story about eating before I came to the banquet and for the next thirty seconds Ray and I got along fairly well. That's about how long it took him to eat my meal and lick the plate clean. After that I felt pretty good, because Ray sat there watching Doc Pleban eat his meal and I started a conversation with Mike Webster and Jon Kolb. I figured that everything was going to be okay, but at the same time, I felt that I owed my loyal friend something. And I'm not talking about a royalty check, either.

Doc Pleban warmed up the crowd and finally I had my turn at the podium. I told a few football jokes, talked about the great Steeler athletes in attendance, made a joke about Ray always trying to break my legs, and then started on the book. Without any hesitation I immediately hit the Franco Harris and Lynn Swann issue, and I hit hard. I said, "Since the publication of *They Call Me Assassin*, people ask me if I really believe that Franco Harris and Lynn Swann are gutless chickens." Damn, that banquet hall really settled down. It was more quiet than a funeral parlor after hours, and I noticed that Ray was staring at my legs again. Clearing my throat, I continued, "I myself don't think that Franco and Lynn are gutless chickens. If you want to know why it was written in the book, you'll have to ask Bill Kushner. You see, Bill wrote that part." Everyone in the audience laughed, and what's more, they actually believed me. I didn't stop there and before the night was over, I blamed every controversial area in the book on Bill. What the hell, he wanted me to have the spotlight, and I would never be the one to disappoint a friend.

About five minutes into my routine, I could see someone toward the back sneaking out. With the exception of the main table, the lights were turned off; so I couldn't be positive who was leaving the banquet during my hilarious show, but I had a pretty good idea I would be in need of a ride back to Bill's home. After everything was over, I looked high and low for Bill, but I couldn't find him. So, I asked my long-time friend Ray Mansfield to drive me over to Bill's house.

On the way over to Bill's, I started a casual conversation with Ray. Inadvertently, I casually mentioned that Bill cheats on the golf course. Ray really perked up at that and wanted to know what I meant. I told Ray that Bill had a phony handicap, that he used the smaller, illegal British ball, that he'll move the ball in the rough, and that he rarely counts all of his strokes. I had Ray's attention and so I explained that Bill put vaseline on his driver to keep the ball from slicing and hooking, and I threw in a few other things, too.

Ray told me that he and Bill played a lot of golf, but he never saw the man cheat. "Sneaky, Ray," I answered, "Bill's really sneaky …" I left everything at that point because I could see the wheels turning in Ray's head. I had a feeling he was going to ask Bill some golfing questions.

When we got to Bill's house, I naturally invited Ray in for a cup of coffee. Bill was sitting there watching television, trying to be his usual cool self, pretending that nothing happened. When Ray brought up the subject of golf, I decided that "two's company, three's a crowd." With a smile on my face, I bid Ray and Bill a good night.

In the morning, Bill never mentioned anything about their discussion and I never brought up the subject. But it's like I said, Bill has a knack for convincing people he's right, regardless of the situation. His legs weren't broken and there were no bruises on his face. I figured he talked his way out of another sticky situation. About a year later, I did hear, from a reliable source, that Ray and Bill have joined forces and are often seen representing the Pittsburgh Steelers in the NFL's Super Bowl of Golf Tournament in Florida.

When I returned to Oakland, I began to perfect a "Blame Bill" routine. With a little practice, I got to where I could blame just about anything on Bill and it sounded sincere. But hell, Bill did write several parts of my story the way he "thought" they should have happened and not the way they actually did happen. Whenever his version of my life was better than reality, I took the credit. If it sounded bad, I would raise my eyebrows, shake my head back and forth and say, "That writer I had wasn't worth a damn. He got everything screwed up except ..." then I would tell all the good stories he wrote, taking full credit, of course.

The more I thought about Bill and his involvement with the project, the more fascinating litigation was beginning to sound. If push came to shove, and the NFL really wanted to take me and the book into a courtroom, I'd make sure that Bill was there. If I ever put Bill on the stand to testify, everyone in the courtroom would end up with a frustrating, Excedrin headache.

I know that statement doesn't make a lot of sense, but Bill wins his argument by wearing down and frustrating the opposition with a barrage of words and logic that only he can understand. When a person gets frustrated and tired, Bill starts twisting little facts and details around to suit his views. Before long a person finds that he has just agreed with Bill, but knowing full well Bill was wrong.

Bill did some word twisting and phrase turning when we wrote the book. Actually, I should back up and tell the entire story, because I never had any thoughts about doing a book. Then my attorney from Pittsburgh called one February morning at 5:30 a.m. Just because it was 8:30 in Pittsburgh and he was up, he thought I should be up, too.

I was explaining the three hour time difference between

Pittsburgh and Oakland when he interrupted. He said, "I know, I know, but this is important." That's when he told me that Bill something or other wanted to write my story. "Jack, he said, if you trust him, it will be a best seller!" Without even thinking, I said yes, hung up the phone and went back to sleep. Later in the day, my attorney called again, and informed me that the deal was set.

I checked Bill out and discovered that he did a book with Joe Namath's mother, Rose, titled *Namath My Son Joe.* I also learned that he spent some time in the New York Jets' training camp in 1970 as a quarterback. Obviously, he knew a little about football so everything looked pretty good. But then I talked to a couple of people who actually knew Bill. They thought my doing a book was a great idea, but wanted to know if I had ever met the writer.

I asked, "What's wrong?" They looked at each other in a peculiar way, shook their heads and just stared at me. Once again I asked for an explanation, but all they would say was, "When you meet the man, then you'll understand."

I flew into Pittsburgh, and Bill, along with Bobby Jones, a friend of his, met me at the airport. So far everything seemed fairly normal except that neither Bill nor Bobby helped me with my luggage. My three suitcases weren't that heavy so it wasn't a big deal.

It was early March and by Pittsburgh weather standards a fantastic day. The temperature was right around freezing, the sky was an ominous dark gray and I couldn't tell if it was going to rain or snow or both. Walking through the parking lot, my luggage was getting to be a little much so I mentioned it to Bill and Bobby. They stopped and looked at each other like I was some kind of a dummy. Finally Bobby said, "Take a rest, we'll wait."

I put the suitcases down just as it started to rain. Bill and Bobby stood there in the rain and waited for me to rest up. Finally, I took the initiative and explained that if each of us carried a suitcase, no one would get wet or tired. It made sense to Bill, because he told Bobby, "That's right, help Jack with his luggage."

A moment later we were moving through the parking lot. Bobby was carrying a suitcase, I was carrying two, and Bill was walking ahead of us jingling his car keys. By now the rain was coming down pretty hard and the only car in sight was a Lincoln at the far, far end of the parking lot. I was just about ready to ask the obvious question when Bill said, "I hope you don't mind a little walk. It's just that I don't like people banging against my car, so I parked where it's safe."

Driving from Pittsburgh to Brookfield, Ohio, took about ninety minutes. During that time I heard Bill and Bobby talking about a workout. I couldn't get a real grasp on their conversation, but it almost sounded as though Bobby was going to run some pass patterns, Bill was going to throw the football, and they had elected me a defender. A little workout session would be okay, but only if they were planning an indoor session or perhaps waiting for a warm day in June. But if I was hearing right they, or we, were scheduled for this afternoon and outdoors.

I glanced out the window and saw a damp and depressing world. The rain was coming down at a steady pace but Bill figured the weather was going to change. He said, "Looks like we're going to hit it lucky … I think the rain is going to change to sleet, maybe even snow."

Bobby turned to me and explained, "I don't mind the snow or even sleet, but workin' out in the rain is a bitch."

I just shook my head and said, "Yeah."

The car didn't smell from marijuana and I couldn't see any roach clips so I figured Bill and Bobby were straight. Therefore, it had to be some kind of a joke. Yeah, I told myself, they're only playing some kind of a joke on me. I had experience with people from this area of the country before and I knew that some of them were a little strange. I went along with everything and asked, "What's the reason for working out on a day like this?"

Bill explained that he had contacted the New York Jets and made arrangements for them to take a look at Bobby as a wide receiver. He wanted to make sure that Bobby was in shape and could run sharp patterns. When I considered that Bobby looked more like a skinny kid just out of high school, not an NFL receiver, I was positive that they were pulling my leg or else they were completely nuts.

I started a conversation only to discover that Bill had convinced Bobby that with a little dedication and hard work, he could become an NFL receiver. Then Bill went out and convinced the Jets that Bobby was NFL caliber and guaranteed Jets' scout Carroll Huntress that Bobby would make the team. Going with the flow of the joke I asked, "Bobby, where did you play your college football?"

I wasn't surprised when he told me that he had never played college ball. After all, it was a joke … right?

"I was gonna walk on at Youngstown State University," Bobby explained, "but when the equipment manager gave me some old black high top shoes and a leather helmet without a face mask, I quit."

Still going along with the joke I said, "And Bill figured that instead of wasting your time with college football, you should go into the NFL … right?"

"Not exactly," Bill interrupted. "I contacted several colleges but they saw Bobby play in high school and weren't interested in giving him an athletic scholarship. So, since he couldn't go into the NFL until his collegiate eligibility ran out, we figured to spend that time lifting weights, running patterns and learning how to catch the football. Couple of years and he'll be ready for the NFL. Right, Bobby?"

And Bobby shouted, "Right! One hundred percent right!"

The more I listened to these characters talk the more I began to suspect that they were, as strange as it all sounded, serious. During my playing days at Ohio State, I ran into other bizarre individuals and they were usually from the northeastern Ohio and western Pennsylvania areas of the country. It got to where I could spot those dudes from Youngstown, Canton, Erie, Pittsburgh, or any of the other towns in that particular region, from the way they would walk into a room. I began to suspect that there was something in the drinking water in that area of the country that made people act strange and say and do the damnedest things. Just like Bill and Bobby.

Bobby had no college experience and had never caught a pass during a high school football game, but nonetheless, Bill had convinced this skinny kid that he could play in the NFL. Not only that, Bill told everyone in town that Bobby would play for the New York Jets. Bill said, "If Bobby wants to look like a fool, he won't work hard. That way he'll come home with his tail between his legs. But if he guts it out and works hard, he'll play in the NFL. Don't want to look like a fool, do you Bobby?"

And Bobby shouted, "I ain't gonna look like no fool, I'm gonna make it!"

All the positive talk and hard work in the world isn't worth a damn if a person's dream is unattainable. Bill had talked Bobby into an impossible dream, and Bobby, in order to believe, was obviously drinking the water.

Admittedly, they played a tough brand of high school football in that area of Ohio and western Pennsylvania, but the caliber of play in the NFL was light years away. Even if Bobby could work himself into a physical condition where he could take an NFL hit, he would still need the experience of college football to give him a fighting chance. Was Bobby that gullible or was Bill the greatest salesman in the world? Or was it simple a matter of the drinking water getting the better of reason and logic?

Listening to their conversation, I had the feeling that if Bill told Bobby that with a little hard work, he could jump over the moon, Bobby would run outside and start trying. But high diddle diddle, that's a bunch of bullshit. Jumping over the moon would be easy in comparison to playing wide receiver in the NFL without ever having caught a pass on any level of competition! Bobby was in for an embarrassing awakening unless I could talk some sense into him.

"But Bobby," I tried to reason with the young man, "If you never caught a pass in high school you must realize the odds against your making it in the NFL are a million to one."

Then Bill chimed in, "Yeah, he never caught a pass in high school, but he never dropped one, either. In my book Bobby has a perfect record. In fact, that's what I told the Jets ... I said I've never seen him drop a pass. Right, Bobby?"

Bobby answered in the affirmative, then quickly explained that his high school coach believed that only 'sissy teams' used a passing game. Bobby told me it wasn't that he couldn't catch, but simply a matter of no one ever having thrown him the ball. His high school football experience was strictly up the middle and helmet to helmet. Still, this kid actually believed he was destined to play in the NFL as a wide receiver. It was obvious that I couldn't sway Bobby from his impossible dream. Bill had convinced this kid that he was going to play in the NFL, and success was just a matter of a little hard work and dedication.

I glanced out the window and saw blizzard conditions. Perhaps Bobby and Bill were going to work out, but there was no way I would be joining the dynamic duo on this windswept, cold and snowy day. I wouldn't work out on a day like this even if the Raiders were holding practice and paying me to participate. "I'd like to work out with you people," I told the boys, "but I don't have football shoes, and I think I'm coming down with a cold." It wasn't a real strong statement, but deep down inside, I was adamantly entrenched in a position of no compromise. Bill might have talked Bobby into a war zone without a gun or bullets, but I wasn't going to be a party to anyone's suicidal venture.

Bill looked in the rear view mirror, established eye contact with me and asked, "What's the matter, you a pussy or just afraid of getting burned by a skinny kid?"

I had made up my mind and, no matter what Bill said, I wasn't going to run around like a damn fool chasing after Bobby on a day like this, or on any day, for that matter.

Bill turned up his power of persuasion. He was slick, but there was nothing he could say or do that would change my mind. Nothing!

The first pattern Bobby ran was a little slant. Without cleats I couldn't get any traction. I slipped and fell into a puddle of mud just as Bobby caught the pass. He ran about two hundred yards down the field, spiked the ball and did a little dance.

I know my reading audience is looking for a couple of missing paragraphs to this little story, but that's sort of what happened to me. I didn't lose any paragraphs, but it was almost like I had misplaced some time. We got to Bill's home all right. I even remember meeting his wife and kids, nice people, too, but that's when everything got a little hazy. Bill started talking real fast about the workout. I remember asking his wife for a couple of aspirins. The next thing I knew we were out on this muddy field and running around like damn fools. I was wearing someone's old blue jeans, a pair of Boston Celtic green tennis shoes and, of all things, a Pittsburgh Steeler jersey with Franco's number and name on the back. I couldn't believe it, but there I was, chasing a skinny kid around a muddy field on a cold and snowy March day.

I didn't realize it back then, but later I learned that people who know Bill never argue with him. Bill gets his way and it doesn't matter what the circumstances are. In my situation, there was no way anyone could have convinced me that I would have worked out on a dismal March day, but I did. When everything was over, I spent the rest of the evening trying to convince myself it never happened. I don't remember what he said, but somehow, much to my dismay, his powers of persuasion were stronger than my will to resist.

Several years later, after I had retired from the game of football, Al Davis invited me to Los Angeles to watch the Raiders play against the New York Jets. I was standing on the sidelines talking with Jim Garner of "The Rockford Files" fame and heard someone yell, "You pussy! I know why you retired!"

I looked across the field and saw one of the Jets' players pointing at me and shouting for the world to hear, "Yeah! You! I'm talking to you, Jack Tatum!"

Jim Garner asked, "Who's that?"

"I don't know," I answered. "Who's number 89 for the Jets?"

Number 89 for the Jets started walking toward me while shouting, "You chicken! You retired because you were afraid of getting burned by me! The field's dry and I'd really fry your ass today! You big chicken!"

Suddenly, I recognized the voice. Damn, if it wasn't Bobby Jones! I couldn't believe it, and yet in a way I could. The first time I saw Bobby run and catch, I knew that he had a lot of ability even though he didn't have any experience. Still, there were extenuating circumstances in Bobby's rise from high school mediocrity to NFL status. First of all, he grew up drinking the water in that area of the country. Sometimes a person will start drinking the water, forget reason and logic, and simply leap before looking. If Bobby had stopped long enough to think about the impossibility of his dream, he probably wouldn't have even listened to his big brother. But the water, coupled with Bill's continuous chattering, a few years of hard work and suddenly, Bobby had arrived.

The odds of a high school player going into the NFL without any experience are probably a billion to one. But Bobby played for six years in the NFL and had developed a reputation as a fearless, catch-anything receiver. I figured that if a certain person could convince a skinny high school player from Brookfield that the NFL wasn't an impossible dream, I knew that same person would have a pretty good shot of convincing Pete Rozelle that Jack Tatum wasn't such a bad guy after all should we end up in the courtroom.

In a strange way, I began to hope the NFL would pursue a course of litigation. I could see Pete coming into the courtroom thinking about a lynching and walking away with a declaration naming me as the first saint inducted into the Pro Football Hall of Fame.

Of course, I had to consider the down side, too. There was the haunting memory of my Gravy Train Award and the fact that Bill had failed to convince journalist Steve Bisheff that Jack Tatum was a-okay. Bill doesn't win his debates all of the time, just most of the time.

I started thinking about the occasions when Bill failed to connect, and there weren't that many that I was aware of. I thought about Bill's friend, J.J. Cafaro. I'd have to classify J.J. as one of the times Bill had a communication problem, but a person can't hold him entirely responsible. It's just that J.J. thinks on a different level than most people.

Let me tell you about J.J.'s home, for example. J.J. wanted to build a big home. However, J.J.'s idea of big greatly differs from your average standard of big. I've heard conflicting reports as to the exact size of J.J.'s home. Some people say J.J.'s home is only 27,000 square feet while others maintain that it's more like 33,000 square feet. When J.J. gave me a tour of the dwelling I didn't have a ruler handy; but I would venture a guess that we were talking somewhere between 27,000 and 33,000 square feet. J.J. had what he referred to as "a complete home with two bowling lanes and two theaters in the basement." It's like I said, J.J. thinks on a different level and that's probably what threw Bill a little off stride.

J.J. and Bill actually began their friendship over, of all things, a book. J.J. wanted Bill to write a book about his father, Mr. William Cafaro. In the beginning, everyone was on the same wavelength except for Mr. Cafaro. J.J. wanted to surprise his father with the book and therefore, had made arrangements with his family and friends to help out with the details of the story. Bill actually figured that he had a best seller in the making and perhaps even a movie.

The story goes that Mr. Cafaro started out poorer than most people, but ended up an extremely wealthy land developer. I know it sounds like a typical all-American story of hard word and dedication, but you've got to remember that this was Youngstown, Ohio. Even though Mr. Cafaro is a wonderful human being and the salt of the earth, some of the other characters in the story were drinking the water, so to speak. Bill told me the story had all the elements of a blockbuster and he couldn't wait to get started. That's when J.J. and Bill reached their impasse.

J.J. was going to form his own publishing company, fund everything, and pay Bill a substantial amount to write the book. But there was a little problem as to how many books they should print. Bill thought a first printing of about 30,000 books was in line. But J.J. figured that Bill's estimate was 29,999 books too many. That's right. J.J. was only interested in having one copy of the book printed. J.J. always had a problem buying his father a Christmas gift. Dwell on that one for a moment. If your father was extremely wealthy and had everything, what would you get him for Christmas?

Well, this year J.J. had a special gift all picked out for his father and it was going to be the only copy of Mr. Cafaro's biography. Of course, J.J. planned to use the finest paper and was thinking about a twenty-four karat gold cover. It was a unique idea, only one copy of the book in print, but Bill was thinking about hitting the charts with a best seller. When it came to fast talking, Bill was slicker than a peeled onion, but J.J. had a mind of his own. I couldn't see Bill taking the time to write a book where the total sales would be only one, nor could I see J.J. wanting to flood the market with a Christmas gift anyone could give to his father.

I went out for dinner with Bill and J.J. the night they had their final discussion about the book. The festivities and their conversation were something to see and hear. J.J. took us to an exclusive restaurant, but we didn't have a dinner reservation. It was the weekend. The place was crowded. The head waiter couldn't be bribed and it didn't look as though we were going to get in. Bill suggested that J.J. buy the place and fire the head waiter. Coming from Bill, it was a logical statement, but J.J. had a better idea. He roused the owner out of an office somewhere in the back and within a minute or so, we were en route to our table.

Bill, being more of a McDonald's man, was completely lost. He accidentally smeared butter over the linen table cloth and, while he tried to clean up that mess, he spilled his wine. Just about then, J.J. thought we were sitting too close to the orchestra, so he opted to move to an empty table in the far corner of the room.

We arrived at the other table just in time to see the head waiter bringing in a party of six. The head waiter stopped in his tracks and glared at us. If looks could kill! I had a feeling our clean table with the fresh linen was reserved for his customers. but maybe not, at least J.J. didn't think so. The waiter turned and took the party of six over to the table we had just vacated. That's when I heard one of the ladies tell the head waiter, "This table looks as though a pig was here waddling on the tablecloth!"

The evening wore on and I was enjoying myself. The food was excellent and the entertainment was outstanding — I'm talking about Bill and J.J. Bill was at his best, but J.J. had a mind of his own. It was obvious from the beginning that J.J. was only going to print one copy of the book, but there was no quit in Bill. Damn, now I could understand why I ended up working out with Bill and Bobby on a dismal day in March. Bill was overpowering but, at the same time, I really admired J.J. for his ability to resist. Bill was coming at him from all angles, but J.J. didn't waver an inch. Bill told J.J., "Best seller." And J.J. answered, "One copy." Then Bill said, "Major motion picture." And J.J. answered, "One copy." The Bill said, "Academy Awards!" J.J. said, "One copy." Then Bill said, "Nobel prize for literature." And J.J. said, "One book." It was beginning to sound like one of those "tastes great — less filling" commercials.

I could see Bill was getting frustrated and even desperate. Finally Bill brought out the heavy artillery as he said, "But J.J., think about it, we can make a million dollars!" I knew the discussion was over when J.J. answered with a ho-hum expression, "So what."

J.J. was interested in only one copy of the book, while Bill was interested in a best seller. There just wasn't any room for compromise. Bill couldn't convince J.J. to print more than one copy and J.J. couldn't convince Bill to write a book where there would only be one copy. Bill wasn't interested in taking the money and running, and J.J. wasn't interested in making money from a book.

J.J. and Bill were involved in something called a no-win situation. Now some people go to the extremes and find themselves caught up in a lose-lose dilemma. And that's kind of what I figure happened to Pete Rozelle. Pete as I've already pointed out, had a tendency to get stuck in those precarious positions to where, no matter what direction he turned, he still lost. When my book came out, I felt that Pete had opened his mouth prematurely, got his foot and ankle stuck against the back of his throat and, after that, couldn't make any intelligent sounds. He went around gagging about the NFL rejecting a certain philosophy and didn't know what the hell he was even talking about. Pete made a lot of noise, turned several different colors, but in the end he coughed up his shoe and rode quietly off into the sunset with his rope dragging along behind. All of the talk about litigation was simply a lot of talk and nothing but talk. No one was going to ban me from the NFL or take the book off the shelf at the stores. To be perfectly honest, I had hoped for a little excitement in the judicial arena because I truly believed Bill would end up with another best seller. Matter of fact, I would have let Bill defend me. And even if J.J. was there representing the NFL, I still had by backside covered. I'd simply blame the book on the drinking water back in that area of the country. I'd tell the judge that we were working on the book, I was drinking water and, suddenly, something came over me.

It all sounds a tad ridiculous, but believe me, I am keeping everything in proper perspective. And also, I'm quite positive there really is something in the drinking water in the Cleveland–Pittsburgh area of the country. Sometimes a person will drink that water and strange things start to happen. I can't say for certain, but to this very day I believe that Arrowhead Holmes drank some Pittsburgh water and after that his personality changed.

Arrowhead Holmes was actually baptized Ernie Holmes. Ernie was a normal dude from somewhere in Texas until he signed on with the Pittsburgh Steelers as a defensive lineman. After moving to Pittsburgh, his personality began to change. Everyone figured it went with the new turf, because this was, after all, Pittsburgh. My thoughts on the subject ran a little deeper. I suspected that Ernie had started drinking the water. If Ernie was into using the water, then I figured the people in that area would see a drastic character alteration before long. It's not that Ernie was a bad guy, I just felt he had the potential to be different even by Pittsburgh standards.

Trouble quickly started following Ernie around and, before long, he had a couple of typical Pittsburgh beer-joint scuffles — nothing more serious than some bumps and bruises and a broken nose or two. Fortunately Ernie had a way of escaping unscathed, but the people around him usually ended up running into walls or they managed to jam their faces into his fists. Ernie claimed that since moving to Pittsburgh something would come over him and all of a sudden he'd get to feeling mean. Ah, ha … the water! Ernie was probably drinking the water.

Another time, the story goes, Ernie got this mean feeling and, before it passed away, he bashed a dude with a stool and urinated all over a barroom in downtown Pittsburgh. That's actually putting it mildly because the real story I heard was triple X. Folks back there simply figured that Ernie wanted to be one of the boys. In downtown Pittsburgh that kind of action is sort of your average weekend tomfoolery and nothing out of the norm.

When I heard that story, it only cemented my suspicions about Ernie drinking the water. If he was into doing the water, then I was pretty sure Ernie would show Pittsburgh a thing or two before long. It's like I said, Ernie had potential. The incident never made the headlines, just a small write-up in the newspaper; and with that particular incident behind him, Ernie finally adjusted to Pittsburgh. Well, some people claim that instead of adjusting to Pittsburgh, Ernie adjusted Pittsburgh. But regardless, Ernie Holmes, all six feet three inches and 290 pounds of him, was finally accepted by the football fans of Pittsburgh as a member in good standing of their celebrated Steel Curtain Defense. And drinking water or not, Ernie Holmes was one helluva football player.

I realize that some people are going to find this hard to believe, but Brian "The Boz" Bosworth was not the originator of Creative Hairdo, Unlimited. Ernie Holmes was, and one night he showed the football world a thing or two about haircuts.

Any fool can dump a bottle of peroxide on his hair and then stick his head under a lawn mower for the finishing touch. But with Ernie, his new haircut was creatively different. There was a purpose, a legitimate reason why Ernie had styled his hair, and it didn't have anything to do with free publicity. Hell, Ernie forgot more about publicity stunts than Boz, in ten lifetimes, will ever dream up. Publicity stunts followed Ernie around and happened naturally. Unlike the Boz, Ernie never had to sit around trying to dream up cheap ploys to get attention. Whenever Ernie pulled off one of his famous attention grabbers, one could be absolutely certain that he wasn't thinking.

Actually Ernie's hair styling career began with one of those spontaneous "something came over me"s that he was now so famous for. And, on a Monday night football game, Ernie unveiled the new look — the Arrowhead Haircut.

Ernie had shaved around his ears and formed this arrowhead haircut over the top of his head. I know it sounds a little "Bosworthish," but seriously, it wasn't a cheap publicity stunt. There was a reason for it all. Arrowhead, he insisted on being called Arrowhead, told Howard Cosell that the new hair style would give him balance and keep him pointed in the right direction. See, I told you there was a legitimate reason for the new haircut.

Arrowhead explained that he would sort of aim his haircut in the direction of the quarterback and run toward the target. And with that clear and concise explanation, everyone in the television audience understood perfectly how the arrowhead haircut worked. Well, everyone except Howard Cosell. Howard was a little slow to catch on.

It was strange, almost impossible to believe, but for once in his life, Howard Cosell was actually caught dumfounded. Howard sort of stammered and stuttered, hemmed and hawed, but was, for his first time ever on *Monday Night Football,* actually making sense.

When I heard the arrowhead story I simple shrugged my shoulders. Hey, what the hell! It was Pittsburgh and things like that were par for the area. After all, when you stop to think about it, Arrowhead was drinking water from the Ohio, Allegheny and Monongahela rivers. One polluted river is bad enough, but three are something else.

At that time, no one would believe me, but it all had something to do with the drinking water. People drink that water and begin doing weird things. And weird is a way of life not only in Pittsburgh, but in Cleveland, Canton, Akron, Youngstown, Erie and all the little towns in that region. Nothing, and I mean nothing, could ever happen in that area of the country that would shock me. In fact, I wasn't shocked or even slightly surprised the time Arrowhead finally did make the headlines. Sooner or later national recognition was inevitable because Arrowhead was obviously doing the water in Pittsburgh.

Arrowhead's rise to national prominence began the day he went for a quiet drive in the country. He was minding his own business; but then, about one hour out of Pittsburgh, something came over him. Arrowhead stopped his auto along Interstate 80, west of Girard, Ohio, and, with rifle in hand, climbed up a small hill. Finding a comfortable spot on the muddy slope, Arrowhead sat down and proceeded to open fire on passing trucks and autos. He wasn't shooting at people, just at the passing vehicles. Something came over him. I understood. He probably had a drink of water just before something came over him.

Eventually, something must have come over a passing motorist because the police finally received a phone call about a strange looking dude with an arrowhead haircut sitting out by the freeway taking shots at passing trucks and cars. I'll bet anything that the individual who called the police was from way, way out of state and wasn't drinking the water, either. Hell, Arrowhead could have set up shop on some rarely traveled rural route and he'd still be there shooting passing cars and trucks and no one would give him a second thought.

Several minutes later, a police helicopter was on the scene. Arrowhead stopped shooting and began watching the helicopter. It was fascinating, this flying machine with twirling blades and rapid, thumping engine hovering over the freeway. Arrowhead was mesmerized.

Then a bull-like voice came from inside the helicopter, "Put down your weapon and place your hands over your head!"

The voice panicked Arrowhead. There was no telling what went through his mind as the natural instinct of self-preservation took over. Without even aiming his haircut, Arrowhead started blasting away at the helicopter.

It was obvious that the dude flying the chopper was into purified, bottled water. To this day I believe that, had the pilot been under the influence of regular tap water, he would have hovered around while he tried to figure out if Arrowhead was only shooting at the helicopter, if Arrowhead was shooting at him, or if could it be that both he and the helicopter were targets?

If given a little time to zero in, you know, sort of point the haircut in the direction of the helicopter, I'm positive that Arrowhead would have claimed the title of Top Gun in the NFL. Seriously, I could just see a little decal of a helicopter on Arrowhead's Steeler helmet. But the pilot didn't request a court order before taking his leave.

Next came a state trooper. The trooper arrived and promptly ordered Arrowhead off the hill. Ordering Arrowhead off the hill was the wrong thing to do. Eventually, Arrowhead would come down, but he never liked people ordering him around.

Well, Arrowhead got a little ticked and fired a few more shots. Then the trooper got all riled up because Arrowhead slightly nicked and scratched the highway patrol car with a few 30.06 bullet holes. Finally, Arrowhead came down the hill, was arrested and, later on, was placed in a lineup. But since his excursion to Girard, Ohio, came under the heading of "no blood, no foul," the lineup belonged to the Pittsburgh Steelers. That's right, the prosecuting attorney's case couldn't hold water, and Arrowhead was back on the turf of Three River Stadium, wearing the gold and black and aiming his haircut, instead of a rifle, at opposing quarterbacks.

I'm not picking on Arrowhead, because he was one of the friendliest dudes I've ever met. Seriously, Arrowhead has a bubbly personality and was forever with a smile on his face. But then, something would come over him, and everything would change. Believe me, it all had to do with the water.

I know that most of the legal minds reading this would try to shoot holes in my defense. Of course, J.J. would have a fighting chance against Bill, but my final document of evidence would have been irrefutable even in Pete's kangaroo courtroom.

July 30, 1988, Mike Ditka, Jack Ham, Alan Page and Fred Biletnikoff were inducted into the Professional Football Hall of Fame at Canton, Ohio. Two days prior to the actual induction ceremony, Charles Gibson, of ABC's *Good Morning America*, interviewed these former NFL greats as they stood outside the Hall of Fame.

Gibson pointed out that all four of these men were from this region of the country. Mike and Jack grew up in the Pittsburgh area, Alan was from Canton, Ohio, and Fred came from Erie, Pennsylvania. Gibson made reference to the fact that this area was considered a hotbed for high school and college football players. He even went on to explain that an uncommon, almost unnatural number of these athletes have gone on to become professional football players of the NFL. A curious Charlie Gibson asked Alan Page, "Is there something in the water that creates these types of hard-nosed football players?"

I was watching the program from my home in Oakland. With the mention of water, I suddenly perked up and waited for Alan to answer.

"It's not only the water around here," Alan said, "but it's also in the air."

And with that, I rest my case!

Slant Patterns were not allowed.

7

Hypocrites,
Hitmen and Assassins

Hypocrisy is as much a part of the NFL as are touchdowns and tackles. Believe me, the hypocrites are just as visible as the big hits or long touchdown runs, but a person has to look beyond the football field to understand what I'm talking about.

I've already given examples of hypocritical sportswriters, so there's no need to beat that particular horse to death. As for hypocrisy and the football fan, I can almost understand the kind of mentality that would, because of loyalties to the home team colors, give some spectators a one-sided view of the game. The home team fans call it a great defensive play when their boys flatten the opposing quarterback, but a blatant cheap shot when it works the other way. The fans cheer their heroes for the kill-hits and big victories, but trash the other team for hitting too hard or running up the score.

We live in a hypocritical society, but most people couldn't spell the word or even tell you what it means. Our children are taught not to lie because lies are wrong and can hurt other people, but we fail to understand the same holds true for hypocrisy and the hypocrite.

I believe Chuck Noll, head coach of the Pittsburgh Steelers, is one of the biggest hypocrites in the game of football. Of course, I realize that some knowledgeable fans and several coaches around the league will argue the hypocrisy issue with me while claiming that Chuck is the NFL's number-one complainer and crybaby. And I have to agree, but that's only because Chuck Noll is a complex character and hypocrite is only one of his many faces.

When you travel back over the career of head coach Chuck Noll, it's an interesting journey to say the least. For openers, Chuck Noll brought the Lombardi Trophy to Pittsburgh four times. That's remarkable, because if a person ever listened to Chuck, he would swear Chuck never had a legitimate NFL quarterback.

During the 1970s, Chuck complained about his number-one

draft choice, quarterback Terry Bradshaw. And then Chuck complained about replacement quarterback Joe Gilliam, and then Chuck complained some more about Terry Bradshaw, and then there was someone called Mark Malone who Chuck didn't think too much about. I'm sure if I checked the record there are a few more names I could add to the list because quarterback woes have always haunted poor ol' Chuck.

Backing up for a moment, I have to spend a little time on the Noll-Bradshaw scenario that took place during the Steeler glory years. According to Chuck's way of thinking, Terry Bradshaw wasn't smart enough to be an NFL quarterback. Bradshaw's lack of intelligence became a major issue with Chuck Noll; and wouldn't you know it, the press and fans lapped everything up. Even to this day many fans think that Terry Bradshaw wasn't too bright. Hey, I understand! Terry Bradshaw isn't too bright, Jack Tatum has no sensitivity and Mike Tyson built a reputation beating up bums.

I realize there is a big difference between hindsight and fore-sighted vision, but even during the early 1970s it didn't take much imagination to recognize that Terry Bradshaw, brain or no brain, was an exceptional athlete. Sure, Terry looked and sounded like a country bumpkin, but so did a thousand other great athletes who came out of the south. Chuck Noll might find it difficult to believe, but the true measure of greatness has little or nothing to do with how a person looks or talks or scores on the ink blot tests.

With his career over, and all things said and done, I'd have to think that four Super Bowl rings, All-Pro status, Super Bowl MVP honors and being a 1989 inductee into the Professional Football Hall of Fame would have to say something about Terry Bradshaw's ability to play in the NFL. But for all the Chuck Noll fans, I guess we can only sit back and forever wonder what an intelligent quarterback would have accomplished under similar circumstances.

I don't know if Terry Bradshaw was the most intelligent quarter-back to ever play the game of football or the dumbest. It's a tough question to answer because IQs are not part of the NFL's library of statistics. In my estimation there are many factors that go into the making of a great quarterback, but I've never looked at a scouting report to see how intelligent the man is.

I could never figure out why Chuck Noll was always trashing Terry Bradshaw. Speaking from experience, Terry Bradshaw was a defensive player's nightmare. Terry was one of the most gifted athletes to ever play quarterback, and he could put more pressure on a defensive team than anyone in the game. Terry Bradshaw was big and strong, and defensive linemen had a difficult time bringing him down. To complicate the situation, Terry was fast and elusive, and could scramble around for five or ten seconds buying extra time so that his receivers could get open. He had a quick release, a cannon for an arm, and he could throw right while running left. If everyone was covered, then he would simply tuck the ball under his arm and become a fearless running back.

I think Terry's success finally came because of his mental toughness. Hey, he was a great athlete and somewhere along the line, in spite of all the negative flak, he came to realize his own potential. Even if Terry never won the respect of his head coach and some of the fans, it was obvious that he certainly won the respect of his team-mates and his peers.

Franco Harris won the MVP award for Super Bowl IX, but gave Terry Bradshaw credit for the Steelers' victory. Franco said, "Terry had us all relaxed in the huddle. We had control of the situation."

In my first book I mentioned the perfect quarterback would be Kenny Stabler's mind in Terry Bradshaw's body. Having been a team-mate of Stabler's, I felt that he was more cerebral and less physical than Terry. Now don't get me wrong, because that statement wasn't a slap at Terry's intelligence any more than it was meant to question Stabler's courage or toughness. The fact is that Kenny would belly up to the bar with the best of them and wasn't afraid of taking on any-one in the house or on the field. And when a person listened to Bradshaw's wit and sense of humor, he had to realize there was a pretty sharp mind behind the hillbilly drawl. But during a football game, physically speaking, Bradshaw could do things that Kenny Stabler couldn't, and Stabler did things that Bradshaw never thought about. Yet, when it came down to the bottom line, both men were winners.

When any individual, even Chuck Noll, complains loud enough and long enough some people will begin to think there is validity to it all. Chuck Noll put a monkey on Terry Bradshaw's back; and, to this very day, some fans question Terry's intelligence, even his ability. But it's like I said, I don't know if Terry was the smartest or the dumbest quarterback in football. But, I do know one thing; he was one of the greatest ever to play the game.

Terry Bradshaw had his problems with Chuck Noll. I've had mine and, believe me, we are not in the minority. Check the record and you will soon discover that Chuck Noll has taken shots at just about everyone in the league. That's his style.

When Chuck Noll uttered his infamous words, "criminal elements in professional football," and then named names, he and George Atkinson became entangled in their own little problem. According to NFL procedures, Chuck Noll was wrong for giving that kind of slanderous statement to the press. The implication was that George and myself were something less than legit. I resented being called a criminal element, but George carried resentment a step further.

George hired an attorney and filed a two million dollar lawsuit. I honestly figured that George had a fighting chance in a courtroom battle. After all, Chuck was wrong and George was right. That counts for something, but this time out something meant nothing.

The NFL, being the NFL, put their legal staff to work in Chuck's corner. George was never quite sure why he lost his case or why the NFL defended Chuck, but obviously it had something to do with a twist in the law that states a little guy can't fight the establishment.

Those stories are just about ancient history now and things have a way of changing. George, Terry and I have retired and seem to be mellowing with age. Most of us do, you know, mellow with age, but that doesn't apply to a complex character like Chuck Noll.

In recent years, the Steelers have fallen on hard times. Even though Chuck managed to get rid of 'at thar' dumb quarterback, he's had other persistent quarterback problems nagging at him: more dumb quarterbacks. If the quarterback situation in Pittsburgh wasn't enough for Chuck to complain about, then there was the problem with his punter, an inept offense, a shaky defense, not to mention the Houston Oilers and their coach, Jerry Glanville.

To understand the Houston-Pittsburgh drama of today, one must first remember the Houston-Pittsburgh rivalry of the '70s. During the Pittsburgh glory days, Chuck Noll would turn loose the Steel Curtain Defense and give the Houston Oilers two serious whippings a year. Now mind you, the beating had nothing to do with winning or losing the game on the scoreboard. I'm talking about a beating that turned powder blue uniforms into bloody red. On an average, run-of-the-mill day at the stadium, the Steelers left their opponents bumped and bruised, cut and bleeding, mangled and broken. However, the Steeler-Houston rivalry was usually something more than an average run-of-the-mill day. Whenever they played against Houston, the Steelers were intent on transforming the spirit of football rivalry into something that resembled the aftermath of a good old-fashioned Texas chainsaw massacre.

There was no denying the fact the Steelers had a great defensive team, but the Houston Oilers had this guy from Tyler, Texas, Earl Campbell. I've already mentioned Earl. He was big and fast and, if he got a full head of steam, it took at least two guys to bring him down. Unfortunately for Earl, the Steelers used their full complement of eleven defensive players. Even more unfortunate was the fact that most of the Steeler defensive team had nasty dispositions long before they started drinking the water in Pittsburgh.

Earl "The Tyler Rose" Campbell was a great running back, but quite frankly, Salman Rushdie would have a better chance selling autographed copies of *The Satanic Verses* on the streets of Tehran than Earl did lugging the football against the Steel Curtain Defense. But it was all simply a part of the game and Earl never complained.

Amazingly, during Steeler-Campbell rivalry, Chuck Noll never once complained. He would pace the sideline with a mused expression on his face as the likes of Mean Joe Greene, Mel Blount, Jack Lambert, Jack Ham, L.C. Greenwood, Arrowhead Holmes and the rest of his boys gave Earl a serious ass-whippin'.

I really want to emphasize the point that Chuck Noll never complained about the action of those brutally physical games. Not that he had the right or need to complain, but every once in a while Earl would get cranking with a full head of steam and knock a Steeler or two into next week. But again, Chuck Noll never once complained. After all, aggression and violence are simply a part of the game. In fact, eleven defensive players honing in on one offensive player was good for the integrity of the game, good for the fans, good for the TV ratings, and good for ol' Chuck's ego.

On the other side of the coin, no one ever took issue or complained about Earl needing a proctologist to surgically remove his helmet every time he played in one of those games. But what the hell, things like that are part of football. Damn, if you can't stand the heat, get out of the kitchen. Right?

A few years back the Oilers hired Jerry Glanville as their head coach. I have to believe that Jerry spent some time in and around Cleveland or Pittsburgh because he came to Houston under the influence of the water. That was obvious even to the casual observer.

For openers, Jerry has a bizarre sense of humor. He's left game tickets at the Will Call window for Elvis and James Dean. When Elvis and James were no-shows, Jerry then left tickets for Burt Reynolds and Loni Anderson. Burt and Loni never showed up either, and that, I can understand. If a man is married to Loni Anderson, he probably has more pressing matters to work on than spending a day with Jerry Glanville and the Oilers.

If I ever hear that Jerry Glanville left tickets for Jack Tatum, he can be certain that I will attend the game. I am a Jerry Glanville fan. Furthermore, if the game happens to be one of those Steeler-Oiler get-togethers, I'll beg or steal a sideline pass. I don't want to miss any of the action. I know Chuck Noll's infamous Steel Curtain Defense resembles something more of a soggy cardboard box, and Earl Campbell has retired. Nevertheless, there are a few interesting twists that keep the ratings up.

Jerry Glanville brought some spirit and class to the Oilers' organization. He's a fiery character with enough personality to warrant his own sideline, instant replay camera. But more importantly, Jerry is a coach who understands that the basic factor of winning football is to demoralize your opponents through physical aggression. The Raiders once played with that type of aggression, the Bears won a Super Bowl with that style as did the Giants and the Redskins, and the Steelers built their dynasty on that physical fact.

Jerry's a bright guy and a student of the game. For all I know he studied the NFL's *Crunch Course* video of those winning traditions, those many criminal elements of the game paving the way to victory after victory. Then, in order to truly understand the anatomy of the winning edge, Jerry probably went into the Oilers' film library and studied yesterday's brutal encounters with the Pittsburgh Steelers.

Suddenly, the Oilers started developing a reputation as a physical team. They weren't afraid to go out and crack heads with anyone in the league. In fact, the more physical the game, the better Jerry Glanville's Oilers liked it. I heard stories about the Oilers getting their fair share of limp-offs, knockouts and double knockouts. Then rumor had it the Oilers were keeping score on broken face masks. I heard Glanville's boys had crushed fifty of their opponents' face masks with aggressive tackling. However, the boys of ABC's *Monday Night Football*, Al, Frank and Dan, clarified that malarkey about the Oilers hitting so hard they were busting face masks. Actually it wasn't broken face masks causing all the stir. Instead, the Oilers were breaking the area where the face mask and helmet connected. And it wasn't fifty helmets either, it was only forty-six.

Houston was winning through aggressive football, the Astrodome was filling up with fans, television ratings soared, but, to quote Chuck Noll, "It's bad for the game!" "It's bad for the game" was simply Chuck Noll's way of telling the football world the Steelers ran into a good old-fashioned ass-whippin' compliments of the Houston Oilers and head coach Jerry Glanville. "It's bad for the game" meant that Chuck was thrashed so horribly he wouldn't even shake Jerry Glanville's hand after the game. And that's exactly what happened. The Oilers came to play and Chuck's boys didn't.

In fairness to Chuck, I should explain that he was spending a considerable amount of time complaining and bitching about his dumb quarterbacks, a sagging offense, and a defense that had more holes than a hunk of Swiss cheese. There are just so many hours in a day, and with Chuck spending most of his time bitching and complaining about his team, he probably never got around to a game plan. So, Jerry Glanville and the Oilers strolled into the stadium and promptly kicked some ass. Chuck Noll, being true to character, had to get the last word in, "It's bad for the game."

I find it interesting that Chuck Noll never thought his aggressive Super Bowl teams were bad for the game. And a real interesting fact is that Earl Campbell never thought those same aggressive Steeler teams were bad for the game. But then again, Earl Campbell wasn't a crybaby or a hypocrite. You see, only a hypocrite would win four Super Bowls with an aggressive and physically dominating defensive team and then complain when that same style of defense pounds his team into submission. I don't know how many people feel sorry for Chuck these days, but I don't think any of the Houston players or their fans are losing sleep over this dilemma. Neither am I.

Giving credit where credit is due, the Steelers had one of the truly great dynasties of modern football. The Pittsburgh Steelers won a record four Super Bowls and did so with a defensive team that simply laid waste to most opponents. However, contrary to what Chuck Noll will say or try to make you believe, to my knowledge, no members of Chuck's defensive football teams, present or past, are on the Vatican's list for canonization. The original founder of the Pittsburgh Steelers, Mr. Art Rooney, God rest his soul, might well be under consideration for sainthood and justifiably so, but the Steel Curtain Defense of Pittsburgh had absolutely no on-field redeeming qualities. But then again, no winning defensive team does.

That last statement isn't a put-down. In fact, it's one of the highest forms of compliment I can pay to another defensive unit. Football, especially defensive football, is savagery, a continuing violent clash of wills to win coupled with outstanding physical abilities. But the truly great defensive players take everything one step further as they become obstinate and brutally mean in their assignments. They try to hit harder and more violently. They strive to be more physical in every aspect of the game. During the heat of battle that desire to win will often translate into a sucker punch, a kick, or perhaps a late hit out of bounds. Action like that isn't a premeditated attempt to hurt an opponent or a sign of criminal intent. It's an impulsive, usually retaliatory, reaction of which all great defensive players have, at one time or another, been guilty. A great defensive football game is played in a physical rage.

I know how the Steelers played and they know how they played. Their rise to glory was a case of pure athletic abilities and a flaming passion to win. It had nothing to do with coaching or clean, crisp tackling. On the field, most of those great Steeler defensive players were a little guilty of felonious assault. But that's not bad, because any athlete who can reach that near criminal level of football intensity does it. Those who can't wish they could. That type of aggression is worthy of the big bucks in the NFL and anyone telling you differently is a hypocrite.

According to Chuck Noll, George Atkinson and I were among the criminal elements of the game. Maybe we were, but the only difference between the Raiders and Steelers of the '70s was the color of their uniforms. Okay, so the Steelers have four Super Bowl rings and I have only one, but the no-mercy attitudes of combat were exactly the same. The Steelers punched, kicked and gouged for every inch of turf and so did the Raiders and so do all the other winners. Make no mistake about it, when the championship games begin, the nice guys and true sportsmen of football are usually on vacation.

Some fans have a distorted view of football and the athletes of the game. It's easy to understand how that can happen. The average fan will read articles on the sports page and actually believe the hypocrisy and lies. They hear a one-sided fabrication and believe they've heard the whole truth.

Listening to Chuck Noll complain, a person would have had to believe that Terry Bradshaw was the dumbest quarterback in the history of football and that Jerry Glanville's Oilers were nothing but a bunch of cheap-shot artists. Neither assumption is even remotely accurate, but a person has to know how to sort through the lies and hypocrisy before he can get to the truth.

For example, the true story of winning football in Pittsburgh began during the 1970s when the Steelers drafted the best athletes they could. I'm talking about tough guys, the type of characters that Al Capone would have had riding shotgun on the beer trucks of Chicago. If we're going to talk about criminal elements and the Raiders, then let's mention Al Capone football and the Steelers. Criminals? Hardly. Winners? Yes.

However, if you ever listened to Pittsburgh radio during football season, chances are you would have heard Myron Cope tell his all-Pittsburgh version of Father Chuck Noll and Pittsburgh's Boys Town. Myron is famous for hypocrisy and the cliché. Even though Myron Cope has a voice that sounds like Mickey Mouse's gangster brother, his tales of Father Chuck and the boys have the fragrance and lingering taste of good ole Irish whiskey on a cold, damp night. The true story, however, reeks of garlic, gunpowder and gangrene.

Myron Cope will argue that Father Chuck's Boys never wore trenchcoats or fedoras, but many NFL receivers and running backs can attest to the fact they didn't spend their Sunday afternoons passing out communion, either. They were nasty, mean, aggressive, intimidating, insensitive and brutally violent! But hell, I'm not complaining because they were everything a great defense should be. They were fantastic!

There are times when I actually wonder how it would have been had I played for the Steelers. While wearing the silver and black of the Raiders, Chuck Noll and Myron Cope considered me a criminal element, and worse. Admittedly, I played a mean, nasty, aggressive, and violent game of defensive football – just like the Steelers. But let's remember the rules and the fact that I was not overly flagged, nor were the Steelers.

Playing in Pittsburgh and wearing a different color uniform certainly wouldn't have changed my aggressive mode, but drinking the water and running around with Arrowhead Holmes would have intensified and magnified the Mr. Hyde living within. As one of Father Chuck's boys, Myron Cope probably would have dubbed me Saint John and defended my style as compassionate hitting.

It's called hypocrisy and the NFL is cluttered with it. Furthermore, a person doesn't have to sift through ancient NFL history to find it because hypocrisy is a common everyday occurrence.

Tom Landry coached the Dallas Cowboys through a miserable 1988 season. The Dallas press and fans were calling for Tom's head. They wanted him fired, axed, terminated, cut loose, banished from football, and run out of the state of Texas. According to Dallas loyalists, Tom was old, senile, his coaching techniques outdated, his mind warped by twenty-nine hard years at the helm of America's team. The Cowboys needed new blood, a young, aggressive, innovative coach. Presto, it happened.

During a weekend transaction, the Cowboys were sold to Jerry Jones, an Arkansas oil man, and Jimmy Johnson, one of the most successful collegiate coaches in recent history, was hired to replace Ol' Tom. With the exception of Ol' Tom, a person would have to think that everyone in Dallas was going to be elated over the change. After all, Tom Landry was gone and the Cowboys had their transfusion of new blood. Jimmy Johnson was the young, aggressive, innovative coach everyone wanted.

Instead of a celebration, the Dallas press and fans were livid over the fact that Tom had been unceremoniously axed and Jimmy Johnson hired. The same individuals who were asking for Tom's head on a platter were now rushing to his defense. All of a sudden the press was writing positive stories about Tom Landry's twenty-nine years of dedication to the Cowboy organization. They were remembering those many division championships Tom brought to Dallas, five trips to the Super Bowl, and two championship rings.

It was all for naught, because Jimmy was in and Tom was out. Football is a callous and insensitive business, as Jimmy Johnson found out. Jimmy's first press conference turned out to be an apologia. He stood in front of a group of idiot reporters and tried to justify his reasons for being there. Jimmy was born and raised in Texas as a Cowboy fan, he had paid his dues as an athlete and earned a reputation as a truly great collegiate coach. Jimmy shouldn't have to justify his being hired or Tom's being fired because that kind of action is simply part of the game. I have to believe that if an oil man pays something like one hundred and fifty million dollars for the Dallas Cowboys, then he has the right to fire and hire anyone he chooses. Tom Landry understood and left football the same way he coached, with class. But Jimmy Johnson had to face the angry mob, the same mob that had originally screamed for Tom's head. "Please, give me a chance." I'm pretty sure that's what Jimmy said, but with hypocrisy being hypocrisy, and journalists being journalists, and fans being fans, Jimmy better win and win and win.

By NFL standards, Tom Landry's story is kind of your average day at the office. Survival in the NFL is a matter of what you can do right now, instead of what you did yesterday. It works that way for rookies coming into the system, seasoned veterans and coaches. Day-by-day performance is all that counts, so don't miss many tackles or drop touchdown passes or have a losing season, because someone else is waiting in the wings to take your place.

Football is a strange business, where even doing the right things aren't enough sometimes. About ten years ago, Bum Phillips was the head coach of the Houston Oilers. Bum was fired for doing a great job and being a quality human being. It might be difficult to believe, but it's true.

I spent my last year of professional football in Houston playing for Bum Phillips. He was a player's coach, but more importantly, he was a great human being. Bum cared about the athletes and they truly cared about him. Harmony between the head coach and players doesn't necessarily translate into winning seasons, but it does mean a team will play harder for a Bum Phillips than a Chuck Noll. Bum sincerely cared about his people whereas Chuck Noll cared only about himself.

The Oilers had their summer training camp in San Angelo, Texas. That's where I first learned a little about Bum Phillips. We were four hundred and fifty miles from Houston and in the middle of two-a-day sessions when Bum heard that a hurricane was going to hit the southeastern Texas coastline. It was supposed to be a killer storm. Bum told us that he was going back to Houston to be with his family. But, he made special arrangements for a charter flight so that the players could go home, too. Bum thought that helping our families weather the storm was more important than a football training camp, and it was. Bum had a different set of rules that he lived and played by. Bum thought that playing hard and to the best of your ability was more important than winning every game. He knew the Oilers couldn't win every game of every season. No team can. He stressed the importance of always trying to play to the full potential of our abilities. Bum felt that if we could do that, then the Oilers would win their share of games.

During my career, I always gave football my best effort, but for a man like Bum Phillips I found myself trying harder. Sometimes human nature will cause us to be a little lazy, and if one is just playing for oneself maybe he will dog it once in a while. But if he is playing for a real man, like Bum, then he goes one hundred percent all the time.

That season, the Oilers rallied behind Bum Phillips and we finished with 11 wins and five losses, and made the playoffs. It was a great season by Houston standards, but for Bum's efforts, and a great effort it was, the Oilers fired him and hired Eddie Biles.

Originally, Eddie Biles was my defensive coach with the Oilers. In my estimation, he didn't know the difference between a football and a doorknob. Further complicating the situation was the fact that Eddie had a personality closely related to a hemorrhoid. Quite frankly, Eddie Biles was an asshole and a phony. Most of the time I can tolerate assholes, and even phonies, but Eddie Biles was also a liar. Hypocrisy is one thing, but a liar is the bottom of the garbage can.

When I went to Houston, Eddie told me I wouldn't be a starter in his defensive secondary. I didn't find a problem with that, but Eddie had to carry everything one step further. He said that Pete Rozelle was watching me. He was afraid that if I played physical and hurt anyone it would create serious problems for me and the team. He made a big issue of my physical style and emphasized the point that Pete didn't want me roughing anyone up.

The truth of my not starting had nothing to do with Pete Rozelle or aggressive play. Eddie Biles was contractually obliged to start free safety Mike Reinfeldt. Eddie figured by telling me a lie, I'd get pissed off at Pete and not him. However, I knew the true story going in. You see, Mike Reinfeldt and I went back a long way. In fact, I taught Mike the ropes when he was with the Raiders. Maybe Eddie didn't understand, but players have a way of talking among themselves.

When I arrived in Houston, I was at the end of my career. Going into the NFL, God willing, my plan was to play for ten years and retire. I had nine pretty good seasons with the Raiders, and I was thinking that one more year, maybe two with Houston, and it would be time to move on to something else. So in truth, I don't think I was as interested in starting for the Oilers as I was in sharing some of my experience with their defensive backs. I know when I came into the league, the experience of wide receiver Fred Biletnikoff made a difference in my career. Fred taught me more about receivers than any coach. He warned me that receivers were the biggest bunch of con men in the game. A receiver will give a defender two, three, sometimes four phony moves before he breaks for the ball. Fred taught me to recognize and understand what was real and what wasn't. It made me a better player and maybe I could teach some of the Houston defensive players those techniques.

During one game, we were getting burned in the secondary. It was obvious that Eddie Biles had his people in the wrong places. The Raiders made the same mistake one time and the problem was correctable with a few minor adjustments. I tried to talk to Eddie but he didn't want to listen. When I went out on the field we made the adjustments and they worked. Eddie got pissed off and started screaming and cussing at me for interfering. Eddie said that I was a player and should stop trying to coach his team.

Hell, the Oilers were in a war and getting slaughtered. I wasn't trying to make Eddie look bad any more than I was trying to make me look good. If your people are in a fight and gettin punched in the face because their hands are too low, you tell them, "Get 'em up! Your hands are too low, get 'em up!" But Eddie would rather see a slaughter than admit he made a mistake.

Interestingly enough, the very next week, Eddie came up with a brilliant new scheme for positioning the defensive secondary. It was exactly the same alignment I suggested on Sunday. Eddie went around patting himself on the back while taking all the credit. I never said anything nor did anyone else. If that's what it took to keep Eddie happy and Bum's Oilers winning, then it was fine with me. The most interesting thing of all was that when Eddie finally became the head man in Houston, he took Bum's winning team and put them in the toilet. I think Eddie only won three or four games during the next two seasons. The Oilers were basically the same team, but the difference between being winners and losers was a head coach.

Football, on any level of competition, is like that. You'll find a combination of real pros, hypocrites, phonies, idiots, not to mention the egos and liars like Eddie Biles. I don't like liars, but I think idiots and egos can really do a tremendous amount of harm to the athletes, especially young athletes.

I watched a high school team working out once. It was said to be strictly conditioning, but the coach, a real taskmaster, was into sadistic punishment. It was brutal. He was torturing the kids. Then, worst of all, if one player faltered, the coach made everyone repeat the drill. He would punish the entire team because one or two athletes were, in his estimation, dogging it. The whole scene was ridiculously stupid, but the coach continued.

I watched several defensive backs running forty yard sprints against a kicker. The defensive backs were beating the kicker. They should because as a rule, they're faster. I could see that the kicker was really putting out, trying his best and running harder than the defensive people, but he lost every sprint by a couple of yards. The coach kept screaming and cussing, and made them run the sprint over and over again until everyone was on the ground puking. In his estimation the kicker wasn't trying.

I thought about running a few sprints against the coach, and then kicking his ass all over the field when he couldn't keep up. But, I just bit my tongue and tried diplomacy. In a mild way I talked about the difference between coaching and torturing athletes. The coach was obviously blinded by his own brilliance and couldn't see my views. For some reason he didn't understand that his part-time athletes were full-time human beings. Sometimes all the words in the world are a waste of time because, no matter what you say, it isn't going to register.

Afterward I talked to the kicker and the defensive backs. It turned out the slowest defensive back ran a 4.8 forty yard dash and the kicker's best time ever was a 5.2. All things being equal, no matter how hard the kicker ran, he would never beat the defensive people. But an idiot blinded by his own ego would never understand the mathematics of that fact.

Most fans never get the overall view of the entire story of football. Some people think that coaching determines outcomes, others believe that athletes do. In reality it is a combination of both plus a little luck and then a whole lot more. For example, all winning teams have their hitmen and assassins, but some fans and journalists believe that football is a gentlemanly game of finesse and clean crisp tackles. Not true.

Football belongs to hitmen and assassins. Contrary to the stories a hypocrite might tell, I wasn't the only assassin ever to play the game of football. Believe me, most championship teams are built from the foundation of devastating defensive play. In order to achieve that kind of aggressive and physical defensive football the services of hitmen and assassins are needed. Without these intimidating characters patrolling the defensive side of scrimmage, the team becomes part of the also-rans.

The average football fan thinks that hitmen and assassins are the same type of creature. Once again, not true! A hitman is simply a good hitter, and he will get his opponent's attention. When a hitman is involved in a tackle, the receiver or running back will get up and stagger over to the sideline looking for the trainer.

Trainer will say, "Hitman got you, eh."

"Think so, but I'm a little fuzzy."

A couple of Excedrin, some Preparation H, and the trainer will say, "Okay, pull up your pants and get outta here. But be more careful next time you see the hitman."

Make no mistake about it, receivers and running backs do keep a watchful eye out for the hitman because it can be a painfully embarrassing situation. But in football circles, running into a hitman is considered nothing more serious than a stiff headache and a pain in the lower extremity. However, an encounter with an assassin is more complex and much more devastating. First of all, when an assassin lays the wood to a receiver or running back there are no questions asked such as, "Who or what hit me?" An assassin is actually football's answer to medicine's anesthesiologist — only quicker.

A person goes to the hospital for an operation expecting to be sedated. Ten, nine... eight... seven... and they're asleep. But a receiver comes wandering over the middle expecting to catch the football and suddenly he can't remember going to sleep but, nonetheless, he's waking up from a journey into limbo. There was no pain, no counting backwards, no indication that he was sleepy and yet he is coming out of a deep sleep. Most of the time, after one shot administered by the assassin, a receiver is only capable of uttering the single football word, "Whatthefuckhappened?"

The neurologist will explain to the receiver exactly what happens to the brain during a knockout. Dangerous dude, that assassin. Next, the psychiatrist will attempt to convince the receiver that it's safe to go back in the water, so to speak. But deep down in the subconscious chambers of the mind the receiver knows he's still out there waiting for him, and it's frightening. The receiver will tell himself that he's macho and not afraid, but deep down he knows differently. He is afraid, very much afraid. Why? Well, because pain hurts and pain is one of the common threads associated when a receiver meets the assassin.

Finally, a couple of weeks later, just before the receiver returns to the field for the first time since the encounter with the assassin, the trainer will give him a bottle of Keopectate to drink.

The receiver complains, "But I don't have diarrhea."

"I know, I know," the trainer will explain. "But you remember the last time all of this happened ... took the cleaners a week to get the stains out of your football pants." The first encounter with an assassin isn't that scary. But it's waking up and then having to face him a second time that can be embarrassingly frightening.

Frank Gifford is still part of the professional football scene, but his work is confined to the press box announcing games for ABC's *Monday Night Football.* In his day, Frank could run with the best of them. Galloping out of Southern Cal in 1952 and onto the NFL scene he became an instant swashbuckling hero. Frank was part of the history-making New York Giants and if you ever want to talk football and assassins, sit down sometime and have a conversation with him. Somewhere in the dialog Frank will mention his most regrettable moment in football — he thinks. Frank usually begins by making you believe it's a vivid and unforgettable memory. But when he starts stammering and stuttering about a football game when he was hit between the eyes with a sledgehammer and then run over with a cement truck, he's only trying to explain his on-the-field encounter with Concrete Charlie Bednarik. Frank will swear that it's a vivid and yet hazy memory — hazy in the sense that he doesn't remember, vivid in the sense that he can't forget. That's usually the way it happened when running backs and receivers met Concrete Charlie Bednarik. Simply stated: Concrete Charlie was an assassin working for the Philadelphia Eagles.

Hard-hitting football players are not criminal elements. They never have been. But if you listen to lies and hypocrisy long enough the real story becomes a distorted image. The next time you watch a football game, turn off the sound and see what really goes on. You'll be surprised, because the truth is, Charley's a tuna and Sylvester's a pussy, and neither one of them ever won a Super Bowl ring. I'm talking about a fish as in chump, and a pussy as in pussy. Think about it.

If you're still having trouble figuring everything out, then consider this. The San Francisco 49ers and Cincinnati Bengals gave the fans a great Super Bowl this past season because both teams were physical. They each had their share of hitmen and assassins. They fought and clawed and scratched for every damn inch of real estate and took turns busting each other up. The outcome wasn't determined until the last seconds of the game. Physical, aggressive, violent, but in the end, the 49ers won a thriller.

However, in recent years, only one physical team showed up at the stadium for Super Bowl Sunday. The Bears, Giants, and Redskins were physical teams loaded with hitmen and assassins. They easily won the championship because of competition that resembled Charley the tuna and Sylvester the pussy. Once in a while Charley or Sylvester will get lucky and make it to the big game because even the fish and pussy teams of the NFL are made up of professional athletes. But the Super Bowl is a matter of all-out violence and aggression. It's a matter of attitude and intimidation. Three hours of war and you take no prisoners.

Once again, Charley's a tuna and Sylvester's a pussy. It's like I said, neither one of them have a Super Bowl ring. Simply stated: don't bet on fish and pussies when it comes to championships because hitmen and assassins wear the Super Bowl ring.

8

Inside the Real NFL

March 5, 1989, began like any normal Sunday morning. I got up, had a little breakfast and glanced over the sports page. However, this particular Sunday was of monumental consequence because I read an article that gave me second thoughts about Pete Rozelle. I spent the better part of my adult life believing that Pete Rozelle was a complete boob. Firsthand experiences with Pete had, over the years, led me to that rather irrefutable conclusion. But now, reading the morning paper, I found myself actually wondering if I had been wrong in my assessment of Pete. Perhaps he wasn't a complete, inept, bungling boob after all.

This Pete Rozelle story started about ten years ago. Actually, in the beginning, it wasn't even a Pete Rozelle story. But Pete, being Pete, just sort of stumbled into an ugly mess out in Oakland, California. I know it's a long stumble from New York to Oakland, but Pete isn't the most coordinated guy in town. He has a tendency to stumble into sticky situations, so to speak.

It all started when Al Davis and his Raiders ran into some problems with the Oakland Alameda County Coliseum Commission. Al Davis is kind of a strange man, contractually speaking, of course. Al is a tough negotiator but when he signs a contract he will live by that agreement. That's the way it should be, but not everyone will agree. I've read about a number of athletes negotiating and signing multi-year contracts. Six months later the same athletes are unhappy and looking to renegotiate or trying to get out of the original agreement. It's that way with a lot of people, not just athletes.

I believe that was the problem in Oakland with the Coliseum Commission. A long-term agreement was signed between the Raiders and the coliseum officials with both sides agreeing to do certain things. Al Davis and the Raiders agreed to play in Oakland and the coliseum officials agreed to make certain stadium changes and improvements over the years. Al Davis was doing a pretty fair job of fielding a football team and keeping his side of the agreement, but not everyone can say the same. Al expected stadium improvements to be made, but officials were sort of dragging their feet. A person has to understand that Mr. Davis is kind of a no-nonsense guy. Knowing Al the way I know Al, I would have taken him quite seriously when he made the statement about moving the Raiders to another city unless improvements were made at the Coliseum. But some coliseum officials called the NFL and got word from the top brass, aka Pete Rozelle, that Al Davis couldn't move the Raiders.

Pete Rozelle and the NFL have always had this notion that rules, regulations and laws governing little things like monopolies, and in this case, antitrust violations, don't apply to football. Al Davis thought differently. In spite of Pete telling coliseum officials that Al couldn't move, Al did exactly what he said he would do. He moved. The fact is that Al Davis had the Raiders set up in Los Angeles quicker than Pete could say Oakland Alameda County Coliseum Commission.

All of a sudden, attorneys were involved and from there everything became rather complicated. Lawsuits were filed, counter lawsuits were filed, appeals were filed and everything else attorneys do in order to justify hefty fees. In the end, as expected, Pete Rozelle was again in the doghouse. But this time he was licking about a thirty-four million dollar wound plus those miscellaneous costs that had to occur during years and years of litigation.

Originally, the court awarded the Raiders and the Los Angeles Coliseum something in the neighborhood of thirty-four million dollars in damages. Damn, Al Davis was right. Antitrust laws did apply to the National Football League, too.

Yogi once said, "It ain't over 'til it's over," and that's why Pete and his people decided to appeal the thirty-four million dollar figure. Normally, a person would think that renegotiate would mean less money. But with Pete involved, that wasn't necessarily true. I honestly believed that before Pete was finished with negotiations, he would prove conclusively that he was the biggest boob to ever walk upright. I would have bet my car and the house that if Pete was in the room during renegotiations, the settlement figures would soar into the hundreds of millions of dollars. Hell, with Pete handling renegotiations, Al Davis had a pretty fair chance of ending up as the owner of the NFL. So I thought.

However, reading the newspaper that Sunday morning in March, I learned that Pete and his people actually saved the NFL about fourteen million dollars. Incredible as it all sounded, Pete and the boys renegotiated everything down to a final settlement of about twenty million dollars. For the first time in my life, I had to give Pete some credit.

I realize that every smart-ass in the country is going to look at the antitrust suit from a negative point of view. There will be a large number of critical individuals who will attempt to make a case out of the flimsy fact that the whole ruckus never should have happened in the first place. They'll blame Pete for a whopping twenty million dollar loss and not give the man credit for saving the NFL fourteen million. Some folks will maintain that if Al Davis wanted to move the Raiders, Pete should have kept his nose out of the problem and just left well enough alone. That way, there never would have been any need for litigation, not a twenty million dollar settlement or all the other ridiculous expenses.

This may come as a surprise to everyone, but regardless of the overwhelming evidence, I'd still like to argue in Pete's defense. I understand a little about antitrust laws, and I admit that Pete and the NFL had no right dictating where the Raiders could or couldn't play. Okay, so Pete did make a little twenty million dollar error, but let's not be so quick to condemn the man before we total up the rest of the story.

Admittedly, Pete became involved in a sticky situation with Al Davis. From the very beginning it was never a question of who would win, but simply a matter of how badly Pete was going to get his ass kicked. When it came to a tussle, mentally speaking, Al and Pete are not in the same league. Courtroom or no courtroom it was almost criminal for a heavyweight like Al Davis to mentally joust with a fly-weight. But on the other hand, some people constantly go around asking for it, and Al Davis was more than willing to oblige. You see, Al has always been more of an eye-for-an-eye personality rather than a turn-the-other-cheek man. There isn't a damn thing wrong with that philosophy and when Pete came looking for a fight, I was positive he would get one. The NFL and Pete Rozelle were going to lose and all the courtroom drama was simply to determine how much.

I've always believed that everyone should be entitled to one mistake, even if his name was Pete Rozelle, and it eventually became a twenty million dollar mistake. I know that twenty million dollars, to some folks, might sound like a major league blunder, but let's analyze everything. First of all, when a person stops and thinks about twenty million dollars against the growing rate of inflation, it's really not a lot of money. I'm serious.

For a mere pittance like twenty million dollars, a person wouldn't even make Robin Leach's *Lifestyles of the Rich and Famous*. To be rejected by a dude called "Leach" must tell you something about the true worth of twenty million dollars.

Leach? I never could figure out if that was his name or his occupation. I'm serious. I've seen Robin Leach travel all over the world with millionaires and billionaires. The man seems to end up in the most exotic places, eat the finest foods, and all I can do is wonder, who's picking up the tab?

All this talk about Robin Leach reminded me of Jim and Tammy. I'd have to believe that for twenty million dollars Jim and Tammy would warm up to a person. But who in his right mind could take all those tears and smeared mascara?

Okay, on the serious side, for twenty million dollars a person could buy a Ferrari for every day of the week and a Rolls Royce or two. And sure, if he watched his purse strings he could afford a villa on the fabulous French Riviera, a home in Palm Springs, a little abode in Aspen, a dwelling on Park Avenue, and something in Beverly Hills. If he counted pennies he could purchase a Lear Jet, afford a chauffeur-driven limousine, and have a butler and a couple of maids. But after that he'd be down to his last ten million dollars.

All right, twenty million dollars is a lot of money, but I'm just trying to make a point on Pete's behalf. Pete did make a little mistake; but in this situation, if he had not been paying attention, the loss to the NFL could have been three times as much. Instead of picking on Pete for a twenty million dollar loss, I'm going to give him credit for having saved the NFL at least forty million dollars. Let me explain.

Sure, Pete said the Raiders couldn't move, and Al Davis proved beyond any reasonable doubt they could. It was an expensive lesson; but, with Pete Rozelle attending class, one would automatically think that several refresher courses would be needed before the whole scheme of antitrust violations would sink in. It's nearly impossible to believe, but Pete learned his lesson the first time out.

Interestingly enough, Pete was still in the process of straightening out Al Davis, or getting himself straightened out on the antitrust issue when other problems plagued the NFL. The Colts decided they didn't like Baltimore and, without NFL blessings, they moved to Indianapolis. They packed up in the middle of the night and left town, but Pete didn't give them any flak. He could have, you know, but he didn't. To my way of thinking, that was a savings of at least twenty million dollars.

With the Colts playing in Indianapolis, the St. Louis Cardinals decided the climate in Phoenix was better for their financial health. They moved. And guess what? Once again Pete didn't say a word. Hell, fifteen years ago, the Pete Rozelle I knew would have ended up in courtroom battles with the Colts and Cardinals. The Pete Rozelle

I knew wouldn't care what jurors had to say, or what decision a judge had previously handed down. The Pete I knew would have banged his head against the wall, held his breath, and probably cost the NFL sixty million or more. So, if a person takes into consideration a mere twenty million dollar loss against the potential of a sixty million dollar ordeal, I'd say the NFL is forty million dollars ahead. Of course, if that guy I mentioned before, Elmer Fudd, was commissioner of the NFL, there probably wouldn't have been a loss in the first place.

A person has to understand that the Pete Rozelle I knew never considered the right or wrong of any particular situation. He always did what he damn well pleased and his system of kangaroo justice was final. In the past, Pete never let things like facts, truth or the law of the land confuse his thought process or interfere with his system of justice. Pete never cared if a quarterback had a right to own a nightclub. If Pete said, "Sell the club or get out of football," that's exactly what he meant and the facts or a person's rights never entered into his decision-making process. If Pete dropped a fine on a defensive back for allegedly breaking rules, but the films proved otherwise, it still didn't matter. Pete was the first and last word on any subject because he was the boss man. Being boss man meant Pete could say or do anything he wanted. If Pete so desired, he could even change an NFL rule just prior to kick-off, outlawing the no-huddle, quick-snap offense, and then change the rule back next week. If he so desired.

When everything was said and done, I was disappointed in Pete. Even though Al Davis gave him a big-time beating, I still expected Pete to go after the Colts and Cardinals. What the hell, it wasn't as if Pete had lost twenty million dollars of his own money. I honestly felt that he would saddle up and head west in search of the other deserters, but he didn't. That could only mean one of two things. Maybe Pete was getting a little sharper in his old age and finally realized that two wrongs don't equal a right. Then again, it might have been that someone with a little more sense than Pete, and that's not a whole lot of sense, pulled back the reins and said, "Let 'em go, Pete." And he did.

If I was disappointed in Pete Rozelle, I was jumping up and down with excitement for Al Davis. I'm not talking strictly about the twenty million dollar settlement, although Al Davis' courtroom victory had me chuckling a little. Actually, the best part of this story took place on January 20, 1984. That was the day the "LOS ANGE-LES" Raiders played the Redskins in Super Bowl XVIII. If Al Davis' Los Angeles Raiders won the Super Bowl, someone would have to present him with the Lombardi Trophy. Traditionally speaking, that someone would be the Commissioner of the NFL, Pete Rozelle.

When the Los Angeles Raiders won the AFC West with a 12-4 record. I started rooting for them to go all the way. Call me sadistic, if you so desire, but I wanted to see Pete Rozelle hand Al Davis the Lombardi Trophy. You see, about this time, with all the litigation going on, Pete and Al were sort of on the outs. I guess a person could go as far as to say they were mortal enemies and probably hated each other's guts. I just thought it would be an interesting twist to watch Al and Pete in the same room holding the Lombardi Trophy.

The Raiders, at their criminal element best, opened the playoffs by mugging Chuck Noll's Steelers 38-10. A week later they beat the Seahawks 30-14. From there it was on to Tampa Stadium and the Super Bowl. The day belonged to Al Davis and his Los Angeles Raiders as the Redskins were pounded into submission by a score of 38-9. It was great, watching Pete standing in the winner's locker room, his tanned face turning red as he choked and gagged on his own words proclaiming the Los Angeles Raiders as world champions of football.

And what about Al Davis? Well, with a wonderful sneer on his face, Al accepted the Lombardi Trophy and said that these Los Angeles Raiders were "the greatest Raider team of all time." Who could argue with that? No one, not even Pete.

Shortly after the twenty million dollar blunder was put to bed, I had a conversation with some Raider fans — Oakland Raider fans. Some folks around the Bay area still resented the fact that Al Davis took the Raiders south. They felt betrayed and I can understand that. Sure, there were many loyal Raider fans who believed they were left out in the cold, but moving to Los Angeles was strictly a business judgment. Al Davis did what he felt was financially best for the Raiders and, as Pete learned the hard way, Al had that right. It was no different for the Colts or the Cardinals. Their decision to move to a different location had to do with making money, more money.

Management tries to keep the stadiums filled but, more importantly, they're always looking for angles to improve the television ratings. Holding a fair share of the television market translates into dollars and cents, and that's the bottom line when it comes to football – money.

In the ratings battle it helps to be a winning franchise, but winning teams aren't the only thing that sells tickets or lures the advertising dollars into paying for prime time slots. Heated rivalries are marketable, as are coaches who don't like each other. It's all business, a violent form of show business and, believe me, the NFL and television marketing people rarely miss an opportunity to capitalize on the best possible match-ups.

For example, no one has seen the Green Bay Packers and the Atlanta Falcons playing on national television in recent times. Check their records and maybe you'll understand. Furthermore, there's nothing controversial about the players or coaches on those teams. Who is coaching Atlanta and Green Bay these days?

Atlanta and Green Bay on the same field will not sell tickets or bring in the advertising dollars. Therefore, they're not going to receive a prime time invitation for the game of the week time slot. The same thing holds true for Tampa Bay and Detroit. Last season the Bucs beat the Lions 23-20 in a thriller at the Silver Dome. But don't expect to see those teams in a prime time TV rematch. Only 25,000 fans showed up at the stadium for that game, and no one in his right mind is going to put something like that on national television and expect advertisers to pay the bill.

The fans want to see the winners at the stadium and on television. They want to see the controversial characters of football; those fiery coaches, and aggressive players who make everything worth the price of admission.

The Chicago Bears had one of the all-time great running backs in Walter Payton, but the fans went crazy when William "The Refrigerator" Perry, a three hundred and fifty pound lineman carried the ball. As a running back, William Perry isn't a threat to any of Walter's records, but he was and still is different. The Refrigerator was a controversial kick, a different kind of high, and all of a sudden his exploits as a running back were major news and prime time.

Football is a form of show business and sometimes a character actor is more valuable than a great athlete. Fredd Young, for example, was a linebacker with the Seattle Seahawks. He was a seasoned All-Pro, but didn't have a controversial personality. Along came Brian Bosworth and the Seahawks went Hollywood.

Giving the Boz the benefit of the doubt I'll say that he was and still is an untested rookie with potential, but certainly not in the same league as a proven vet like Fredd Young. Boz was, however, a controversial character with a bizarre haircut. Furthermore, Boz had a knack for opening his mouth at the right time or wrong time, and he didn't care what he said. The Seahawks gave Boz an eleven million dollar, multiyear contract, and Fredd Young got the shuffle treatment.

Fredd didn't like the thought of an unproven rookie making more money than he. Naturally, he wanted a bigger slice of the pie, and rightly so. But instead of more Seahawk money, Fredd was promptly traded to the Colts and the Boz became the big man on campus in

Seattle. Fredd is playing football in Indianapolis, but Boz has only been a part-time performer on the field for the Seahawks. In defense of Boz I will say that he has been quite busy, though. He went in for some surgery, wrote a book, has made a number of television appearances, has a few commercials running, started a little company to market and sell Boz items, and I've heard he's even planning a movie. All of that doesn't have a lot to do with playing football and winning championships; nevertheless, Boz, in uniform or not, still sells tickets and brings in the prime time viewers. Maybe Fredd Young was a running back's worst nightmare, but Boz is definitely a marketing man's dream.

No one is involved with major league football just for the love of the game. For the players and owners alike, it all comes down to money. That's why I never had any problem with Al Davis wanting to move the franchise to Los Angeles. Al has the right to make as much money as he possibly can. At the same time, I think that basic right should also apply to the players.

I don't really want to get into the problems between management, the weakening union and the players because those issues will be resolved in a court of law. However, I do believe that the NFL is going to be scrutinized and major changes, constitutionally speaking, are forthcoming.

In general terms and briefly, I want to mention a little about free agency. To play in the NFL an athlete has to give up some of his basic rights and go wherever the wind blows. I know the NFL has recently adopted a program where each team can only protect thirty-seven players. The unprotected players then become conditional free agents and can negotiate with any team in the league. The new system is simply a Band-Aid for a major wound.

In order to become a conditional free agent, the player must fall into the categories of injured, old or mediocre. In some instances, free agents have signed on with other teams and will earn more money. Still, this form of free agency is a quick whistle stop before the end of the line which is also known as the unemployment line.

I know the argument about the NFL striving for parity, and it's a weak one. In my estimation, true parity is pure boredom. I'd rather see a team trying to hit the high note of an undefeated season rather than two teams with losing records slugging it out for a wild card playoff spot. I'd rather see a complete blowout or an upset rather than mediocrity.

I thought the Jets-Colts match-up in Super Bowl III was better for the game of football than so-called parity and many of our recent championship games. Super Bowl III was played before the AFL and

NFL merged. With two separate leagues coming after the talent, the owners found themselves in a bidding war in order to hire the best money could buy. Financially it was good for the athletes and it wasn't bad for football, either. Actually, if we put aside Super Bowl XXIII, the big game and parity have recently produced some ridiculously one-sided Sunday afternoons. Maybe it tells us that there is no such thing as true parity, but some teams do reach mediocrity.

I think it would be great for football if there was a dynasty or two. I'm talking about a truly great team, loaded with all the talent money could buy. That way, every Sunday, a team would have the opportunity to prove it was the best, while the other team would reach for the high note while trying to beat the best.

During my career, I never liked to be written off before the game was played. I remember my sophomore year of college when we played the number-one ranked team in the nation, Purdue. We were a young, inexperienced team and the Boilermakers were loaded with talent. Purdue also had a great running back, Leroy Keyes. For one week we read stories about Leroy using us as his stepping-stone to the Heisman. If we were to believe the headlines, then we never should have played the game. Maybe the journalists were right, but there was one way to find out the truth: Purdue and Leroy had to go out on the field and prove they were number one to Woody Hayes and his kids.

As a team we reached inside of ourselves and found something special. It was an awesome feeling, an astounding high I rarely experienced as an athlete. Instead of stepping stones, the Buckeyes turned out to be the roadblock on the trip to Leroy's Heisman Trophy. We pounded Leroy into submission and went on to beat Purdue 13-0. We finished the season undefeated, won the Rose Bowl and the National Championship.

My point is that when athletes are involved, the game is played on the field and not on the pages of a newspaper. The journalists write about a heavily favored team before the game, but on Monday morning, the sports page has a story about an upset. I don't know, maybe I'm wrong, but seriously, I'd rather see a blow-out or an upset, but not parity.

It's been said that if the NFL had total free agency, Al Davis, along with Eddie DeBartolo, Jr., and his 49ers and a few other real heavy financial hitters, would load up with the best athletes and ruin the NFL. Eddie and Al, with their checkbooks in hand, probably would go after the best money could buy, but it wouldn't ruin football. They've been paying for the best possible team money could buy. They've been doing it for years. It's no secret that the Raiders and the 49ers pay top dollar and go first class. And history will tell you they've played in a total of seven Super Bowls and have six championship rings among their franchises. With or without parity, it all comes down to the fact that winners are winners and losers are losers.

I know some smart-ass critic is going to point out that during recent times, Al Davis and his Raiders haven't been winning. That's true, but it has nothing to do with parity. Al Davis and the Raiders have fallen on some hard times, but it's not as bad as some people will lead you to believe. As of late, the Raiders haven't been part of the playoff picture, but let us remember, Al Davis still claimed two Lombardi Trophies during the '80s. The last few years have been lean, but Al will get back to the basics and win again.

The basics of Raider football was many things. Offensively, it was stretching out the field by going with deep pass patterns, then buckling up and stuffing the ball down the opposition's throat. No trickery, nothing fancy. When you played the Raiders you knew just what to expect because Al drafted and traded for that type of athlete. Offensive football wasn't a science, it was an attitude, a mean and contemptuous attitude. Nowadays the Raider offense has too many Daryle Lamonicas and not enough Kenny Stablers.

In my first book I questioned the courage of one of our quarterbacks, Daryle Lamonica. Actually, the final printed word on Daryle was different than what I meant. Daryle was, in his own right, a great quarterback, but he didn't fit the Raider image. That's the trouble with the Raiders today: they're really not true Raiders.

Daryle Lamonica was a perfect textbook athlete even to the point of looking the all-American part. Daryle was always clean-shaven, his hair cut and combed and he probably changed his underwear and socks every day. That put him in the minority with the Raiders right off the bat.

If Daryle got knocked down he never bitched or complained. A true Raider would get up and spit on the man for knocking him down, or at least cuss. When a Raider got slapped, he punched him back. If he got punched, then a true Raider would kick in retaliation. If an opponent said go to hell, a Raider would motherfuck that person in return. Anything less, and you weren't a Raider. Worst of all, if you just sat there and took it, everyone would start questioning your courage — even your own people. Sure, Daryle always bounced up after getting hit, but he never retaliated. That simply wasn't the Raiders' style.

I realize some athletes are like that and it has nothing to do with courage or lack of courage. Hell, I punished Dolphin wide receiver Howard Twilley for years and he never said a word. I hit him, beat him groggy and bloody, rubbed his face in the mud. I even knocked him out a number of times. He always came back for more but never lost sight of his mission: catching the football. I couldn't intimidate the man and it used to bother me. I never liked Howard Twilley on the football field, but to this day, I greatly respect and admire the man.

Maybe that's the way it was with Daryle Lamonica. Maybe the players around the league respected him, but he wasn't carrying on in the Raiders' tradition. If he let his hair grow and didn't look so damn squeaky clean and bitched a little, or just said something, then maybe he would have been true Raider material.

After my book came out, I went on a fishing trip with some of the Raiders. We were in a restaurant one night talking football with some fans. One dude was talking to me about tough quarterbacks in the league. All of a sudden he looked toward the door and said, "Here comes the roughest, toughest quarterback of all time. What do you think, Jack?"

I turned around and there was Daryle Lamonica. He glared at me and said, "That's not what he wrote about me in his book. He said I was a coward."

Damn! I thought Daryle was going to ask me to step outside. Suddenly his face broke into a smile, he laughed and said, "Tate, I didn't know you were going to be here."

Daryle pulled up a chair, sat down and we started talking over old times. A few drinks later we go into the book and straightened everything out. Before the evening was over I told Daryle exactly what I felt about him and how my old buddy the writer twisted everything around a little. It was a good night, a good fishing trip, and even to this day Daryle and I are golfing buddies.

When Kenny Stabler came along, we knew immediately he was Raider material. It had nothing to do with Kenny being a better athlete than Daryle, or for that matter, more courageous. But Kenny didn't comb his hair. He rarely shaved and he would get on a receiver for running the wrong pattern or motherfuck a defensive lineman who had just flattened him.

Kenny and Daryle were different. Kenny had a Raider personality and Daryle didn't. What I mean to say is that if Daryle would blow his nose in a handkerchief and pass gas, then Kenny would pick his nose, wipe snot on his jersey and fart. It might sound crude, but proper etiquette never won a football game. Besides, most of the Raiders ate soup with a fork. Remember, the Raiders were rogues and misfits, football's equivalent to Hollywood's Dirty Dozen. We had a reputation and played to the boos.

To play defense for the Raiders during my day, an athlete had to have a really twisted personality off the field and a screw-you attitude on the field. We didn't have many defensive formations or strategies. We simply got after the opposition any way we could. Most of the time it wasn't very pretty, but it was effective.

Intimidation was always a factor in our games, but it didn't necessarily have to be physical. I remember playing against the Dallas Cowboys when George Atkinson had to cover an old friend of his, Bob Hayes. George was a track star and he was damn fast. Bob Hayes was faster. Speed is difficult to defense, but George had a plan that would slow an old adversary.

Even before the game started, George was talking to Bob. He said, "Hey, Bob, I want to warn you about Tate. Damn, I don't know what the hell you did to him, but he's pissed off. He's out to get you today. Be careful 'cause you know how vicious he can be."

To this day, Bob Hayes doesn't know the truth, but George was playing with his mind. George figured that if Bob Hayes was worried about me, then his job of covering blazing speed would be easier.

Bob said, "But Ack, I didn't do anything to him. What's he pissed off at me for?"

Bob Hayes had world-class speed, but George is a world-class instigator. He knew exactly what to say and how to say it. "Must of been something you said. I'm telling you, Bob, I've never seen Tate like this. He's gonna kill you first chance he gets. Be careful."

"But Ack, you gotta tell Tate, I'm sorry. Whatever it was, I didn't mean it."

Between plays George and Bob had a dialogue going. Bob was so worried about me that he forgot about running pass patterns. George continued adding wood to the fire and by the second quarter, Bob came up to me and apologized. I didn't know what the hell he was talking about. Since I had my game face on, I gave him a dirty look and went back to our huddle.

A little later in the game, we huddled up and our defensive captain, Willie Brown asked, "Tate, what the hell did Bob Hayes do to you?"

"Nothin'," I answered. "Why?"

"He wanted me to tell you he's sorry. I told him you were a crazy motherfucker and I wasn't going to get involved."

Bob never caught a pass that day and I never accepted his apology. To this very day, Bob Hayes never knew that George had found a little edge and worked it for all it was worth. It has got to be that way, because when the game starts, the man wearing a different colored uniform isn't your friend. He's going to try to beat you any way he can, and it's your job to kick his ass any way you can. Sometimes, a friendly conversation is all you need, while other times it takes a little more.

One game, our cornerback, Nemiah Wilson and George were having trouble with Riley Odoms, a tight end with the Denver Broncos. Riley would split out wide or move in a slot formation. Depending on Riley's split, it would create a one-on-one situation with either George or Nemiah. Denver was working the formation and Riley for big yardage. To complicate the matter, he outweighed George by at least fifty pounds and Nemiah by seventy.

Unlike Bob Hayes, George knew that conversation alone wasn't going to stop Riley, so he asked for a little help. We called it "outside-inside." George played Riley to the outside. A smart tight end would think he could beat George to the inside. Well, Riley was smart and that's why we called it "outside-inside."

Riley did beat George on a little slant pattern, or at least he thought so. I was waiting. It was the best hit of my career and, without a doubt, a two-point knockout. While the trainers and doctors were working on Riley, George came up to me. His face was pale and, in a dead serious tone he whispered, "I'm thanking God I was only a spectator."

Our defensive team would do things like that, make adjustments to where we could lower the boom on a receiver or running back. Sometimes we got burned, but most of the time it worked in our favor. Often, when players started moving all over the field making last-second adjustments, coaches will get pissed off. Unlike Houston coach Eddie Biles, our coaches were different. They would study game films, see how far out of position we were, and just shake their heads in disbelief. Once in a while a coach would ask, "What the hell kind of a defense was that?" George or I would explain the method to our madness and the coach would just shake his head.

The Raiders were a collection of characters. What else could you call Skip "Doctor Death" Thomas? Skip was truly one of the greatest athletes in football, but had the most bizarre personality I've ever been associated with.

Doc had a passion for fast cars and motorcycles. He took me for a ride in his Corvette … one time! Normal people don't paint skulls and crossbones on doors of Corvettes or any automobile for that matter. But that's my point: Doctor Death wasn't normal. Skip Thomas would give a friend the shirt of his back, but I repeat, Doctor Death wasn't normal.

My first and last ride with Doctor Death started at our training camp in Santa Rosa. Exactly one hour and ten minutes later we were back in Santa Rosa. During those seventy minutes, Doc had taken me on a quick tour of San Francisco, over the Golden Gate Bridge, through Oakland, back over the Bay Bridge, once again through San Francisco and then north to Santa Rosa.

Getting out of his 'Vette, I dropped to my knees and kissed good old mother earth. Then, I made a solemn vow never to be a passenger in a car driven by Doctor Death. Doc couldn't understand why. To him, a little ride to Oakland wasn't a big deal. He did it all the time. "It was only sixty miles," he said in his defense.

I quickly pointed out that sixty miles south to Oakland, plus sixty miles north to Santa Rosa equals one hundred and twenty miles. I also explained that if a person ran every red light, drove like a maniac with restless abandon and shattered every legal speed limit, it would still take a good fifty minutes to drive that course ... one way. I also mentioned that going over the Bay Bridge at 135 miles an hour wasn't a rational thing to do.

Doc justified everything by telling me, "Damn, Tate, we didn't even come close to breaking my record." Doc's record for the trip was sixty-five minutes.

If you haven't guessed by now, then let me say it, George Atkinson was another character. George rode with Doc even after I had warned him not to. If it wasn't for rush hour traffic, Doc and George might have set a new Santa Rosa-Oakland-Santa Rosa record.

After that ride, George vowed, he would never again sit in Doc's Corvette. George said, "Only a damn fool would get in that 'Vette with Doc." George was adamant about never riding with Doc, but obviously that only applied to rides in the Corvette. I never was able to figure out what kind of logic would possess an intelligent, rational human being like George to go for a ride with Doc on a motorcycle, knowing how fast he drove a Corvette. The Corvette was fast, but the bike was faster! The Corvette had seatbelts, the bike didn't!

It happened after we broke camp and moved back to Oakland for the start of the season. I was driving to our practice facilities when I saw Doc coming toward me on his motorcycle. Zoom! He's gone! Damn! He had to be going over a hundred miles an hour!

I glanced in my rear view mirror and watched Doc vanishing into the background. I wasn't positive, but it sure looked as though Doc had suckered some damn fool into going for a ride with him. It looked as though someone was on the back of the bike hanging on for life.

Several minutes later, I was still putting along with the flow of traffic at a modest sixty miles an hour. I was enjoying my ride to work, listening to soft music, minding my own business, when all of a sudden … ZOOM! Doc and his passenger blew out of sight. A minute later, I saw Doc coming again. ZOOM! This time, as they passed by, I finally caught a glimpse of the passenger, George Atkinson.

Later in the day, when George finally got his legs under him and was able to make intelligent sounds, he told me his reason for going on a motorcycle ride with Doc. George said, "Doc promised he wouldn't drive fast."

Doc was a man of his word. If he said he wouldn't drive fast, then he wouldn't drive fast. However, George failed to get an interpretation of exactly what fast on a motorcycle meant in relation to fast in a Corvette. Anything less than one hundred and fifty miles an hour in the Corvette wasn't, by Doc's standards of speed, considered all that fast. On the other hand, Doc's motorcycle was considerably faster than the Corvette.

Doc and George only hit speeds of 120 miles per hour. By Doc's calculations, one hundred and twenty miles and hour, even by Corvette standards, "ain't fast."

To be honest, I was shocked to think that George would even consider climbing on the bike with Doc regardless of any solemn promise not to speed. Three weeks earlier, George and I, along with half the Raider football team, witnessed Doc's motorcycle accident. He wasn't driving fast that time, either.

It happened early in the morning. Most of the players were sitting outdoors, eating some breakfast when Doc ZOOMED through the parking lot on his motorcycle. I'd guess he was only going a conservative fifty or sixty miles an hour, but that "ain't fast."

Doc sure could handle that bike. He was weaving in and out of parked cars, doing wheelies, everything imaginable. Doc was really putting on a show, but he had a legitimate reason. For the last week or so, Doc had been talking about getting an Evel Knievel outfit. Actually, his girlfriend was making him the outfit, and from the stories we heard, it was really something. It was said to be made from black leather, had zippers, metal studs, beads, fancy fringe, his name, DOCTOR DEATH, across the back, and just about everything a serious Knievel outfit would have and then some. Watching Doc zoom around the parking lot wearing his new outfit, we could see pride bursting from all over him. I had to admit, Doc's Evel Knievel outfit was really something.

Just about then, Doc ZOOMED down a straightaway and attempted to make a quick turn. He lost control, hit the curb, revved up through the ice plant and suddenly was airborne. Doc was about twelve feet above the ground. He fell off the bike and landed flat on his back in the ice plant. A split second later, his trusted bike flipped over in mid-air and came crashing down on top of him. I've never seen anything like it, but the bike landed upright on Doc's leg. Strangest of all, the bike seemed to set there for a second and then, almost as though it had a mind of its own, revved the motor and peeled out all over Doc and his new Knievel outfit.

A couple of the younger players got all excited, but the rest of us didn't make a lot to do over the scene. After all, this was Doctor Death and things like this were normal whenever he was involved. To settle down some of the rookies, George asked, "Doc, are you okay?"

Doc rolled over on the ice plant, looked at George and mumbled something that sounded like an affirmative response. He struggled to his feet, brushed himself off and went inside the locker room without saying another word.

My locker was next to Doc's, and even if he thought he was all right, his brand new Knievel outfit certainly wasn't. The entire right side of his leather suit was shredded beyond repair. His new threads had to be trashed.

Doc felt pretty bad about ruining the outfit, but I started feeling pretty bad for Doc. He was battered, bruised and shredded from his right ankle all the way up to his right ear and over the top of his head. Tread marks had peeled away most of Doc's skin and had also given him a bit of a haircut. Doc looked bad even for Doc.

Doc studied his wounded body and finally asked, "Tate, what the hell should I do?"

"Well," I casually answered, "whatever you do, you better do it fast because we have a game this Sunday."

For practice, Doc smeared vaseline over his wounded body and taped himself up like a mummy from a low-budget horror film. He had a Band-Aid over his ear, gauze wrapped around his head, an Ace Band-Aid twisted around his right arm, padding along his rib cage and more gauze and Ace Band-Aids down his right leg. He was, to say the least, a strange-looking sight walking onto the practice field.

To be a Raider coach in those days, an individual had to expect the unexpected. Naturally, when Coach John Madden saw Doc walk onto the field, he was a little curious. Even for Doctor Death, the whole scene was a little bizarre. I'm sure, had it been someone else coming to practice taped from head to toe, John might have asked a question or two. But this was Doctor Death. John Madden shook his head and quietly walked away.

Doc survived practice, played in the game on Sunday and did a helluva job. A different coach, someone other than a John Madden, probably would have gone berserk over an incident like that and caused a big scene. Doc was a starter, and starting cornerbacks aren't supposed to do stupid things off the field. The loss of a starter can change coaching strategies and have an adverse effect on the entire team. John never said a word because he knew the damage was already done and there was no sense complicating the situation.

It all came down to the fact that John Madden is a great man and was a terrific coach. He was a player's coach, and that's what it took to coach the Raiders in those days. He treated all of us as human beings first and professional athletes second. With John, we didn't have a lot of rules and regulations restricting us. We were given flexibility, left pretty much on our own, but when it came to the game, John expected us to be in condition and ready to play to our full potential.

John was responsible for overseeing all the coaching strategies. He called the shots, but winning or losing was a team effort. Some coaches waddle in the glory of a win, but criticize their athletes for the loss. But not John.

John wasn't fancy or pretentious. He was a solid, both-feet-on-the-ground individual. That's why, wherever John Madden travels, success seems to be there waiting for him to arrive. John Madden can go into any arena and win because he's a genuine, first-class act. The Raiders saw that quality in John when he coached and the rest of the world can see it now.

It took a special individual to handle the likes of Doctor Death, or some of the other characters who played for the Raiders. John was able to identify and work with each personality and for that, everyone respected him. Some of the players called him Coach, others referred to him as John. To some he was known as Big Red, and Doc called him "Pinky." Don't misunderstand, because it's like I said, we respected the man and most of us would have gone to hell and back for John. But he only asked us to always give it our best shot. And we did!

When analyzing yesterday's Raiders, I have to give John Madden much credit for the success. At the same time, I can't forget the man who put everything together, Al Davis.

Building a winning football team is actually a full time job. To create a winner, someone had to sit behind the scenes and work to bring all the fragile harmonies together. Winning football is the blending of coaches, athletes, and those intricate strategies that are best suited to your personnel.

Al Davis built the Raiders from the ground up. He drafted a group of great, but sometimes wacky athletes. He took on castoffs from other teams, those players who were said to be over the hill or troublemakers. The younger athletes came into the Raiders organization knowing they would get a fair chance. The rejects came to Oakland knowing it would be their last chance. Al made it work. He made us a family.

Actually, there were two sides to Al Davis: the businessman and the loyal friend. When it came to contract talks, Al Davis was a tough negotiator, but he was also fair. He paid top dollar and went first class. Putting the businessman aside, Al Davis was also a loyal friend. That's important to me because it pulls a team together.

I know there was a story circulating that Al Davis traded me to Houston because of the book and all the controversy over the accident with Darryl Stingley. The story wasn't true. Al traded me for several reasons, none of which had anything to do with controversy or an accident. Al Davis never ran from controversy.

First of all, Al wanted a running back with speed to break the long ones. Houston had that back, Kenny King. Secondly, Al knew that I had plans to play football for ten years. I had already played nine season and one more would make ten. The trade was good for both Houston and the Raiders. In fact, during Super Bowl XV, Kenny King took a little swing pass from quarterback Jim Plunkett, and 80 yards later ended up in the record book. The Raiders went on to win, 27-10.

To this very day, Al and I are friends. Periodically he invites me to Los Angeles for a game, and we still talk about old times. Even Al's wife, Carole, was part of the team and family image. Just like Al, Carole cared about the players. Sometimes it was simply a pat on the back, sometimes just a friendly word, but you knew she was always there and, what's more, she cared.

When I think about yesterday's Raiders, I can see that Al didn't build a squeaky clean or textbook perfect team. I'm not saying that Al hired crooks or criminals, but I am saying that football isn't a squeaky clean sport. Football is a brutal business, blood and guts, dirt and grime, kick ass or get your ass kicked. Sorry, but there isn't a pretty way to win a football game; and Al's little saying, "Just win, baby, win," simply meant, go out and kick ass! Win or lose, we always did kick ass.

I think the Raiders of yesterday played a more aggressive game. Offensively and defensively we simply went out and attacked. It wasn't an issue of winning or losing. It was a matter of physically beating up your opponents. If you beat on the opposition hard enough and long enough, the scoreboard usually has a way of totaling up the pain and punishment in your favor.

Lately, the Raiders are playing a different game. Offensively, they're trying to be deceptively clever, maybe even sneaky. It's as though they're walking on thin ice, afraid of falling into the water. They have to stop worrying about screwing up and start beating up the opposition.

Defensively, some of the Raiders are tentative. I think it comes down to coaching philosophies. The Raiders seem to be attempting to use a textbook perfect scheme, a sit-back, prevent type of defense instead of trying to kick some ass. I think they have to stop trying to look pretty and get back to a more physical game. They need to take chances, set up the opposition to where the defenders can get a few of those "outside-inside" collisions. Ask Riley Odoms if it works.

Also, I think a little knockout and limp-off competition is good for a team. If the defense is going after the opposition and really hitting, the scoreboard will take care of itself. Sure, an aggressive defense will get burned once in a while; but when a team develops a nasty reputation, the opposition will have a tendency to slow down.

It takes a little work to establish that type of reputation. You know what I mean: to be hated. But in the long run it's worth it. When I played for the Raiders, I loved to be hated. To be hated meant we were winning. But don't worry because the real truth is that not everyone hates a winner. Whenever we went traveling into the enemies' camp, we found out that, if their men hated us, their women loved us. I loved to be hated, especially in Pittsburgh.

I know that Al Davis and his Raiders will be back in the winner's circle again. The truth is that winners are winners and losers are losers. Al Davis knows how to win and, believe me, he's going to win again.

Al Davis has always been a winner but he never received the credit he truly deserved. The problem is that some people consider him a maverick, a renegade who does things the way he wants. Perhaps that's true but only because Al Davis isn't going to follow a blind leader stumbling through today when he's already seen tomorrow.

Al Davis could spot a weakness in his team. Then he knew how to correct the problem with the draft and by the trade. Al made tight ends running backs, running backs tight ends. He took rejects from other teams and turned them into All-Pros. Even troublemakers found a home with Al. Simply stated: Al Davis has always been an innovative leader and nothing less. He was good for the NFL and good for the athletes. Yet, he's always been criticized and has come under the gun for making the moves that brought results.

It's a travesty that Al Davis isn't in the Professional Football Hall of Fame. He should have been there years ago, but he's a victim of hypocritical sportswriters who selected the inductees into the Hall of Fame. Sometimes getting into the Hall of Fame becomes an issue of who you are and what you have accomplished. If they had judged Al on his accomplishments, he would have been inducted into the Hall of Fame a long time ago ... but they didn't, and he isn't.

I think Pete Rozelle was another reason Al never received due credit. I have to believe that Pete didn't like Al's aggressive, take charge style. And moving a football team from Oakland to Los Angeles after the commissioner said, "No," didn't help their relationship or Al's chance for a trip to Ohio in July.

Seriously, though, if a person were to check out the truth of their individual contributions to the NFL, it becomes difficult to imagine Pete Rozelle being in the Hall of Fame and Al Davis not. But hell, I can't imagine why anyone would have elected Pete to the Hall of Fame in the first place. I guess either way you look at it, it's an injustice. But when the NFL lets sportswriters select the inductees, those kinds of blunders are bound to happen.

The Professional Football Hall of Fame is said to be the highest honor an NFL player can receive. Maybe it is, but I don't know. Then again, I really don't care. Sorry, but that's how I feel. You see, there are many NFL greats who deserved to be enshrined in the Hall of Fame who aren't. That's wrong. And there are a number of NFL players who shouldn't be there, but they are. And that's wrong, too.

It's a bad system when mediocrity receives a place in the history of the NFL and some of the truly great men who contributed to the game never get their fair share of the glory. John Mackey put the T in tight ends, but he's not in the Hall of Fame. And Bob Brown, check out his credentials and then tell me why he's not in the Hall of Fame.

I could go on and give examples of NFL greats who have been overlooked and at the same time, I can give you a list of also-rans who are enshrined at Canton, Ohio. I find the whole system of induction into the Hall of Fame bewildering. Damn! Sportswriters blow assignments and interviews on a day-to-day basis. Most of them can't get the facts straight when they're at the stadium during the game or in the locker room afterwards. Yet, they are given the power to scrutinize NFL history and say who goes to Canton and who doesn't. It's a piss-poor system.

Don't get the idea this is my way of attracting attention in some vain hope of my gaining admittance into the Hall of Fame. Believe me, that's not the case. Now don't get me wrong, because I'm sure that if someone were to total up the highs and lows of my career, I'd probably have the credentials to one day make it into the Hall of

Fame. However, I'm positive that yours truly will never take that trip to Canton, Ohio. And it's really not difficult to figure out why. Hypocrites who write the stories about athletes are, for the most part, the same hypocrites who vote inductees into the Hall of Fame. I don't like hypocrites and they don't like me. So be it.

However, there's another reason keeping me out of the Hall of Fame, and that reason is me. Even if some bizarre twist of fate were to occur and I, under the present system of nomination, would gain admittance to the Hall of Fame, I'd decline. That's right, I'd say, "Thanks, but no!"

It comes back to the fact that too many NFL greats worthy of Hall of Fame honors have been overlooked. Also, it's like I said, in some instances mediocrity has been more than enough to immortally bronze a number of NFL players who never deserved the honor in the first place.

However, the worst thought of all would be the fact that if I did become part of the Hall of Fame, I would forever be enshrined in the same building with Pete Rozelle. Damn! I just couldn't imagine a bust of me spending eternity under the same roof with a bust of Pete Rozelle. So, as long as Pete Rozelle is in the Hall of Fame, I won't be there!

That might sound like a heavy statement. It is, but only because Pete Rozelle has been given a spot in NFL history that he doesn't deserve. Sure, Pete spent twenty-nine years as commissioner, but there is a difference between what he actually accomplished and the inevitable. The league was going to grow with or without a Pete Rozelle. Expansion was inevitable, but popularity of the sport and not Pete Rozelle assured that. Television contracts were inevitable, but again, popularity of the sport and not Pete Rozelle was responsible.

Recently, I saw a program on television that had me laughing. Pete was busy telling a group of reporters that his greatest accomplishment during his twenty-nine year tenure as commissioner of the NFL was the Super Bowl. What did he mean by that? Was he taking credit for the championship game or was he taking credit for dubbing a championship game the Super Bowl?

Perhaps Pete and his spellbound audience of sports journalists didn't remember, but there was a championship game long before the first Super Bowl. I know it might get confusing to some people, mainly Pete and a number of journalists; but, even during the early days of the sport, before the merger of the two leagues, at season's end there was a championship game. Seriously. If you don't believe me, check it out. It's all there in the Hall of Fame.

Okay, so someone changed the name of the big game and it's

called Super Bowl. Maybe a new title to an old theme was Pete's idea, but it doesn't mean he invented championship Sunday. And sure, the NFL moves the site of the Super Bowl around the country, usually to warm weather and sunshine locations, but we don't need Einstein to calculate the mathematics of that dollar and cent logic. Even Pete wouldn't want a Super Bowl in Green Bay when those tanning rays are shining on other stadiums.

Seriously, does anyone in his right mind honestly believe that Pete was directly responsible for the growth of the NFL, the merger, championship week and the big game called Super Bowl? Would anyone be so stupid as to give Pete credit for bringing television to the NFL, and one hundred and fifty million fans to the television on Super Bowl Sunday?

Pete Rozelle could have been shipwrecked on a deserted island for the last twenty-nine years and the NFL wouldn't have missed a beat, a step or a dollar. Who knows? Perhaps without Pete, the NFL could have ended up with thirty teams, five billion dollars in growth, no games when a nation mourned the death of President John Kennedy, no players' strikes, no pending litigation, no twenty million dollars antitrust settlement, better relationships between owners and players, less of a drug problem, etc., etc. ...

Think about it because the truth isn't that difficult to see. Open your eyes and check the record, because it's all there. The growth and popularity of pro football, college football, and even high school football had nothing to do with Pete Rozelle. It was inevitable. It was going to happen and, in spite of Pete Rozelle, it did happen.

The entire notion of Pete Rozelle actually coming to the rescue of the NFL is ridiculous. The inevitable and progress moved the NFL into another dimension. It happened with baseball, basketball, hockey, golf, even boxing, and it's not hard to understand why. Technology has reduced the size of our world. That same technology has given modern man an abundance of time to enjoy and experience other adventures of life. Football just happened to be there when modern man came looking for something to do on a lazy fall afternoon. To hear some people talk, a person would start to believe that Pete invented football, the lazy fall afternoon and the television audience.

I heard it said that Pete was the greatest commissioner in the history of sporting franchises. I laughed and laughed and laughed some more. My goodness! Saying something like that was bad enough, but did anyone really believe it? I hope not!

I also heard someone say that two commissioners would be needed to replace one Pete Rozelle. I'm inclined to agree with that last statement, but only in part. To efficiently run the NFL, it's probably going to take two full-time, responsible individuals with leadership qualities. However, replacing Pete is only a matter of hiring Jethro or Colonel Klink. Either one would be more than an adequate replacement for Pete.

Howard Cosell was asked the question about Pete's reign as commissioner of the NFL. Was it a good job, bad job, or what? Howard pulled no punches. He rarely does. His answer was what I expected to hear. Howard felt that Pete did a "50-50 job." Where I went to school, fifty percent was always a failing grade.

Pete Rozelle spent twenty-nine years stumbling around the National Football League ducking the real issues and taking credit for the inevitable. It's not a bad way to go if you can pull it off. Evidently he did.

Pete Rozelle left the NFL with a number of problems clouding the horizon. With Pete fading off into retirement, I'd like to believe the NFL can effect a cure for some of the cancers growing within the ranks.

First of all, professional football is made up of two elements: owners and players. One can't survive without the other. Maybe everyone will soon understand that simple fact.

The 1987 strike was bad for owners and players alike. I know the owners have all the money and power and those are pretty big guns in any battle. During the strike, the owners went ahead and played a few games without first-line athletes. I don't know if it really proved anything or not. Personally I felt the owners lost a little, but then again, so did the real NFL players.

If the commissioner was on the job during the 1982 strike or on the job during the other strikes, perhaps he could have taken steps to resolve the differences between players and owners. But during the heated strike of 1982, when leadership was so desperately needed, Pete was out to lunch. It was a long lunch and nothing was resolved. Maybe the courts will straighten everything out and both parties will be happy with the end results. I hope so because there are good people on both sides of the issue.

Pete has made a career of being out to lunch whenever serious problems hit the NFL. There were other strikes during Pete's administration and, like I said, he did nothing. For the longest time, Pete handled the NFL drug problem exactly the same way: he did nothing. This time he had a legitimate excuse. With drugs running rampant through our society, Pete didn't think they were much of a problem within the NFL.

Concerning the drug situation in the NFL, there was a lot of talk about not doing drugs; but for the longest time no one did anything in the way of establishing drug prevention programs or rules governing offenders.

In recent years, the NFL has started taking the drug problem seriously. They've made some changes and are working in the right direction. Last year nearly two dozen players tested positive to drugs and were suspended.

In 1989, the owners finally addressed the steroid issue. First time offenders caught with steroids in their systems will get a thirty-day suspension. Second time offenders will get the boot for the entire season. Maybe some people will get the message, perhaps not.

I don't want to make a lot to do about the drug problem in the NFL even though it's very serious. At the same time, I don't want to get into naming names or telling locker room stories about drugs. The problem is there. It's major and the NFL is finally aware of it. The tragedy is that something wasn't done sooner.

Drugs were a part of the NFL when I showed up on the scene in 1971. In fact, when I developed a painful hip-pointer, a teammate gave me a cure-all: a couple of black beauties. I took the pills and felt pretty good. At least I thought I did.

Buzzed up and running around the field jumping on piles of bodies, I thought I played a helluva game. Afterwards, I didn't sleep for two days, lost my appetite, and got sick. When I saw the game films I realized how stupid drugs were.

That was the first and last time I ever popped a pill. It made such a lasting impression on me that I started working with young people, teaching them how to say "NO" to drugs. Sometimes it is hard for young people to say no. They're confronted with peer pressure and, compounding the problem, they read about their heroes doing the same things we say are bad. Young people are smart and we, as adults, can't tell them one thing and do something contrary.

I'm going to mention one NFL name involved with drugs, and this isn't to put the man down. I'm talking about Lawrence Taylor, linebacker, New York Giants.

I saw a group of young people on television being interviewed outside of the New York Giants' stadium after Lawrence had been suspended from play for thirty days because a controlled substance was found in his system. It was the second time Lawrence had this problem, but after his first bout with rehabilitation he went out and told young people to say no. I admired Lawrence for working with the kids, but now he was down again.

During the interview a teenage boy said, "I believed Lawrence … trusted him when he said don't do drugs, but now this. It's disappointing, man, disappointing. I thought Lawrence knew better. I thought he was strong but he turned out to be weak."

The young man's statement was an honest reaction to a disappointment. Lawrence was his hero and, because of that, it hurt all the more. I could understand that, but Lawrence Taylor isn't weak. On the football field, Lawrence is one bad dude. But drugs are something else. Once you start, it's difficult to stop.

If Lawrence Taylor came to a party in a surly mood and was looking for a fight, no one in his right mind would go outside with him. Lawrence Taylor is an imposing physical force. Maybe Rambo can whip him in the movies; but on the football field and in real life, Lawrence is as tough as they come. But Lawrence tangled with drugs, two times that the world knows about, and got his ass kicked all over the place. So if you're thinking about doing drugs, don't. That way you won't have to worry about getting your ass kicked.

Steroids! That is a real tough issue because there is no doubt about it: steroids work. You get cheaters who use steroids, legit players who don't and, it's true, the bad guys get to the finish line first.

Lately I've had a number of conversations with young people about steroids. It's estimated that 500,000 teenagers are using steroids. That's probably a conservative number.

It's frightening because I honestly can't tell a young person that steroids don't work. They do. There's no argument, steroids work one hundred percent. Steroids will make a young body bigger, stronger and faster. But remember, steroids also prevent middle age. It's called premature death, and death is part of the complete steroid picture.

Unfortunately, dead people don't have much fun. Dead people don't run fast, jump high, lift heavy weights, breathe air or see the future. Dead people just lay there. There's no argument, steroids work, one hundred percent.

When tomorrow gets here, remember, I told you so! Enough said.

9

Move Over
Spuds MacKenzie,
Here Come the Dawgs

Spuds MacKenzie is one cool dude. Every time I turn around I see that Spuds is into something else. I've seen Spuds run his paws over the ivory keyboard of a piano and pound out a mean tune. He plays the guitar, moon-walks, and is an Olympic star. The stories they tell about the back seat of Spuds' limo and those beautiful women, damn, what a lucky dog.

Spuds receives his fair share of publicity and deserves most of it. But I have a real problem with Spuds still claiming the title of "Number One Party Animal." I admit that Spuds, for the longest time, was number one, but he never had any competition. Lassie was a homebody. Rin Tin Tin was always running around in the wilderness chasing crooks and getting the fleas. Cujo was a slobbering psycho. Who's left? Alex is an alcoholic, Benji's a wimp and Pluto's a cartoon. So it's like I said, Spuds never had any real competition. But then Hanford Dixon, a defensive back with the Cleveland Browns, opened the Dog Pound at Municipal Stadium. Forget it, Spuds. The Dawgs of Cleveland are number one and you're a distant second.

They say that seeing is believing. The first time I saw the Dawgs, I shook my head and whispered to myself, "Unbelievable, simply unbelievable."

The Dawgs of Cleveland are football fans, the human kind, I think. At least they stand upright and have hands instead of paws … well, some of them do. Actually you have to see the Dawgs because the English language doesn't have the words to describe them. They are different.

During football season the Dawgs of Cleveland gather in the east end zone and bark and growl and howl at the opposition. I repeat, the whole scene is beyond description. A person has to watch a

Cleveland Browns game to understand what I'm talking about, and even then it is baffling. Mind you, I'm not criticizing. In fact, the Dawgs, in my estimation, are probably the most entertaining sports fans in the world. I like 'em. I really like 'em.

Some of these characters wear dog masks and hard hats, others paint themselves like dogs, and still others don costumes of were-wolves. The Dawgs bring a variety of bones to the stadium: big bones, small bones, soup bones and even dog biscuits. Some of the bones are used as jewelry while other bones and the biscuits are thrown at the visiting team or officials. Some are even for consumption. Honest, I've seen several of the Dawgs chewing on big soup bones. Strangest of all, I even saw one of the Dawgs eating from a can of dog food.

The whole thing started a few years back when defensive back Hanford Dixon mentioned something about the Browns' defense getting nasty and playing like a pack of wild dogs, or maybe it was junk yard dawgs. A week or so later a couple of dudes showed up at the stadium dressed like dogs and you know how that goes, doggie see doggie do. With Hanford visiting the pound on game days, his pets really responded.

Nowadays the Dawgs are an epidemic. It's contagious. Officially the Dog Pound began in the east end zone, but lately everyone in the whole stadium seems to have come down with it. One of the innovative Dawgs must be in business or something because I see Dawg T-shirts, Dawg bones, Dawg hats … it's really catching on. Hey, don't stop, because it's the best show in town. The Dawgs are hilarious and they deserve more camera time.

When the Browns are on defense the Dawgs really get into the game, especially when it's a goal line stand at the east end zone. They go wild! The Dawgs start barking and howling, going completely berserk. It's so loud the opponents can't think, much less hear the quarter-back's signals. When the opposition does score, I can assure you, no one in his right mind does any kind of victory dance in that end zone.

In 1988 the Colts came to Cleveland for a Monday night game. Clarence Verdin, the Colts' punt return man, took one back 73 yards. It was a great run-back and he got a little excited. Without thinking, Clarence started a victory dance in the east end zone. Man, that was dumb! You don't go into the Dog Pound and taunt the Dawgs. Any fool knows that. When Clarence started dancing, about five hundred pounds of dog biscuits and bones flew out of the stands in his direction. If a person thought the punt return was something, they should have seen Clarence running from the Dog Pound, ducking biscuits and bones.

Later in the season, Houston and Cleveland had a big game at the stadium. The Oilers were trying to score at the east end zone and the Dawgs, as usual, were going bonkers. The noise was incredible. No one could hear, but Houston ran a play and then scored.

One official signaled touchdown and was promptly pelted with a couple of dog biscuits. But wait! Among the bones and biscuits, on the green turf of the stadium, was a yellow penalty flag. The officials began sorting everything out while the barking continued.

The television boys doing the game were a little confused about the penalty. Was the penalty on the offense? The defense? Was it a major penalty? Did the touchdown stand? Was instant replay needed for this one? There was quite a delay. Something was wrong, but what?

It was great television work. The home audience could read the official's lips as he asked the obvious question, "Well then, who the hell threw the flag?"

"Not me," the line judge answered. "Not me," the back judged replied. "Not me!" "Not me!" And, "not me."

Hell, someone had to throw the flag. Whodunit?

Bark, bark, bow-wow! This had to be the first time in the history of the NFL that a Dawg flagged the opposition. Things really got nasty when the official went over and picked up the flag and waved off the penalty.

The Dawgs help to support my theory about the water and the air in that part of the country. I'm serious, a person drinks the water and breathes the air and there's no telling what can happen. The fans go to extremes and it's not only Cleveland. During my career I've played in all the NFL cities, but there's nothing quite like the Great Lakes fans even though Lake Erie seems to get most of the exposure.

In 1981, the Raiders had to go through Cleveland en route to the Super Bowl. A football game in Cleveland during the regular season is tough, but in the dead of winter, impossible. It gets cold in Cleveland during the winter. Damn cold! The Siberian Express begins on the frozen tundra of Russia, whips down through Alaska, accelerates over Canada, picks up more speed while crossing the Great Lakes and slams into Cleveland's Municipal Stadium like an avalanche of rock-hard, bone-chilling ice. In 1981 it was a cold December day, even for Cleveland. In fact it was one of the coldest December games on record and the Raiders were in town for a football game.

I hated playing cold weather games, but today was different. For the first in many years I didn't mind the thought of a frozen stadium. I didn't mind because I was home in Oakland sitting in front of my television. Remember? In 1981 I played for Houston, but my heart was still with the Raiders.

It was kind of a strange feeling. There I was in Oakland sipping on a glass of iced tea as the television camera was panning the frozen stands of Municipal Stadium in Cleveland, Ohio. They sure love their football in Cleveland and a packed house of faithful Browns supporters was testimony to that. Thank God they were bundled up for the game because the wind chill factor had already reached a dangerous and deadly thirty below zero. Even with parkas, heavy boots, fur-lined hats and gloves, it was going to be a real sacrifice for these Browns loyalists. Once again, I thought, thank God they're all bundled up.

Suddenly, while panning the frozen arena, the camera stopped on three dudes wildly waving their hands and arms, cheering for all they were worth. They were obviously Cleveland fans because they wore brown and orange stocking caps. However, the only other article of clothing I could see were faded blue jeans. I mean to say these looney-tunes were wearing stocking caps and blue jeans, but no shirts or jackets.

Normally I don't talk to the television set, but this scene warranted a conversation. "Damn, fellas, it's thirty below zero! Where the hell are your shirts, your jackets, your gloves and your brains?" They never answered my question, but they hung in there for the entire game. Every so often the camera would zoom to the stands for a shot of stadium stupidity. But it happens that way in Cleveland and in other Great Lake stadiums.

In the early 1970s, *Monday Night Football* went to Buffalo. The game was going along quite nicely when all of a sudden the camera zoomed to something high above the stadium. Dangling from a wire strung across the stadium was a Great Lakes football fan.

The wire, in most stadiums around the league, was used to hold up the netting behind the goal posts. In Buffalo that same wire took on new meaning. With just a little imagination and a set of balls so large that a person would have to carry them around in a wheelbarrow, a skinny wire opened up an entire frontier of adventure for a football fan. I mean this dude, supported by only a thin wire, moved, hand over hand, as he dangled high above the stadium floor. If he lost his grip, it was a long way down. You're talking about the possibility of becoming an instant, prime-time television smash hit.

I'm telling you, it's in the water. It gives some people a bad case of the extremes. Just like Woody Hayes. Woody used to do a lot of recruiting in that area and he was a man of extremes. I don't think Woody ever got the water completely out of his system.

My junior year at Ohio State, for example, Woody took us up to Michigan for the big game. We were undefeated, rated the number-one team in the country and expected to whip up on Michigan. We didn't!

Woody wasn't too happy with everything, but he controlled himself. For Woody to control his temper under these circumstances was a major effort. When the final gun went off, Michigan had 24 points and we only had 12.

It was a bad day for Woody and the Buckeyes. For many of us, it was the first time we had lost a college game. And Woody had just lost his chance for the possibility of back-to-back national championships. The old man was fuming.

After the game both teams started toward the tunnel at the far end of the stadium. Some of the Buckeyes were shaking Wolverine hands while wishing them well in the Rose Bowl. I guess the whole scene was more than Woody could stand. He stepped up and shouted, "Don't shake their hands! Let's kick their ass!" Of course, Woody didn't kick anyone's ass, at least not that time, but it did take two or three big linemen to drag him into our locker room.

After my college days, I stayed in touch with Woody. I did him a couple of favors and he did me a few. I was working in a drug prevention program with some other NFL players and we wanted Woody to come out to the Bay area and be our guest speaker at a fund raiser. Woody accepted the invitation, came out and did a helluva job for us.

Afterwards, Woody, Tim Anderson, an Ohio State teammate of mine, Delvin Williams, a running back with the 49ers and later Miami, and I went out for a drink. It was a good evening, good people, good conversation, but then it happened. Several tables away from us four dudes were having a few drinks and getting fairly loud. I could tell Woody didn't like it, but he was cool. Later on, after a few more drinks, the dudes got louder and started cussing. Now that was bad.

Several ladies were sitting at a table opposite ours. If we could hear the cussing, the ladies could hear those foul words, too. Suddenly, Woody got up and stomped over to the dudes' table. Woody was cool as he leaned on their table and explained, "You fellas are disturbing everyone in here with your foul mouths. Now you can shut up and start acting like gentlemen or you can get up and leave. If you don't like either of those choices then we can go outside and I'll kick your butts all over San Francisco."

Delvin Williams was concerned. He asked, "Shouldn't we go over and back up Woody?" It was a good question, but only if you didn't know Woody.

The dudes were younger, bigger and no doubt stronger than Woody. However, Tim and I spent four years of our lives with Woody, and during that time we saw the old man get into a few scuffles. Tim looked at me and I looked at him. Finally Tim answered, "Naw, there's only four of them. If the old man wanted help, he would have asked."

Tim was right. If Woody had been alone that night he would have gone over to their table and said exactly the same thing. And, if push came to shove, Woody would have taken them outside and I wouldn't bet against the old man. The four dudes never said a word. They paid their check and quietly left.

Woody Hayes knew the difference between right and wrong, but he was an impulsive character capable of extremes. Most football fans only remember Woody for those time when he jumped off the deep end. Sometimes Woody was downright nasty, but those were isolated incidents. For every photographer Woody slugged he probably worked at a thousand charitable functions. It's like I once said, Woody was a prick and a prince.

When he came west to help with our drug program for young people, Woody didn't charge a cent. We had a suite reserved for him at an expensive hotel, but he insisted on a small room at a less expensive place. We wanted him to travel first-class. We'd pay. He came by coach. We gave him a limo; he took a cab.

Woody was no different than most of the people back in the Cleveland-Pittsburgh area of the country, good people who some-times go to extremes. Sure, I've had some fun with stories about the many characters I've met in and around Cleveland and Pittsburgh. To be honest though, I really like the people back there. I have a lot of friends in that area and it used to be that I had a lot of fans too, even in Pittsburgh. You play in their cities against their athletes and you get to know the people.

I know that every NFL city has its characters, but not like that area of the country. Fans come to the stadium to enjoy the games, to let off steam, to have some fun. Some places go to extremes whereas other places don't. In Washington, the offensive line is known as the Hogs. So, some of the Redskin fans dress up like pigs, polite little pigs. The Giants have a group of screaming, cheering Lawrence Taylor fans. They wear his jersey, number 56, to all the games, but that's it. Florida, they sort of sit back and suck up the sun. California is even more laid back. However, there's nothing laid back about the fans in Cleveland, Pittsburgh and a few other of those NFL cities. Good people, but damn, they sure can go to extremes.

We played a game in Pittsburgh after the "criminal element" incident. During the game there was a group of fans wearing "criminal element" T-shirts and really getting on George and me. They were wild, brutal, belligerent! We beat up the Steelers to a chorus of boos. After the game a group of these Pittsburgh fans jumped from the stands down onto the field. It looked like trouble. But guess what? They wanted our autographs. We signed the autographs and then George asked one of the dudes where he could get a "criminal element" T-shirt. I guess they were selling the T-shirts all over the city, but the fan took the shirt off his back and gave it to George.

That's what I mean about the people back there. During the heat of battle they'll try to rip the shirt off your back. When it's over, most of those same people will give you the shirt right off their back. They're loyal fans, yes, but they're also damn good people.

Eight or nine years ago, Bill Kushner called and asked if I would come to Youngstown, Ohio to help out with a fund raiser for Danny Thomas' Saint Jude Children's Research Hospital. Of course I would. It turned out to be a real experience.

The headquarters for Saint Jude Children's Research Hospital is actually in Memphis, Tennessee. But in 1950 Mrs. Elizabeth Beshara brought a chapter of Saint Jude's to Youngstown, Ohio. The local patients are still diagnosed in Memphis, but then return home to the Youngstown area for treatment.

I expected this particular fund raiser to have a local flavor to it. You know what I mean ... a few hometown heroes from Youngstown supporting Saint Jude's. I've been to this type of function before. They have a little radio time going for them and, if they're lucky, they get mentioned on television, but nothing in the way of a major event.

I knew that Youngstown had been hit by the closing of many steel mills and factories. Unemployment was up and the people of that area were suffering from the effects of hard times. When people don't have money to pay for everyday necessities, you can't expect much in the way of a big time charity event.

Bill met me at the airport and nothing had changed. I still had to carry my own bags, but this time I only brought two. While driving to his home, Bill mentioned that a "few" of the Cleveland Browns and a "couple" of the Pittsburgh Steelers were coming in to help promote the affair. Then he mentioned that Eddie DeBartolo, Jr., had made arrangements for a "49er or two," and most of the daytime activity was going to be staged at Southern Park Mall. The mall was owned by the DeBartolo family. It was beginning to sound like something more than a one-day fund raiser for Danny's kids. It was!

The affair lasted for days, maybe five days, I don't remember. The "few" Browns that Bill mentioned turned out to be about thirty players. The "couple" of Steelers were a couple of dozen. O.J. Simpson came in as did the man himself, Danny Thomas. They had radio going for them, live television, and fund-raising events from sunup to sundown. I've never seen anything quite like it. The town of Youngstown and the surrounding area really responded. I met more caring people during that week of my life than ever before. I'm sure it had a lot to do with the cause, Danny Thomas' Saint Jude Children's Research Hospital, but at the same time, I think it had a lot to do with good people doing good things for little children.

Bill and I spent some quality time with Danny. He told us the history of Saint Jude's, how and why he came to start it and what it represents. I couldn't do justice to Danny's story and I wouldn't want to try. Only Danny Thomas can adequately explain the beauty of a young man's prayer and solemn promise to a Saint of hopeless causes. The long and short of the story was that Danny Thomas received his miracle, and because of that and a promise he fulfilled, many innocent children, afflicted with once hopeless forms of cancer, now receive their share of miracles. Saint Jude's is all about good people doing good things for little kids.

Youngstown went all out for Saint Jude's and I couldn't have been happier about my being able to participate in this work. Looking back, it turned out to be a great week. I guess what really impressed me was the people of Youngstown and those surrounding areas, poor people and rich people alike. They pulled together and because of that, some young children were given the chance to see tomorrow.

On Saturday night, Bill, his wife, Anna, and I went to a party at Eddie DeBartolo, Jr.'s, home. Eddie invited several hundred of his friends and really put on a spectacular affair. Eddie paid for everything, but he expected one thing of his guests: their check made out to Saint Jude's. The people really responded, but it's like I said, good people and a good cause.

Sunday night everything came to a close. Mrs. Beshara's son, Jimmy, organized a big banquet. They sold hundreds and hundreds of tickets. It was a sellout. People came from all over. They came from Pittsburgh, Cleveland, Canton, Akron, and all the little towns in between. Toward the end of the affair, the master of ceremonies, Attorney Ron Galip, introduced a singer by the name of Panfilo. Why Panfilo never made it to the big leagues I'll never know, but on that night, he hit the highest note of all when he sang *Danny Boy*. I know what they meant when they said, "He brought the house down."

Whenever I hear about Cleveland or Pittsburgh, naturally, I think about football and those fans who go to the outer limits. No one will ever accuse the Dawgs or Terrible Towel Pittsburgh fans of not enjoying themselves at the stadium. They really do and during the football season they get their fair share of exposure.

I watch a football game coming from Cleveland or Pittsburgh and I have to laugh. Some funny things go on in those stands. Then, and it never fails, I begin to reminisce. I start thinking back about good times and good people.

I don't get back to Ohio or Pennsylvania very much anymore, but I think about the DeBartolos, the Besharas, and the other wonderful people who live and work in that area. I also think about Danny Thomas and Saint Jude Children's Research Hospital.

Danny is building a three hundred million dollar addition to the clinic in Memphis. And thanks to some wonderful people in the Middle East, he even has a hospital in Saudi Arabia. Also, the doctors at Saint Jude's are working in AIDS research and treatment for little, innocent kids who have been struck down by the disease. In Youngstown, Saint Jude Children's Research Hospital, at the present time, is giving hope to forty-two kids.

Woody Hayes, the Pittsburgh Steelers, Cleveland Browns, Terrible Towels, Dawgs, and Criminal Element T-shirts! Every so often I think back and remember those people, those places and things, I shall never forget.

Jack Tatum looking for trouble.

10

Fried Ice Cream

It was an ugly March day when George Atkinson called for a game of golf. I was a little reluctant to go because it looked like rain, but George insisted he could see the sun breaking through the clouds. George only lives about twenty minutes from me, so I didn't put much credence into what he said. If it looked like rain at my place, it wasn't any different where he lived. Even if it was raining, George would sill think he saw sun breaking through the clouds. Simply stated, George is an optimistic dude with an unbelievable passion for the game of golf.

I finally agreed to meet George at the golf course, but it had nothing to do with his powers of persuasion. I have a passion for the game of golf myself and I happen to believe it never rains on a golf course.

While playing the front nine, George ran into some hard times. Generally speaking, George and I are evenly matched, but today everything was going my way. At the turn he was already five down, but it didn't have anything to do with great shot-making on my part. I was lucky and George wasn't. For example, while playing one hole, my ball hit the cart path, bounced three times and landed on the green were I proceeded to make a fifty-foot putt for birdie. George actually hit a great shot, but a sprinkler head and a bad bounce sent his ball so deep into the woods that a hound dog couldn't have found it.

At the turn, George bought a few beers and I quickly pointed our golf cart in the direction of the tenth tee. When things are going well, I'm not going to waste time hanging around the clubhouse listening to George complain about bad luck and a little rain. Today, believe it or not, it was actually raining on the golf course. For some reason, I didn't mind.

I started the back nine with a good bounce par while George had a terrible bounce bogey. He was six down with eight holes to go and for all intent and purpose this match was history. On the way to the eleventh tee George drank a beer, cussed, and mumbled something about Pete Rozelle. At the time, Pete was still commissioner of the

NFL. It might be difficult to believe, but George never gave Pete very high marks.

If you're reading this book to any young children you had better skip the next few pages or ask them to leave the room. When George gets frustrated or upset, he has a tendency to bring up Pete Rozelle. After that he's liable to say anything and his dialogue usually contains some rather explicit football language. I figured George was about one bad shot away from starting a heavy conversation about Pete Rozelle's NFL.

I sliced a one iron into the right rough. George snap-hooked his drive left. George wasn't happy about the shot and en route to his ball I heard him mumble Pete Rozelle's name again. Arriving at his ball, George grumbled, "How far to the green?"

"Hit the four iron," I answered.

He dubbed the shot, cursed, looked directly at me and said, "Problems of the league are continually compounding, serious drug problems, litigation, still no contract with the players, and what the fuck does Pete do? He sits around his fancy New York office with one finger up his nose and a thumb up his ass. If anyone believes that Pete is doing a good job as commissioner of the NFL, then they'll go for fried ice cream."

Whenever George is trying to emphasize a point he'll mention fried ice cream. It's the equivalent of that old saying about selling a stupid person the Brooklyn Bridge. George wasn't saying that Pete was stupid. He simply meant that a person would have to be an idiot to believe that Pete Rozelle was doing a good job for the NFL. And please don't misunderstand my rather lengthy explanation of everything because I'm certainly not inferring that all of my reading audience are so stupid they would miss George's point. It's just that somewhere along the line a certain retired commissioner of the NFL is going to get wind of this book and I want to make sure he doesn't overlook the impact of George's statement or the point I'm making. George is saying that a certain NFL executive has done a terrible job, and I believe that same person would, if given the opportunity, purchase that bridge in Brooklyn.

I drove George to his ball and said, "Seven iron, George, easy seven iron. Smooth it out."

George steadied himself and hit a pretty good shot. The ball was dead on line, but plugged just short of the green. "I knew I should have hit a damn six iron!"

We cut across the fairway to my ball as George continued. "Hell, even the president of the United States can only serve two terms. After eight years Ron's out and George is in. Eight years! Ever think about that, Tate?"

George wasn't expecting an answer so I drove on while he continued. "They just don't want any one man to become too powerful. Power corrupts a person. He loses touch with reality and fails to understand what's important."

"George," I said, while looking up at him. "I'm trying to hit my shot."

George suddenly realized I was standing over my ball ready to hit. "Sorry 'bout that, Tate. I just get so pissed off when I start thinking about that motherfucker in New York."

I stroked a smooth eight iron, but even before my ball landed in the trap to the right of the green, George was already back to explaining the pitfalls of power. "Hell, he was corrupted before he became commissioner, and, after twenty-nine years, he's ten times as bad."

What George was referring to was an incident Pete was involved in when he worked for the Los Angeles Rams. Pete went out into the college ranks and signed a young running back, Billy Cannon. Under normal conditions that's not illegal, but the signing took place before the draft and that wasn't exactly kosher even by NFL standards.

We proceeded toward the green as George continued, "Do you remember what that motherfucker said at our hearing in New York? Remember when I got into that argument with him about his crooked system of justice and how he was always shittin' on the players?"

"Yeah," I answered. "Pete said he was 'paid to be neutral.'"

George was getting into it as he shouted, "Who pays him, Tate? That motherfucker is paid to be neutral by the owners. The owners pay him pretty close to a million dollars a year and he expects us to believe that he can be neutral. Paid to be neutral. I've heard it all. What's more, Pete's a racist, too."

George hit a good chip shot and had about a four-foot putt left. I blasted out of the sand, two-putted for bogey and waited for George to finish. George pulled his putt and ended up with a double bogey. He was now seven down with seven to go. For some reason, winning or losing didn't seem to matter to George anymore, but Pete Rozelle did.

Walking off the green toward the golf cart George said, "He's got to be one of the stupidest motherfuckers I've ever met. If you put Pete's brain in a bird's head, it would fly backwards. Poor bird would migrate north instead of south in the dead of winter."

George tied me on the next hole but the match was over. When I reminded him that he had lost, George turned to me and asked, "Did that motherfucker ever send your five hundred dollars for expenses? He promised to pay our expenses. I never got mine."

I've already mentioned it, but in 1976, when George and I went to New York to appeal our fines, Pete said that the NFL would pay our expenses. I don't want to call Pete a liar, but we never did receive expense money.

Our round of golf continued and George brought up a few more Pete Rozelle memories. For a while, it got to be kind of funny. We talked about Pete's blunders. There were many. We nearly fell out of the golf cart laughing about the whipping Al Davis had recently administered to Pete during the antitrust litigation.

Finally, George got around to Super Bowl XI when we beat the Vikings. That's when the conversation became serious. After the Super Bowl, Pete came into our locker room and presented the Lombardi Trophy to Al Davis. On the way out George got right up in Pete's face and said, "I know you didn't want to see us win. I'll be this kills you … coming in here and having to give us that trophy. Eat your heart out, motherfucker."

Under normal conditions George doesn't verbally assault civilians in our locker room. There have been a few times that we ousted a reporter or two, but those kinds of incidents happen throughout the league on a daily basis and most of the time the reporter deserves it. However, this time it wasn't a jerk reporter. George was coming down hard on the commissioner. George was so upset that he was right in Pete's suntanned face telling him like it was.

Pete stammered a little, then looked over at me and said, "You two guys are great athletes when you play by the rules."

If there ever was a straw that broke the camel's back, then that stupid statement was it. I did play by the rules! Pete Rozelle didn't! He never did, but yet, he was in the locker room on the biggest day of my athletic career, mouthing off about playing by the rules. I earned my reputation through aggressive, hard hitting, and not by breaking the rules. I was tired of those accusations and with that I jumped up and screamed at Pete, "Get your fuckin' ass out of here!"

I was loud and my reaction took Pete by surprise. Then George started. "Yeah, Pete," he was screaming too, "get your motherfuckin' ass outta here!"

Bernie Jackson, head of NFL security, stepped between Pete and us saying, "Hey fellas, settle down." Bernie was a brother, but we motherfucked him out of the locker room, too. George and I often have a good laugh about that incident, but when it happened back in 1977 it wasn't funny.

Surprisingly, we didn't get fined. Pete probably realized that if he did fine us, George and I would come to his office in New York and motherfuck him all over the place.

When Pete left the locker room George and I were the center of attention. We were shaking more hands than a politician. Not just players, but other people shook our hands and patted us on the back for a job well done.

I know that I've used rather explicit language in telling this story, but I wanted my reading audience to have the full impact of that particular day. I'm not saying that George and I never used profanity around the locker room, because we did. Everyone does. But for George and I to motherfuck a civilian out of our locker room, that individual would have to be a real asshole.

It started to rain harder. Since George had already lost, we decided to head for home. On the way back to the clubhouse, I mentioned that I was going to San Diego for a little work on the new book with Bill Kushner. I invited George to come. He could tell a few of his Pete Rozelle stories and play some golf.

While we were flying to San Diego I told George a little about Bill and why I decided to write a second book. I had been thinking about doing another book for several years, but Bill's decision to participate was a spontaneous reaction followed by a little confusion. Whenever Bill gets involved in any project, one can expect impulsive reactions and a degree of disorder. That's why, when I deal with Bill, I forget about reason and logic. I just sort of go my own way and sooner or later we both seem to arrive at the same conclusion or point in time.

Actually, I could say we began the second book one night while I was watching the late, late movie. Michael Landon, Edward Woodward, Jergen Prochnow and Priscilla Presley were in the movie, but something wasn't right. The movie was filmed on location in Thailand and even with an all-star cast, for some reason, it was turning out to be a real bow-wow flick.

I was having another problem with this picture too. During several scenes I saw a dude in the background who looked like Bill. I hadn't talked with Bill for two or three years, but just seeing someone who looked like him brought back old memories ... the kind of memories you laugh about and then try to forget.

The television was still on, but I was dozing off. For some reason I couldn't get into the movie. Then, suddenly, I heard an old familiar voice. It sent chills up my spine. I quickly opened my eyes and there he was, stepping out of the shadows of an ancient temple while asking a good-looking Thai lady something about the Golden Triangle. It was Bill, playing the part of a spy. It was a serious part, but for some reason, I was laughing. Maybe it was that I knew him, or maybe it was his name in the picture, Clive. When the chick called him "Clive," I fell on the sofa and rolled around on the floor laughing.

Then suddenly, everything hit me! It used to be that I would mention Bill's name or simply think about him and he'd call or show up on my doorstep. It's not that Bill's a bad guy, but whenever I spent any time with him I always walked away with a massive headache. Once again, I'm talking about reason and logic. Whenever he's confronted with a problem, Bill usually arrives at the right answer, but it's how he gets there that would defy reason and logic.

Clive's big spy scene cut away to Michael Landon struggling against overwhelming odds. Michael was under water all duded-up in scuba gear as a boatload of Oriental soldiers were dropping hand grenades into the water. I glanced at the telephone half expecting it to ring, but Clive didn't call. With that, I turned off the TV and went to bed.

In the wee hours of the early morning the telephone started to ring. I rolled over in bed, gained a sense of composure, thought about the late show and reluctantly answered the phone with a hesitant, "Hello."

"Tate, where can I find Lyle Alzado?"

It was Clive! Honestly! It was six o'clock in the morning and I hadn't talked to him for several years. He never said good morning or asked how I was doing. He began the conversation with a question about Lyle Alzado.

It took a while, but I finally learned that Clive's daughter Theresa worked for an airline company. On a flight east she met Lyle Alzado and recognized him as an ex-Raider. Theresa mentioned her Uncle Jack, her dad Clive, and a certain book. Lyle and Uncle Jack always got along pretty well, he loved the book and thought that Clive was a great writer. In fact, Lyle told Theresa that if Clive ever wanted to write a book about his life and career, he was ready.

"*The Aftermath of Violence*, Tate. We'll call it *The Aftermath of Violence*. I'll make Lyle famous." Bill was using that same old line. He was saying famous, but did he mean infamous?

Bill wanted me to get in touch with Lyle and I honestly tried. I called the Raiders' office and left a message. After a couple of weeks nothing happened. Bill figured that he had a great title for a book and he didn't want to waste it. Bill dropped a few subtle hints about doing a book with someone other than Lyle. All he needed was an ex-NFL player, "a hitter," he said, "with a nasty reputation." I wondered who Bill had in mind for his ex-NFL player with a hitter's reputation. Well, since I was ready to do another book and evidently Bill was all primed up, we decided to go for it. However, I managed to convince Bill to save his other title for Lyle Alzado.

Bill wanted me to fly to San Diego so that we could get started. He said that we could do some work and play a little golf. Knowing

Bill, that meant a little work and a whole lot of golf.

I was going to be in the San Diego area anyway. I had some business in Los Angeles. After that, I was going to drive down the coast to Carlsbad and pick up my new set of golf clubs at the Taylor Made factory.

Bill started me golfing about twelve years ago. With retirement and a little extra time on my hands, I really got serious about the game. I became a student of golf. I studied everything from techniques to equipment, and equipment was my reason for going to the Taylor Made factory.

In 1986, while watching the Skins game, I saw Lee Trevino perform a little golf club magic. He eagled a par four with a little flip wedge and won over a hundred thousand dollars for the shot. The next year he came back with a firm six iron for a hole in one and $175,000 in prize money. Lee played Taylor Made equipment as did a number of PGA pros. There had to be a reason.

I called Tim Huet, Director of Program Promotions with Taylor. Tim's originally from Ohio and a Buckeye fan. One thing led to another and before long Tim connected me with John Steinbach, Director of Advertising and Public Relations. I called to order a set of golf clubs, but if I was reading between the lines, Taylor Made wanted me to be on their celebrity staff.

I finally made it to Carlsbad and spent a day with Bob Vokey and his assistant, Don Blue. Bob builds the custom clubs for all the PGA pros who play the Taylor Made equipment. Bob put the finishing touches on my equipment and after that, we sneaked out for a quick nine holes. The new equipment really boosted my confidence.

I spent the night with a couple of friends who lived near the beach in Lajolla. The next day, Bill and I were to meet at the golf course, San Luis Rey Downs. Needless to say, I was looking forward to having a match with Bill. After all, he started me golfing and I felt that I had come a long way since that first lesson.

For my first lesson, Bill took me to the golf course, handed me a club, a ball and tee, and then pointed toward the rising sun and said, "That's the first green. I'll give you two strokes on the par fives, a stroke on par fours. We play the threes even and the loser buys lunch." I never made the bet, but I bought lunch anyway. Bill figured I owed him a lunch for the golf lesson. Well, I told myself, there would be other days. Perhaps the other day had arrived.

Most of the time, Bill tries to stay one step ahead of the competition. That's because he's a bad loser. And for that matter, he's really not a very gracious winner. When he wins, he never lets you forget it. When he loses, he'll make up a thousand excuses or simply convince himself it never happened. If there wasn't a George Atkinson, then Bill would be the world's worst loser and the world's least gracious winner. With George around, Bill can only claim half of that title.

Arriving at San Luis Rey Downs, I discovered that Bill wasn't there yet, but I was about to learn this wasn't your average run-of-the-mill golf course. I saw at least a hundred people milling around the tenth tee. Then I heard someone mention "Gary McCord." Gary is a part-time tour professional and a full-time television golf analyst. I had to see what was going on.

It didn't take me long to understand why Bill played golf at San Luis Rey Downs. Bill, like most all of my friends, is a little different. Obviously "birds of a feather all flock together" and the nest was San Luis Rey Downs.

It was the strangest damn thing I had ever seen on a golf course. Gary McCord was standing on the tenth tee blindfolding a dude. I mean to say, Gary was doing one hell of a job with the blindfold. Gary had wrapped an Ace Band-Aid over the dude's eyes and was completing the job with some duct tape. He then took a burlap sack, placed it over the dude's head and faked a few punches to the face. The dude, he reminded me of the Elephant Man, never flinched. Gary seemed satisfied the dude couldn't see and turned to a lady and said, "Get ready to start the clock."

Curiosity got the best of me. I had to ask one of the spectators what was going on. It turned out that Gary and the Elephant Man had been sitting in the clubhouse drinking a few beers and debating golf — San Luis Rey Downs golf, that is. Now, remember, I said they had been drinking a few beers; nevertheless, the Elephant Man still felt that he could walk from the tenth tee to the tenth green and pull out the flag within thirty minutes. So, there it was. A few beers, a blindfold, turn the Elephant Man in a circle three times to confuse him a little and let the games begin.

The Elephant Man was pretty smart, though. He had taken off his shoes. I guess he figured that bare-footed he could sort of feel his way along the cart path and get started in the direction of the tenth green. I had a feeling that his journey would prove interesting. The cart path only went part way, and after that, if he strayed left or right, there was trouble. To the Elephant Man's left was a ditch and water hazard. To his right there was a lake. Three hundred and fifty yards ahead of him was the green.

After stumbling down a hill, tripping, nearly falling off a narrow bridge, the Elephant Man reached the fairway. He got his bearings, but his calculations were a little off. He headed directly for the lake. Once he stepped onto the slippery, sloping bank of the lake it was history.

He slid down the muddy slope and hit the water with a splash. Neck deep in the water, the Elephant Man sort of doggy paddled back to shore. The more difficult part was crawling up the muddy slope and getting his feet on dry land.

It took a while, but the Elephant Man finally crawled out of the lake, up the muddy slope and back on to the fairway. Outside of several more trips back into the lake, and bumping his head on the low-hanging branch of a tree, his journey to the tenth green was uneventful. But damn, what a mess!

To make a long story short, the Elephant Man walked back and forth across the green, until finally, he stumbled upon the pin. With just several minutes left on the clock, he pulled the pin for his well-deserved victory. The Elephant Man had won, and Gary McCord had lost. With that, everyone headed back to the clubhouse.

Several minutes later Bill showed up. We talked a little, but then it was down to real business, golf. I told Bill, "I get two strokes on the par fives, one on the par fours and we'll play the par threes even. Just like the first time only the loser buys dinner."

Bill made some snide remark about "once a hacker, always a hacker." I didn't know if that meant he had accepted the bet or not, but when I opened the trunk of my car and took out my brand new Taylor Made equipment, I could see the smug expression on his face melt away. He looked at the bag with my name on it, glanced at my new irons and woods and forced a weak smile.

"Oh, by the way," I said in a cocky tone. "I forgot to mention it, but I'm on Taylor Made's celebrity staff."

"Yeah, I see," he answered. "Just think, Tate. If it wasn't for me doing a fabulous job on the first book you'd be just another over-the-hill football player without celebrity status."

We went over to his car. He opened the trunk and took out his clubs. Damn! He had a Taylor bag with his name on it exactly like mine. And he had brand new Taylor irons and woods. Then, and with an arrogance that only Bill could display, he said, "I'm on Taylor's celebrity staff, too. I'm a movie star. Remember?"

Clive-the-Movie-Star's best golfing buddy is the production manager at Taylor, Ron Lavoie. Ron made the introductions for Bill at Taylor and Bob Vokey built him a custom set of clubs identical to mine.

I spent several enjoyable days golfing and even some time working on the book. A few days after I got home, I received a phone call from Bill. He began the conversation by saying, "Hey, dummy, did you forget something?" Bill then informed me that I had accidentally put my seven iron in his bag. With identical bags and clubs it wasn't a difficult thing to do. It seemed, however, that Bill wasn't going to send me the seven iron unless I agreed to play him even up the next time out. Well, I quickly informed him that when I received my seven iron, I'd send out his nine iron. Earlier in the day I went to the driving range and discovered two nine irons in my bag, but no seven iron. Guess who the dummy was that put his nine iron in my bag?

Our plane landed in San Diego just as I finished my golf story. If my last trip to San Diego was worth a humorous hour of conversation, then this trip could be worth a lifetime of laughs. First of all, a person has to understand that George and Bill had never met. Those two characters on the golf course or just sitting around in the same room discussing anything would really be something. George and Bill are not your average human beings. They are unique to say the least.

George is an instigator, but so is Bill. Bill gives everyone a nick-name, but so does George. George is a poor loser and not a very gracious winner, but that's exactly the way Bill is. What's more, they will argue with anyone about anything and most of the time win the argument even when they're wrong. And both George and Bill enjoy a good laugh just as long as it's at someone else's expense.

One time, George showed up at a party with a beautiful lady. He told me that his lady friend had a roommate, a "real foxy lady," who was in love with Jack Tatum. George wanted to know if he could give the lady my phone number. I figured there was no harm in that. I said yes.

The lady called and we talked. Something didn't sound right but I couldn't put my finger on it. At practice the next day I told George the lady called and she wanted to go out. I never had much luck with blind dates so I passed. That's when George really turned it on. George said, "Tate, seeing is believing, and you've got to see her. I'm serious, Tate. You thought my lady friend was something; well … her roommate is twice the lady." It sounded tempting, but once again I was reluctant.

I received several more telephone calls from the lady but something still didn't seem right. And every day at practice George would tell me she was really something to see. Finally curiosity got the best of me and I made the date.

I drove over to the lady's apartment and George's girlfriend answered the door. She was even more beautiful than I had remembered. If her roommate was, like George said, "twice the lady," then I could hardly wait.

All of a sudden the apartment started shaking. Then, I saw what George meant by "twice the lady." At first I thought a small crowd was coming down the stairs. Actually, the crowd was my date. I didn't have a scale handy, but I would venture a guess she was more than "twice the lady." Triple the lady would have been a more accurate assessment.

I went through the date but it wasn't a long drawn out affair. Practice! Yes, I had to get up early in the morning for practice. I explained to the lady that we would only go for a short drive — a real short drive. She didn't seem to mind.

The lady really liked to talk. Before long she was telling me the whole story, even the part about paying George Atkinson's Dating Service one hundred dollars for Jack Tatum's unlisted telephone number. Damn! George sold me out for a hundred bucks. A hundred bucks! That's all our friendship was worth. A hundred bucks!

Last year Dwight Hicks, a retired defensive back with the 49ers, wanted to write a book about his career. During a round of golf, we started talking about the publishing business. Dwight had several questions that only Bill could answer. Without thinking, I gave him Bill's telephone number. That was the last time Dwight ever talked to me.

I found out that Bill answered all of Dwight's questions, but then they started talking about golf. Dwight told Bill I had been beating him with regularity. He felt I was "lucky" but my old buddy Clive-the-Actor set him straight. Since Dwight was going to listen, then Clive was going to talk. My old buddy told Dwight that I cheated on the golf course. He told Dwight that I didn't count all of my strokes, that I've been caught teeing up the ball in the rough and the legitimate golfers ran me out of San Diego County for sandbagging. None of the accusations were true, but it's like I've already said, George and Bill enjoy a good laugh, just as long as it's at someone else's expense.

This trip to San Diego was going to be sweet revenge. I figured with a little prodding I could get things going between George and Bill. I'd encourage each of them to go after the other while I sat back and enjoyed the best of both worlds.

Bill and a friend of his, Al Ritchie, met George and me at the airport. Six months ago, Al was a pretty strait-laced businessman, but then he met Bill and all of that changed. Al is now a part-time businessman. The rest of his time is spent playing practical jokes on people or having Bill play practical jokes on him.

Receiving the usual airport treatment, I struggled with two suitcases and my golf clubs while Bill carried his car keys. Al was different, though. He carried George's clubs and that really proved to be something.

Al is kind of a hyper little guy. He only stands about 5 feet 6, but walks like a man ten feet tall. Al has a long, quick stride and a tendency always to want to be the leader even when he doesn't know where he's going.

One time, Bill, Al and I had a meeting in downtown San Diego.

Bill was the only one who knew where we were going, but Al managed to lead the charge. Bill parked the car and pretended to move toward an adjacent building. Al quickly rushed ahead of us, ran up the stairs and was twirling his way through the revolving doors when Bill looked at me with a wry grin and said, "That ain't our building, Tate." He then pointed over his shoulder and said, "That's where we're going."

I've seen that happen more than once to Al. Bill will feint a move in one direction and Al will charge only to discover that Bill is going the other way. But today was different because Al knew where Bill had parked. It wasn't long before Al was seventy yards ahead of everyone. Al sort of had George's golf bag slung over his shoulder as he vanished into a tunnel that led to a secondary parking lot.

We were moving along at a normal pace when suddenly George saw a golf club in the middle of the parking lot — one of his golf clubs. Then, there was another golf club and another. The clubs were strung out in a line. George screamed, "My clubs! What the hell is going on here?"

About a hundred yards ahead of us, there was Al with George's golf bag still slung over his shoulder. It looked as though George's travel bag had come undone and the golf clubs were dropping out. I had a suspicion it was only Al's warped sense of humor at work.

Needless to say, George and Al didn't see eye-to-eye on the golf club joke. As for me, I loved it. We had only been in San Diego for about five minutes and already George was getting a taste of his own medicine. I could hardly wait until he and Bill got tangled up in a practical joke or even a conversation.

We spent our first day golfing and George won. Well, at least George beat me. However, Bill conveniently managed to get lost and he never did finish the round. Bill was down two holes with two to go. He hit a big drive on the 17th hole, probably too big. I thought the ball went through the fairway and out of bounds. Well, Bill went up ahead to check everything out and he just sort of vanished. After the round was over, we found him on the putting green. He didn't have much to say. I mean, it was absolute silence. It didn't matter though, because George was doing enough talking for both of them. I thought the scene was a classic example of a poor loser and a not very gracious winner.

We got in the car and George continued pouring it on. "Bill," he said, "Tate told me you were a bad loser, but to quit in the middle of a round because you were getting your ass kicked ... I wouldn't have believed it if I hadn't seen it for myself."

Bill put on a Willie Nelson tape, switched the speakers to the back seat and turned the volume up full-blast. George continued screaming something as Bill sang along with Willie. And me? I only sat there quietly minding my own business.

The next morning it became evident that George was in for a serious beating on the golf course. I heard Bill moving around early in the morning. Then I heard this soft music and the sound of a golf club swinging. "SyberVision," I told myself. I knew that Bill was watching his Al Geiberger video called SyberVision.

Several years ago, Al Geiberger made a neuromuscular programming video. The theory goes that if a person watches Al Geiberger's perfect swing over and over again, they will begin to mentally picture and experience that same swing. It's supposed to slow a person's tempo down and help groove the perfect swing. Bill swears by it.

If SyberVision wasn't enough, then Bill made arrangements for us to play Meadow Lake Country Club in Escondido. I knew the golf professional at Meadow Lake, Brad Booth, and I had even taken some lessons from the Director of Golf, Jim Gilbert, a former touring pro. Either one of those pros would tell you that Meadow Lake is one tough track — especially if a person has never played the course before. It was one of those golf courses that featured a lot of doglegs and blind shots.

Bill had a friend of his, John Davis, join us. I made sure that George and John were partners. Then I made double sure that Bill negotiated the strokes. Bill played John and George like a Stradivarius. He cut their strokes in half, doubled mine, tripled the bet from yesterday and we teed off first. Driving up the first fairway, Bill winked at me and said, "Like a couple of bananas, Tate. Those two goofs are going to get peeled like a couple of bananas."

We played three holes and Bill had two birdies. That's when John looked over at Bill and said, "Slick, what's got into you today?"

George came over to me and said, "Why'd John call him Slick?"

"That's one of his nicknames," I answered.

"Tate," George said with a sober expression, "where I come from a nickname means something."

Slick shot a smooth 74, and George "The Weasel" Atkinson found out the hard way that nicknames meant something in San Diego, too. In fact, all the way home, George had to listen to Slick give a blow-by-blow account of the golf match and the story about a sucker being born every minute. George was seriously abused on the golf course and was verbally assaulted all the way home. However, the real blow to George's ego came that night at dinner.

We all went out to eat. It was a quiet little restaurant, good food and I was enjoying my meal. Then it started. I wasn't paying any attention to exactly what set George off, but I heard him say to Al

Ritchie and his wife Helene, "If you two believe that, then you'll go for fried ice cream."

Al and Helene jumped all over George. According to them there was something called fried ice cream. They started going back and forth on the issue. Finally, George wanted to see some fried ice cream on a menu, any menu. George said, "If there's such a thing as fried ice cream, then I'm a duck."

Al started quacking as George quickly retorted, "I'll tell you what. If there is such a thing as fried ice cream, I'll buy some for everyone here. If there isn't, then you and Helene have to buy dinner for everyone tomorrow night."

"Great bet, George!" I added my two cents worth. And it was a great bet. I didn't care if someone was buying me dinner tomorrow night or dessert tonight.

We had to travel across town, but in a small Mexican restaurant, George "The Weasel" Atkinson, aka: Daffy Duck, had his first taste of fried ice cream. For some reason, I thought the taste of that particular brand of fried ice cream was a palatable delight. In fact, it was the best fried ice cream I had tasted.

Later that evening we went back to Bill's home, sat around and talked about everything and anything. George and Bill had a couple of minor disagreements, but nothing serious. Then they got into a heated discussion as to what year the professional football leagues merged.

When the argument started, they were both wrong. George said 1966, and Bill argued it was the year the Jets won the Super Bowl. It was a great match-up. Bill sat on the edge of his chair and continually interrupted George. And George sat on the edge of his chair and continually interrupted Bill.

Ten minutes later George had somehow managed to weasel around the issue and now he was shouting, "Nineteen-seventy was the first season of the merger." And Bill, living up to the nickname Slick, maintained, "The first Super Bowl after the merger was Baltimore and Dallas." George was shouting "season" and Bill was screaming "Super Bowl." They were right! The merger was completed for the 1970 season, and the first Super Bowl under the new alignment was in 1971. Baltimore beat Dallas 16-13.

They were still arguing when I got up, walked over to the refrigerator and looked inside. "Bill," I interrupted their debate, "do you have any fried ice cream in here?"

The ladies laughed, Bill laughed, Al quacked like a duck and finally George broke down and laughed, too. From there we started talking about our new book. George read some of the excerpts and acted out several of our scenes with Pete Rozelle. It was getting funny. Then it became hilarious when we got into the Philyaw, Doctor Death and Arrowhead Holmes stories.

Seeing everyone with tears of laughter rolling down their cheeks, I suddenly thought about our ex-literary agent, Dom Abel. Dom didn't think the book was funny. In fact, Dom ripped the project from beginning to end. He found the material "dated," and didn't think my latest venture was controversial or even vaguely humorous.

I don't know, maybe I'm wrong, but I thought my honest statements about Pete Rozelle were as controversial as it got. And right now, a room full of people were laughing at the same stories an agent thought were humorless. Suddenly the thought of publishing another book was a little frightening. Would the general public see what an agent saw? I could only hope they would read the book and have the intelligence to understand what I had written.

At the same instant, Bill blurted out, "Tate, do you remember what Dom said about this material?"

My mouth dropped open and I just stared at Bill. Our minds were working in unison. We were starting to think alike. Damn! What a frightening thought.

Bill told everyone the story about Dom's insulting rejection of the book. "Not to worry," Bill laughed. "That's pretty much Dom's style."

I thought about it. Bill was right. Dom originally rejected the first book. He didn't think it was much of a story either — no humor, nothing controversial. It wasn't until Bill really pressed the issue that Dom went out and halfheartedly came up with a publisher.

I started feeling a little better about the chances of my latest book making it. I did this book because I have something to say. I've written a sequel, so to speak, believing that sports fans would find it interesting, informative, humorous and, at times, sensitive. Sure, some folks, just like a certain literary agent, will miss the rather obvious points of the book. And perhaps some people will consider my story "dated material." And still others won't give a damn about the continuing trials and tribulations of yesterday's assassin. It comes back to the fact that you can't please everyone all the time. But I still believe enough football fans are going to read this book and see the other side of football's assassin.

Even though a so-called New York expert rejected the book, I still had to believe my audience was out there. Journalists continually ask me for interviews, television personalities want me on their programs, and I receive my share of fan mail urging me to do another book. Without fail, every month or so, I receive a phone call or two from booksellers wanting to know where they can get copies of the original story. Last month a bookseller in Los Angeles wanted 300 copies of

They Call Me Assassin; the month before that a fan in northern California wanted sixty.

Just then, Bill's son came home. Entering the family room he handed me a magazine: *Football Digest*, March 1989. He said, "Page ninety-two, Tate. They just won't quit."

Joe Fitzgerald of the *Boston Herald* was at it again. His article was titled "Yesterday's Heroes." It was about Darryl Stingley. That's the way it usually goes. I can be sitting around with good people, having fun, laughing, but then it begins all over.

Someone called it "dated material" and yet a major leaguer like Joe Fitzgerald was using yesterday's news in order to sell today's magazines. Dated material, and yet, here we go again.

Just about ten years ago, Joe Fitzgerald started the uproar. He used slanted and twisted words, a small sampling of excerpts from my book and then made mention of a lynching. With that, I knew Jack Tatum was going to carry the brand of football's villain for a long, long time.

And Pete Rozelle, the stammering, blundering boob that he was, helped to fortify the notion that I might well be the predicted coming of 666. It's like I said, Pete spent twenty-nine years taking credit for the inevitable, but was always out to lunch on issues of importance. With the publication of my first book, Pete didn't have to make a big deal out of it either way. All he should have done was tell the truth. And the truth was that I have written an honest book.

Seriously, I've tried to figure out exactly what I did that was wrong. Sure, I tackled hard and played aggressively. Forgive me, but I always believed that football was and still is a hitter's game — the harder the hit the better the hit! Football just happens to be one of those sports where a passive player is rejected and an aggressive player is rewarded. I didn't set the standard, I only played by it.

What was my sin? Okay, so I wrote a controversial book and made some controversial statements. Sorry, but I can't be sorry for that. I have a difficult time believing that controversy has made me a minority of one. The honesty factor of my book might well give me minority status, but not the controversial aspects.

Looking back and analyzing everything, I know that my image problem stems from the Darryl Stingley accident. Even though we're talking about an accident, someone figured there had to be a bad guy and there had to be a good guy. I walked away, Darryl didn't. Okay, he's right and I'm wrong. Is that what everyone expects me to say?

Once again, forgive me for being honest, but there wasn't a right or wrong to my tackling Darryl. And there wasn't a right or wrong to Darryl running a pattern and trying to catch a pass. He was a receiver paid to catch the ball and I was a defender paid to tackle. It's unfortunate, even unfair; nevertheless, it happened. Neither one of us can go back and erase that segment of our lives. My heart bleeds for Darryl, but how does one repent when he hasn't committed a sin?

Joe Fitzgerald, in his most recent article, wrote, "A gifted wide receiver, Stingley, who was 26 that August day in 1978 and starting his sixth season with the Patriots, was violently tackled by defensive back Jack Tatum of the Oakland Raiders, a hit which left him paralyzed, which made him a quadriplegic, a hit the unrepentant Tatum (he's never said he's sorry) boasted of in a subsequent book entitled, *They Call Me Assassin.*"

"Unrepentant," in this instance, is a tricky word. The inference is that I did something wrong. I didn't. If my career had ended that August night instead of Darryl's, would that have made him wrong and me right?

"Boasted" is another tricky word. Reading Fitzgerald's article, a person would think that I wrote a book to brag about a tragic accident. Joe Fitzgerald, of all people knew the whole story. He was there when it began. He knows the truth.

They Call Me Assassin was the story of my life and career. Unfortunately, Darryl Stingley was a tragic part of the story. That doesn't mean I was boasting about an accident where another human being was seriously injured. And it doesn't mean that I was trying to capitalize on another person's misfortune. I wasn't. But someone is still writing negative trash about the accident and turning a profit.

Just for the record, I've always felt terrible about the fact that Darryl Stingley didn't walk away from that hit. At the same time, I'm never going to apologize for doing my job on a football field. That doesn't mean I'm an insensitive thug, either. It simply means we had our jobs to do. Darryl was trying to do his job to the best of his ability and I was trying to do my job to the best of my ability.

The truth is that Darryl was simply reacting to the ball. He wasn't thinking about Jack Tatum or concerned about injuring himself or, for that matter, worried about injuring someone else. And it was exactly the same way with me. I instinctively reacted to a situation. Every defensive back in the NFL reacts the same way and with the same intent. Take a close look at a football game and maybe then you will understand.

If my critics were to check the record they would discover the truth. Believe it or not, receivers and defensive backs have been slamming into each other ever since the forward pass was invented. When collisions are inevitable, accidents are going to happen. Sometimes serious accidents will happen, but that doesn't mean there was a right or a wrong.

It's sad, but there will always be a Joe Fitzgerald, a Morton Downey, Jr., or some other insensitive hypocrite who will try to make you believe that there was a good guy and a bad guy on a football field that August night. Sadder yet, some people will believe that trash. What can I say?

I'm not denying that Darryl Stingley is newsworthy. He has taken extreme adversity and converted it into something positive. I've heard that Darryl travels around the country lecturing to young people about the pitfalls of doing drugs. The truth is, I have a lot of respect and admiration for Darryl. He's making his life count and because of his tremendous efforts, young people will really turn off to drugs. Believe me, Darryl's work really means something in this day and age.

Print the positive stories about Darryl's life because he deserves the credit and support. And go ahead, write about a tragic August night in 1987 when his career ended and a mountain suddenly rose up in front of him. Mention my name, if you so desire, but don't print your trash about Jack Tatum being unrepentant or insensitive or boasting about a hit that crippled another human being.

Once again, and for the record, I did try to see Darryl after the accident, twice to be exact. I was told that he was heavily sedated and only family was permitted to see him at that time. Afterwards I heard that Darryl didn't want to see me. He was quoted as having said that he blamed me for what happened. I could understand that. After all, he was carried away from an accident — I walked away.

I decided to give everything a little time. With the publication of *They Call Me Assassin*, I knew the controversy over the whole incident was going to promote the book. I didn't want it that way, but it wasn't something I could change. I wanted Darryl to know that I cared, so I made arrangements for him to share in the royalties. I never asked, but even Bill wanted to give up part of his royalties for that cause.

Helping Darryl financially wasn't the complete answer to the tragedy, there was no cure-all solution, but it was a beginning. Also, I started working on a plan to set up a Darryl Stingley Fund. Once again, it was only money, but I wanted to help Darryl with expenses and perhaps help some other individuals who would suffer a similar injury. From there, I believed that Darryl and I would eventually face each other and even talk I was certain that one Darryl looked into my eyes, he would understand that I cared.

My attorney called Jack Sands, Darryl's attorney. We told him the plan; sharing royalties and setting up the fund. They didn't want our help. Jack Sands went as far as to accuse me "grandstanding." That was Jack Sands' word, "grandstanding."

It was an accident; nevertheless, there was a good guy and, forever, there had to be a bad guy. So be it! Brush the dust from your sandals and move on.

It's been a long time, much too long. It has to end. I want to get together with Darryl, just the two of us. After Darryl and I have our private moment, and we will, then I want someone with intelligence and sensitivity asking the questions football fans want answered. Maybe Oprah or Phil, Roy Firestone, or some nighttime personality like Johnny or Arsenio will be interested in letting the world see and hear how Darryl and I feel about the incident and about each other.

I know some of my critics are going to say I'm only using Darryl to hype a new book. Believe me, it has nothing to do with "grandstanding" to promote a book. This book is going to do all right on its own. I just feel that Darryl and I both want to put yesterday behind us and get on with tomorrow.

By now everyone should realize that *They Call Me Assassin – Here We Go Again,* is more than just a football story. After all, football has only been a small segment of my life. It was my job, but let's not forget, I've retired and there's the rest of my life waiting for me. I'll still probably have some ups and downs, some bad times and good times, but we all have to pass through some storms in order to see the sunshine. Life, what an experience!

During the pages of this book I've introduced some of my friends as a way of saying that I, too, can laugh. In fact, I enjoy a good joke and I like to be with people who know how to laugh. Everyone does. And I'm sure everyone has known similar characters, individuals exactly like my friends. Even Skip Thomas. Everyone knows a Doctor Death. Don't they?

Actually, Skip is a pretty basic guy... these days, that is. Skip lives in Kansas City. He works with the police department and has a pig farm. I don't know how or why Skip came to work for the police department and I'm not even going to ask why he decided to raise pigs... Everyone knows a Skip Thomas... right?

After reading this book, maybe people, when they see me coming down the street, won't turn and run away. Maybe mothers won't hide their children behind their skirts, and maybe fathers won't whisper in fear, "Look... that's the Assassin..." Yesterday I was the Assassin, but only on a football field. Today and forever more, I'm simply Jack.

When you see me coming, say hello. Don't be afraid. I won't tackle you or cuss and scream. I left my game face on the football field and that was a long time ago. Besides, the truth is, I've always liked most people ... especially kids.

Just mentioning kids I'm reminded of the problems they are confronted with on a daily basis. I don't like some of the things that go on in our society, especially the drug scene. As long as we have a drug problem, I'll be out there working with kids. I'll teach them how to say, "NO!" Sometimes the littlest words are the most difficult to say.

I'm going to do some work with Danny's kids, too. Saint Jude Children's Research Hospital is important, and I want to help Danny. And there's also the Torrey Pines Kiwanis Disabled Skier Program. A number of NFL players are working in that program. Can you imagine a person with one leg skiing down a mountain? It's called courage.

I'm going to keep busy with my life. I have a lot of things to do. I'll still be a part of the football scene, but only as a spectator. Who knows, I might even watch a game from the Dog Pound in Cleveland or wave a Terrible Towel in Pittsburgh.

Lately, though, I've started thinking about a seat at the Coliseum in Oakland. Rumor has it that Al Davis might be moving again, this time back to Oakland. I hope so! Once an Oakland Raider, always an Oakland Raider.

Naturally, I'm going to do a lot of golfing. Bill and I have talked about playing some of the great courses in the country. I mentioned the courses in and around the Monterey area and several of the new PGA courses. Bill said, "Willie Nelson."

According to Bill, Willie is supposed to have his own golf course somewhere in Texas. At least that's what Bill thinks. He told me about Willie's rules, too. Only twelve players to a foursome. I thought about it and that's a good rule. I like people and four to a foursome doesn't seem fair.

Willie also permits players to throw the ball out of sand traps. What's more, a person can pick up his ball and walk it out of the woods. No penalty strokes, either. Those are good rules because there's nothing more frustrating than a woods full of trees or a plugged ball in the sand. Golf is supposed to be relaxing and fun and Bill said that Willie's rules assure that. He was right.

Bill also told me that Willie has wild animals running all over the course. According to Bill, there's supposed to be a special harmony between nature and man on Willie's golf course.

The more I listened to Bill, the more I had to agree, someday, somehow, we had to get together with Willie for a round of golf. I kept going back to the one thing that Bill said, "There's supposed to be a special harmony between nature and man on Willie's golf course." What a beautiful thought — harmony between nature and man. It's got to be a great golf course.

Right now, I've set my sights on tomorrow. Someday I'd like to get a place on the island of Maui. It's quiet and peaceful. I like it that way. Quiet and peaceful.

FINAL CONFESSIONS

of NFL ASSASSIN
Jack Tatum

by Jack Tatum with Bill Kushner

About a year ago I was browsing around a card show in Sacramento when I saw two copies of the book and the price tag — $180.00 each. I shook my head in disbelief. In 1980 the book sold for $9.95.

Granted, the books were original hard cover copies of *They Call Me Assassin*, and in mint condition. But would anyone actually pay $180.00 for a copy?

Starting a conversation with the guy selling the books, I asked him about the price tag.

He said, "At one hundred and eighty bucks, they're a steal. These books are collector's items. They represent ever."

"Ever? What do you mean by ever?" I asked.

"Best football book ever! And the hardest hitting, most feared football player ever. These are the last two original copies of Jack Tatum's story."

With my baseball cap pulled slightly down covering most of my face, I picked up a copy of the book, flipped over several pages and said, "Jack Tatum … never heard of him."

"If you never heard of Tatum, you never heard of football," the man responded. "Jack Tatum was known as the Assassin. You heard of the Assassin, didn't you?"

Still casually flipping over the pages of the book and without looking up I answered, "Nope."

"The Assassin was the meanest, dirtiest, biggest cheap-shot artist the Raiders ever had. And that's when the Raiders were the Oakland Raiders, not a bunch of Los Angeles wimps," the man explained.

I couldn't dispute the fact that the real Oakland Raiders were right up there with the dirtiest teams in football. But that's one thread in common all winners have, they cheat.

In recent years the Dallas Cowboys and the San Francisco 49ers have had a monopoly on the Super Bowl trophy. At the same time, both offensive teams are notorious for using such illegal tactics as holding, the pick, and the chop block. In other words, they cheat.

For years the 49ers have run receivers all over the field working the pick to perfection. Then, in Super Bowl XXX, the Cowboys showed the world, and Steeler linebacker Jerry Olsavsky, they had their own version of the pick.

The pick is quite simple, but illegal. Yet the officials rarely call it. All the offensive team has to do is get a receiver to block or just get in the way of a linebacker or defensive back and then bring the hot receiver into the pattern.

Ask Steeler linebacker Jerry Olsavsky how that one worked for the Cowboys in Super Bowl XXX. The Steelers were in a goal line defense and Jerry was an inside linebacker. Naturally, once the play started, Jerry's first responsibility was to check run. Within a second, Jerry recognized pass. His responsibility now became the outside flat. Jerry turned to his right and WHAM! The Cowboys picked Jerry off with a tight end and Troy Aikman completed a one on none touchdown pass to Jay Novecek. One on none means there wasn't a Pittsburgh Steeler within ten yards of Novecek.

On the subject of holding, it's not that other teams don't know how to hold, it's just that the 49ers' and Cowboys' offensive linemen have perfected holding techniques.

If you don't believe me, then ask Green Bay Packer, Reggie White, about holding during the 1996 NFC Championship game in Dallas. Reggie had more fingerprints on his jersey than an ink pad in the fingerprint department of the New York City Police Department.

Of course, holding is one thing, but the chop block is another story. The 49ers and Cowboys openly deny it, but both offensive teams are taught the chop block as the last resort in protection for the quarterback. When beaten by an opponent, the Cowboys' and 49ers' offensive line will go for the back of the opponent's leg. The tactic will not only slow the advance toward the quarterback, but one well-placed chop block will usually blow out the knee of the biggest and toughest defensive lineman.

Ask Packer defensive lineman John Jurkovic about the chop block he received during the 1996 NFC Championship game in Dallas.

Of course, Cowboy offensive lineman Eric Williams called it an "accident," and John Jurkovic called it "reconstructive knee surgery," and I called it "cheating." But the Cowboys won the game and went on to the Super Bowl and John Jurkovic went in for surgery.

Just for the record I have more than a general understanding of cheating, cheaters, dirty play and dirty players. After all, I played for the Oakland Raiders when the Oakland Raiders were the real Oakland Raiders. And what's more, we used to play against the Pittsburgh Steelers when the Steelers were the Steelers and not some team trying to live off past glories.

However, there is a major difference between breaking a rule and stretching one. Personally, I felt the Raiders and Steelers played some extremely physical games. And both teams stretched the rules, but rarely did we engage in blatant dirty play.

Now don't get me wrong because during the Steeler-Raider rivalry, there were some occasions when penalty flags flew. I'm not talking about calculated picks, holds or chop blocks. I'm talking about those times when emotions gave way to spontaneous retaliations.

There is one incident in my mind that really stands out during our rivalry with the Steelers. Lynn Swann was running a pattern over the middle, but Terry Bradshaw dumped the ball off to Franco Harris. As Franco was about to be gobbled up by our defense, Lynn Swann made the mistake of running a little too close to me. I blasted him into the cheap seats, knocked him cold. It was a legal play, and if I had it to do over, I'd hit Lynn harder.

Ray Mansfield, the Steeler center, saw what happened and came after me. Ray clipped me, got my knee. So, I kicked him between the eyes, split his head wide open. Ray retaliated to what he thought he saw, and I retaliated to what Ray did. Neither action was dirty. It was simply emotions giving way to spontaneous retaliation.

During my career I stretched every rule to the max. When head-hunting was legal, I was a head hunter personified. When the Hook was in, I had a better Hook than Joe Louis. When defensive backs could bump and run, I bumped and ran and beat up receivers all over the field. I mean to say that anyone who came near me during a game wearing a different colored uniform was going to get blasted. BUT, I wasn't a dirty player or a cheap shot artist. Physical, yes. Dirty, never.

So, I had to take exception with that one thing the man had said. With my head still buried in the book I told the man, "You don't mean Tatum, you mean George Atkinson. George Atkinson was the cheap-shot artist and Jack Tatum was strictly legit, always by the rules."

With an agreeable nod the man answered, "Atkinson ... George Atkinson, yeah, I gotta agree with you. Hell, I still remember him sneaking up on Lynn Swann and clubbing him during a championship game at Oakland. Broke Lynn's nose, caused a concussion. That combination had to be a receiver's worst nightmare. If Tatum wouldn't get you, then Atkinson would. But wait a second. If you never heard of Tatum, how come you know Atkinson?"

Then the wheels started turning in the man's head. He peeked under my hat and with a surprised expression said, "I'll be damned ... Jack Tatum. You're Jack Tatum."

The first thing the man wanted me to do was sign the last two original copies of *They Call Me Assassin*.

"Okay," I said. "I'll sign the books but only if you can answer one question. Who was the cheap-shot artist of the real Oakland Raiders?"

"George Atkinson," the man said.

I signed the books. And then the man reached under his table, pulled out a box and asked, "Could you sign a few more copies?"

"I thought these were the last two copies of the book."

"Not exactly," the man answered.

The man had a box of books, originals and in mint condition. It turned out he owned a book store and, back in 1980 when *They Call*

Sammy White being punished for crossing the middle.

Sammy White... later!

Me Assassin hit the stands, he sold hundreds of copies.

"I couldn't keep it in stock," the man said. "As fast as I would order it, I'd sell out. So, I ordered five hundred copies. I put half the copies on display and the others in storage. Then, last week I was cleaning out my storage room and found the box."

I signed the books, kept a couple for myself, and then hung out at the man's table for a while. Interestingly enough, the price went from $180.00 a book to $250.00. And even more interesting was the fact that the books were selling.

We carried on a conversation. Actually it was more of a question and answer session than a conversation. The man asked the kind of questions that people always ask me. What's wrong with the Raiders of today? What was John Madden like as a coach? Did Al Davis really call the plays? On the Immaculate Reception, did the football bounce off me or Frenchy Fuqua? Have I ever talked to Darryl Stingley since the accident?

Then the man got around to asking the question. "Did you and George Atkinson really make bets as to who could knock more opponents out?"

Interestingly enough, I get asked the "knock-out" question as much as any question. I don't know why, but when I first wrote about "knock-outs" and that I always went for the devastating hit, the NFL cringed. My value to the Raiders and the NFL was that I hit hard, harder than anyone in the game. I wasn't paid to intercept passes or score touchdowns. I was paid to hit people, paid to beat up receivers, paid to knock people senseless, paid to strike fear into the hearts of our opponents, paid to be the intimidator, paid to be the Assassin that no winning team is without. And guess what? Every receiver, ball carrier and offensive man in the NFL knew exactly who I was and what I, if given the opportunity, would do. But then I wrote a book, two books, told the truth, and all of a sudden the NFL is shocked. Why?

Well, George and I did have our competition and I always won. However it was "knock-out" and "limp-off" competition. A knock-out was awarded only if the hit rendered the receiver unconscious and he didn't return to the game. Knock-outs were worth two points.

However, if the hit put the man down for a charged time out, but he was able to limp off and then later return to the game, that was called a "limp-off" and worth only one point.

George was good competition only because he was sneaky. He knew how to position himself in order to deliver the effective blind side hit or the Hook. But the bottom line was I always won the knock-out competition. After all, I've always claimed, and to this day maintain, that my best hit bordered on felonious assault. George was more of a mugger.

In fairness to George, I should mention that although he had a reputation as being a dirty player, he really wasn't. Oh, there were a few times when the camera caught George getting a little too overly zealous, but he really wasn't a cheap shot artist. He was an Oakland Raider.

Most of George's reputation, and mine too, was a direct result of the Raiders' persona. Black and silver uniforms, pirate decal, a maverick owner who did things his own damn way, the wildest, toughest fans in football, and a winning tradition that stemmed from a 'burn the village and children, too' style of play gave us the bad-boy image of football. From there it was just a few good nicknames such as Doctor Death, Snake, Kick 'em, and yours truly, the Assassin. With all of that going for the Raiders, all we had to do was add a couple of good hits — the two-point kind — listen to a certain coach

1976 Super Bowl, Soul Patrol: Skip Thomas (26), Jack Tatum (32), Neal Colzie (20), George Atkinson (43), Willie Brown (24) and Charles Phillips (47).

making reference to "criminal elements," openly protest the fines the NFL was always dropping on George and me, and suddenly, the Raider persona became the Raider mystique.

With that we developed an attitude, a winning attitude. And by the mid-1970s we had taken the characteristics of the Raiders and transformed it into the knowledge that we were the meanest, toughest and best team in professional football. And every time we took the field we went the extra mile to prove that point to our opponents. Whatever it took, it was simply just "win, baby, win."

I played in many games where our opponents were intimidated by our just showing up on a Sunday afternoon. That was always a bad move on the part of any opponent because we showed no mercy, we took no prisoners. We came! We conquered! We annihilated everything in our path! They say cowards die many times but the brave taste of death but once. It was true.

And of those encounters with the brave, those games when a team said they couldn't be intimidated … well, they were mistaken, flat-out wrong. By simply admitting that we were intimidators the process of intimidation had begun.

In those kinds of games, it took a little longer than walking over the chumps. But by playing like the Raiders were supposed to play, aggressive and violent, the opponent's will to win would eventually warp.

We may have lost some games on the scoreboard, but on the field another standard of measuring victory was set. Win or lose, we rarely left the opponent with cause to celebrate the outcome.

During the 1995 season, the Los Angeles Raiders made the move back up the coast to Oakland. The fans said, "The Raiders are back."

For the Raiders' first home game against the St. Louis Rams, I stood in the crowd and watched as the team stepped off the bus and walked into the locker room. Right then and there I knew the Raiders weren't back. The persona wasn't there, the mystique was gone, lost along the highway from Oakland to Los Angeles and then back to Oakland.

I remembered going into Pittsburgh to play a game at Three Rivers Stadium. Being one of the first guys off the bus, I stood outside the locker room door and had a conversation with my attorney. Glancing back toward the bus I watched as my teammates walked toward the locker room.

These were the Oakland Raiders, a professional football team, but my first thought was to hide the women and children. It was the arrogance, the absolute confidence, the disdain, the invincibility; large men wearing black leather coats, dark sunglasses, almost something of

Darth Vaders moving through the eerie silence of a Sunday morning. A person had to see to understand, but this was the Raider mystique.

I thought, my God, I'm glad I'm playing with them and not against them.

When the Raiders were the real Raiders, persona and mystique weren't things we worked at or talked about. Hell, most of the guys playing for the Raiders during those days wouldn't even have known what persona and mystique meant. Persona and mystique were things that just happened.

To be perfectly honest, I never heard much about the Raider mystique while I was playing for the Raiders. In fact, I really didn't hear much about the Raider mystique until the Oakland Raiders became the Los Angeles Raiders and they started losing. Then the Raider persona and the Raider mystique became something of a conversation piece. You know, a lot of talk about the Raiders reclaiming the persona and mystique, but only talk and no action.

How many times must the Raiders lose to a mediocre team before someone gets pissed off?

How many times must the Raiders start the season by talking about playing in the Super Bowl before Al Davis hires the type of guys who want to win football games ... every game?

During my day we would have never let Kansas City make us their chumps. The Oakland Raiders were never anyone's door mat. Furthermore we would have refused to let Denver out-physical us twice in one season. We would have just gone out and found a way to do what Al expected us to do. And that was "just win, baby, win."

In February 1996 the Raiders had an induction ceremony for the Bay Area Hall of Fame. Gene Upshaw, a former teammate of mine from the Raider glory days was being inducted. It was a gathering of the real Raiders and the phonies who now brought shame and disgrace to the silver and black.

After dinner Al and I got to talking about the Oakland Raiders of today. I've always had a great relationship with Al, a completely honest and frank relationship with him.

Al knew he had problems in Raiderland, major problems, and he didn't need to hear that from me. But I did tell him a solution to the problems. I told him how to stop the bleeding.

"If I were you," I said in a rather loud and adamant way, "I'd back up a bus to the stadium, load it with about half the guys you have on the team, and drive it into the bay. Get rid of the troublemakers, the whiners and the pussies who talk about winning but don't understand kicking ass it the only way to win in this league. Get back to Raider football! Back to just win, baby, win instead of lose, baby, lose."

Three of the best: Willie Brown, Lester Hayes and Jack Tatum.

I glanced around and everyone in the room was looking at me. The old Raiders, my former teammates, echoed those same sentiments. Just win, baby, win.

However, the new guys, the kids disgracing our silver and black just dropped their heads and walked away. It was sort of like the new Oakland Raiders taking an ass-whipping at the hands of the Kansas City Chiefs. You know what I mean. They spend the week talking about reclaiming the Raider mystique, but then lay down for the Chiefs. And worst of all, after the game they just walk away and start talking about getting the job done next week.

Al saw what happened. He knew what I meant. He understood when the real Oakland Raiders ended up on the short end of the scoreboard it was a bad scene. And come next week someone sure as hell was going to pay the price. But nowadays, a loss is a loss and no one except Al really gives a damn.

Al said, "You're right. Yeah, you're right. Maybe I will clean house."

Even if Al cleans house I'm not sure the Raiders can ever recapture the glory and mystique of years gone by. I think professional football is played in a different arena today.

You see, because of the salary caps and free agency, there's not much in the way of team unity or team chemistry. The emphasis is on money. Everyone wants to make as much money as they can. Not that there's anything wrong with making a lot of money, but this year's Dallas Cowboys are going to look and play a lot differently than last year's team.

During my playing days, the Raiders made changes ever year – new faces, new personalities, new nicknames. But I couldn't imagine starting a game without George, Doctor Death and Old Man Willie playing in the secondary with me. The Raider mystique was one thing, but the chemistry and experience we developed over the years in the secondary gave us the confidence to take chances in order to make great plays. We knew each other's weaknesses and because of that we played to each other's strengths.

If George, Doc, Willie and myself were playing during this day and age, free agency and the lure of big money would have probably found us Raiders for only a short time. Team unity and chemistry would have been replaced with the security of a big bank account.

Okay, I can understand the guys going for the big bucks, but I'll never fathom why the Raiders of today play without any heart. I'm sorry, but I'll never understand how anyone can go out on a football field and not give a damn about winning.

I was still hanging out at the man's table as he sold the last copy of the book. He then suggested that I write another one, but this time do something on the changes within professional football during the past twenty years. It was an interesting thought, but the truth of the matter is that as much as things change, they stay the same.

During my day, Pete Rozelle was commissioner of the NFL. Today it's Paul Tagliabue. Okay, Tagliabue is a lot taller than Rozelle and has more hair. But as different as Tagliabue and Rozelle might seem, they are the same.

To be the commissioner of the NFL a person has got to be weak. You know, subservient, a boot licker, an ass kisser. In the case of Pete Rozelle, being stupid was also part of his job description.

Sure the commissioner is supposed to balance everything between the players and the owners, but who hires the commish? It's not as though the owners and players get together and vote on a commissioner. The owners hire the commissioner and say lick. And if the commissioner wants to keep his job he asks, "Left boot, or right?"

Let me explain this so Pete Rozelle could understand it. The owners control the game and the commissioner has always been the owners' puppet. It takes a weak man to be a puppet. Rozelle was weak. Tagliabue is weak. What more can I say?

On the subject of the game itself, some people think the last twenty years have produced some dramatic changes. I'm not sure that is necessarily true.

Since its very beginning, football has always been a contact sport that features violence. The NFL would never admit it, but the popularity of football is the result of big, strong and fast people slamming into other big, strong and fast people. I've always maintained that football is legalized mayhem. If I did the same thing on the street that I once did on the football field, I'd be arrested and sent to jail.

Of course, the players are a little bigger today, perhaps a little stronger and faster. But Lombardi's Packers aren't playing Jerry Jones' Dallas Cowboys. The point I am making is that as much as things change, they stay the same.

Now if we are looking for a real change in football, I think we should look at the rules. During the leather helmet era, clotheslining and clipping were legal. Dangerous stuff, so the NFL changed the rules.

When I came into the league, the Hook was legal. In my first book, *They Call Me Assassin*, I did a terrific job of describing the Hook. For a brief description, the Hook was simply trying to catch the receiver's head between my forearm and bicep. It was designed to strip the receiver of the ball, his helmet, head and courage. The Hook was effective.

Naturally, George Atkinson was one of the experts with that particular technique. And it goes without saying that George taught me the Hook. Damn! After only one lesson I had a lethal weapon.

In college I had knockout potential on every tackle and the Hook wasn't a part of my arsenal. But now, as an NFL hit man, I felt the Hook would only increase my knockout potential. It did. And I spent the better part of my career licking my chops, sitting back and just waiting for a receiver to run a pattern over the middle.

Then one day, Pete Rozelle called me into the office. He said, "Frankly, Jack, I think you hit too hard."

For once in his life, Pete Rozelle was right about something. I did hit too hard. The Hook was outlawed and I stopped using the technique. Rules are made to be stretched but not broken.

About the same time the NFL was outlawing the Hook, it started working on rules to protect the quarterbacks. That particular action prompted Pittsburgh Steeler linebacker Jack Lambert to say, "Put dresses on the quarterbacks."

During the games, I was never a quarterback lover. But I didn't see anything wrong with offering the QBs a little protection by

Raymond Chester and Jack Tatum inspect a golf course project in Placerville Co. Ray and Jack are partners in the project.

Raymond and Jack with Jim Ward majority partner in Gold Creek Golf Project.

changing. And, of course, I'm not talking about rules that might include dresses for the quarterbacks.

Actually, the NFL made some changes in the rules that helped to protect the quarterbacks especially in the late or questionable hit department. There's nothing wrong with protecting the quarterback from late hits. But the NFL is getting ridiculous in its definition of what is late.

Okay, a quarterback releases the ball and there should be some protection concerning the late hit. But give the defensive man some time to react. In other words, stop flagging and fining defensive people because they might hit the quarterback a fraction of a second too late.

I get the feeling the NFL thinks defensive people should be able to change direction or intent while in mid-air. They can't, and because of that there has to be a happy medium. If the rules continue to be slanted in the quarterbacks' favor, we'll need three digit scoreboards. Any NFL quarterback, if given enough time and protection, will pick a defense apart.

Yet, the NFL continues to make other changes in rules to protect quarterbacks. It has gotten to the point where quarterbacks actually play by a different set of rules. Take the hook-slide rule for example.

The hook-slide means quarterbacks can run all over the place and just prior to contact hit the ground and slide to safety. In other words, quarterbacks can attack the defensive player much like a running back, but the defensive player has to be extremely cautious when attacking the quarterback.

Now I, for one, wasn't opposed to protecting the quarterback in the pocket, but only in the pocket. Once the quarterback steps outside the pocket, he should be a fair and legal target.

The problem with letting the quarterback slide to safety is the defensive man is placed at a disadvantage. Instead of reacting to the situation, the defender has to sit back and wait on the quarterback. For the defensive man it becomes a second guess situation. If he does go for the hit on the quarterback just as the quarterback begins his slide, the officials will throw the flag. If the defender sits back and waits too long, the quarterback has the opportunity to lower his shoulder and plow for extra yards.

I've seen quarterbacks scramble down the field instead of sliding; they lower their shoulder and try to run over the defensive man. Hell, anyone, even a quarterback, has the potential to run over a defensive back if they catch the DB standing flat-footed and waiting for contact instead of initiating contact.

As I look at football today, I think the NFL is doing much too much in the way of attempting to protect quarterbacks. At the same time, the NFL has also gone overboard on new rules to protect receivers.

Think about this. A receiver catches the ball coming over the middle and the defensive back goes for a high hit in an attempt to not only make the tackle but cause a fumble. Well, it's now illegal to hit too high. Hits to the head will draw flags and flags mean fines — major money fines.

What's next, throw away helmets and should pads and play flag football in the NFL?

My God, what a horrible thought. I'm almost agreeing with Jack Lambert. But seriously, if the NFL continues to punish hitters because they hit too hard or they hit a fraction of a second too late, then football is going to suffer the consequences. Fans just don't want to see bitch-slapping. Fans want to see men kicking the hell out of each other.

I think about my style when I played the game — attack, attack, attack. My object was not only to bring the man down as quickly and violently as possible, but to punish him, to discourage him from coming back. That meant I hit high, low, in the ribs, in the back, wherever I could find a clean target to project myself through. I would try to drive my helmet or my body through the man. If I were playing under the thin line of today's rules, I'd need free agency and Deion Sanders' mega-bucks contract to pay my fines.

If the NFL continues to hit the hitters with penalties and fines, then professional football is going to truly become Deion's game. And does the NFL really want that? Does anyone really want that?

I could be wrong, but I just don't think that Deion Sanders tackling empty space or even dancing in the end zone will sell as many tickets as an Assassin knocking some receiver from a Sunday afternoon into next Tuesday. Believe me, one well-timed hit can do more to discourage the opponent than a chorus line featuring Deion the Dancing Queen.

Suddenly, I began to realize that there was one major difference in the game – Deion Sanders. Twenty years ago defensive backs were paid to cover and hit. But now, Jerry Jones, owner of the Dallas Cowboys, has introduced a new type of defensive back, the Dancing Queen.

I've just had a funny thought, perhaps even hilarious. Picture Deion playing football twenty years ago. And Deion's team? Well, none other than the men who wore silver and black, the real Oakland

Raiders. With our personalities and penchant for beating the hell out of our opponents, I just couldn't see any of the original Oakland Raiders warming up to a Dancing Queen. Sissy stuff and fag dancing just wasn't a part of the Raider mystique.

There is no doubt in my mind that after one day in camp Deion would have packed his bags and headed for the baseball field in San Francisco. You see, when football was a hitter's game, baseball would have been Deion's only chance at sports. And as for his dancing, well, there are plenty of bars in the San Fran area where the boys would have enjoyed that kind of stuff.

Then again, if Deion was playing in my position on August 12, 1978, Darryl Stingley wouldn't be confined to a wheelchair. But he wasn't, and there's no way to change yesterday. I was paid to hit, the harder the better. And I hit, and I knocked people down and knocked people out. But sooner or later they would always get back up. Yes, they got up every time except one.

Several years ago, I received a call from Oprah's people. I was told that Oprah was going to have Darryl as one of her guests. And she wanted me to be on the show, too.

My first reaction was to do it. It's been a long time since the accident and I'd really like to see Darryl. I'd like to have a talk with him. But then they told me the show was going to be about People You Love To Hate … or something like that. I turned them down.

I was paid to hit. Darryl was paid to catch the football. He was trying to do his job. I understand why Darryl is considered the victim. But I'll never understand why some people look at me as the villain.

As the man sold his last copy of *They Call Me Assassin*, his customer, a lady, answered my question. She said, "It had to do with the Raiders' persona. You could have played for another team, been the same Jack Tatum, made the same tackle with the same results and instead of a victim/villain scenario, it would have gone down as a football tragedy."

I shrugged my shoulders. "Perhaps you're right."

The card show was over and I began walking out with the man who sold the books. He asked me if I ever see Darryl, what will I say.

I told him, "If and when it happens, it will be right off the top of my head, non-rehearsed, just let it all go wherever it goes."

Then the man said, "Someday, I believe you'll see him."

"Maybe," I said. "Maybe someday Darryl Stingley and I will get together and talk."

"You will," the man replied as he patted me on the back and headed toward his car.

I hope the man is right.